Global Governance in a World of Change

Global governance has come under increasing pressure since the end of the Cold War. In some issue areas, these pressures have led to significant changes in the architecture of governance institutions. In others, institutions have resisted pressures for change. This volume explores what accounts for this divergence in architecture by identifying three modes of governance: hierarchies, networks, and markets. The authors apply these ideal types to different issue areas in order to assess how global governance has changed and why. In most issue areas, hierarchical modes of governance, established after the Second World War, have given way to alternative forms of organization focused on market or network-based architectures. Each chapter explores whether these changes are likely to lead to more or less effective global governance across a wide range of issue areas. This provides a novel and coherent theoretical framework for analyzing change in global governance.

Michael N. Barnett is University Professor of International Affairs and Political Science at the George Washington University. His previous books include *Rules for the World: International Organizations in World Politics* (co-authored with Martha Finnemore, 2004) which won several prizes, and *Power in Global Governance* (co-edited with Raymond Duvall, 2004).

Jon C.W. Pevehouse is the Vilas Distinguished Achievement Professor in Political Science and Public Policy. His research interests are in the field of international relations and political methodology. He is the recipient of the Karl Deutsch Award and multiple teaching awards. He served as the editor of *International Organization*.

Kal Raustiala is the Promise Institute Professor of Comparative and International Law at the UCLA School of Law and Director of the UCLA Burkle Center for International Relations. His previous books include *Does the Constitution Follow the Flag?* (2009) and *The Implementation and Effectiveness of International Environmental Commitments* (co-edited with David G. Victor and Eugene B. Skolnikoff, 1998).

◂ STI ▸

Social Trends Institute
FOSTERING UNDERSTANDING

The Social Trends Institute (STI) is a nonprofit international research center dedicated to fostering understanding of globally significant social trends. To this end, STI brings together the world's leading thinkers, taking an interdisciplinary and international approach.

Currently, STI's areas of priority study are the future of work, technology and ethics, and the thriving society. Findings are disseminated to the media and through scholarly publications.

The individuals and institutions that support STI share a conception of society and the individual that commands a deep respect for the equal dignity of human beings, and for freedom of thought, as well as a strong desire to contribute to social progress and the common good.

Carlos Cavallé, PhD, is President of the Social Trends Institute. Founded in New York City, STI also has a delegation in Barcelona, Spain. Visit www.socialtrendsinstitute.org.

Global Governance in a World of Change

Edited by

Michael N. Barnett

George Washington University

Jon C.W. Pevehouse

University of Wisconsin–Madison

Kal Raustiala

University of California, Los Angeles

CAMBRIDGE
UNIVERSITY PRESS

CAMBRIDGE
UNIVERSITY PRESS

University Printing House, Cambridge CB2 8BS, United Kingdom

One Liberty Plaza, 20th Floor, New York, NY 10006, USA

477 Williamstown Road, Port Melbourne, VIC 3207, Australia

314–321, 3rd Floor, Plot 3, Splendor Forum, Jasola District Centre,
New Delhi – 110025, India

103 Penang Road, #05–06/07, Visioncrest Commercial, Singapore 238467

Cambridge University Press is part of the University of Cambridge.

It furthers the University's mission by disseminating knowledge in the pursuit of
education, learning, and research at the highest international levels of excellence.

www.cambridge.org
Information on this title: www.cambridge.org/9781108843232
DOI: 10.1017/9781108915199

First published 2022

A catalogue record for this publication is available from the British Library.

ISBN 978-1-108-84323-2 Hardback
ISBN 978-1-108-82411-8 Paperback

Contents

Figures

Tables

Contributors

Liliana B. Andonova is Professor of International Relations and Political Science and Co-director of the Centre for International Environmental Studies at the Graduate Institute Geneva.

Deborah Avant is Director and Chair of the Sié Chéou-Kang Center for International Security and Diplomacy at the University of Denver.

Michael N. Barnett is University Professor of International Affairs and Political Science at the George Washington University.

Vincent Bernard is Executive in Residence at the Geneva Center for Security Policy and the former Editor in Chief of the *International Review of the Red Cross*.

Orfeo Fioretos is Associate Professor of Political Science at Temple University.

Jessica F. Green is Associate Professor of Political Science at the University of Toronto.

Miles Kahler is Distinguished Professor the School of International Service at American University and Senior Fellow for Global Governance at the Council on Foreign Relations.

Michael W. Manulak is Assistant Professor of International Affairs at Carleton University.

Suerie Moon is Co-director at the Global Health Centre and Professor of Practice in International Relations & Political Science at the Graduate Institute Geneva.

Susanne Mueller is Visiting Lecturer in Politics at Mount Holyoke College.

Jon C.W. Pevehouse is Vilas Distinguished Professor of Political Science at the University of Wisconsin–Madison.

Anne Quintin is head of the Advisory Service on International Humanitarian Law at the International Committee of the Red Cross.

Kal Raustiala holds the Promise Chair in Comparative and International Law, and is the Director of the Ronald W. Burkle Center for International Relations, at the University of California, Los Angeles.

Leonard Seabrooke is Professor of International Political Economy and Economic Sociology at the Copenhagen Business School.

Ole Jacob Sending is Director of Research at the Norwegian Institute of International Affairs.

Duncan Snidal is Professor of International Relations and Fellow of Nuffield College at the University of Oxford.

Jonas Tallberg is Professor of Political Science at Stockholm University.

Acknowledgments

One of the participants in the project recently reminded us that this volume has been a very long time in the making. Although we think the comment was intended for other purposes, we choose to take the high road and see it as a reminder that we have many people to thank for their insights, involvement, and patience. First and foremost, the survivors who can count this outcome as a reward. It might not be much, but, like global governance itself, it is probably better than the alternatives. Many of the contributors to the volume were part of the project from the very beginning, while others joined later. Regardless of their length of service, they were great company and critics, making the ride both more enjoyable and intellectually stimulating. And we do want to thank all the participants for their persistence and resilience. In many ways the project could have been a self-study in modes of governance, but that might be an overly generous description of the editors' leadership.

All projects have benefactors and we have three that helped fund the three workshops. The first workshop was held at the George Washington University and was funded by the Provost's office through Michael Barnett's research funds. The second workshop was funded by the Social Trends Institute (STI) and held in Barcelona. We cannot thank STI enough, and our dear friends Dr. Carlos Cavallé and Tracey O'Donnell for their generous financial support and friendship. They were incredible hosts and the best funders any project could ever hope to have. They also helped to fund the third workshop, which took place at the Graduate Institute of International and Development Studies in Geneva. We are indebted to Liliana B. Andonova for initiating this possibility and then putting together a coalition to help make the workshop possible. We would like to join Liliana in thanking the Center for International Environmental Studies (CIES) and the Center for Trade and Economic Integration (CTEI), both of whom supported the Geneva meeting. Dr. Joelle Noailly (CIES) and Theresa Carpenter (CTEI) facilitated the organization of that meeting.

Over the years, workshops, and invited lectures, we received many comments from many colleagues, some of whom also wrote memos and papers for our early conferences. We are going to try and name them all, but undoubtedly will miss a few, and apologize in advance: Ayelet Berman, Joost Pauwelyn, Tom Hale, Oliver Westerwinter, Esther Brimmer, Tana Johnson, Tim Maurer, Aisling Swaine, Bill Burke-White, Tom Weiss, Abe Newman, Martha Finnemore, Ken Abbott, Erik Voeten, Kate McNamara, Susan Sell, Stewart Patrick, Amitav Acharaya, Henry Farrell, David Bosco, Janice Stein, Ilona Kickbusch, and Jacqueline Best. We have individually given presentations and received helpful feedback on the Introduction at the following universities: Princeton University, the Graduate Institute in Geneva, and Temple University.

We received terrific research assistance from graduate students at UCLA, the University of Wisconsin–Madison, and George Washington University, including Mara Pillinger, Dani Gilbert, Miles Evers, David Silverlid, Anne Jamison, Ryan Powers, and Nishant Sabnis. Dario Piselli of CIES served as a rapporteur of the Geneva meeting.

We have the great fortune of becoming accustomed to thanking John Haslam for his support and candor.

Introduction
The Modes of Global Governance

Michael N. Barnett, Jon C. W. Pevehouse, and Kal Raustiala

Global governance began in the mid-nineteenth century and accelerated after the First World War. But it came of age in the post-Second World War era. In response to the lessons learned from the collapse of international order between the wars, and the need to rebuild after the devastation wrought by the Second World War, states, with the USA in the lead, set out to create a new and comprehensive set of international organizations to tackle a growing list of shared global challenges. Led by legendary statesman like Harry Dexter White, John Maynard Keynes, Dean Acheson, and Jean Monnet, states collectively recognized that their joint interests in a reshaped world required new forms of interstate cooperation, coordination, and collaboration. Their lengthy negotiations often resulted in the creation of a big and sometimes powerful international institution, anchored by a comprehensive treaty, and with aspirations to global and even universal membership. These mid-century institutions typically had large secretariats housed in imposing buildings in New York, Washington, or Geneva. States remained very much in control, bureaucracies were expected to use their authority and expertise to carry out the decisions made by states, and their growing size and scale meant that these new international organizations (IOs) had a global reach. States and their IOs created and regulated global governance in this era on a scale and with a scope that had not been seen before.

There remain plenty of examples of this postwar modernism, with states and IOs standing at the center of ambitious efforts to address global challenges. But scholars are increasingly using different language, discourse, and imagery to try and capture what they now see, some seventy-five years later, as a much more complex system of global governance.[1] Exactly how to describe these developments is a matter of

---

[1] For overviews of the broad trends in global governance, see Zürn 2018; Coen and Pegram 2018, 107–113; Acharya 2016; Pouliot and Therien 2017, 1–10; Kahler 2018, 239–246; Weiss 2009, 253–271; Kennedy 2009; Murphy 2013; Ruggie 2014, 5–17; Weiss and Wilkinson 2014, 207–215; Patomäki 2014; Murphy 2014, 216–218;

debate – and competition. Westphalian global governance has given way to one that is post-Westphalian.[2] The modern has succumbed to the post-modern.[3] Good-bye old multilateralism; hello new multilateralism.[4] We are now in a Copernican world.[5] Global governance is now orchestrated.[6] There has been an increase in delegated authority.[7] But not all authority is delegated. Because of world-historical processes, authority has become more fragmented and dispersed across the globe, enabling new kinds of actors to have a voice.[8] We have now entered an era of partnerships and "multistakeholderism."[9] Global governance is best seen as "networked."[10] Some talk about clubs.[11] Others discuss the "layering" of global governance.[12] Maybe global governance is less layered and more multilevel.[13] Layering and multilevel suggest that there is fixed arrangement, while those who work with regime complexity suggest the existence of a much less stable and predictable order.[14] An even messier possibility is that the new governance arrangements have all the characteristics, and perhaps even entropy, of a spaghetti bowl.[15] In short, there is widespread agreement that something fundamental in the form and structure of governance has changed, but there are competing views on exactly what has changed – and how. What is clear is that global governance has become much more diverse and complex. States and IOs are still often the stars of the show, but they increasingly work with an ensemble cast, including non-governmental organizations (NGOs), public–private partnerships, multi-stakeholder arrangements, transnational networks, private organizations, corporations, and foundations. A good example is the Global Alliance on Vaccines, known as Gavi. The primary partners include existing global institutions (World Health Organization, World Bank) as well as foundations (the Gates Foundation), private

---

Pegram and Cueto 2015; Avant et al. 2010; Hampson and Heinbecker 2011, 299–310; Van Langenhove 2010, 263–270; Cooper 2010, 741–757; Cooper and Pouliot 2015, 334–350.

[2] Dryzek 2012, 101–119.   [3] Ruggie 2004, 499–531.

[4] Hampson and Heinbecker 2011, 299–310; Van Langenhove 2010; Cooper 2010; Cooper and Pouliot 2015, 334–350.

[5] Jentleson 2012, 133–148.   [6] Abbott et al. 2015a.   [7] Lake 2010, 587–613.

[8] On fragmented authority see Rosenau 1995, 13–43; Held 2013; Guzzini 2012; Hooghe et al. 2017; Raustiala 2014; and Halliday and Shaffer 2015. Also see Coen and Pegram 2015, 417–420.

[9] Raymond and DeNardis 2015, 572–616.

[10] Slaughter 2005; Kahler 2009; Sikkink 2009; Kendall 2004.

[11] Tsingou 2015, 225–256; Graz 2003, 321–340.   [12] Bartley 2011, 517–542.

[13] Zürn 2012; Stephenson 2013, 817–837; Hooghe and Marks, 2001.

[14] Alter and Raustiala 2018; Special Focus: Regime Complexity 2013; Keohane and Victor 2011, 7–23; Raustiala and Victor 2004, 277–309.

[15] Baldwin 2016, 1451–1518.

sector organizations (the International Federation of Pharmaceutical Manufacturers Association), and governments.

Alongside this change in the kinds of actors there has also been a change in the relationship between them. States and IOs used to be the major players, and sometimes the only players, but increasingly they govern with others. This suggests that there are new patterns of inclusion. But inclusion does not mean equality and inclusion often creates some with more and others with lesser authority and those who still remain excluded altogether. Additionally, these actors conduct their relations in different kinds of spaces. Previous governance arrangements used to be formed by treaties and often overseen by secretariats in buildings. Now they can be quite informal and have the barest sort of physical presence.

Are these changes good or bad for addressing the world's problems? Each position has its defenders. More actors might mean more kinds of knowledge and the ability to benefit from the wisdom of diverse views; or it may mean more veto players and more opportunities to drive outcomes to the lowest common denominator. Change may reflect a rational, functional adaptation. In this view the old forms of governance, while perhaps appropriate for the twentieth century, are insufficient for the current age; the new forms of governance better reflect the demands of the twenty-first century. In short, because the world is messier, denser, more tightly coupled, and more interconnected it naturally requires a global governance that is subtler, fluid, and pluralistic.[16] It is becoming "fit for purpose." But global governance does not necessarily rationally adapt – form does not necessarily follow function, supply does not necessarily follow demand, and efficacy often outweighs efficiency. These less than functional, perhaps dysfunctional, outcomes are often attributed to politics and power; states and other actors are often more interested in defending and advancing their own short-term interests than they are in solving collective problems.

These new governance mechanisms may also reflect and produce much less ambition and vision. The global organizations created after 1945 had far-reaching goals and attempted to establish rules that would regulate an entire issue area. The World Bank took on the challenge of creating development, and later fighting poverty in the Global South. The International Monetary Fund would handle issues related to international financial stability. The United Nations (UN) and its specialized agencies covered an array of large global public goods, from refugees to

---

[16] Slaughter 2005; See also Farrell and Newman 2014, 331–363.

education, not to mention policing international conflict via the Security Council. The European Coal and Steel Community's rather dull name betrayed a rather far-reaching agenda that included creating the basis for greater economic openness and regional security in an area decimated by two recent total wars. These were broad and deep agendas.

Global governance in the twenty-first century has become much less ambitious, characterized by provisional and improvisational action, piecemeal incrementalism, more modest goals, and experimentalism. Perhaps these more modest approaches will eventually provide the foundation for a more ambitious undertaking. Yet while these scaled-back ambitions might deliver more identifiable "successes," they might not sum to a solution. More agreements between municipalities on reducing carbon emissions might be welcome, but would not be enough to meaningfully combat climate change. Amid the 2019–2020 Covid-19 global health pandemic Dr. Michele Barry, director of the Center for Innovation in Global Health at Stanford University, lamented:

But one of the things about epidemics is it's really important to have what I call shared global governance. And I don't think in this world it's great that we don't have a stronger central governance of our world health. We have a World Health Organization that has a budget that is less than many of our hospitals in the United States.[17]

This volume is an intervention in the debate about the evolving architecture of global governance. The chapters herein reassess what is happening, why it is happening, and what effects ensue. We understand global governance to be the institutional arrangements used to identify problems, facilitate decision-making, and promote rule-based behavior on a global scale. Scholars of global governance agree that it has changed, and usually focus on the number and kinds of actors now involved. By these measures there is no disputing the change. We approach the question of change from a somewhat different vantage point, one that we think offers a superior way of getting to the core issue: how do these new architectures reflect the changing relations between the actors involved in global governance? In order to better understand whether and how relations among the now myriad key actors have changed we use the lens of *modes of governance*.

We focus our analysis on three ideal-typical modes drawn from economic and sociological institutionalism: hierarchy, network, and

---

[17] "Doctor: As Coronavirus Cases Spike Worldwide, We Need Global Cooperation to Halt Spread," *Democracy Now*, March 20, 2020.

market.[18] While we go on to say more about these modes, the core distinction revolves around how rules are produced, sustained, and enforced. *Hierarchical modes* are characterized by top-down, centralized, organizational forms that regulate relations between relatively dependent actors and enforce the rules through command and force. The traditional IO is a classic example of a hierarchical mode of global governance. *Market modes* are organized around non-hierarchical principles that regulate relatively independent actors, often associated with a "hidden hand" or competition among independent actors. Whereas hierarchies are centralized, markets are decentralized. *Network modes* are characterized by relatively interdependent (and possibly formally) equal actors with a common purpose that voluntarily negotiate their rules through bargaining and persuasion and then maintain and enforce those rules through mechanisms of trust. Although scholars might disagree on what a networked world means, many nevertheless seem to agree that it exists.

In broad terms the existing literature on global governance tends to claim, often implicitly, that hierarchical modes of governance such as traditional IOs are losing their prominence, and networks and market modes are increasingly prevalent and significant.[19] This is the basic description we began this chapter with. However, we challenge this claim for two reasons.

First, while this view captures an important truth it is not the whole truth. As the chapters illustrate, there are areas of global governance in which this has occurred and is occurring, but there are others where it has not. In short, there is heterogeneity across issue areas. Furthermore, changes between these ideal-typical forms may take a variety of pathways. Some are linear, others not. Some occur quickly, others over decades. Some are permanent transitions, others reverse or follow yet another path. Some paths taken in one period will increase the likelihood of others in the future.

Second, even where there has been a shift from hierarchies to markets and networks the former remain alive and well, even if less visible. We argue that there is a significant "shadow of hierarchy" in many areas of global governance. Just as economic markets cannot operate without legally enforced property rights protections, global networks and

---

[18] For economic institutionalism see Williamson 1975; and Williamson 1991, 269–296. For sociological institutionalism, see Powell 1990, 295–336. For other useful statements on these three modes, see Treib et al. 2007, 1–20; Estwistle et al. 2007, 63–79; Jung and Lake 2011, 971–989. For other scholars that operate with a similar taxonomy in the area of governance, see Stephenson 2016, 139–148; Keast 2016, 442–454; and Tenbensel 2005, 267–288; Blatter 2003, 503–526; Dixon and Dogan 2002, 175–196.

[19] Abbott et al. 2015b, 247–277.

market-driven governance typically require rules that have some modicum of support from states. Although we use these three modes to mark change in global governance, this volume emphasizes how they intersect and combine in complex and interesting ways.

This volume also looks to the underlying causes, or drivers, of these shifting modes of global governance. We identify nine major drivers of change that are present to one degree or another, all of which reside at the structural level: (1) geopolitical change, such as the relative decline of US power and rise of China; (2) shifts in the global economy; the sheer "crowding" in the global governance space, both in terms of (3) the number of actors and (4) the pluralization of actors; (5) the increasing complexity of global problems; (6) changes in ideology and trends in governance theory; (7) the global turn to expertise as a way to rationalize governance; (8) technological change; and (9) domestic political change, for example in the form of rising populism and nationalism.

This is a rather lengthy list of drivers, and all along we aspired to reduce it to the fingers on one hand – but the history of global governance would not play along. At this point the chapters provide no grounds for removing any from consideration. Also, these drivers also are not independent but rather interdependent. For instance, technological change has enabled the rise of non-state actors in global governance. Moreover, there also might be other factors, such as legitimacy, as suggested by Jonas Tallberg in Chapter 11 and Michael Zürn in his work, or growing legalization, that also deserve independent status and can alter the path of these drivers.[20] Lastly, structures can impose but actors choose, even if not necessarily under the conditions of their choosing. The history of global governance illustrates this point over and over again. There are underlying forces that help us sort through some of the important patterns in global governance, but there also are state and non-state actors, and more of them in different kinds of relationships, that create a space for creativity and agency. However convenient it might be to reduce the world to structure, the world rarely abides.

We are interested in the shifting modes of governance not only because they provide a different way of thinking about patterns and trends in global governance but also because of their material and normative consequences. The demand for change in global governance is often driven by the desire to solve major global problems. Accordingly, the major measure of outcome is effectiveness – and many of the chapters understandably make this a major concern, even if they are unable to

---

[20] Zürn 2018; Hooghe et al. 2019, 731–743.

provide airtight assessments one way or another. But in many instances they note how a mode of governance is judged not only on material gains but also on normative evaluations. At such moments they raise issues of legitimacy, fairness, justice, accountability, and other normative scales. And these normative measures refer not only to distributional outcomes but also to process and whether those who are affected by the decisions have a voice in shaping them.

The remainder of the Introduction is organized as follows. This first section lays out how scholars have tended to mark transformation and presents our alternative. Specifically, our view is that the transformations many have documented are better understood not in terms of changes in actors but rather *changes in relations* among actors. Consequently, we examine the modes of global governance in terms of hierarchy, markets, and networks, which almost always involves a change in actors. The second section reviews the various forces behind the change, ties these individual arguments to shifts in the modes of governance, insists on looking for multiple and interacting causes, and emphasizes the necessity of examining both structures and preferences. The third section addresses what is at stake in this debate. The fourth section provides an overview of the remaining chapters in this book.

Global Governance Today

Students of global governance have used various markers of transformation, but many if not most note the often dramatic shifts in the number and kinds of actors that are involved in governing the world – at times a kind of Cambrian explosion compared to the initial postwar approach. Because there is no official "census" of "global governors" it is impossible to offer decisive evidence of demographic change.[21] However, the available data suggest that there has been a major quantitative and qualitative change.

Figure I.1 graphs the changing number of IOs, NGOs, networks, and transgovernmental initiatives over time. The data provide a reasonable approximation of their comparative numbers, but the population figures have to be taken as suggestive rather than definitive.

The overall story is that while states and IOs remain central to most governance relationships, they increasingly share space with other non-state actors.

---

[21] But for an overview see Avant et al. 2010.

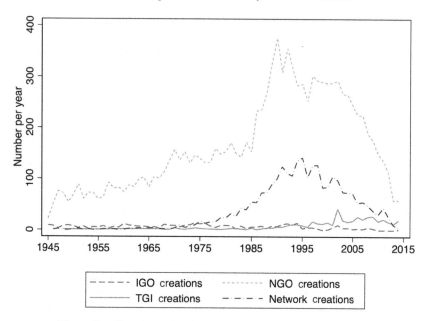

Figure I.1 Creation of new organizational types, 1945–2005.

We have an accurate count of the number of states, and we know that this number has increased several-fold since 1945. We have a reasonable approximation of the relative change in the number of IOs: their numbers grew substantially after the Second World War, and then again after the end of the Cold War, but have plateaued since then. Data on IO creation paints a comparable picture, which tells us that if the population of IOs has plateaued it is due not only to death rates but also birth rates. IOs are going through their own demographic transition.[22]

Although such counts tell us about the numbers of IOs they do not quite capture the variation in IOs in terms of their inclusion of non-state actors. One minimalist definition of an IO is a permanent collaborative arrangement established by three of more states, but the members of an IO can also include other IOs, NGOs, and other private actors. It has become commonplace to note that the participants in global governance have diversified – not only as formal members, but also as informal participants in a range of decision-making and discussion forums. In particular, a wide array of studies has pointed to the varied ways in which

---

[22] Abbott et al. 2015b; Pevehouse et al. 2019.

NGOs and other non-state actors are participating in global governance.[23]

The data on NGOs support this view.[24] There are more NGOs than ever before, playing various roles – from shaping the agenda, to negotiating agreements, to monitoring rates of compliance by states with those agreements.[25] There also are more networks than ever before. There is no best way to tally the number of networks, in part because there is no consensus definition on what is a network. Assuming that self-identification – do actors see themselves as part of a network? – provides at least a reasonable first cut, there are far more networks than ever before. As shown in Figure I.1, self-described networks significantly increased in the mid-1970s, but the rate of increase has leveled off in recent years.[26] This strikingly large increase can be read as consistent with the argument that traditional forms of global governance are in decline – with the decline of more formal IOs in the issue area, networks rise to fill "global governance" gaps. Alternatively, it can be read as consistent with the claim that traditional hierarchical IOs are stable, but increasingly inclusive and open in their operation. In other words, perhaps traditional IOs and networks are complements, not substitutes. This line of argument, addressed in some of the chapters, suggests a denser and more complex array of institutions and actors.[27] In addition to networks there are other kinds of groupings, formal and informal, that are increasingly being recognized. Public–private partnerships have grown in significance and number, although as seen in Figure I.1 (where they are measured as transgovernmental initiatives (TGIs)) their numbers do not yet rival that of self-identified networks or NGOs.[28] Corporations have always had an important impact on global governance, but they too are increasingly visible.[29] Municipalities and "nation cities" are also more active today, often because they are frustrated by the inaction of states.[30]

Expert communities, originally referred to by social scientists as epistemic communities,[31] are also not new, but scholars have become more aware of the multiple functions they perform. These and other

---

[23] Tallberg et al. 2013; Raustiala 1997, 719–740.   [24] Bush and Haddon 2019.

[25] Boli and Thomas 1997, 171–190; Grigorescu 2020.

[26] We generated these data by scraping all organizations from the *Yearbook of International Organization* that self-describe as a "network." We were also able to scrape those organizations' years of origin to create this graph.

[27] Bernstein and Cashore 2012, 585–604; Abbott and Snidal 2010.

[28] Andonova 2017. The data on TGIs are taken from Westerwinter 2017.

[29] Avant 2005; Ruggie 2017, 317–333; Eberlein 2019, 1125–1145.

[30] Emanuel 2020; Bloomberg 2015.   [31] Haas 1992, 1–35.

associations of private actors have many informal roles. But most strikingly they have increasingly received formal roles – as full-blown members of public–private partnerships; as (perhaps nonvoting) participants in more traditional IOs; as advisors to state delegations; and as interlocutors in a range of multilateral bodies, many of which have adopted rules that allow for private actors to participate in a range of discussions and debates.

We can learn a lot from a census of global governance, but it cannot address whether there has been a change in its very organization.[32] A rise in the number of NGOs in and of itself tells us little unless it is embedded in an understanding of whether and how this has affected the mechanisms of global governance. Our elevation of relations over numbers is consistent with our earlier (and others') definition of global governance – how institutionalized rule systems coordinate actors. And it provides the justification for the concept we use to capture the different ways that societies can organize social relations: modes of governance.

Modes of governance can be distinguished according to various criteria, but in the interest of parsimony and comparison we highlight the primary mechanism used to coordinate social action. Following sociological and economic institutionalists we identify three modes: hierarchies, in which social action is organized through regulation and law that demand some kinds of action and prohibit others; markets, in which decentralized institutions such as markets provide costs and benefits for different actions; and networks, in which independent, purposive actors negotiate the rules that will regulate their relations.

Because we treat hierarchical, market, and network modes of governance as ideal types, we must recite a few common words regarding the conceptual and methodological advantages and limits of ideal-typical analysis.[33] To begin with, ideal types are the attributes associated with a social phenomenon in its purity. Observers often disagree about what these attributes are. For instance, Max Weber's concept of the state has been turned into an ideal type, but his is not the only formulation, for there are rival Marxian and liberal alternatives. Furthermore, types are often decomposed into subtypes, and the justification for doing so is because it provides a more useful, granular concept for comparison within the ideal type. For instance, scholars that draw from Weber's ideal type of the state often subdivide it into weak and strong variants. These subtypes should have distinctive attributes. For instance, the

---

[32] See, for instance, Pegram 2015, 618–639; Barnett 2013, 379–398.
[33] Swedberg 2018, 181–196.

attributes associated with weak states should not also define strong states. Moreover, these types and subtypes provide the basis for comparison across cases and over time. We can use the ideal types of strong and weak states to provide meaningful comparisons between the USA and Argentina at a moment in time, and also to measure historical changes in state power in the United States. Lastly, there is no assumption that any existing case will map perfectly onto an ideal type; in fact, the assumption is that such ideal types do not exist concretely. Ideal types are purified abstractions and the real world is filled with muddy complications. The USA is a strong state in some ways and a weak state in others.

This outline of ideal-typical analysis guides our use of modes of governance. Modes of governance concern how societies organize social relations.[34] Although there are various ways in which these three ideal types can be distinguished from each other, we focus on the mechanisms that organize and pattern their actions. Hierarchies are organized around command and control, markets on decentralized institutions that produce incentives for action by independent actors, and networks on negotiated agreements between purposeful actors. These different modes of governance provide the basis for analysis across instances and history. Has there been a change in the social organization of trade, emergency relief, pandemics, carbon emissions, or small arms? We can use these ideal types to make comparisons across these different issue areas, for example to claim that small arms is more networked while trade is largely hierarchical. We also can use these ideal types for historical analysis, for example to claim that the direction of global governance has moved from hierarchical to markets and networks, or that a single issue-area like humanitarianism has become less networked and more hierarchical. The chapters also blaze the warning that actual examples of global governance will not map perfectly onto any of the three modes of governance. Instead there is considerable overlap, blending, and layering between two or more modes. That said, these ideal types provide a

---

[34] Another possible point of differentiation regards who has authority and what kind of authority they have. Discussions of hierarchy in international politics tend to focus on the legal authority of the state and the rational-legal and expert authority of international organizations. Discussions of networks in international politics tend to rely on expert authority, with professional networks and NGOs being premier examples. We do not find a comparable form of authority associated with markets for the primary reason that authority is dependent on social recognition and is typically conferred on an actor. But markets are not actors but instead represent a way to organize social relations. However, sometimes the market is invested with "authority" and there are private authorities. We leave the concept of authority as an area for other scholars to engage with and prefer instead to focus on questions of organization.

common basis for judging whether and how there has been a change in the dominant mode of governance.

Although the concept of modes of governance is intended to be general enough to be applicable to almost any social setting, heretofore much of the literature deploying these modes has focused on domestic governance. International relations scholars will be quick to point out the key difference between domestic and global governance: whereas the former is defined by hierarchy because of the presence of a state, the latter is defined by anarchy because of the absence of a supranational authority. A Waltzian view might add that the absence of hierarchy does not mean that governance is organized around anarchy, but rather that states can be likened to firms and their relations are akin to firms in markets.[35] The literatures on global governance and hierarchy suggest that the absence of a supranational authority does not mean the absence of hierarchy in governance. In fact, one of the interesting parallels between the literature on domestic and global governance is that each, for different reasons, have observed a change from hierarchies to markets and networks.

In what follows we define the three modes in greater detail. *Hierarchical modes* are characterized by top-down, centralized, organizational forms. Or, as Herbert Simon put it, "[I]n a hierarchic formal organization, each system consists of a 'boss' and a set of subordinate subsystems."[36] The state, the bureaucracy, and the military are the prototypical forms of hierarchical organization. The state has the authority, legitimacy, and coercive power to issue commands and laws and expect them to be followed – or else. The bureaucracy is characterized by a head that can issue orders to subordinates with the expectation that they will be implemented. The military operates with a chain of command and can punish for failure to obey.

Two critical wrinkles must be addressed when discussing hierarchical modes of global governance. To retrace our earlier steps, the first is whether it is even warranted to consider hierarchy in a world of sovereign states. Although the concept of the modes of governance has not been widely applied to global governance, there is a substantial literature on EU governance which accepts that hierarchies can exist.[37] One advantage that

---

[35] Waltz 1979.   [36] Simon 1962, 140.

[37] The concept of modes of governance has been discussed alongside the concept of governance in general, but most of its application has been to the realm of domestic governance and EU governance and differs quite substantially from ours. Eberlein and Kerwer 2002; Kohler-Koch and Eising 1999; Héritier 2002, 185–206; Knill and Lenschow 2004; Blauberger and Rittberger 2015, 367–376; Héritier and Rhodes 2011. There has been relatively little application to the area of global governance. However, see Bartolini 2011; Provan and Kenis 2008, 229–252. Héritier and

EU governance has over global governance more broadly for making claims about the existence of hierarchy is the presence of law and tight linkages between the domestic and the regional. But none of our cases of hierarchy are built around such conditions. Instead they point to two alternative forms of hierarchy. One is hegemonic or imperial arrangements. The other is IOs, which is where many rules are debated, legislated, implemented, and (sometimes) enforced. The objection to considering IOs as a form of hierarchy is that they rely on borrowed authority. Simply put, (a limited number of) states stand behind IOs and keep them on a short leash. But there are four justifications for treating IOs as a form of hierarchy: they operate on delegated state authority; they regulate through norms and soft and hard law that impose rules on states and others; they are organized around the bureaucratic form; and they often have (or work to create) considerable discretion and even the authority to make nearly unilateral decisions that shape social action.[38]

The second and related wrinkle regards the distinction between formal and informal arrangements. IOs are formalized arrangements, which are most of the cases in the volume, but there are two cases in this volume of informal hierarchies. In Chapter 2 Kahler points to the interesting case of cartels, which exist when a small number of actors create an agreement that regulates the actions of others for private and public interests. Cartels are informal (though often quite visible) because they are not typically created through a legal agreement. Consequently they do not regulate in a heavy-handed way but rather, in his case of trade, use softer rules and prices to do so. Barnett uses the concept of a club to capture how a set of states, IOs, and nongovernmental organizations create a set of rules and norms among themselves that are then intended to regulate the broader network of humanitarian governance. And beyond the two cases of informal hierarchy in this volume a growing number of scholars now point to the power of informal organizations, possessing many of the characteristics one would come to expect of traditional hierarchies.[39]

Market modes of governance are organized around non-hierarchical principles, often associated with a "hidden hand" that steers action through incentives. Hierarchies command; markets incentivize. Central to the market is price, which contains information about costs and

Lehmukhl offer a definition of modes of governance that is quite different from ours because it focuses not on social organization but rather on actors – the inclusion of private actors outside the normal democratic channels. Héritier and Lehmkhul 2011, 49–51. Koenig-Archiburgi and Zürn 2005 use the concept of modes as another way to express the growing diversity of governance arrangements. Koenig-Archiburgi and Zürn 2005, 236–254.

[38] Barnett and Finnemore 2004.   [39] Vabulas and Snidal 2013, 193–220; Stone 2011.

benefits and creates incentives and disincentives for different actions. There is no need for a regulator to command the merchant to lower the price because the market communicates what to do. One of the distinct advantages of markets, therefore, is that they are efficient; a "hidden hand" is cheaper than law and machinery to enforce the rules. Yet, under some conditions, especially when transaction costs are high, hierarchy can be even more efficient. This is one reason firms exist.[40] Furthermore, markets require some form of hierarchy – usually in the form of law, property rights, and courts – to function.

Market modes of global governance are quite common. One of the most famous uses of markets for governance is cap and trade in the area of climate governance (as discussed by Green in Chapter 3); in this instance there was no existing market for CO_2 emissions – it was created specifically for the purpose of trying to reduce its level. Similarly, in Chapter 10 Andonova outlines efforts by private firms using market mechanisms in the area of clean energy. Various NGOs want to regulate firms through certification measures, such as fair trade or the living wage; in doing so they create incentives for firms to alter their behavior to conform with international norms. Other examples of market modes of governance include benchmarking and rating systems, which can cause actors to change their behavior to maintain or elevate their reputation, thereby altering their stream of benefits.[41] Some of the most interesting innovations in global governance, such as forest certification, are built on the logic of markets.[42]

Network modes consist of a "set of actors, or nodes, along with a specific set of relations that connect them."[43] In this broad definition, markets and hierarchies also can count as networks – the former have enduring ties and the latter are tied formally. We follow those scholars and practitioners that use the concept of network to capture not the fact of ongoing exchange but rather the quality of the exchange and how governance is produced.

Specifically, networks have the following characteristics. The actors that form a network are interdependent, in contrast to hierarchies (defined by dependence) and markets (defined by independence). There is a common purpose or interest among the actors. There is relative and formal equality between the participants. They create agreements that are voluntary or quasi-voluntary, are negotiated with little or no coercion and are freely entered into. Disputes and differences of opinion are arbitrated and

[40] Coase 1937, 386–405.   [41] Kelley and Simmons 2015, 55–70; Kelley 2017.
[42] Cashore et al. 2004.   [43] Seabrooke and Henriksen 2017, 3.

resolved through negotiation and persuasion.[44] Because of the voluntary, interdependent nature of the exchange, and the absence of any enforcement mechanism, trust is central for producing order.[45]

There has been a visible rise of networks in global governance.[46] There are human rights networks, in which various NGOs and other non-state actors collaborate to create, monitor, and enforce human rights. Networks are credited with helping to put and keep climate change on the global agenda. In Chapter 9 on the International Committee of the Red Cross (ICRC) Bernard and Quintin argue that a coalition of networks, led by the ICRC, working in conjunction with a select number of allied states, shaped the regulation of armed conflict – including banning landmines.[47]

By conceptualizing the transformation of global governance through hierarchies, markets, and networks the volume addresses four central issues. The first is the considerable diversity in global governance arrangements. This is not a novel claim, but the focus on the social relations and organizing principles in this volume offers additional light on this development.[48]

Second, by treating the three modes of governance as ideal types we are able to provide an assessment of change in global governance. As suggested earlier, we do not assume that these ideal types correspond exactly to what exists in empirical reality. The world is always more complicated than our models. Accordingly, our analysis is attuned not only to whether there has been a change in the mode of governance but also the changing relationship between the modes of governance, with the possibility that they might become layered, entangled, and intersecting.[49] In this way, and following on Rhodes's observation two decades ago, "it's the mix that matters."[50] And indeed many of our authors, including Avant, Moon, Barnett, and Seabrooke and Sending, find that their issue area is now characterized by hybrids of our ideal types.

Third, the same issue area might exhibit different modes across different functions of governance. Conceptually speaking, effective governance requires several core functions, including: the identification of the problem to be governed; the creation of a forum where parties can negotiate and legitimate the rules; a body (however skeletal) that implements and interprets the rules; the monitoring of compliance with the

---

[44] Podolny and Page 1998, 59.   [45] Thompson 2003, 31; Rhodes 2000, 61.
[46] Kahler 2009; Kendall 2004.
[47] A developing literature in international relations explores the hierarchies that exist within networks, particularly as some actors have more authority and perform various gatekeeping roles. Carpenter 2011, 69–102; Stroup and Wong 2017.
[48] Kahler and Lake 2003.   [49] Also see Heupel 2008, 7–29   [50] Rhodes 1997, 40–53.

rules; and enforcement. Theoretically speaking, different modes of governance can coexist in these different functions in a single field. For instance, hierarchies might be important for problem definition and normative legitimation, but networks for monitoring. For example, in Chapter 4 Mueller and Pevehouse argue that hierarchical arrangements still dominate rule-making in trade, but that networks have become more common in compliance monitoring.

The fourth is the "shadow of hierarchy."[51] The claim is critical: even when markets and networks appear to dominate there is almost always a hierarchy casting a shadow and doing important work.[52] Or said otherwise, it is possible to imagine hierarchies without markets and networks, but nearly impossible to imagine networks and markets operating effectively without some form of hierarchy. Even the austere Austrian school of economics, led by Friedrich Hayek, had difficulty conceptualizing a stable, globalizing market without international law (and courts) standing behind it.[53] Summarizing the literature on economic governance, Robert Jessop similarly observes "meta-governance":

> Political authorities (at national and other levels) are more involved in organizing the self-organization of partnerships, networks, and governance regimes. They provide the ground rules for governance; ensure the compatibility of different governance mechanisms and regimes; deploy a relative monopoly of organizational intelligence and information with which to shape cognitive expectations; act as a "court of appeal" for disputes arising within and other governance; seek to rebalance power differentials by strengthening weaker forces of systems in the interest of system integration and/or social cohesion; try to modify the self-understandings of identities, strategic capacities and interests of individual and collective actors in different strategic contexts and hence alter their implications for governance failure. This emerging meta-governance role ... take[s] place "in the shadow of hierarchy."[54]

But what counts as the shadow of hierarchy? In market and network modes of governance the shadow is often quite latent, such as the existence of property rights and law that allow these modes to function. But it can become much more present and much less shadow-like when there are trends that threaten the continued pattern of regulation.[55]

---

[51] Héritier and Lehmkhul 2008, 1–17; Jessop 1997, 561–581; Rhodes 1997, 40–53.
[52] For a comparable claim, see Granovetter's 1985, 481–510 concept of embeddedness.
[53] Slobodian 2018.   [54] Jessop 1997, 575.
[55] The metaphor of shadow might refer not only to how rules constrain but also how they constitute actors. In other words, rules can be regulatory and produce self-regulation. This is consistent with both Gramscian notions of hegemony and Foucaldian notions of governmentality. For Gramscian approaches see Nelson 2015; Cox 1993, 259–289; Rupert 2000; Murphy 1994. For Foucauldian approaches, see Guzzini and Neumann 2012; Joseph 2012; Jaeger 2007, 257–277; and Sending and Neumann 2006, 651–672.

In situations of domestic governance it is the state that provides that shadow, looming over networks and markets armed with coercive and legal tools of enforcement. In global governance this "backstop" is often the function of powerful states working on their own or through IOs. In this vein, Barnett argues that while the humanitarian sector has network-like attributes, IOs and the states that fund them can use their funding (and the threat of its withdrawal) to bring aid agencies into line.

Explaining the Transformation

We use modes of governance to measure change. For the purposes of simplicity and clarity we consider adaptive change to be slight alterations in a particular mode of governance and transformational change to be a salient shift from one mode to another. Most of the chapters document transformations, but of varying magnitude. Manulak and Snidal, focusing on the supply side of global governance, observe a modest but significant shift from formal hierarchies to informal hierarchies plus networks. Andonova chronicles an energy field that was largely dominated by a few major states to a much more complex and networked system of governance. Moon traces global health governance that seems to move from hierarchy to networks to a modest return to hierarchy. Seabrooke and Sending observe the rise of a transnational expert network on post-conflict reconstruction in the midst of a presumed UN hierarchy. Avant compares two different areas of security: in the area of small arms it remains lightly regulated and has the characteristics of a market, whereas in the realm of private security it has moved from market to hierarchy. Green argues that climate governance has become more reliant on markets and networks.

In other areas, though, change has been muted. Kahler argues that economic governance has been relatively hierarchical over the decades, though the form of hierarchy has changed from cartel to regimes and beyond. Mueller and Pevehouse also note the continuity of hierarchy in trade, though with the important qualifier of a shift from global to regional hierarchies. Bernard and Quintin argue that despite many wars and changes in the international order the ICRC remains at the center of a hybrid form of governance that combines hierarchies and networks. And Barnett argues that emergency relief has evolved from a disorganized and disjointed sector to have hierarchy-like characteristics in a club of Western-based actors, and proven quite adept at fighting off any push to make the club more inclusive.

Our nine drivers described later in this section (geopolitics, global economics, technological change, a rise in the number of actors, a pluralization of the kinds of actors, low-hanging fruit, ideologies of governance, global rationalization, and domestic change) account for many of the changes examined by the authors. Not all nine are equally prominent across the chapters. Instead, many of the chapters identify a primary and secondary factor. In other words, transformation is rarely the result of a master cause, but rather is a product of conjunctural causation. For example, the end of the Cold War was a great disrupter, but it alone would not have produced many of the shifts in modes of governance; instead, the end of the Cold War created space for these other factors that were already quite present.

Again, our drivers are largely structural. How states and other agents respond also plays an important role. All the chapters reference how states and non-state actors engage in strategic choice as they consider the desirability of one mode over another in the context of the structural changes we outline. There is no single environment that shapes equally all areas of global governance. Trade, security, and climate, for instance, are nested in distinct contexts, with the implication that there will be different drivers interacting in different ways. Nor will one kind of driver produce one kind of change. The most that can be said is that certain drivers will create the underlying conditions for the likelihood of change from one mode to another. For instance, new forms of technology are associated with a shift from hierarchies to markets and networks. But, as Manulak and Snidal suggest, these new forms of technology may produce only a shift from formal to informal hierarchies. Technological determinism is tempting, but power and politics usually have a say. Drivers can also shape one another. The complex interaction between drivers is found in several chapters in this volume. Avant identifies how policy gridlock in the area of security led to policy entrepreneurship, which, in turn, created opportunities for policy innovation and multi-stakeholder arrangements. Seabrooke and Sending examine rationalization and transnational expertise in the context of global ideology and geopolitical changes to produce greater reliance on networks. Green identifies shifts in great power interests and rationalizing processes that led states to consider climate change to be a technical issue and to open up new forms of governance. Kahler highlights how postwar economic and political developments led to a growing regulatory state. Andonova points to the growing intersection of different markets and spaces of governance for driving more hybrid forms of global governance.

In what follows, we examine each of the nine drivers we identify in greater detail.

Geopolitics

For many international relations theorists there is no more intuitive explanation for changes in global governance than shifts in the distribution of power. A standard argument is that hegemony or a coalition of powerful states will create a hierarchical global governance, and that a shift in the distribution of power will lead to a shift in the pecking order of the hierarchy and the rules of governance.[56] This argument informs many discussions of contemporary global governance.

After the Second World War, the USA enjoyed an unprecedented degree of power. The USA used this power to reshape the global order and create a set of institutions that reflected its interests and its belief that multilateral institutions were the best way to promote cooperation and secure its hegemony at the lowest possible cost. Although it encountered turbulence in the 1970s, the existing global governance institutions endured because of American "go it alone" power.[57] After the end of the Cold War the USA used its relative power to help sponsor a new round of institution building, but arguably for different reasons – to slow its relative decline, spread the costs of cooperation through burden-sharing, and freeze the existing order.[58] Importantly, the USA and its allies began to turn away from hierarchies and toward both smaller groupings and multistakeholderism in part because they believed each would better preserve their power in a time of change.[59]

At the same time there were rising powers in the post-Cold War world who imagined a different kind of change. The rapid rise of China and other BRICs (Brazil, Russia, and India) created considerable uncertainty regarding the future of global governance.[60] Would China be a status quo or revisionist state? Would it play by the existing rules or would it want to change the rules? Would it choose to work with the existing institutions or choose to develop its own? Although many Asian states are nervous about China's growing power, its economic policies, including the Asian Infrastructure Investment Bank, are attractive at a moment when the existing institutions appear weak or strained.[61]

Several of our authors note the importance of shifts in power. For Tallberg the diffusion of material power after 1945 led to increasing questions about the legitimacy of the existing order. For Green and for

---

[56] This view is not limited to realists; see e.g. Ruggie 1982.   [57] Gruber 2000.
[58] These arguments are nearly owned by Ikenberry. See, for instance, Ikenberry 2012.
[59] See e.g. Raustiala 2016.
[60] Mukherjee and Malone 2011, 311–329; Gray and Murphy 2015; Haas 2015, 434–441; Mandrup et al. 2016.
[61] Acharya 2011, 851–869; Hanquin 2007, 83–93.

Mueller and Pevehouse the growing voice of the developing world brought new demands to climate governance and harder negotiations over the trade regime, respectively. For Avant the relevant geopolitical shift was the end of the Cold War – the move from a bipolar distribution of power – creating new demands for governance. Seabrooke and Sending argue that the end of the Cold War led to calls for governance in heretofore unexplored areas.

A Changing Global Economy

Global economic change is associated with some of the most important shifts in global governance.[62] Arguments about interdependence often highlight how changing patterns of trade, finance, and capital lead to changing rules of the international economic game. (Labor is rarely included in these discussions, but recent political upheavals around immigration have led to some attention.) The nearly twenty years of failures in the Doha Round of trade talks has encouraged more states to consider minilateral and bilateral trade arrangements. The changing structure of international trade with its complex supply chains and high levels of intrafirm trade have led some to question whether existing governance hierarchies should be fundamentally transformed.[63] Kahler echoes this argument, as he contends that globalization – with its attendant changes in cross-border flows – brought pressures on governance hierarchies that they were not able to withstand.

Marxist-oriented scholars take a different tack, tracing the relationship between transnational capitalism, global governance, and imperialism.[64] There are a host of arguments that link various configurations of capitalism to global governance, including how the postwar governance institutions were intended to produce a "compromise" between labor and capital that would unequally benefit the latter. Some argue that the phases of industrialization led to changes in international organization.[65] The rise of neoliberalism promoted an influential vision of how to encase the market in society.[66] The Washington Consensus became a central dimension of the policies of international financial institutions, profoundly benefiting foreign and domestic capital at the expense of the poor and marginalized.

---

[62] See, for instance, Taylor 2004, 773–789.
[63] See Chapter 4. Also see Baldwin 2014, 261–283.
[64] Callinicos 2002; Rupert 2005, 205–222; Chimni 2017, 41–78; Biel 2003, 77–88.
[65] Murphy 1997; Tooze 1990, 273–280.   [66] Polanyi 2001.

Increase in the Number of Actors

It has become part of the conventional wisdom that the rising number of states in the international system will slow down if not clog global governance.[67] At the signing of the UN Charter in San Francisco in 1945 there were only fifty states present. Today the membership stands at 193, and the degree of difficulty is not additive but logarithmic. Because of this gridlock states often try to form smaller, more manageable groupings (which in theory could possess a hierarchical character).[68] Increasing numbers may also account for more informal and networked modes of governance.[69] But it also has led to more obstacles on the way to "yes." It is no surprise that alongside "multi-stakeholder dialogue" phrases like "conference fatigue" and "treaty congestion" began to be widely invoked in the 1990s. In short, not only were the problems of the post-Cold War era likely harder to tackle, there were many more –and more diverse – actors that were at the table and had to be satisfied in some fashion.

Pluralization of Kinds of Actors

Does the rising diversity of the actors in global governance presage a shift in the modes of governance? While states have traditionally preferred hierarchical arrangements, other actors, such as corporations, are more likely to prefer markets, and NGOs and transnational actors are likely to prefer networks. The creation of hierarchical governance has also carried the seeds of pluralization. As states created (hierarchical) IOs this encouraged the emergence of new actors relating in different modes.[70] A variation on this theme is that the staff of IOs will create emanations (non-independent organizations) or ally with NGOs to evade their state masters.[71] Thus, the shift to more networked forms of governance could be driven (ironically) by bureaucracies attempting to reduce the shadow of hierarchy. Private and public authorities now frequently mingle, as emphasized by Andonova's and Avant's chapters, creating hybrid forms of governance that defy easy categorization.[72]

---

[67] Hale and Held 2013.   [68] Naím 2009, 136.
[69] Hale and Held 2017 argue that gridlock could be dissolved by several forces, including a change in great power interests, adaptive international institutions, expert groups, and the convergence of different kinds of actors around common goals and norms.
[70] According to Seabrooke and Sending, this is the case in the area of post-Cold War security policy – as professional networks engaged in advocacy to respond to fragile states.
[71] Johnson 2015.   [72] Büthe and Mattli 2011.

Another nascent but profound change is that private actors, as well as substate actors, have increasingly circumvented the traditional negotiating forums and taken the lead in designing their own governance structures. As Moon notes, the Gates Foundation was instrumental in getting Gavi and the Global Fund off the ground. And a new wave of networks, often in the regulatory arena, began engaging globally without going (directly) through their foreign policy apparatus. The International Organization of Securities Commissions (IOSCO) is one of the many transnational regulatory networks that illustrate this process.[73] IOSCO is largely standard-setting and consensus-based; the participants coordinate domestic actions but importantly coordinate principles and norms and share best practices. Thus, the rise in the number of NGOs, private actors, and public–private networks suggests a potential diffusion of authority away from the top of the hierarchy into networks and market-oriented modes.

Low-Hanging Fruit

Fruit and its height on the tree are often in the eye of the beholder, but a widely accepted observation is that negotiated agreements were easier to achieve in the early postwar years than in the later years because there were clear overlapping interests. But as the difficulties increase, the desire to find alternative governance modes increases. One scenario is that because states do not want to spend time and resources on difficult problems they delegate authority to non-state actors to solve these problems. This could be especially true in issue areas that were traditionally considered "low politics" – why spend scarce resources on issues which are viewed as unimportant or marginal? Note that the logic of these arguments are akin to an adverse selection problem: these newer, or at least later-tackled, problems typically require much more detailed coordination and compromise and agitate new sets of interest groups.

Mueller and Pevehouse note how the General Agreement on Tariffs and Trade (GATT) initially dealt with tariffs and trade in goods, leaving aside far touchier areas such as trade in agriculture, non-tariff barriers, services, and cultural goods. There were plenty of issues to fight over, but also a relatively clear path forward and broad consensus on goals. In short, the low-hanging fruit was there to be picked, and for many decades the harvest was good. In contrast to the first four trade rounds that lasted an average of six months, Doha has run for twenty years – and counting.

---

[73] Gadinis 2015, 1–57; Raustiala 2002.

Among the reasons are disagreements over intellectual property provisions (something no early GATT negotiator paid attention to) and agricultural trade (something GATT negotiators left off the table for political reasons). As Manulak and Snidal note, it is the issues that are nettlesome and not well defined that have forced changes in solution concepts in governance.

Ideologies of Governance

Ideologies of governance can be shaped by cultural expectations regarding what kinds of governance solutions are generally most efficient and appropriate. As we noted at the beginning of this chapter, modes of global governance are often said to have shifted from hierarchies to networks and markets. Changes in ideologies of governance can help explain this transformation. In the early postwar years the assumption was that governance required a strong role for the state.[74] As Kahler argues, it was this mid-century victory of the "regulatory state" that also gave rise to strong hierarchies in global governance. Beginning in the 1980s, and especially evident with the rise of neoliberalism, there was a growing belief that governance is done best and is most efficient when the state steps back. Moon notes that beliefs about efficacy help account for the shift from hierarchical to market and network modes of governance in global health. To many this represents a positive development that produces a more efficient, democratic, and effective system of governance. There is a greater interest in having business and technological sectors' solutions applied to longstanding global problems such as poverty. The recent US assault on the existing global governance system also reflects ideologies of governance. A small government, pro-sovereignty worldview is almost necessarily anti-global governance. The Trump White House was championed by nationalists who saw globalism as a threat to the identity and interests of the USA.[75]

Global Rationalization

Among the various explanations for the changes in global governance, global rationalization is the most "cultural." Rationalization is a multi-layered process that broadly refers to the movement of societies from tradition to modernity. For our purposes it underscores some features that help explain the shift toward networks. To begin with, rationalization

---

[74] Slaughter 1992.   [75] White House 2018; Bolton 2000.

is bound up with a new kind of authority – a rational-legal authority whose authority claims derive from being constituted by law and following sound, scientific objective reasoning. Rational-legal authority is both rational and legal. The preferred manner of making decisions is through standardized calculations that can produce more efficient and effective responses to environmental demands. Modern governance of all kinds displays this type of reasoning and authority. Additionally, legitimacy is increasingly conferred on bureaucratic principles such as hierarchy, specialization, and routinization. In other words, it is not just hierarchy that matters, but hierarchy that conforms to specific organizing principles. IOs, in this view, are increasingly valorized to the extent that they present modern bureaucratic characteristics.[76] And law, whether it is hard or soft or something in-between, figures more importantly in global governance than ever before. Indeed, it is often viewed as the gold standard for the legitimation of rules, the paragon of objectivity, and the depoliticizing mechanism that any enduring order needs.[77]

Via rationalization expert knowledge is increasingly valued over lived or learned knowledge. Governance authorities are not only supposed to be staffed by experts with the right training and advanced education, but experts can become something of a class unto themselves and form their own networks that circulate in the environment and influence global governance.[78] Moreover, expertise, standardization, and specialization has led to the emergence of distinct fields that define rules for regulating activity, standards of legitimacy, and notions of competence and best practices.[79] Rationalization processes are also associated with standard-setting, benchmarking, and governing through indicators.[80]

Technological Change

While the emergence of new issues and the pluralization of participants has soured many on solutions based on large, bureaucratic multilateral organizations, technological change has created the possibility for more networked, flexible, and innovative governance solutions. As Manulak and Snidal argue, one no longer needs a formal secretariat convening meetings in a headquarters to facilitate governance. The influence of

---

[76] Barnett and Finnemore 2004.   [77] Roger 2020.

[78] Sending 2015; Cross 2013, 137–160; Barnett and Finnemore 2004; Cutler 2010, 157–185; Dezalay and Garth 2010, 113–130.

[79] Bernstein and van der Ven 2017, 534–556.

[80] Davis et al. 2012; Larner and Hue 2004; Cooley and Snyder 2015; Kelley 2017; Broome and Quirk 2015, 813–818; Best 2017, 163–181.

technology goes beyond methods of communication, however. Information that was once hard to get is now easily grabbed with Google, and easily crunched by cheap computing. Social media facilitate communication, lower monitoring costs, and ease the implementation of programs and policies.[81] Air travel makes it much easier for groups of various sizes to gather. Technological changes have revolutionized communication and coordination, even making it possible to gather in a virtual space: Zoom governance as the new global governance. Governance once limited to vertical links has become increasingly horizontal; and horizontal and vertical links have begun to coalesce into networks. One consequence is that network governance has become the (hyped) solution, touted as more democratic, flexible, and innovative, more capable of learning, and more efficient. All of these developments permit, or encourage, new forms of governance.

And as these technological changes pervade the globe they enable non-state actors to coordinate more easily. Setting aside the question of whether NGOs have wrestled any real power or authority away from states, technology has allowed them to level the playing field in the areas of coordination, information, and even resources. Some of these changes are closely linked to the shift in reigning ideologies of governance discussed earlier in this section. It is hard to say what came first, and perhaps this is a chicken and egg question never to be answered. But it seems clear that as technology has shaped the sense of the possible in governance, so too have ideas about the best models for governance shifted.

Domestic Change

The first eight drivers introduce the role of domestic forces but without necessarily giving it its proper due. There is, however, an established literature in international relations that considers the "second image" and its effects on international order in general and on global governance specifically. Changes in voting patterns, coalitions, regimes, and governments are often attributed to a shift in the state's strategy toward specific agreements and global governance possibilities. These strategies are molded by domestic actors in power. There also is the "second image reversed" that considers how various global forces – growing interdependence, responses to specific treaties, multilateral arrangements, and

---

[81] Castells 2009; Shirky 2011, 28–41.

international financial institutions – can influence domestic politics and institutions.[82]

Some of this literature hits closer to the subject of this volume, particularly as it considers how domestic coalitions prefer one governance mode over another. There is, for instance, a growing literature on the role of domestic actors in the shift from hierarchies to networks and markets. Illustrative are the groups that have called for an end to hierarchical arrangements altogether (e.g., the International Criminal Court or Trans-Pacific Partnership) or to renegotiate them (e.g., the North American Free Trade Agreement), and the growing role of municipalities and regional governments in transnational networks on climate governance.

The chapters suggest various reasons why domestic actors might become mobilized around governance. For example, Moon argues that the HIV/AIDS crisis and its resulting domestic social pressures led directly to the evolution of governance in global health. Domestic activists might perceive the existing arrangements as inadequate to solve the global problem or want to create arrangements that give them a greater voice. On the other hand, some domestic actors, such as corporations, may wish to preserve hierarchical arrangements because they shut out other non-state actors – a form of regulatory capture. And then there is rising nationalism, which tends to target hierarchical modes of governance because they appear most threatening to sovereignty, because they are the most visible symbols of global governance, or because they are blamed for the perceived degradation of economic welfare and the "purity" of the nation. The two infamous examples are Brexit and the election of Donald Trump, and in both cases a particular form of domestic politics led to a desire to cut the taut ties to global institutions.[83] However, in contrast to the prevailing wisdom that global institutions are losing their legitimacy and popularity, Tallberg argues that they actually retain considerable support.

One last but critical point is that when accounting for a change in the modes of global governance the chapters rely not only on the drivers we have detailed but also on actors' preferences, interests, and strategies. Indeed, because these drivers are structural they create underlying conditions of possibility and impossibility, tightening and loosening constraints for particular kinds of action, and recalculating strategies for maintaining and extending power. All the chapters acknowledge how actors are central to the story of change, whether the actors are the

---

[82] Gourevitch 1978.
[83] For a review of this narrative, see Copelovitch and Pevehouse 2019.

USA, the ICRC, professional networks, corporations, NGOs, or UN agencies. Both stasis and change are produced not only by environmental forces, but also by actors that believe that a shift in the mode of global governance must be resisted or engineered. And the reasons for their positions reflect not only a desire to produce more efficient and effective global governance, but also to protect and advance their private interests.

What Is at Stake?

We began this project because we wondered about the state and the trajectory of global governance. Like many before us we were struck by the transformation of global governance, frequently described as "old" and "new." But the more we dove into the attributes that seemingly marked the change between the past and the present the more convinced we became that, while important, they did not adequately capture the "how" of global governance and the ways it had evolved. Modes of governance provided an alternative way of approaching this critical issue. But what does our focus on modes say about the state of global governance? We reject pat conclusions that might suggest the new is better than the old, or that one mode is necessarily superior to the others. As with everything in life, it depends. For those seeking verdicts we have only hung juries.

But the chapters provide varied ways to unpack the current state of global governance. Each engages, in its own way, two separate but entangled dimensions of the quality of global governance: effectiveness and ethics. Consider effectiveness. Many chapters note that actors sought change because the existing mode was perceived to be ineffective. Did they get what they hoped? The results were mixed. In Andonova's study of global energy governance, earlier state-dominated governance was unable to produce the kind of collaboration required. Yet it proved difficult for non-state actors to figure out how to slot into a much more decentralized governance framework. Almost all the chapters capture some sort of trade-off that both advances and frustrates the ability to mobilize effective action. Effectiveness is of course a notoriously difficult concept to operationalize, and its evaluation is inherently value-laden: effective for what? Still, the chapters suggest, perhaps unsurprisingly, that clear advances in effectiveness are rare.

Complicating any evaluation of effectiveness, moreover, is that the authors adopt different definitions of effectiveness. Rather than seeing this as a problem, we treat this as an important finding. Effectiveness is an inherently varied concept. For the participants in a given regime effectiveness could mean shaping outcomes, establishing norms or laws, or even changing the mode of governance. Green echoes this sentiment on the issue of climate governance: the change in mode of governance itself is often seen as an effective outcome, yet its long-run influence on the ultimate goal, reversing climate change, is still unknown. Perhaps this is an example of the weary embrace of "good enough governance," or perhaps it reflects a more meaningful belief that gains in process are critical for gains in substance.

Further complicating any evaluation of effectiveness is that shifts in the modes of governance often led to a change in *what* was governed. Many of the chapters note how debates about the mode of governance often had the knock-on effect of changing the subject of governance. As Seabrooke and Sending observe, for example, the substance of governance is not independent of the mode. And if the content has changed, then presumably so too does the meaning of effectiveness. Moon notes a similar dynamic in global health: as new modes of governance have led to more effective responses to certain types of crises, other aims have fallen off the table, making net effectiveness difficult to determine. Moreover, some of the push for new modes in global health are as much a reflection of an effort at retaining power (on the part of traditionally powerful actors) as an effort at improving effectiveness.

The second dimension of quality includes ethics: legitimacy, fairness, accountability, transparency, and democracy, among others. Many studies of global governance tend to fall into a depoliticized stance, to treat governance as a technical accomplishment: all means to the neglect of ends. But ethics is always in the background, and often in the foreground, of global governance. The chapters often refer to legitimacy, accountability, and other normative claims. Legitimacy is not incidental to global governance but central, because it focuses on whether global governance and its institutional arrangements are accepted and decisions followed. In this sense legitimacy is both a deontological concern and an aspect of effectiveness: more legitimate systems tend to be more effective and, perhaps, more efficient. Indeed, it is worth remembering that the concept of global governance became the term of choice for describing new forms of cooperation that were presumed to represent a more legitimate form of international order. The question of legitimacy is expansively covered by Tallberg, so we need not say much here.

Legitimacy traditionally has two components. Process legitimacy regards whether decisions go through the right process. In contemporary international society the right process is often assumed to be participatory and democratic. Output legitimacy asks whether decisions are largely consistent with the values of the community. It is possible to have one and not the other but legitimate institutions ideally have both.

Hierarchical modes of governance may be effective but they are routinely accused of lacking legitimacy and running a democratic deficit. In response, demands for inclusivity have risen.

But does inclusion necessarily generate more legitimacy? Many of the players newly included claim to speak on behalf of the "public good" or the "people" but this self-presentation seems to be based on a combination of self-assuredness, ideology, and hubris. Kahler reminds us that private modes of governance, once considered normatively acceptable and legitimate at the beginning of the twentieth century, have become more contested in the twenty-first. Manulak and Snidal point to a variant of the inclusion–legitimacy relationship: that transnational actors can themselves be legitimized by their inclusion in informal international organizations. This has implications for effectiveness but from a particular standpoint: the head of government, who can now avoid a potentially complex and stultifying domestic bureaucracy.

Expanding the circle of inclusion is not infinite but rather has clear boundaries – some actors or stakeholders are always left out, and these exclusions shape whose interests are represented and whose voice counts. Moon points out how the inclusion of drug companies as part of multi-stakeholder efforts in global health has the potential to delegitimize governance efforts in the eyes of some. Similarly, Barnett suggests that a combination of hierarchy and networks dominates in the area of humanitarianism, but important actors in the Global South are summarily excluded from what he labels as the Humanitarian Club. This is consonant with those who claim that global governance lacks legitimacy because it fundamentally represents Western interests and values. As Amitav Acharya and others have emphasized, global governance, and its sidekick the liberal international order, were never very legitimate in the eyes of the Global South.[84]

The chapters reinforce the growing sense that global governance will also be judged on other normative standards. A global governance arrangement might be effective but nevertheless rejected if it is seen as unfair or unjust. But the chapters also reinforce the view that it is difficult to harmonize these culturally and historically bound judgments. Trade agreements have to provide economic gains for both sides, but there are instances in which a trade proposal is rejected by one side because it is seen as insulting. The International Criminal Court has run into various situations in which "global justice" is in tension with "local justice."

[84] Acharya 2018.

Power can also be understood as part of the normative dimension of global governance. Although in many of the chapters forms of power are used to discuss why some actors were able to achieve their preferred mode of governance, considerations of power also figure centrally in the consequences of a change in the mode of governance. There are distributional consequences, which of course link to questions of fairness. There are questions of arbitrary power, which is most apparent in the growing demand for accountability and transparency and the desire to ensure that there are mechanisms in place so that those who are in power can be held to account by those who are affected by their decisions.[85] And, as just noted, there are matters of representation. Many of the chapters point to the demand for greater inclusion to limit the influence of the powerful. Sometimes this happens within hierarchy, as when a small group of states move to include other states. Sometimes this happens within networks. Several of the chapters question whether these moves toward greater inclusion present a real opportunity for giving voice to the marginalized, or rather are merely ways of giving the appearance of growing equality while maintaining the status quo.

Do effectiveness and normativity reinforce or undercut each other? Avant suggests that a more inclusive global governance will be more effective. Other chapters suggest that while more voices might lead to improved outcomes, they could also lead to the lowest common denominator or simply more veto players. In many of the chapters the search for more effective global governance arrangements went in the direction of markets and networks, which appeared to unleash more activity than ever.

The big question is whether change has actually increased the prospects of solving global problems or instead provides only the illusion of improvement. Some argue that there is no substitute for hierarchies when it comes to solving big global problems, and often point to the golden years of global governance after the Second World War and the end of the Cold War. Mueller and Pevehouse echo this idea when they question the move to regionalism in trade: the classic building blocks versus stumbling blocs debate in trade liberalization. Regional arrangements may have advantages in terms of legitimacy and perhaps effectiveness for participants, but from a global welfare perspective economists would argue that such regional arrangements are suboptimal. The question of effectiveness for what or whom is always present.

---

[85] Slaughter 2004; Bexell et al. 2010, 81–101; Dutta 2012; Grant and Keohane 2005, 29–43; Koppell 2010; Keohane 2015, 343–353; Pillinger et al. 2016, 70–86.

Others argue that these hierarchies are part of the problem – lumbering dinosaurs that must yield to nimbler, fluid, and inclusive networks and markets to deliver the goods.[86] Hierarchies are for planners, while markets and networks are guided by searchers.[87] Hierarchies are anti-democratic while markets and networks are more inclusive and capture the wisdom of the public. But are the major challenges of today fixable or even manageable via piecemeal, incremental, and disorganized efforts?[88] Moreover, if the "shadow of hierarchy" is omnipresent this mode of governance can never be replaced in an anarchic world, only managed. In sum, hierarchical modes just might prioritize effectiveness through a concentration of power – a concentration that is increasingly considered illegitimate. Whether this is an insurmountable tension is not clear.

Market modes of governance promise greater efficiency and effectiveness, and (usually) the diffusion of power across units within markets. Yet, except in abstract models, markets are never perfect. Markets require property rights and regulation to remain robust from predation (and the illegitimacy that follows) and competitive. Property rights and regulations are never value neutral and often have their own mechanisms of inclusion and exclusion, creating their own forms of hierarchy. Networks modes of governance are frequently championed as legitimate and effective: offering a voice for many, efficient allocation of expertise, local expertise for legitimacy, and the diffusion of power away from traditional stakeholders. But some of our authors suggest that the sum may not be more than the whole of the parts. Decentralization can lead to a lack of efficiency and worse: to competition and cross-purposes. And where is the accountability point in networks? A boss may be more easily tamed than a hydra-headed monster.

Actors are constantly tweaking and sometimes attempting to transform modes of governance with the hope that they will improve their effectiveness and be more fair, accountable, and just. But the chapters suggest that effectiveness and ethics are something of a balancing act in global governance, and rarely do all good things go together. And what might be prescribed as the best fit for the social situation is often elusive. Studies of global governance have been quite good at spinning prescriptions, but the empirical reality is often quite different because states care about more than just effectiveness and ethics; in fact, an argument can be made that often effectiveness and ethics is the last thing on their minds. Perhaps the world gets the global governance it deserves.

---

[86] Plesch and Weiss 2015, 197–204.   [87] Easterly 2006   [88] Hale and Held 2013.

Overview of the Chapters

Global governance is a huge topic and this is an ambitious book. Yet there is much we left out. Although the volume has a fixed set of concerns and questions we decided to avoid the focus-structured comparative method in favor of allowing the contributors to address the foundational questions we raise in this Introduction in the manner that made the most sense to them. Although the obvious disadvantage of this open-ended approach is that we lose something in the ability to draw firmer generalizations, the decisive advantage is that we open the aperture and possibly capture processes that might otherwise be overlooked.

Perhaps the most difficult decision was selecting the featured areas of global governance. This was complicated for a few reasons. First, the standard way of dividing global governance is by issue area, but there are issues areas that have expanded, converged, and layered (which is one reason we have regime complexity), and there are some issue areas that are so large, such as the environment, that it makes greater sense to disaggregate into different subareas, such as climate change, energy, biodiversity, and so on. Second, this is a book that is about the transformation of global governance writ large and not the individual stories of different issue areas. Those stories are important, but we want to keep a focus on the forest as much as the trees. Consequently, while it might make sense to pick the "superstars" of global governance, such as climate change, arms control, financial regulation, peacekeeping, and so on, it is difficult to know a priori whether these issue areas tell us everything we want to know about the transformations that are taking place. For instance, one of the major innovations in global governance occurred decades ago with the establishment of the World Commission on Dams (a coalition of NGOs and international financial institutions), which was not exactly a marquee issue at the time.

Given these very important limits on case selection we decided in favor of something much more practical, inductive, and intuitive: to identify some of the important areas of global governance, with importance defined in terms of what they might say about the evolution of different modes of global governance. The consequence is that we believe the chapters provide a sufficient range of coverage, but there are areas that are not covered that we wish had been, for instance gender, development, cybersecurity, and refugees. Our claim is not to be comprehensive. Rather, we (hope to) demonstrate the importance of the question of transformation in the architecture of global governance and, in the chapters to come, map out the broad contours of that phenomenon. We are demonstrating and beginning to map out a phenomenon, not testing a theory.

In Chapter 1, Deborah Avant compares the architecture of global governance across two security issues: the regulation of private militaries and of small arms. In the former case she argues that a multi-stakeholder arrangement engaging a panoply of actors has replaced a largely hierarchical structure previously dominated by states. In the latter, networks reign in particularly contentious fashion, leading Avant to suggest a governance deficit in this issue area. Avant argues that geopolitical changes and an emergence of new actors lead to an opening in the area of private militaries that was filled by Swiss policy entrepreneurs. For the small arms area, while networks have actively sought solutions, and policy entrepreneurs have attempted to build momentum for cooperation, a continued attempt to create a hierarchical structure has met with less success. Avant concludes that governance strategies that are more open to different actor types are better able to generate governance coordination.

In Chapter 2, Miles Kahler argues that the post-Second World War architecture of hierarchical, centralized global governance is the historical exception rather than the rule. The interwar period, according to Kahler, contained mostly instances of marke- and network-based governance encouraged by less interventionist central governments. These less centralized institutions were replaced by strong, state-led hierarchies after the war – in order to constrain both markets and states. Yet, as the recovery progressed, more informal and private modes of governance reemerged to challenge the hierarchical model. For Kahler the past presages the present both in terms of governance patterns but also in terms of the key driving factor: globalization. The height of hierarchical modes of governance occurs at a time of closed markets and the rise of the regulatory state. Kahler investigates three areas to review the variety of interwar governance arrangements, their immediate postwar regulation, and subsequent shift to less hierarchical governance: international monetary and financial affairs, cartels, and international commercial arbitration.

In Chapter 3, Jessica F. Green examines the global regime in climate governance. Although climate governance is a relatively new issue, Green argues that we have already witnessed change in the previous two decades. Moreover, she argues that conventional wisdom about the two central pieces of climate governance – the Kyoto Protocol and the Paris Agreement – misdiagnoses key features of their architectures. The conventional top-down (hierarchical) view of Kyoto misses key market- and network-based aspects of governance, while states remain in an important role in the (supposedly) bottom-up Paris Agreement. Green argues that changing geopolitical factors, namely the rise of the BRICs as well as the process of global rationalization, led to the failure of the Kyoto approach. This failure gave rise to a more flexible and politically viable Paris Agreement, which reserved important roles for states. And while Green contends that this flexibility has made Paris more politically palatable, it also leaves the success of the effort more uncertain. Indeed, she concludes by noting the move to new architectures of governance: often dubbed "experimentalism," these offer promise but uncertainty in the area of climate change.

In Chapter 4, Susanne Mueller and Jon C.W. Pevehouse discuss the emergence of an increasingly complex set of governance mechanisms in the area of global trade. At its core the postwar trade regime was hierarchical: the GATT was a state-led organization that governed with a light touch. Members of the GATT promised to abide by a principle of fairness in tariff-setting, while compliance with that principle was governed by the GATT and its state members. Nongovernmental actors were only allowed very limited access to the governance process. Yet, two challenges brought shifts in the governance architecture. First, states began to exploit the regionalism exception in the GATT, creating separate agreements regarding tariffs – still closed to non-state actors – but potentially in competition with the GATT. This created a multi-peaked hierarchical system. Second, because of rising domestic opposition and the success of trade governance, governance became less about trade and more about non-trade issues: labor rights, the environment, and human rights. The linking of policies and non-trade policies has created an opening to networks to play some role in the trade governance process.

In Chapter 5, Michael Barnett argues that humanitarian governance has the characteristics of a club. Humanitarianism – the attempt to provide life-saving relief to distant strangers – has a long history but without much governance. Prior to the end of the Cold War emergency agencies largely acted on their own and marched to their own beats, with the exception of the Second World War when governments established various controls on them. The end of the Cold War and several high-profile failures in the field caused a handful of elite aid agencies to begin thinking about establishing rules to govern emergency aid. In the process of creating these rules they created a humanitarian field and a Humanitarian Club with themselves as core members. The members of the club had characteristics of both a hierarchy and networks: the donors called many of the shots but the aid agencies and the UN system largely collaborated to create many of the rules and codes of conduct for relief. Excluded from the club, though, were Southern aid agencies, which were the vast majority of agencies and often the first responders. In reaction to this pattern of exclusion and inclusion there have been many reform efforts. Using Bourdieu's notion of capital to understand power and distinction, Barnett argues that these Southern aid agencies are locked out because of a combination of self-interest and paternalism from the members of the club.

In Chapter 6, Michael W. Manulak and Duncan Snidal argue that some areas of global governance that once were organized around formal hierarchies have added a strong layer of networks and become informal hierarchies. Once upon a time many areas of global governance ran as follows: when there were clear and well-defined issues, government heads created cooperative arrangements and then these arrangements were implemented transgovernmentally within a formal, hierarchical organization. This process still operates, but with an important twist: confronting issues that are not well defined, governments leaders meet to come to a common understanding and develop trust within informal international organizations and then assign their networked national line departments to implement their agreement. What happened to produce this change? The growing role of information. Information has two dimensions: technical information, which concerns how problems are diagnosed and remedied; and political information, which is how polit-ical leaders decide what is to be done. Political information becomes more important when there is issue uncertainty and must be addressed before those with technical information can find solutions. And we live in a world in which there is greater uncertainty about the issues than ever before. They use the Proliferation Security Network to illustrate their argument.

In Chapter 7, Leonard Seabrooke and Ole Jacob Sending examine how the creation of the category of "fragile states" led to the development of a professional network of individuals who claimed expertise in pro-moting resilience. They make several claims. Beginning in the post-Cold War period states that were in the thick of war, conflict, or instability became defined as a "problem" for the international community. In addition to the UN there were states, NGOs, and for-profit agencies that began to offer action plans and remedies. But, according to Seabrooke and Sending, there was a synchronicity between these actors, suggesting that there was a common background factor – a developing professional network that influenced these other organizations through their creden-tials and their employment in them. Seabrooke and Sending argue that such expertise was not an accomplished fact but rather required a struggle for jurisdictional control in their relationships with other profes-sional networks, such as those in development or human rights. These experts on fragile states used to focus on the process of liberal peacebuilding, but after 9/11 began to shift toward issues of "protection" and stabilization. This move, however, reopened a space for the UN and other military organizations that introduced a stronger hierarchical element into the network.

In Chapter 8, Suerie Moon argues that the governance of global health has evolved considerably since the mid-nineteenth century – from a thin, limited set of formally agreed rules within the health sector in 1850, to a more centralized and traditional approach with the World Health Organization at the center, to today's more complex, dense, yet fragmented system featuring many networks, non-state actors, and multistakeholder processes. Many of the currents underlying broader changes in global governance, Moon argues, also impact the health sector, such as a globalizing economy, the demographic transition, neoliberal and cosmopolitan ideation, and technological change. But key features of the contemporary governance system also owe much to the particularities of the HIV/AIDS pandemic and the social responses to it. Despite many weaknesses, the World Health Organization's central role – not as a directive coordinator but rather as a convener, legitimator, and political arena – is likely to endure in an increasingly fragmented yet ambitious Westphalia-plus, Great Powers-plus system.

In Chapter 9, Vincent Bernard and Anne Quintin examine the evolution of the governance of international humanitarian law (IHL). IHL governs how states fight, and, as law, is established and revised by states. States established the ICRC as a quasi-IO to implement, guard, and teach IHL, and since its creation in 1864 it has been central to the governance of IHL. In addition, the ICRC established red cross societies across the Euro-Atlantic world. Although these red cross societies were supposed to defer to the ICRC, because they needed domestic support, they often became co-opted by their home states. The ICRC saw itself as the guardian of IHL and sought to ensure centralization and consistency in IHL. Bernard and Quintin call this a hybrid model of global governance. Although this situation might have encouraged the ICRC to try and defend its turf, in fact it tightened its internal cohesion and it adopted a strategy that welcomed new entrants. This governance model remained unchanged until the post-Cold War period when there were several critical challenges to IHL, including new forms of war, the growing incorporation of human rights into humanitarian law, the development of international criminal law, the need to get non-state actors to accept IHL, and the relationship with the red crescent movement. Despite these major trends, Bernard and Quintin contend that this hybrid form has endured and proved flexible and responsive to these developments.

In Chapter 10, Liliana B. Andonova argues that changes in clean energy governance can be characterized as decentralized complex governance. The shadow of IOs looms over networks of actors, yet those decentralized networks principally guide the norms and functions of governance. Andonova contends that immobilism, brought about by geopolitical differences, has led to the emergence of this decentralized complex governance. In addition, the complexity of the clean energy problem has contributed to a growing need for a variety of expertise. These factors provide the demand side explanation for the move from centralized, hierarchical governance. However, Andonova emphasizes that they do not explain the emergence of the particular decentralized complex arrangements. Rather, governance entrepreneurs and their political coalitions play a central role in shaping institutional form in clean energy. These entrepreneurs use existing intergovernmental hierarchies to help garner political support and legitimacy in their efforts. The result, for Andonova, is the emergence of decentralized, yet cooperative, efforts between public and private entities.

In Chapter 11 Jonas Tallberg explores the relationship between legitimacy and the change in global governance. Legitimacy is often argued to be critical to global governance and the decline of legitimacy directly tied to the demise of and change in global governance. Tallberg finds limited support for both claims. Many of the most prominent theories of global governance change, including those that highlight geopolitics and domestic politics, use legitimacy as an intervening variable – a change in these other variables alters the legitimacy for existing IOs. But citing public opinion surveys, Tallberg argues that IOs are actually doing just fine in terms of legitimacy. The consequence is that it is difficult to argue that a decline in the legitimacy of IOs might be the reason for a shift to other forms of global governance. Indeed, he finds that these alternative forms might have less legitimacy and that elites have higher confidence in the traditional hierarchical IOs. Why is this? Some of this owes to their familiarity and their representativeness, but perhaps most important is that the more confidence that elites and publics have in their own institutions the more likely they will be to treat these traditional IOs as legitimate.

In the Conclusion Orfeo Fioretos observes how the global institutional arrangements that structure contemporary relations between states and other actors have grown beyond past benchmarks of diversity. This institutional diversity accentuates some challenges for contemporary global governance, including how states and global actors strike a balance in the integration of institutions. While in some periods and areas there have been successful efforts to integrate global governance arrangements, a sense has long prevailed among contemporary policy-makers and scholars that global governance has become conspicuously fragmented. Institutional incompatibilities that stem from diverse designs are one reason why the world is thought to be poorly equipped to effectively manage global challenges in the security, trade, finance, health, environmental, and other policy domains, especially when these intersect. This chapter probes the contributions of comparative institutional analysis for explaining past and present institutional diversity as well as answers to why institutional integration remains an elusive goal in contemporary global governance.

References

Abbott, Ken and Duncan Snidal. 2010. Strengthening International Regulation through Transnational New Governance: Overcoming the Orchestration Deficit. *Vanderbilt Journal of Transnational Law* 47 (2): 501–578.

Abbott, Kenneth, Phillip Genschel, Duncan Snidal, and Bernhard Zangl. 2015a. *International Organizations as Orchestrators*. New York: Cambridge University Press.

Abbott, Kenneth, Jessica F. Green, and Robert Keohane. 2015b. Organizational Ecology and Institutional Change in Global Governance. *International Organization* 70 (2): 247–277.

Acharya, Amitav. 2011. Can Asia Lead? Power Ambitions and Global Governance in the Twenty-First Century. *International Affairs* 87 (2): 851–869.

ed. 2016. *Why Govern: Rethinking Demand and Progress*. New York: Cambridge University Press.

2018. *Constructing Global Order: Agency and Change in World Politics*. New York: Cambridge University Press.

Alter, Karen and Kal Raustiala. 2018. The Rise of International Regime Complexity. *Annual Review of Law and Social Science*: 329–349.

Andonova, Liliana. 2017. *Governance Entrepreneurs: International Organizations and the Rise of Global Public–Private Partnerships*. New York: Cambridge University Press.

Avant, Deborah. 2005. *The Market for Force: The Consequences of Privatizing Security*. New York: Cambridge University Press.

Avant, Deborah, Martha Finnemore, and Susan Sell. 2010. *Who Governs the Globe?* New York: Cambridge University Press.

Baldwin, Richard. 2014. WTO 2.0: Governance of 21st Century Trade. *The Review of International Organizations* 9 (2): 261–283.

2016. Multilateralising Regionalism: Spaghetti Bowls as Building Blocs on the Path to Global Free Trade. *The World Economy* 29 (11): 1451–1518.

Barnett, Michael. 2013. Humanitarian Governance. *Annual Review of Political Science* 16: 379–398.

Barnett, Michael and Martha Finnemore. 2004. *Rules for the World: International Organizations in World Politics*. Ithaca, NY: Cornell University Press.

Bartley, Tim. 2011. Transnational Governance as the Layering of Rules: Intersections of Public and Private Standards. *Theoretical Inquiries in Law* 12 (2): 517–542.

Bartolini, Stefano. 2011. New Modes of European Governance: An Introduction. In *New Modes of Governance in Europe*, edited by A. Héritier and M. Rhodes, 1–18. London: Palgrave Macmillan.

Bernstein, Steven and Benjamin Cashore. 2012. Complex Global Governance and Domestic Policies: Four Pathways of Influence. *International Affairs* 88 (3): 585–604.

Bernstein, Steven and Hamish van der Ven. 2017. Best Practices in Global Governance. *Review of International Studies* 43 (3): 534–556.

Best, Jacqueline. 2017. The Rise of Measurement-Driven Governance: The Case of International Development. *Global Governance* (23): 163–181.

Bexell, Magdalena, Jonas Tallberg, and Anders Uhlin. 2010. Democracy in Global Governance: The Promises and Pitfalls of Transnational Actors. *Global Governance* 16 (1): 81–101.

Biel, Robert. 2003. Imperialism and International Governance: The Case of U.S. Policy towards Africa. *Review of African Political Economy* 30 (95): 77–88.

Blatter, Joachim. 2003. Beyond Hierarchies and Networks: Institutional Logics and Change in Transboundary Spaces. *Governance* 26 (4): 503–526.

Blauberger, M. and B. Rittberger. 2015. Conceptualizing and Theorizing EU Regulatory Networks. *Regulation & Governance* 9: 367–376.

Bloomberg, Michael. 2015. City Century: Why Municipalities Are the Key to Fighting Climate Change. *Foreign Affairs* (September/October): 67–79.

Boli, John and George M. Thomas. 1997. World Culture in the World Polity: A Century of International Non-governmental Organization. *American Sociological Review* 62 (2): 171–190.

Bolton, John. 2000. Should We Take Global Governance Seriously? Presented at the American Enterprise Institute Conference, Trends in Global Governance: Do They Threaten American Sovereignty?, April, Washington, DC.

Broome, André and Joel Quirk. 2015. The Politics of Global Numbers: The Normative Agendas of Global Benchmarking. *Review of International Studies* 41: 813–818.

Bush, Sarah and Jennifer Haddon. 2019. Density and Decline in the Founding of International NGOs in the United States. *International Studies Quarterly* 63 (4): 1113–1146.

Büthe, Tim and Walter Mattli. 2011. *The New Global Rulers: The Privatization of Regulation in the World Economy*. Princeton: Princeton University Press.

Callinicos, Alex. 2002. Marxism and Global Governance. In *Governing Globalization*, edited by D. Held and A. McGrew, 249–266. New York: Polity Press.

Carpenter, R. Charli. 2011. Vetting the Advocacy Agenda: Networks, Centrality and the Paradox of Weapons Norms. *International Organization* 65 (1): 69–102.

Cashore, B., G. Auld, and D. Newsom. 2004. *Governing through Markets: Forest Certification and the Emergence of Non-state Authority*. New Haven: Yale University Press.

Castells, Manuel. 2009. *The Power of Identity*. Oxford: Wiley Blackwell.

Chimni, B.S. 2017. International Institutions Today: An Imperial Global State in the Making. In *Globalization and International Organizations*, edited by Edward Kwakwa, 41–78. New York: Routledge.

Coase, Ronald. 1937. Theory of the Firm. *Economica* 4 (16): 386–405.

Coen, David and Tom Pegram. 2015. Wanted: A Third Generation of Global Governance Research. *Governance* 28 (4): 417–420.

    2018. Towards a Third Generation of Global Governance Scholarship. *Global Policy* 9 (1): 107–113.

Cooley, Alex and Jack Snyder. 2015. *Ranking the World: Grading States as a Tool of Global Governance*. New York: Cambridge University Press.

Cooper, Andrew and Pouliot, Vincent. 2015. How Much Is Global Governance Changing? The G20 as International Practice. *Cooperation and Conflict* 50 (3): 334–350.

Cooper, Richard. 2010. The G20 as an Improvised Crisis Committee and/or a Contested "Steering Committee." *International Affairs* 86 (3): 741–757.

Copelovitch, Mark and Pevehouse, Jon C.W. 2019. International Organizations in a New Era of Populist Nationalism. *Review of International Organizations* 14 (1): 169–186.

Cox, Robert. 1993. Structural Issues of Global Governance: Issues for Europe. In *Gramsci, Historical Materialism, and International Relations*, edited by S. Gill, 259–289. New York: Cambridge University Press.

Cross, Mai'a K. Davis. 2013. Rethinking Epistemic Communities Twenty Years Later. *Review of International Studies* 39 (1): 137–160.

Cutler, Claire. 2010. The Legitimacy of Private Transnational Governance: Experts and the Transnational Market for Force. *Socio-Economic Review* 8 (1): 157–185.

Davis, Kevin, Angelina Fisher, Benedict Kingsbury, and Sally Engle Merry. 2012. *Governance by Indicators: Global Power through Classification and Rankings*. Oxford: Oxford University Press.

Dezalay, Yves and Bryant G. Garth. 2010. Marketing and Selling Transnational "Judges" and Global "Experts": Building the Credibility of (Quasi)judicial Regulation. *Socio-Economic Review* 8 (1): 113–130.

Dixon, John and Rhys Dogan. 2002. Hierarchies, Networks, and Markets: Responses to Social Governance Failure. *Administrative Theory and Practice* (24) 1: 175–196.

Dryzek, John. 2012. Global Civil Society: The Progress of Post-Westphalian Politics. *Annual Review of Political Science* 15: 101–119.

Dutta, Nikhil. 2012. Accountability in the Generation of Governance Indicators. In *Governance by Indicators: Global Power through Classification and Rankings*, edited by Kevin Davis, Angelina Fisher, Benedict Kingsbury, and Sally Engle Merry, 156–198. Oxford: Oxford University Press.

Easterly, William. 2006. Planners vs. Searchers in Foreign Aid. *Asian Development Review* 23 (2): 1–35.

Eberlein, Burkard. 2019. Who Fills the Global Governance Gap? Rethinking the Roles of Business and Government in Global Governance. *Organization Studies* 40 (8): 1125–1145.

Eberlein, Burkard and Dieter Kerwer. 2002. Theorizing the New Modes of European Union Governance, European Integration Online Papers. https://papers.ssrn.com/sol3/papers.cfm?abstract_id=307521.

Emanuel, Rahm. 2020. *The Nation City: Why Mayors Are Now Running the World*. New York: Random House.

Estwistle, T., et al. 2007. The Dysfunctions of Markets, Hierarchies, and Networks in the Meta-governance of Partnership. *Urban Studies*, 44 (1): 63–79.

Farrell, Henry and Abraham Newman. 2014. Domestic Institutions Beyond the Nation-State: Charting the New Interdependence Approach. *World Politics* 66 (2): 331–363.

Gadinis, Stavros. 2015. Three Pathways to Global Standards: Private, Regulator, and Ministry Networks. *American Journal of International Law* 10 (1): 1–57.

Gourevitch, Peter. 1978. The Second Image Reversed. *International Organization* 32 (4) 881–912.

Granovetter, Mark. 1985. Economic Action and Social Structure: The Problem of Embeddedness. *American Journal of Sociology* 91 (3): 481–510.

Grant, Ruth and Robert Keohane. 2005. Accountability and the Abuses of Power in World Politics. *American Political Science Review* 99 (1): 29–43.

Gray, Kevin and Craig N. Murphy, eds. 2015. *Rising Powers and the Future of Global Governance*. New York: Routledge.

Graz, Jean-Christophe. 2003. How Powerful Are Transnational Elite Clubs? The Social Myth of the World Economic Forum. *New Political Economy* (8) 3: 321–340.

Grigorescu, Alexandru. 2020. *The Ebb and Flow of Global Governance*. New York: Cambridge University Press.

Gruber, Lloyd. 2000. *Ruling the World: Power Politics and the Rise of Supranational Institutions*. Princeton: Princeton University Press.

Guzzini, Stefano. 2012. The Ambivalent "Diffusion of Power" in Global Governance. In *The Diffusion of Power in Global Governance: International Political Economy Meets Foucault*, edited by Stefano G. Guzzini and Iver N. Neumann, 1–37. New York: Palgrave McMillan.

Guzzini, Stefano and Iver Neumann, eds. 2012. *Diffusion of Power in Global Governance: International Political Economy Meets Foucault*. New York: Palgrave Macmillan.

Haas, Peter. 1992. Introduction: Epistemic Communities and International Policy Coordination. *International Organization* 46 (1): 1–35.

2015. Post Hegemonic Global Governance. *Japanese Journal of Political Science* 16 (3): 434–441.

Hale, Thomas and David Held. 2013. *Gridlock: Why Global Governance Is Failing When We Need It Most*. New York: Polity Press.

2017. *Beyond Global Gridlock*. New York: Polity Press

Halliday, Terrance and Gregory Shaffer, eds. 2015. *Transnational Legal Orders*. New York: Cambridge University Press.

Hampson, Fen Osler and Paul Heinbecker. 2011. The "New" Multilateralism of the Twenty-First Century. *Global Governance* 17 (3): 299–310.

Hanquin, Xue. 2007. Chinese Observations on International Law. *Chinese Journal of International Law* 6 (1): 83–93.

Held, David. 2013. The Diffusion of Authority. In *International Organization and Global Governance*, edited by T. Weiss and R. Wilkinson, 63–76. New York: Routledge.

Héritier, Adrienne 2002. New Modes of Governance in Europe: Policymaking without Legislating? In *Common Goods: Reinventing European and International Governance*, edited by A. Héritier, 185–206. Lanham, MD: Rowman & Littlefield.

Héritier, Adrienne and Dennis Lehmkhul. 2008. Introduction: The Shadow of Hierarchy and New Modes of Governance. *Journal of Public Policy* 28 (1): 1–17.

2011. Governing in the Shadow of Hierarchy: New Modes of Governance Regulation. In *New Modes of Governance in Europe*, edited by A. Héritier and M. Rhodes, 49–51. London: Palgrave Macmillan.

Héritier, Adrienne and Martin Rhodes, eds. 2011. *New Modes of Governance in Europe: Governing in the Shadow of Hierarchy*. New York: Palgrave Macmillan.

Heupel, Monika. 2008. Combining Hierarchical and Soft Modes of Governance. *Cooperation and Conflict* 43 (1): 7–29.

Hooghe, Liesbet and Gary Wolfe Marks. 2001. *Multi-level Governance and European Integration*. Lanham, MD: Rowman & Littlefield.

Hooghe, Lisbeth and Gary Marks, et al. 2017. *Measuring International Authority: A Postfunctional Theory of Governance*, Vol. 3. New York: Oxford University Press.

Hooghe, Liesbet, Tobias Lenz, and Gary Marks. 2019. Contested World Order: The Delegitimation of International Governance. *Review of International Organizations* 14: 731–743.

Ikenberry, John. 2012. *The Liberal Leviathan: The Origins, Crisis, and Transformations of the American World Order*. Princeton: Princeton University Press.

Jaeger, Hans-Martin. 2007. Global Civil Society and the Political Depoliticization of Global Governance. *International Political Sociology* 1: 257–277.

Jentleson, Bruce. 2012. Global Governance in a Copernican World. *Global Governance* (18) 2: 133–148.

Jessop, Robert. 1997. Capitalism and Its Future: Remarks on Regulation, Government, and Governance. *Review of International Political Economy* 4 (3): 561–581.

Johnson, Tana. 2015. *Organizational Progeny*. New York: Oxford University Press.

Joseph, Jonathan. 2012. *The Social in the Global: Social Theory, Governmentality, and Global Politics*. New York: Cambridge University Press.

Jung, Danielle and Lake, David. 2011. Markets, Hierarchies, and Networks: An Agent-Based Organizational Ecology. *American Journal of Political Science* (55) 4: 971–989.

Kahler, Miles and David Lake, eds. 2003. *Governance in a Global Economy: Political Authority in Transition*. Princeton: Princeton University Press.

Kahler, Miles. 2009. Networked Power. In *Networked Power: Agency, Power and Governance*, edited by Miles Kahler, et al., 1–22. Ithaca, NY: Cornell University Press.

2018. Global Governance: Three Future. *International Studies Review* 20: 239–246.

Keast, Robyn. 2016. Network Governance. In *Handbook on Theories of Governance*, edited by Christopher Ansell and Jacob Torfing, 442–453. Northampton, MA: Edward Elgar.

Kelley, Judith G. 2017. *Scorecard Diplomacy: Grading States to Influence Their Reputation and Behavior*. Cambridge: Cambridge University Press.

Kelley, Judith G. and Beth A. Simmons. 2015. Politics by Number: Indicators as Social Pressure International Relations. *American Journal of Political Science* 59 (1): 55–70.

Kendall, Gavin. 2004. Global Networks, International Networks, Actor Networks. In *Global Governmentality: Governing International Spaces*, edited by Wendy Larner and William Walters, 59–74. New York: Routledge.

Kennedy, David. 2009. The Mystery of Global Governance. In *Ruling the World? Constitutionalism, International Law, and Global Governance*, edited by Jeffery Dunhoff and Steve Trachtman, 37–68. New York: Cambridge University Press.

Keohane, Robert. 2015. Nominal Democracy? Prospects for Democratic Global Governance. *International Journal of Constitutional Law* 13 (2): 343–353.

Keohane, Robert and David G. Victor. 2011. The Regime Complex for Climate Change. *Perspectives on Politics* 9 (1): 7–23.

Knill, Christoph and Andrea Lenschow. 2004. Modes of Regulation in the Governance of the European Union: Towards a Comprehensive Evaluation. *European Integration Online Papers*. https://papers.ssrn.com/sol3/papers.cfm?abstract_id=380680.

Koenig-Archiburgi, Matthias and Michael Zürn, eds. 2005. *New Modes of Governance in the Global System: Exploring Publicness, Delegation and Inclusiveness*. New York: Palgrave McMillan.

Kohler-Koch, Beate and Rainer Eising, eds. 1999. *The Transformation of Governance in the European Union*. London: Routledge.

Koppell, Jonathan. 2010. *World Rule: Accountability, Legitimacy and the Design of Global Governance*. Chicago: University of Chicago Press.

Lake, David. 2010. Rightful Rules: Authority, Order, and the Foundations of Global Governance. *International Studies Quarterly* 54 (3): 587–613.

Larner, Wendy and Richard Le Hue. 2004. Global Benchmarking: Participating "at a Distance" in the Global Economy. In *Global Governmentality: Governing International Spaces*, edited by Wendy Larner and William Walters, 212–232. New York: Routledge.

Mandrup, Thomas, Liselotte Odgaard, and Cedric de Coning. 2016. *The BRICs and Co-existence: An Alternative Vision of World Order*. New York: Routledge.

Mukherjee, Rohan and David Malone. 2011. From High Ground to High Table: The Evolution of Indian Multilateralism. *Global Governance* 17: 311–329.

Murphy, Craig. 1994. *International Organization and Industrial Change: Global Governance since 1850*. Cambridge: Polity.

1997. *International Organizations and Industrial Change*. New York: Oxford University Press.

2013. The Emergence of Global Governance. In *International Organization and Global Governance*, edited by T. Weiss and R. Wilkinson, 23–34. New York: Routledge.

2014. Global Governance over the Long Haul. *International Studies Quarterly* 58 (1): 216–218.

Naím, Moisés. 2009. Minilateralism. *Foreign Policy* 173: 136.

Nelson, Marcel. 2015. *A History of the FTAA: From Hegemony to Fragmentation in the Americas*. New York: Palgrave Macmillan.

Patomäki, Heikki. 2014. On the Dialectics of Global Governance in the Twenty-First Century: A Polanyian Double Movement? *Globalizations* 11 (5): 733–750.

Pegram, Tom. 2015. Governing Relationships: The New Architecture in Global Human Rights Governance. *Millennium* 43 (2): 618–639.

Pegram, Tom and Michele Cueto. 2015. Introduction: Global Governance in the Interregnum. *Millennium* 43 (2): 584–597. https://doi.org/10.1177/0305829814562017.

Pevehouse, Jon C.W., et al. 2019. Tracking Organizations in the World: The Correlates of War IGO Version 3.0 Datasets. *Journal of Peace Research* 57 (3): 492–503.

Pillinger, M., I. Hurd, and M. Barnett. 2016. How to Get Away with Cholera: The UN, Haiti, and International Law. *Perspectives on Politics* 14 (1): 70–86.

Plesch, Dan and Thomas G. Weiss. 2015. 1945's Lesson: "Good Enough" Global Governance Ain't Good Enough. *Global Governance* 21 (2): 197–204.

Podolny, Joel and Karen Page. 1998. Network Forms of Organization. *Annual Review of Sociology* 242 (59): 57–76.

Polanyi, Karl. 2001. *The Great Transformation: The Political and Economic Origins of Our Times*. Boston: Beacon Press.

Pouliot, Vincent and Jean-Philippe Therien. 2017. Global Governance in Practice. *Global Policy* 9 (2): 163–172.

Powell, Walter W. 1990. Neither Market nor Hierarchy: Network Forms of Organization. In *Research in Organizational Behavior*, edited by B. Staw, 295–336. Greenwich, CT: JAI.

Provan, Keith and Patrick Kenis. 2008. Modes of Network Governance: Structure, Management, and Effectiveness. *Journal of Public Administration Research and Theory* 18 (2): 229–252.

Raustiala, Kal. 1997. States, NGOs, and International Environmental Institutions. *International Studies Quarterly* 41 (4): 719–740.

2002. The Architecture of International Cooperation: Transgovernmental Regulatory Networks and the Future of International Law. *Virginia Journal of International Law* 43 (1): 1–92.

2014. Institutional Proliferation and the International Legal Order. In *Interdisciplinary Perspectives on International Law and International Relations: A State of the Art*, edited by Jeffrey Dumhoff and Mark Pollack, 293–320. New York: Cambridge University Press.

2016. Governing the Internet. *American Journal of International Law* 110 (3): 491–503.

Raustiala, Kal and David G. Victor. 2004. The Regime Complex for Plant Genetic Resources. *International Organization* 58 (2): 277–309.

Raymond, Mark and Laura DeNardis. 2015. Multistakeholderism: Anatomy of an Inchoate Global Institution. *International Theory* 7 (3): 572–616.

Rhodes, Richard. 2000. Governance and Public Administration. In *Debating Governance: Authority, Steering, and Democracy*, edited by J. Pierre, 61. New York: Oxford University Press.

Rhodes, Richard A.W. 1997. From Marketization to Diplomacy: It's the Mix that Matters. *Australian Journal of Public Administration* 56 (2): 40–53.

Roger, Charles. 2020. *The Origin of Informality: Why the Legal Foundations of Governance Are Shifting, and Why It Matters*. New York: Oxford University Press.

Rosenau, James. 1995. Governance in the Twenty-First Century. *Global Governance* 1 (1): 13–43.

Ruggie, John. 1982. International Regimes, Transactions, and Change: Embedded Liberalism in the Postwar Economic Order. *International Organization* 36 (2): 379–415.

Ruggie, John. 2004. Reconstituting the Global Public Domain: Issues, Actors, and Practices. *European Journal of International Relations* 10 (4): 499–531.

2014. Global Governance and "New Governance Theory": Lessons from Business and Human Rights. *Global Governance* 20 (1): 5–17.

2017. Multinationals as Global Institutions: Power, Authority, and Relative Autonomy. *Regulation and Governance* 12 (3): 317–333.

Rupert, Mark. 2000. *Ideologies of Globalization: Contending Visions of a New World Order*. London: Routledge.

2005. Class Powers and the Politics of Global Governance. In *Power in Global Governance*, edited by Michael Barnett and Raymond Duvall, 205–229. New York: Cambridge University Press.

Seabrooke, Leonard and Lasse Folke Henriksen. 2017. Issue Control in Transnational Professional and Organizational Networks. In *Professional Networks in Transnational Governance*, edited by L. Seabrooke and L. Folke Henrikson, 3–24. New York: Cambridge University Press.

Sending, Ole Jacob. 2015. *The Politics of Expertise: Competing for Authority in Global Governance*. Ann Arbor: University of Michigan Press.

Sending, Ole Jacob and Iver B. Neumann. 2006. Governance to Governmentality: Analyzing NGOs, States, and Power. *International Studies Quarterly* 50 (3): 651–672.

Shirky, Clay. 2011. The Political Power of Social Media: Technology, the Public Sphere, and Political Change. *Foreign Affairs* (90) 1: 28–41.

Sikkink, Kathryn. 2009. The Power of Networks in International Politics. In *Networked Power: Agency, Power and Governance*, Miles Kahler, et al., 228–247. Ithaca, NY: Cornell University Press.

Simon, Herbert. 1962. The Architecture of Complexity. *Proceedings of the American Philosophical Society* 106 (6): 140.

Slaughter, Anne-Marie. 1992. Regulating the World: Multilateralism, International Law, and the Projection of the New Deal Regulatory State. In *Multilateralism Matters*, edited by John Ruggie, 125–156. New York: Columbia University Press.

2004. Disaggregated Sovereignty: Toward the Public Accountability of Global Government Networks. *Government and Opposition* 39 (2): 159–190.

2005. *A New World Order*. Princeton: Princeton University Press.

Slobodian, Quinn. 2018. *The Globalists: The End of Empire and the Birth of Neoliberalism*. Cambridge: Harvard University Press.

Special Focus: Regime Complexity. 2013. *Global Governance* 19 (1): 27–130.

Stephenson, Karen. 2016. Heterarchy. In *Handbook on Theories of Governance*, edited by Christopher Ansell and Jacob Torfing, 139–148. Northampton, MA: Edward Elgar.

Stephenson, Paul. 2013. Twenty Years of Multilevel Governance: "Where Does It Come From? Where Is It Going?" *Journal of European Public Policy* (20) 6: 817–837.

Stone, Randall. 2011. *Controlling Institutions: International Organizations and the Global Economy*. New York: Cambridge University Press.

Stroup, Sarah and Wendy Wong. 2017. *The Authority Trap: The Strategic Choices of International NGOs*. Ithaca, NY: Cornell University Press.

Swedberg, Richard. 2018. How to Use Max Weber's Ideal Type in Sociological Analysis. *Journal of Classical Sociology* 18 (3): 181–196.

Tallberg, Jonas, Thomas Sommerer, Theresa Squatrito, and Christer Jönsson. 2013. *The Opening Up of International Organizations*. New York: Cambridge University Press.

Taylor, Kenneth. 2004. Global Capitalism and the Question of Global Governance: A Socio-Economic Perspective. *International Journal of Social Economics* 7 (8): 773–789.

Tenbensel, Tim. 2005. Multiple Modes of Governance: Disentangling the Alternatives to Markets and Hierarchies. *Public Management Review* 7 (2): 267–288.

Thompson, Grahame. 2003. *Between Hierarchies and Markets: The Logic and Limits of Network Forms of Organization*. New York: Oxford University Press.

Tooze, Roger. 1990. Understanding the Global Political Economy: Applying Gramsci. *Millennium* 19 (2): 273–280.

Treib, Oliver, Holger Bäahr, and Gerda Falkner. 2007. Modes of Governance: Toward a Conceptual Clarification. *Journal of European Public Policy* (14) 1: 1–20.

Tsingou, Eleni. 2015. Club Governance and the Making of Global Financial Rules. *Review of International Political Economy* 22 (2): 225–256.

Vabulas, Felicity and Duncan Snidal. 2013. Organization without Delegation: Informal Intergovernmental organizations (IIGOs) and the Spectrum of Intergovernmental Arrangements. *Review of International Organizations* 8 (2): 193–220.

Van Langenhove, Luk. 2010. The Transformation of Multilateralism: Mode 1.0 to Mode 2.0. *Global Policy* 1 (October): 263–270.

Waltz, Kenneth. 1979. *A Theory of International Politics*. Boston: Addison-Wesley.

Weiss, Thomas. 2009. What Happened to the Idea of World Government? *International Studies Quarterly* 53: 253–271.

Weiss, Thomas and Rorden Wilkinson. 2014. Rethinking Global Governance? Complexity, Authority, Power, Change. *International Studies Quarterly* 58 (1): 207–215.

Westerwinter, Oliver. 2017. Measuring Transnational Public–Private Governance Initiatives in World Politics: A New Dataset. Unpublished. St. Gallen: Switzerland. http://oliverwesterwinter.com/working%20paper/Measuring-Transnational-Public-Private-Governance-Initiatives-in-World-Politics/.

White House. 2018. Remarks by President Trump at the 73rd United Nations General Assembly. https://uy.usembassy.gov/remarks-by-president-trump-to-the-73rd-session-of-the-united-nations-general-assembly/.

Williamson, Oliver. 1975. *Markets and Hierarchies*. New York: Free Press.

1991. Comparative Economic Organization: The Analysis of Discrete Alternatives. *Administrative Sciences Quarterly* 36: 269–296.

Zürn, Michael. 2012. Global Governance as Multilevel Governance. In *The Oxford Handbook of Governance*, edited by in D. Levi-Faur, 730–743. New York: Oxford University Press.

2018. *A Theory of Global Governance*. New York: Cambridge University Press.

1 Governance Shifts in Security
Military and Security Services and Small Arms Compared

Deborah Avant

Scholars commonly doubt the relevance of complex governance for security issues, but it is very much present in the nascent regulation of military and security services. A set of multi-stakeholder initiatives link action by national and international hierarchies, markets, and networks. This complex governance system has eclipsed a largely hierarchical system focused on national and international law controlling mercenaries. Complex governance, however, is a sideshow in the governance of small arms. Here, national hierarchies act with less coordination via one another, diametrically opposed networks battle for their attention, and markets are largely absent (though commercial money from arms flows through both national hierarchies and networks, market modes are not present in governance processes). Concomitant with these institutional configurations, global governance, loosely defined as the coordination of relevant actors, has progressed in military and security services but regressed in small arms. In what follows, I compare the evolution of governance modes in these two issue areas illustrating the interplay of structure and agency that yields change (or not) as well as more and less governance surrounding these two issues. In so doing, I argue that while the "good enough" of complex governance may not be enough in some eyes, it is likely to be the best we can hope for and far more likely to solve problems than forms that rely on top-down, commanding, and forceful measures alone.

Toward the end of the Cold War one would have been hard-pressed to find mention of either "military and security services" or "small arms" as governance issues. But geopolitical changes, combined with proliferating actor types and interactions, generated new problems (and greater awareness of them) in both realms. Different logics of governance offered distinct interpretations of, and paths for managing, these developments. In military and security services an initial disarray of perspectives, proposing competing market and hierarchical responses, led to little change in the 1990s. In the wake of escalating problems, though, policy entrepreneurship by the Swiss government and the International Commission of the Red Cross (ICRC) in the mid-2000s generated a process that both shifted the perspectives of many of the actors involved (including the United States) and articulated new governance processes that joined network, hierarchical, and market mechanisms. By 2016 perspectives had largely coalesced around this system. In small arms, different factions in the 1990s came together around distinct hierarchical perspectives. Evidence of gun violence in civil wars, transnational crime, and domestic shootings led proponents of small arms regulation to optimism for hierarchical governance at the international level by the late 1990s. With US support, however, opponents of regulation disrupted this momentum at a UN conference in 2001. Pro- and anti-regulation perspectives hardened into a clash over whether to govern at all. Both remained focused on hierarchical tools, but pro-regulation perspectives aimed for international hierarchical governance and anti-regulation used national hierarchies to resist. Though there are relevant networks, they oppose one another, and thus they lack common purpose. The bulk of efforts – for or against regulation – aims to be hierarchical. With the United States often supporting the governance resisters, little regulation of small arms has been enacted at the global level since 2001.

A comparison of these two issue areas highlights similar structural conditions and thus the importance of agency for the different responses. The trajectory of military and security services demonstrates how problems without apparent solutions can provide openings for policy entrepreneurship – in this case by the Swiss government – that generate pragmatic processes. Continual efforts by the Swiss and others knitted these solutions, based in a range of different governance forms, into a reinforcing complex governance system. The small arms trajectory reveals how strategies fixed on commanding solutions can limit the space for policy entrepreneurship. Without new connections and the potential to coordinate action among different types of relevant actors, the potential for changed perspectives and innovation was diminished.

This comparison also yields provocative insights into the effectiveness of different governance outcomes. While the complex governance surrounding military and security services has not curtailed their growth, it has shaped rules and norms about proper behavior among service providers and their clients and drawn these into contract law and other regulatory tools that enable enforcement by states, companies, and other organizations. The complex system has tamed what looked like a downward cycle of behavior and holds the potential to influence the range of actor types relevant to this issue. A focus on hierarchical solutions in small arms allowed for clearer wins (and losses) but not for coordination of disparate actors. Pro-regulation networks influenced hierarchy in

Australia in the 1990s but anti-regulation networks did the same in Brazil in the 2000s. Neither side feels that it has solved the governance problem. The global proliferation of small arms has escalated, but how to understand that is disputed. Thus, in these two processes, strategy more open to new actor types and different solutions was better able to generate coordination. Though these new solutions are deemed less satisfying by some, those focused on managing global concerns are unlikely to do better. More focus on specific solutions and forced acceptance generates less of the flexibility, innovation, and buy-in often necessary to solve collective problems.

What Has Happened?

Growth in global markets for both security services and weapons in the 1990s, largely a function of geopolitical changes precipitated by the end of the Cold War as they rippled through different regions and countries, generated a number of problems. These, in turn, spurred calls, and mobilization, for transnational action. The pace, energy, and timing of the action were different in the two issue areas.

Military and Security Services: From Hierarchy to Complexity

Both the use and governance of hired fighters have shifted over the course of Western history. The modern system in Europe began with mercenaries of various sorts prominent in conflict – and governed by the parties that hired them – at national or local levels. This style of recruitment went out of style in the nineteenth century.[1] Changes in practice were largely initiated – and governed – by national governments.[2] But there also developed an international norm against the use of mercenaries.[3]

National regulation and the international norm worked together to "outlaw" guns for hire, even though they never really went away.[4] Governments, rebel movements, and others used them from time to time, more often in the colonial and postcolonial world. During the Cold War, mercenaries were most prominent in parts of Africa.[5] Concerns about mercenaries and their consequences led African states to seek international regulation to formally outlaw them in the 1980s. The 1989 International Convention Against the Recruitment, Use, Financing and Training of Mercenaries was adopted in 1990.[6]

---

[1] Avant 2000.   [2] Thomson 1994.   [3] Percy 2007.   [4] O'Brien 1998.
[5] Mockler 1985.   [6] And came into force in 2002.

By this time, though, the market for military and security services was beginning to expand. Largely coincident with the end of the Cold War, the supply of those with military experience went up with force contractions and demand for services increased as governments undertook new missions and neoliberal thinking led some companies and other non-state actors to increasingly take responsibility for their own security. Though customers (some states, companies, and nongovernmental organizations [NGOs]) saw these forces as useful tools, others saw them as a scourge.[7] The former often referred to them as private security or military companies (eventually private military and security companies [PMSCs]), the latter as mercenaries. Dramatic stories of Executive Outcomes in Angola and Sierra Leone and Military Professional Resources Incorporated working with Croatian forces in the Yugoslavian civil war in the middle of the decade were seized for both purposes.[8]

As the market expanded, laws in the United States (developed for other purposes) provided a basic governance framework for some elements of these services and their export, but many governments had no such laws in place.[9] So, there was little global governance, and in some places there was little national regulation either. The United Nations, and especially the Special Rapporteur on the use of mercenaries, which had been appointed in 1987 to develop and then work to ratify the International Convention, saw the market as a growth in mercenarism and doubled down on its efforts to get it ratified. Once it was ratified in 2002, this office worked to enforce it in ways that would eliminate these forces.[10]

Neither national nor international efforts, though, were sufficient to address concerns around this industry and its use. Both its transnational nature and the growing relevance of different sorts of customers, including companies, NGOs, and international bureaucracies as well as governments, frustrated the ability of any one government to regulate effectively. As the use of these companies escalated during the wars in Iraq and Afghanistan after 9/11, so did increasing evidence of problems.[11]

In response to these problems, the Swiss government and the ICRC initiated a series of meetings among governments, companies, and civil society groups in 2005. These meetings eventually generated a set of

---

[7] Shearer 1998.   [8] Douglass 1999; Musah 2000; Goulet 1998.   [9] Avant 2005.

[10] The United Nations Commission on Human Rights appointed a special rapporteur in 1987 to address the increasing concerns about the use of mercenaries.

[11] *New Yorker*, May 6, 2004; Hammes 2011.

multi-stakeholder agreements that are nested with each other as well as with international, national, and local regulations. To sum up, the Montreux Document outlines obligations and best practices for states; an International Code of Conduct (ICoC) for private security providers spells out International Humanitarian Law and human rights obligations for PMSCs; and the American National Standards Institute (ANSI) and International Organization for Standardization (ISO) standards rely specifically on both of these (as well as the UN Guiding Principles on Business and Human Rights) to articulate standards that can be written into contracts and contracting requirements. These have led to changes in national laws and there are efforts to enhance use of the ICoC and standards by non-state clients (such as the extractive companies) and international organizations. This web of governance links heterogeneous actors – organized as hierarchies (governments), as networks (civil society and industry organizations), and as markets (clients and service providers). There is no hierarchy at the global level, but participants make use of national hierarchical controls and international norms. Market mechanisms and the information exchange prominent in networks also play key roles in this governance process. Each of these different forms is involved in rule-making, rule implementation, rule interpretation, and rule enforcement.[12]

In the terms of this project, governance has shifted from a form in which rule-making, implementation, interpretation, and enforcement were undertaken by national and international hierarchies against using mercenaries, through a moment of contestation in which there was little coordination, to a form in which coordination is accomplished via an interaction among hierarchies, networks, and markets. This complex governance system is characterized by a diverse array of mechanisms and the interaction among them. Government regulation references standards to explicitly generate hierarchical leverage on networks and markets. Markets both rely on and reinforce networks and hierarchies, and civil society networks have worked with state and market mechanisms to generate effect.

Small Arms: Reassertion of Hierarchy

Small arms were largely regulated by national hierarchies at the end of the Cold War. The Cold War's end, though, led to increases in the supply of these weapons as demobilized soldiers sold their weapons to

---

[12] Avant 2016.

black markets and governments upped their sales and transfers of small arms as demand for larger conventional weapons waned even as arms manufacturers grew, spread, and became more interconnected.[13] The number of manufacturers tripled between 1980 and 2000 as the industry globalized.[14] Demand also rose, particularly among substate and non-state actors.[15]

As with military and security services, opinions were mixed about whether this increasing flow was a problem. Those with newfound access to weapons with which to pursue their causes saw arms as a security tool and one that ought not be restricted. But arms control advocates, already organized and connected with one another and with national and international hierarchies via their Cold War efforts, increasingly saw small arms and light weapons as a problem fueling intrastate conflicts in the 1990s.[16] Crime control and disarmament networks joined forces with the United Nations to create a network to combat small arms and light weapons as a threat to global peace and security.[17] Advocates for transnational regulation were initially split over whether to focus particularly on illicit arms in conflict zones or to link up with those seeking gun control in more stable countries. As they came together to launch the International Action Network on Small Arms (IANSA) in 1999, this broader stance took root.[18] IANSA also pushed for a formal international conference at the United Nations to look comprehensively at the small arms issue.[19] A formal process, they thought, was more serious, and would lead to international hierarchy; the kind of binding international commitments that could squarely address the problem.

Connections between domestic groups that had opposed gun control measures in the United States, Australia, and other states, though, also created a network to coordinate resistance to domestic gun control in the mid-1990s. As the network to regulate small arms internationally grew, the anti-control forces turned their attention to combating regulation on the global stage.[20] This network developed an alternative normative perspective, claiming that arms were not the issue; people, not guns, kill.[21] They also argued that legal restrictions would be ignored by criminals and only impact law-abiding citizens. And, drawing on the National Rifle Association's (NRA) use of the Second Amendment in American politics, they argued that people have a "right" to bear arms.[22]

---

[13] Klare 1997; Alves and Cipollone 1998.
[14] Bitzinger 1994; Hayward 2000; Survey 2001.   [15] Laurance 1998.
[16] Boutwell and Klare 1998.   [17] Bob 2012, 111–119.   [18] Bob 2012, 117–123.
[19] Survey 2002, 205.   [20] Bob 2012, 114–117.   [21] Grillot 2011.
[22] Bob 2012, 115.

They formed an international NGO, the World Forum on the Future of Sport Shooting Activities (WFSA). These advocates fought control on weaponry from different normative frames. To combat international regulation, they touted the sovereign rights of nations. To combat domestic regulation, they touted the rights of individuals to bear arms.

Simultaneously, global, regional, and national networks attempted to manage particular problems arising from the flow of weapons – from the Wassenaar arrangement to EU Codes of Conduct and an Organization of American States convention. These regional and nonbinding agreements, though, remained largely separate from the pro- and anti-regulation coalitions. The 2001 UN Conference on the Illicit Trade in Small Arms and Light Weapons in All Its Aspects demonstrated the strength of the pro-regulation movement. The conference results, though – the Programme of Action (a set of nonbinding commitments and an agreement to meet for another conference in 2006) – were sorely disappointing. IANSA and its allies felt particularly betrayed as the USA took a position highly influenced by the NRA and abandoned the fight for regulation. After 2001 rancor grew on both sides. The United Nations established a special rapporteur to issue a report that would demonstrate with hard evidence that human rights abuses were associated with small arms. And IANSA remobilized to push for the insertion of "teeth" in the Program of Action (POA) at the Review Conference (RevCon) in 2006. The NRA, on the other hand, cast the POA as a significant threat to the rights of law-abiding citizens and also geared up for the battle in 2006. Wayne LaPierre, the NRA executive vice president, wrote *The Global War on Your Guns* released in 2006 before RevCon. Its Amazon description reads:

The United Nations wants your guns. They want all of them – *now* – and they've found a way to do it. In fact, the UN is so cocksure it can commandeer the Second Amendment that it chose the Fourth of July, 2006, to hold its global gun ban summit in New York City. If you think there's no way an armed UN platoon of blue helmets can knock on your door to take your guns, this book just became your next must-read.

Sovereignty carried the day in 2006. The POA was not extended, and no additional meetings were planned. IANSA joined with other NGOs to form the Control Arms campaign, which worked with supportive states to focus on a much broader array of weapons. Advocates hoped that including small arms in the entire range of conventional weapons (advanced conventional weapons, tanks, armored combat vehicles, artillery systems, military aircraft, military helicopters, naval vessels, missiles, missile launchers, small arms and light weapons, and combat support equipment as well as parts, components, and/or technology to manufacture, modify, or repair the covered items) would have more success. Their goal, according to Control Arms, was still "a bulletproof ATT [Arms Trade Treaty]" – that is, "a global, legally binding agreement that will ease the suffering caused by irresponsible transfers of conventional weapons and munitions."[23] Despite resistance from the gun rights network, the ATT did pass in 2013 and the treaty does require control systems for export obligations and these are legally binding. The compromise necessary to pass it, however, left provisions for importing, transporting, and brokering small arms weaker than in the nonbinding commitments in the POA. Thus, analysts worry that it could be a step backward in some areas.[24] Also, while the United States engaged with the process and signed the ATT, it carefully avoided its implications for small arms, and it is unlikely to ratify the treaty.

In sum, the hierarchical form of small arms regulation is largely unchanged. It takes place mostly at the national level in an uncoordinated fashion. Though there are some more informal mechanisms, these remain largely unconnected to either national or international regulatory debates.

Why? Similar Structural Shifts and Different Agency

These different stories begin with similar structural shifts. The end of the Cold War generated changes that allowed transnational markets to grow. Increasing transnational connections generated concerns on a scale different from the scale of the nation state. Connections via multinational companies and supply chains generated economic worries about stability in many parts of the world. These were joined by connections among like-minded advocates for conservation, human rights, or humanitarianism[25] created by different sorts of, similarly wide-reaching, worries. These connections, combined with technology and the speed of travel, allowed violence or disorder in one part of the world to generate concern in many others.

Efforts to link these concerns with "national" security and the use of national forces were complicated. So were efforts to build multilateral forces based on concerns of an "international community." Commercial provision of military and security services, arms, or both – no doubt connected with neoliberal ideas of governance – provided a different

---

[23] Lerman 2012.   [24] Survey 2013.   [25] Keck and Sikkink 1998; Barnett 2011.

avenue for governments, commercial actors, and others to respond to this array of concerns.

The increasing demand for private security and small arms was complemented by increasing supply. The contraction of national military forces with the lessening of tensions between East and West led to networks of retired military personnel: potential contractors for those in need of services. And demobilized soldiers sold their weapons to black markets in some parts of the world while arms manufacturers grew, spread, connected, and focused increasingly on small weapons as demand for large weapons systems declined.[26]

The expanding markets, in turn, increased the importance of corporate actors selling services or arms, respectively. They also generated potential governance roles for their customers – a mix of governments, anti-government political groups, commercial actors, and not-for-profit groups.[27] Legal corporate providers contracted openly with governments and commercial clients to deliver military and security services. UN anti-mercenary regulation was of questionable relevance and hierarchically based international arms control did not address small arms at all. The transnational logic of both markets challenged uncoordinated national hierarchical regulation.

Distinct ideologies of governance offered different interpretation of these developments. A focus on international hierarchy and legalization, dominant at the beginning of the post-Cold War era, focused on inadequate controls as a problem and sought binding international agreements. A more libertarian approach suggested regulation was not needed at all, and that these markets were new flexible responses that should be allowed to flourish without interference (or according to the sovereign decisions of independent states). Finally, an emerging stakeholder approach to governance focused less on any particular form and more the process of finding common purpose and buy-in from those surrounding particular issues (including various actor types), often with the advice and participation of experts.

Gathering around Problems, Policy Entrepreneurship, a Pragmatic Process, and Complex Governance Development around Military and Security Services

The growing market in military and security services generated problems. The US experience during the second Iraq war provides a useful

---

[26] Klare 1997; Alves and Cipollone 1998.   [27] Avant 2005.

illustration. The US government contracted with PMSCs from all over the world. Non-US firms, though, were subject to the legal stipulations of the states in which they were incorporated. Some, like South Africa, claimed that contracts were illegal. Other had different screening requirements or offered inadequate insurance in the event of injury or death. Even contracts with US companies were complicated by transnational recruitment. Also, turning to PMSCs in its stabilization effort led the USA to encourage (or require) the use of private security by others. These PMSCs working for different clients (other governments, companies, and NGOs) were not coordinated with US military forces and harmed US counterinsurgency efforts.[28] Other countries had different experiences but none were able to control PMSCs with national tools alone.

International regulation sought to outlaw mercenaries rather than regulate the behavior of the industry,[29] but it was not supported by any of the powerful players, including the three largest exporters (the US, the UK, and South Africa). Some were interested in managing the behavior of these forces rather than outlawing them altogether.[30] The varied type of services offered by private military and security companies and the forms that security privatization took led to different concerns in different parts of the world.[31] The USA was adamantly opposed to international coordination out of concern that would limit its flexibility. And commercial clients of PMSCs were not represented in, or tapped by, government-based arrangements.

The scale of PMSC problems in Iraq and Afghanistan led to disparate reactions. The UN Working Group and some NGOs redoubled mercenary charges. Some NGOs focused on US-based waste and fraud. Others began to investigate potential human rights abuses. While some industry leaders signed on to professional codes of conduct, others highlighted their ability to pursue national interests. Despite some concern in Congress, the US government remained committed to retaining maximum flexibility and resistant to any transnational coordination efforts.

It was at this point in 2005 that the Swiss government and the ICRC joined to introduce the Swiss Initiative. Building on their longstanding commitment to humanitarianism as a reason to host, they acted much as a policy entrepreneur would, capitalizing on a window of opportunity and framing the problem so as to draw in the widest variety of networks.[32] Its first exploratory meeting was in January 2006 and brought

---

[28] *The Christian Science Monitor*, October 21, 2010; Hammes 2011.
[29] Gaultier et al. 2001.   [30] Shearer 1998.   [31] Dunigan and Petersohn 2015.
[32] Kingdon 1984.

together government experts, representatives from the security industry, and civil society. Partly as a tactic to ensure US participation, the meeting sought to produce nothing new – only to catalogue the way existing agreements might affect government relations with PMSCs.

The Swiss set the agenda, as policy entrepreneurs often do, around humanitarianism and human rights as opposed to waste and fraud or mercenarism. In keeping with ICRC tradition, which has inferred obligations for other non-state actors on the battlefield from existing agreements,[33] the Swiss asserted that there was not a vacuum of law surrounding private security. This claim drew in industry and its clients who were tired of hearing arguments about the vacuum of law. But it also drew in members of civil society who were eager to have the legal obligations surrounding the industry acknowledged and met. Discussions at the first meeting were fraught at times but the group did settle on how to define private military and security services and agreed that states had different relationships with PMSCs: contracting states, exporting states, and territorial states. These three relationships provided the structure for another meeting.

Building on this small amount of progress, the second meeting began to chart state obligations according to these different relationships. Subsequently, participants also noted the best practices for each. The resulting Montreux Document in September 2008 simply drew on existing international agreements and was thus "nothing new." But was an entirely new legal framework for PMSCs that highlighted state obligations via PMSCs and the best practices they might follow. It also noted governance gaps – particularly in behavioral standards for PMSCs. The meetings thus ended with both a new document (signed by seventeen governments) and the initiation of another multi-stakeholder process to define appropriate PMSC behavior.

The resulting international code of conduct for private security providers, or ICoC, specifically referenced the Montreux Document and built on extensions of international humanitarian law and human rights obligations to other non-state actors. The ICoC was finalized in October 2010 and then signed by companies in November. It outlines principles that should inform good behavior in delivering private security services, building on the Montreux Document but also the "Respect, Protect, Remedy" Framework developed by the Special Representative of the UN Secretary-General on Business and Human Rights.[34] The ICoC's gravitas grew when it gained key support from the US Department of

---

[33] Roling 1976; Avant 2017.   [34] ICoC 2009, 3.

Defense's (DoD) Program Support Office. This office, set up in 2006 to address contractor concerns, was charged by Congress in 2009 to come up with a standard by which to judge whether private security companies should be eligible for contracts. The ICoC provided an outline for just such a standard, and US officials realized that if they answered the congressional requirement building on a transnational standard they may be able to impact private security contracts with other clients as well. Because these officials were concurrently keeping track of incidents in Iraq, they realized that private security contracts with the US government were only a small fraction of private security in the country. They saw that PMSCs were less likely to be disruptive to US policy if they had the same standard no matter who they worked for. DoD thus reversed its reluctance to engage transnationally and both DoD and threw its support behind the ICoC – and the creation of an association to govern it. They also began a process to build national and international standards based on the ICoC.

DoD joined with US State Department representatives to indicate the usefulness of the ICoC to the world's largest client. Their support also increased both company and civil society interest in the ICoC. Many large PMSCs were committed to be compliant with US requirements and eager to participate in a process that would shape them. Civil Society Organizations (CSOs) saw that US requirements could make the ICoC more biting. Negotiations about the association intensified as the stakeholders saw promise and began to build standards on it, but also became increasingly interested in ensuring that their perspectives were included.

In launching the Montreux process the Swiss government and the ICRC had acted as policy entrepreneurs to open a conversation that generated new thinking about the problems private security generated and how to solve them. This thinking led US participants to craft policy that embraced rather than resisted transnational coordination. The Montreux Document and the ICoC process also shifted the conversation within the industry and among civil society groups. Though PMSCs had long been interested in some regulatory framework to counter the mercenary charge, tension existed between those interested in a broader, transnational approach and those more focused on working for the interests of governments like the United States. The Montreux process began to tip the balance toward a more transnational approach. The International Peace Operations Association (now International Stability Operations Association) called it "the way ahead" for accountability.[35]

---

[35] Mayer 2010.

Well-established civil society voices such as Amnesty International and Human Rights First agreed, embracing the Montreux Document and its recommendations.[36]

The workability of this framework attracted others. The Special Rapporteur on the use of mercenaries was replaced by the "Working Group on the use of mercenaries as a means of violating human rights and impeding the exercise of the rights of peoples to self-determination" in 2005. The working group's initial efforts focused on state use of private military and security companies as a mechanism for impunity. When it was reauthorized in 2008, though, it was asked to prepare a draft of "international basic principles that encourage respect for human rights by those companies in their activities."[37] After over a decade of treating PMSCs as mercenaries, the working group saw them as companies in need of regulation. The "Draft International Convention on the Regulation, Oversight and Monitoring of Private Military and Security Companies," released in July 2009, adopted the Montreux Document's terminology of contracting, territorial, and home states.[38]

The process did not stop there. The US government supported standards process was conducted by the ANSI. Consistent with ANSI practices, it involved stakeholders from all over the world. PSC 1 (Management System for Quality of Private Security Company Operations – Requirements With Guidance), the private security management standard, was published in 2011. It was also elevated, and approved, as an ISO Standard. The ANSI and ISO standards specifically reference the Montreux Document and the ICoC. With the publication of PSC 1, the US DoD required that contractors be compliant with the standard to be eligible to compete for DoD contracts.[39]

Concurrent with the standards development were negotiations within the ICoC's temporary steering committee to create a governance body. A charter was approved on February 22, 2013.[40] The ICoCA was launched in September 2013, after which the US Department of State (DoS) required ICoCA membership for its Worldwide Protective Services contracts. Since then the ICoCA has developed certification and monitoring procedures. It has also reached out to related governance processes such as the Voluntary Principles on Security and Human Rights and the UN Guiding Principles on Business and Human Rights in an effort to make ICoCA certification useful to companies that hire

---

[36] Amnesty International 2008; HRF 2010.   [37] UNWG 2011, 2.

[38] This legislation has since fallen by the wayside. Though the office still hopes for binding regulation, most see this as highly unlikely.

[39] DFARS 2012.   [40] ICoCA 2013.

private security as well. At the five-year anniversary celebrating the signing of the Montreux Document governments created the Montreux Document Forum to continue government-to-government discussion on how best to handle relationships with PMSCs.[41]

Each step in this process was supported by the Swiss government. Again, in keeping with a policy entrepreneurial role, the Swiss invested time, energy, reputation, and money into this process and supported what many see as a workable solution to problems associated with PMSCs. Beyond setting an agenda focused on accepted international law (which also privileged humanitarianism and human rights), though, the Swiss have remained open to different solutions. The open process and interaction among previously unconnected networks generated options that were not seen from the beginning and also led key actors to understand their interests and relationships with the industry in new ways. Thus, while US support for the network led it to have increased gravitas as a "shadow of hierarchy" argument might suggest, the US position was influenced by the network. It is the continual process of linking different initiatives that has generated a system with governance roles for hierarchical, market, and network mechanisms; the continual interaction among these forms is more important than the shadow of anyone.

Disputed Problems, Set Solutions, and Deadlock around Different Versions of Hierarchical Governance around Small Arms

The growing market for small arms and light weapons dramatically increased the number of these weapons in circulation. The increasing flows were linked with a range of transnational concerns in the latter half of the 1990s, including increased conflict intensity, victimization of civilians, large-scale criminal violence, threats to UN and humanitarian workers, and even increasing public health costs.[42] By 2001, "a relatively large consensus (geographically and politically)" had emerged "that the unconstrained availability of small arms and light weapons ought to be addressed as a problem in itself."[43]

This problem was defined, researched, and shaped by individuals who had worked on more conventional arms control issues or crime during the Cold War. Though increasingly networked with each other and, to some extent, the domestic gun control movements in Canada, Australia, and the UK, they were inclined to focus on addressing this problem

---

[41] www.montreuxdocument.org/.   [42] Bob 2010, 188; Krause 2002, 251.
[43] Krause 2002, 251.

within the United Nations. In 1994 experts outlined the relationship between small arms and conflict and steps to address it.[44] The UN was quick to seize on this issue. In 1995, UN Secretary-General Boutros Boutros-Ghali called for "Micro-Disarmament" – focused on land mines, small arms, and light weapons.[45] Also in 1995 the UN General Assembly passed a resolution calling on the secretary-general to research the issue of small arms and lay out options for reducing their numbers.[46] Governments joined to help. Norway, Canada, and Belgium hosted meetings in 1998 to coordinate action among states on small arms issues. These meetings focused on the development and enforcement of laws about civilian possession, improvement of weapons transfer processes, enhancing weapons collection and destruction efforts, and developing weapons export criteria.[47]

UN interest intensified in the wake of the Ottawa Convention to ban landmines in 1999. Concerned that the Ottawa Treaty would set a precedent for negotiations to happen outside of UN processes, advocates pushed for an international conference at the UN on small arms in 2001.[48] Meanwhile, activists who had participated in the campaign to ban landmines turned their attention to small arms and argued for stronger control measures, within countries as well as in exports, all over the world. Activists joined together to form IANSA in 1999 with an aim of obtaining an international agreement similar to the Ottawa Convention at the UN conference scheduled for 2001.

At the same time, though, anti-regulation forces mobilized based on a libertarian philosophy that saw guns as a solution, not a problem. This philosophy may be related to the changes in capitalism and governance ideologies that the Introduction discusses but it is distinct in that access to weaponry was not rooted in a market logic but in a political one. And the logic was not for a different type of governance but a different extent of governance. In response to tightening gun laws in Australia in the early 1990s, the head of the Sporting Shooters Association of Australia visited the NRA's headquarters in Washington, DC and asked the NRA to help establish an international forum on firearm laws to protect the rights of gun owners.[49]

The NRA and its affiliated organizations around the world founded the International Conference on Firearms Legislation (ICFL) in 1993 and then the WFSA in 1997. The WFSA's early members included the NRA and other US gun groups as well as similar groups in mostly European countries. While the ICFL was focused on domestic gun

---

[44] Boutwell et al. 1995.   [45] UNGA 1995.   [46] UNGA 1996.   [47] Grillot 2011.
[48] Bob 2010.   [49] *Foreign Policy*, October 19, 2006; Bob 2010.

control, the WFSA geared up to blunt the UN's efforts to promote international gun control schemes.[50] These groups claimed that legal restrictions on guns were unnecessary (people, rather than guns kill), unfair (they would disproportionately affect law-abiding citizens), and (drawing from the US Constitution) that people have a "right" to bear arms.

Despite a forceful position that took issue with every part of the pro-governance argument, there were small signs that the WFSA as well as the pro-governance forces were open to some conversation in the 1990s. In its efforts at the UN the WFSA argued that it was focused on ensuring that "correct and unbiased information is available to international deci-sion makers."[51] In pursuit of that the WFSA applied for and received status as an NGO with the UN's Economic and Social Council. There were also signs of pro-governance openness at this moment. Pro-governance forces opted not to block the WFSA's status as an NGO to avoid looking as if they were trying to thwart debate.

Neither side in this struggle suggested a role for arms manufacturers, arms dealers, or markets more generally in governance. This is not to suggest that the arms industry showed much interest in engaging in effort for the common good.[52] But there was some movement toward at least the idea of corporate social responsibility in 2000 when President William J. Clinton announced an agreement with Smith and Wesson to adopt new designs to limit gun operation by children and require that its dealers conduct background checks even at gun shows.[53] Pro-regulation forces, though, were suspicious of this development, claiming that cor-porate social responsibility, or any measures short of hierarchical law, would not actually address the problem. Anti-regulation forces had an even harsher reaction, arguing that companies had no authority to make such judgments. Some have claimed that efforts to mediate sales in any way would infringe on individual freedom. And the NRA orchestrated a boycott of Smith and Wesson, leading its sales to plummet.[54]

Similarly, while networks are a big part of the competing mobilization around this issue, neither side advocated for networks as a governance tool. For the anti-regulation coalition, networks were a tool for thwarting governance. Although they exerted heavy pressure on their members, sometimes using market-based tools – as the boycott of Smith and Wesson demonstrates – they did not suggest network governance. The same was true for the pro-regulation forces. They saw networks of

---

[50] Bob 2010, 190.   [51] Goldring 1999, 112; Bob 2010, 190.   [52] Byrne 2007.
[53] White House 2000.   [54] *The New York Times*, May 27, 2013.

experts as important for providing information and analysis of the problem but pushed consistently for "hard," hierarchical governance solutions.

Ironically, however, networks did grow in the 1990s to respond to particular problems. For instance, the Wassenaar arrangement was established 1996 as a nonbinding multilateral agreement among forty-one states.[55] Set up as a successor to the Cold War-era Coordinating Committee for Multilateral Export Controls in order to promote transparency and greater responsibility in transfers of conventional arms and dual-use goods and technologies, it also pertains to small arms. The Wassenaar Arrangement operates by consensus and its decisions are nonbinding, but it has served as a forum for harmonizing categorizations of arms and enhancing transparency. Also launched were the EU's "European Programme for Preventing and Combating Illicit Trafficking on Conventional Arms" (to promote information exchange and the assist developing countries in eliminating illicit trade) as well as its "EU Code of Conduct on Arms Embargo" (setting standards on arms exports). In December 1999 the United States and European Union signed a joint Statement of Common Principles on Small Arms and Light Weapons, a ten-point plan of action that included US support for the EU Code of Conduct on arms exports and the principles contained in its criteria. And, in 1997, the OAS aimed to combat weapons used in the illegal drug trade with its "Inter-American Convention against the Illicit Manufacturing and Trafficking in Firearms, Ammunition Explosives, and Other Related Materials."

The competing mobilizations each had clear solutions, which left less room for a policy entrepreneurship role. The Swiss government was involved with small arms, but rather than pulling together stakeholders to find a new solution they largely supported the regulation proponents.[56]

The pro-regulation forces were successful in pushing for the 2001 UN Conference on the Illicit Trade in Small Arms and Light Weapons in All Its Aspects, which resulted in the POA. Though it raised attention to

---

[55] www.wassenaar.org.

[56] They have advocated for the implementation of an international instrument for the rapid and reliable identification and tracing of illicit small arms and light weapons and for the implementation of the Geneva Declaration on Armed Violence and Development. They also took part in negotiations within the UN for a comprehensive and binding ATT, contributed to a project for the destruction of superfluous small arms and light weapons and to their secure storage in the framework of the Organization for Security and Cooperation in Europe under the Partnership for Peace, supported the Small Arms Survey competence center and countries and NGOs in the implementation of the UN action program.

small arms as an issue and set a framework for agreement, the pro-regulation forces saw its lack of binding rules as a loss. They called the POA disappointing and toothless: "zombie policy" or, as Human Rights Watch suggested, the "Program of Inaction."[57] The language and strategies of the pro-gun groups was reflected in the Bush administration's policy (NRA Board of Directors member Bob Barr was even part of the official US delegation), leading pro-regulation groups to argue that the US position had been hijacked by pro-gun forces.[58] The USA was not alone in frustrating stronger regulation. It joined other governments that resisted different elements of the proposed agreement – China did not want human rights language, Arab states were concerned about transparency, and some southern (non-manufacturing) states were concerned about measures that would limit their access to arms for defense.[59] But without US support international regulation had little chance.

In the wake of the 2001 conference both positions hardened. The pro-governance groups did not acknowledge the small gains made with the POA. On the pro-gun side, the WFSA, the NRA, and other gun rights groups portrayed the POA as the opening gambit of the UN's assault on private gun ownership all over the world. Making claims about the potential for the POA to infringe upon the rights of law-abiding citizens, equating gun ownership with the potential for self-preservation, and even linking disarmament and genocide,[60] they mobilized their forces to roll it back.

The NRA's influence on both US policy and policy in other countries grew in the 2000s. Pro-gun forces aimed to frustrate or repeal both domestic and international regulation on the basis of the self-protection benefits of access to weapons.[61] The NRA's action included lobbying Congress to shield arms manufacturers from lawsuits. With a friendly ear in the Bush administration and the Republican Congress, the "Protection of lawful commerce in arms" was passed in 2005.[62]

The NRA also gave advice to gun rights groups in other countries, most prominently Brazil. There, what looked like a popular proposal to outlaw the commercial sale of arms and ammunition to civilians in 2005 had majority support at the start. In the wake of a campaign advised by the NRA to protect the "right" to bear arms (not a traditional right in Brazil), however, the proposal was rejected by a margin of 2–1. Ads warned that the proposal would not disarm criminals but would take away popular rights and urged viewers: "Don't lose your grip on liberty."[63] The NRA linked with gun rights groups in various countries,

[57] Bob 2010.   [58] Meierding 2005.   [59] Meierding 2005.   [60] LaPierre 2006.
[61] Grillot 2011.   [62] Bob 2010.   [63] Morton 2006.

concerned that any gun control could impact the US. As put by one NRA member before the vote in Brazil, "We view Brazil as the opening salvo for the global gun control movement. If gun control proponents succeed in Brazil, America will be next."[64] Similarly an NRA representative to the UN stated, "We live in a very globalized society, you can't say what happened in Scotland doesn't affect the United States, because it does."[65] The NRA also joined the WFSA in concerted grassroots efforts to block and even roll back the POA at the 2006 RevCon.[66]

The pro-regulation forces remobilized to push for the insertion of "teeth" in the POA at RevCon. Their hopes would have been tough to achieve even with the USA on board, but they were completely unrealistic without it.[67] At RevCon the USA maintained its restrictions on stipulations about civilian firearms and its ability to sell or give arms to whomever it pleased, and even added restriction on the regulation of ammunition. China, Russia, and Arab states that had joined the USA in 2001 were also unchanged. Pro-regulation forces then pushed further later in 2006 for a UN General Assembly resolution for to create a comprehensive ATT. Demonstrating its increasing connection with the NRA's view, the USA distinguished itself by being the only state to vote against this resolution.

When the Obama administration took office in 2009 it reengaged on the UN and the proponents of regulation on the ATT. Even agreeing to take part in the process, however, caused the NRA to send out a press release telling people that the UN was going to regulate private gun owners in the USA. What Obama and Clinton could not get in domestic legislation, the NRA argued, they would try and bring in through the "back door" of the UN. Meanwhile, pro-regulation forces were profoundly disappointed with Obama's efforts. US hesitancy and Chinese resistance led the meeting to consider a comprehensive ATT in 2012 to adjourn at the end of July without reaching any consensus.[68]

Continued negotiations, perhaps buoyed by the Obama administration's recommitment to halt gun violence in the wake of the Newtown shootings, did lead to the passage of the ATT in 2013. The ATT includes little attention to small arms, light weapons, and ammunition and a number of its provisions are weaker than commitments on small arms transfers in the POA.[69] Despite Obama's efforts common ground was hard to find, the arms industry remained unengaged, and the USA signed, but did not ratify, the treaty.

---

[64] Morton 2006.   [65] Morton 2006.   [66] Bob 2010.   [67] Meierding 2005.
[68] *New York Times*, July 27, 2012.   [69] Survey 2013.

What is interesting for the purposes of this book, though, is both sides' continued focus on hierarchical forms of governance as the preferred mode. While some networked schemes are also in place they have remained generally disconnected from this political struggle. And market mechanisms are largely uninvolved in small arms governance.

How Does It Matter?

The process surrounding military and security services moved from hierarchy to a complex governance system involving hierarchy, market, and network mechanisms. Small arms remained largely focused on hierarchy. Just a cursory evaluation of the efforts in these two issue areas demonstrates at least some progress in military and security services since the mid-2000s and no progress, or even some backsliding, in small arms. Nonetheless, many feel unease when looking at the complex governance system surrounding military and security services, often seeing it as a less effective, second-best solution to a "binding," legalized, hierarchical agreement among states. As the Introduction to this volume muses, are major challenges "fixable or even manageable via piecemeal, incremental, and disorganized efforts?"

But ambitious, hierarchical regimes, even in their heyday, were rarely produced in the absence of agreement among consequential parties.[70] Regimes have rarely been forced. And given growth in the array of relevant actor types, a solution built on states alone is unlikely to address the range of governance issues.[71] Bringing different actor types to the table can link previously unconnected networks in ways that yield new ideas and even new coalitions. Complex governance can serve to aggregate, shape, and build toward collective ambition.

Rather than thinking of complex governance processes as second best compared to some finite alternative, a more pragmatic conception of effectiveness evaluates them according to whether they connect relevant stakeholders and enhance the prospect that their efforts will be reinforcing (see Table 1.1). What makes governance tick from this perspective is the relationship between many different venues, perspectives, and mechanisms; it thus incorporates a measure of legitimacy. The web of initiatives that govern private security, for instance, generates more traction if the initiatives work together instead of at cross-purposes.[72] When US government regulations push in the same general direction as British government regulations, and what will satisfy them also satisfies the

---

[70] Krasner 1983.   [71] Abbott and Snidal 2009.   [72] Avant et al. 2010.

Table 1.1 *Pragmatic conception of variation in governance processes*

	Reinforcing efforts	Competing efforts
With a broad set of stakeholders/capacities	(1) Most effective governance processes	(2) Rival governance processes
With a narrow set of stakeholders/capacities	(3) Partial governance processes	(4) Least effective governance processes

Note: Drawn from Avant 2016.

demands of other prominent clients, such as those in the extractive industry, and they lead to fewer complaints that civil society groups catch wind of, PMSCs are more inclined to sign on and observers are more likely to see the issue area as relatively well governed. All of this is more likely to happen if the regulation of military and security services fits under the larger umbrella of business and human rights, and this larger umbrella continues to garner effort and attention.

In both military and security services and small arms there was a proliferation of actor types relevant for governance. They reflected different bases of authority with different constituencies all concerned with problems surrounding the issues. In military and security services different stakeholders were included in the process, while with small arms constituencies were largely funneled through state and international hierarchies.

Recognizing different stakeholders was key to the Montreux Document's articulation of the various relationships states had with private security and the implications of these for quite distinct best practices. Recognizing that clients who hire PMSCs include an array of organizations, from governments to extractive industry groups to a wide array of commercial organizations (including shipping) to implementing NGOs, also had important implications for the process. It led not only to the need to include these constituencies but was also key to convincing many powerful players that an international code of conduct could be useful rather than disruptive. Including a breadth of stakeholders and recognizing their different perspectives and impact on one another was not only important to moving toward some governance in the first place, it also led to harmonization among national processes. And recognizing that ongoing communication and coordination would be necessary led to the successful creation of an organization, the ICoCA, that could link different constituencies as a way of facilitating both responses to new concerns and some sort of communications or coordination among them.

Though the ongoing success of this organization is less certain, the processes of agreeing on it and setting it up have already served to link and coordinate among different clients, industry members, and civil society representatives.

In small arms, on the other hand, industry representatives were not included in governance efforts. The Smith and Wesson initiative at the end of the Clinton administration, though, suggests that there was some difference of opinion on how best to proceed within the industry. One counterfactual to consider is whether acceptance of this by regulatory proponents and/or the NRA could have brought industry voices more directly to the governance table (rather than leaving them to work through interest group influence on governments) and whether this broadening of voices could have widened the debate in ways that allowed for new ideas and/or shifts in how actors perceived their interests.

Complex governance systems also work through lower levels of the bureaucracy. The networks involved are transgovernmental like those that Anne-Marie Slaughter[73] wrote of, but they join hierarchies (governments) and different networks (links across governments and also CSOs, subject matter experts, and commercial actors). Because they operate at this lower level they are often able to get around veto points and other political hurdles.[74] Students of bureaucratic politics have long argued that policy made by those closer to the ground is more responsive to actual problems and more effective.[75]

These systems can face stumbling blocks within hierarchies. Though the system governing PMSCs allowed for harmonization between US regulation (in DoD and one part of DoS) and the ICoC standards, harmonization across United States government agencies (other offices at the State Department and USAID, among others) has been more difficult. Offices relevant to some parts of the regulatory web are not even aware of their role in the framework that governs PMSCs and have sometimes unknowingly made changes that challenged elements of the system. In 2015, for instance, the State Department office of defense trade controls made changes that threatened the degree to which the USA was compliant with its obligations under the Montreux Document.[76] These processes can be likened to the banal authority that McNamara[77] argues the European Union has developed. Problems are solved quietly by closely involved experts in ways that avoid openly

---

[73] Slaughter 2004.   [74] Eilstrup-Sangiovanni 2016.
[75] Thompson and Frizzell 1977.   [76] *Foreign Policy*, October 26, 2015.
[77] McNamara 2016.

"political" manifestations. The solutions may become part of regulatory routines but fail to generate commitment.

Finally, the governance complex surrounding private security has no one central point or pinnacle. This may lead some to worry about "multiple principal" problems: many authorities could compete or move in different directions and weaken effectiveness. For instance, periodic stories that high-level US officials are considering plans to use PMSCs in a way that counters the best practices put forth by the Montreux Document have led to concern among other governments about weakened influence for ICoCA membership and PSC standard certification. Others, though, might point to the various ways different nodes are linked. If firms in the extractive sector continued to see the behavior suggested by the ICoC and standards as important they could buffet participation in these initiatives even if US policy changed. The different connections could thus inject a degree of resilience into governance practices even in the face of policy changes by an important player like the United States. Some have argued that the key to management, even in hierarchies, is shared norms and relationships.[78]

As suggested in Section 1.2, pragmatic arguments about effectiveness incorporate a degree of legitimacy. Governance, by its nature, addresses matters of public – or common – concern.[79] Arguments for including multiple stakeholders hold that pulling those with a stake in common concerns into supporting their governance can yield both effectiveness and legitimacy. When those who will be governed have a say in that governance they are more likely to buy in and this should increase its effectiveness. At the same time their stake also means they are affected and thus should have some say into how an issue ought to be governed.

But both popular and academic language often equates "public" with government and "private" with commercial, narrow, and self-interested. Governments represent the "public sector" and thus ought to be the institutions pursuing common concerns. The legitimacy of private actors working for "public" goals is more suspect. These concerns are amplified by the association of specific processes, like elections and criminal enforcement (typically associated with government and government policy), as *the* tools for accountability. Though multistakeholderism's language of inclusiveness may be appealing, some stakeholders are viewed suspiciously and the processes for participation are not fully specified in ways that challenge their rightfulness.

---

[78] Miller 1992.   [79] Best and Gheciu 2014.

The legitimacy of the military and security services governance system – often termed "voluntary" or "self"-regulation – has suffered from this critique. In the absence of international hierarchical agreements, some have argued that PMSCs have used the regulatory façade to escape the mercenary tag and gain legitimacy but without guarantees that their behavior will serve common concerns. These critiques are aided by evidence that traditional democratic mechanisms are often interrupted, even when governments contract for military and security services,[80] let alone other clients. The comparison of these two issue areas, though, shows that worries over capture should not be limited to complex governance.[81] Indeed, many of those promoting small arms regulation argued that the NRA captured the US position during the George W. Bush administration.

The very nature of complex governance challenges many modern ways of thinking of legitimacy. It could be more promising to think about legitimacy as based not only on who actors are but what they do; whether their actions are public serving or not.[82] This perspective could benefit from imagining publics as not set in stone but situations where people realize their interdependence and take steps to manage it.[83] This is the logic on which the ICoC is based and it follows in a long tradition of pulling non-state armed actors into the International Humanitarian Law framework.[84] This more process-based approach could also inform analysis of participation where legitimacy is tied to processes of deliberation.[85] Finally, the types of power operative in complex governance is relevant to discussions of legitimacy. As demonstrated in the PMSC case, this kind of governance enhances the power of brokers that connect others. The Swiss government, the ICRC, and the Geneva-based Center for the Democratic Control of Armed Forces (the NGO facilitating the Montreux Process and ICoC/ICoCA), for instance, have had an outsized influence on the unfolding of this governance process because of their central position in the governance network and their ability to bring different stakeholders to the table. The process that emerged reflected these organizations' traditional concerns with humanitarianism and human rights even though the concerns people voiced around private security ranged widely.[86] On the one hand, this exacerbates the worries mentioned in the Introduction that the power of the global "haves" will

---

[80] Avant and Sigelman 2010.   [81] Mattli and Woods 2009.
[82] Avant and Haufler 2018; Ciepley 2013.   [83] Dewey 1927.   [84] Avant 2017.
[85] Nanz and Steffek 2004; Castells 2008; see also Ruggie 2013.
[86] Some saw a threat to state control of force, others a threat to military professionalism, a threat to democracy, a tool for corruption, and a threat to the rights of those who work in the industry, among others.

be enhanced. On the other, these organizations constructed power for themselves through connecting with others, and that power is contingent on the maintenance of those relationships. This different sort of power has some element of accountability baked in to it. If relationships break down so does the power that these organizations hold.[87] To gain greater influence the Swiss government, the ICRC, and the ICoCA have worked to connect with companies and civil society groups in many different parts of the world and, once connected, these new organizations gain influence on the process.

Conclusion

What is happening in private security governance is different now than it was twenty years ago. In this project's terms it has moved from a governance system based on hierarchy to one based on markets, networks, hierarchies, and the interactions among them. Small arms governance remains based on hierarchy and the coordination among hierarchies at the global level has lessened. Similar structural changes in both issue areas led to new concerns, but the agency of actors varied. As problems mounted, clear ideas about solutions led initially to greater direction in small arms, but increasingly rigid positions eroded space for creative ideas and new solutions, and the governance process stalled in a stalemate between proponents and opponents of regulation. In military and security services, initial confusion and escalating problems led to policy entrepreneurship by the Swiss government and the ICRC that involved a range of actors and entertained the potential for different mechanisms. The pragmatic process that unfolded shifted the perspectives of key actors and moved the governance process forward.

Given the range of actors that is important for global concerns the proliferation of governance forms makes sense, but the relationships among these various governance forms is critical to effectiveness. Processes that work to aggregate different forms and allow for healthy conflict but manage unproductive rigidity should be most effective. This conceptualization of effectiveness incorporates legitimacy to some extent but it would be useful to devote more thought in academic and popular circles to the processes that connect different forms of governance and the mechanism by which they gain or lose legitimacy. Rigid

---

[87] Avant and Westerwinter 2016.

commitments to specific ideas or forms of governance can lead strategies to minimize the potential for new connections and lessen the possibility for both greater buy-in and creative solutions that can change how actors see their concerns. A focus on hierarchical governance as the best solution can thus erode the potential for coordination altogether.

References

Abbott, Kenneth and Duncan Snidal. 2009. The Governance Triangle: Regulatory standards Institutions and the Shadow of the State. In *The Politics of Global Regulation*, eds., Walter Mattli and Ngaire Woods, 44–88. Princeton: Princeton University Press.

Alves, Gasparani and Daiana Cipollone. 1998. *Curbing Illicit Trafficking in Small Arms and Sensitive Technologies: An Agenda Oriented Agenda*. Geneva: United Nations Institute for Disarmament.

Amnesty International. 2008. Amnesty International Public Statement on the Montreux Document (October). www.globalpolicy.org/pmscs/50736-amnesty-international-public-statement-on-the-montreux-document.html.

Avant, Deborah. 2000. From Mercenaries to Citizen Armies: Explaining Change in the Practice of War. *International Organization* 54 (1): 41–72.

2005. *The Market for Force: The Implications of Privatizing Security*. Cambridge: Cambridge University Press.

2016. Pragmatic Networks and Transnational Governance of Private Military and Security Services. *International Studies Quarterly* 60: 330–342.

2017. Pragmatism, the Just War Tradition, and an Ethical Approach to Private Military and Security Companies. In *The Ethics of War and Peace Revisited: Moral Challenges in an Era of Contested and Fragmented Sovereignty*, edited by Daniel R. Brunstetter and Jean-Vincent Holeindre, 119–138. Washington, DC: Georgetown University Press.

Avant, Deborah and Lee Sigelman. 2010. Private Security and Democracy: Lessons from the US in Iraq. *Security Studies* 19 (2): 230–265.

Avant, Deborah, Martha Finnemore, and Susan Sell, eds. 2010. *Who Governs the Globe?* Cambridge: Cambridge University Press.

Avant, Deborah and Oliver Westerwinter. 2016. Introduction: Networks and Transnational Security Governance. In *The New Power Politics: Networks and Security Governance*, edited by Deborah Avant and Oliver Westerwinter, 1–18. New York: Oxford University Press.

Avant, Deborah and Virginia Haufler. 2018. Public–Private Interactions in the Provision of Security and Insecurity. In *Oxford University Press Handbook on International Security*, edited by Alexandra Gheciu and William Wohlforth. Oxford: Oxford University Press.

Barnett, Michael. 2011. *Empire of Humanity: A History of Humanitarianism*. Ithaca, NY: Cornell University Press.

Best, Jacqueline and Alexandra Gheciu, eds. 2014. *The Return of the Public in Global Governance*. Cambridge: Cambridge University Press.

Bitzinger, Richard. 1994. The Globalization of the Arms Industry: The Next Proliferation Challenge. *International Security* 19 (2): 170–198.

Bob, Clifford. 2010. Packing Heat: Pro-gun Groups and the Governance of Small Arms. In *Who Governs the Globe?*, edited by Deborah D. Avant, Martha Finnemore, and Susan Sell, 183–201. Cambridge: Cambridge University Press.

———. 2012. *The Global Right Wing and the Clash of World Politics*. Cambridge: Cambridge University Press.

Boutwell, Jeffrey and Michael Klare. 1998. Small Arms and Light Weapons: Controlling the Real Instruments of War. *Arms Control Today* (August/September). www.armscontrol.org/act/1998_08-09/mkas98.

Boutwell, Jeffrey, Michael T. Klare, and Laura W. Reed. 1995. *Lethal Commerce: The Global Trade in Small Arms and Light Weapons*. Cambridge, MA: American Academy of Arts and Sciences.

Byrne, Edmund F. 2007. Assessing Arms Makers' Corporate Social Responsibility. *Journal of Business Ethics* 74: 201–217.

Castells, Manuel. 2008. The New Public Sphere: Global Civil Society, Communication Networks and Global Governance. *The Annals of the American Academy of Political and Social Sciences* 616: 78–93.

Ciepley, David. 2013. Beyond Public and Private: Toward a Political Theory of the Corporation. *American Political Science Review* 107 (1): 139–158.

Dewey, John. 1927. *The Public and Its Problems*. Athens, OH: Swallow Press.

DFARS (Defense Federal Acquisitions Regulation Supplement). 2012. Part 252, Subpart 225-7039. www.acq.osd.mil/dpap/dars/dfars/html/current/252225.htm#252.225-7039.

Douglass, Ian. 1999. Fighting for Diamonds in Sierra Leone. In *Peace, Profit, or Plunder: The Privatization of Security in War-Torn African Societies*, edited by Jakkie Cilliers and Peggy Mason, 175–200. Pretoria: Institute for Security Studies.

Dunigan, Molly and Ulrich Petersohn, eds. 2015. *The Markets for Force: Privatization of Security Across World Regions*. Philadelphia: University of Pennsylvania Press.

Eilstrup-Sangiovanni, Mette. 2016. Power and Purpose in Transgovernmental Networks: Insights from the Global Non-Proliferation Regime. In *The New Power Politics: Networks and Security Governance*, edited by Deborah Avant and Oliver Westerwinter, 131–168. Oxford: Oxford University Press.

Gaultier, Leonard, Garine Hovsepian, Ayesha Ramachandran, Ian Wadley, and Badr Zerhdoud. 2001. The Mercenary Convention at the UN Commission on Human Rights: The Need for a New Approach, International Alert (January). www.international-alert.org/publications/mercenary-issues-un-commission-human-rights.

Goldring, Natalie. 1999. Domestic Laws and International Control. In *Light Weapons and Civil Conflict: Controlling the Tools of Violence*, edited by Jeffrey Boutwell and Michael T. Klare, 101–125. New York: Carnegie Commission on Preventing Deadly Conflict.

Goulet, Yves. 1998. MPRI: Washington's Freelance Advisors. *Janes Intelligence Review* 10 (7): 108–112.

Grillot, Suzette R. 2011. Global Gun Control: Examining the Consequences of Competing International Norms. *Global Governance* 17: 529–555.

Hammes, Thomas X. 2011. Private Contractors in Conflict Zones: The Good, the Bad, and the Strategic Impact. *Joint Forces Quarterly* 60 (1): 26–37.

Hayward, Keith. 2000. The Globalisation of Defence Industries. *Survival* 42 (3): 115–132.

HRF. 2010. *State of Affairs Three Years after Nisoor Square: Accountability and Oversight of US Private Security and Other Contractors.* Human Rights First (September). www.humanrightsfirst.org/resource/state-affairs-three-years-after-nisoor-square.

ICoC. 2009. International Code of Conduct for Private Security Providers, Private Security Service Providers Association (November). http://psm.du .edu/media/documents/regulations/global_instruments/multi_stakeholder/icoc/icoc_eng.pdf.

ICoCA. 2013. Articles of Association, Private Security Service Providers Association. http://psm.du.edu/media/documents/regulations/global_instru ments/multi_stakeholder/icoc/icoc_articles_of_association_charter.pdf.

Keck, Margaret and Katheryn Sikkink. 1998. *Activists beyond Borders: Advocacy Networks in International Politics.* Ithaca, NY: Cornell University Press.

Kingdon, John W. 1984 *Agendas, Alternatives, and Public Policies.* Boston: Little, Brown.

Klare, Michael. 1997. East Asia's Militaries Muscle Up. *Bulletin of the Atomic Scientists* 53 (1): 56–61.

Krasner, Stephen D., ed. 1983. *International Regimes.* Ithaca, NY: Cornell University Press.

Krause, Keith. 2002. Multilateral Diplomacy, Norm Building, and the UN Conferences: The Case of Small Arms and Light Weapons. *Global Governance* 8: 247–263.

LaPierre, Wayne. 2006. *The Global War on Your Guns: Inside the U.N. Plan to Destroy the Bill of Rights.* Nashville, TN: Thomas Nelson.

Laurance, Edward. 1998. Small Arms, Light Weapons, and Conflict Prevention: The New Post-Cold War Logic of Disarmament. In *Cases and Strategies for Preventive Action*, edited by Barnett R. Rubin, 135–168. New York: Century Foundation Press.

Lerman, David, 2012. Humanitarian Groups Push for "Bulletproof" Arms Treaty. *Bloomberg*, May 23. www.bloomberg.com/news/articles/2012-05-24/humanitarian-groups-push-for-bullet-proof-arms-treaty.

McNamara, Kathleen. 2016. *The Politics of Everyday Europe: Constructing Authority in the European Union.* New York: Oxford University Press.

Mattli, Walter and Ngaire Woods. 2009. In Whose Benefit? Explaining Regulatory Change in Global Politics. In *The Politics of Global Regulation*, eds. Walter Mattli and Ngaire Woods, 1–43. Princeton: Princeton University Press.

Mayer, Col. Christopher T. 2010. Accountability: The Way Ahead. *Journal of International Peace Operations* 4 (4): 25–39.

Meierding, Emily. 2005. Missing the Target: Light Weapons and the Limits of Global Governance. Paper prepared for the annual International Studies Association Conference, March, Honolulu, HI.

Miller, Gary J. 1992. *Managerial Dilemmas: The Political Economy of Hierarchy.* Cambridge: Cambridge University Press.

Mockler, Anthony. 1985. *The New Mercenaries.* London: Garden City Press.

Morton, David. 2006. Gunning for the World. *Foreign Policy* 152: 58–67.

Musah, Abdel-Farau. 2000. "A Country Under Siege," State Decay and Corporate Military Intervention in Sierra Leone. In *Mercenaries: An African Security Dilemma,* edited by Abdel-Fatau Musah and J. 'Kayode Fayemi, 76–116. London: Pluto.

Nanz, Patrizia and Jens Steffek. 2004. Global Governance, Participation, and the Public Sphere. *Government and Opposition* 39 (2): 314–335.

O'Brien, Kevin. 1998. Freelance Forces: Exploiters of Old or New-Age Peacebrokers? *Jane's Intelligence Review* (August): 42–46.

Percy, Sarah. 2007. *Mercenaries: History of a Norm in International Relations.* Oxford: Oxford University Press.

Roling, Bert V.A. 1976. The Legal Status of Rebels and Rebellion. *Journal of Peace Research* 13 (2): 149–163.

Ruggie, John G. 2013. *Just Business: Multinational Corporations and Human Rights (Norton Global Ethics Series).* New York: W.W. Norton & Company.

Shearer, David. 1998. *Private Armies and Military Intervention.* Adelphi Paper 316. Oxford: Oxford University Press.

Slaughter, Anne-Marie. 2004. *A New World Order.* Princeton: Princeton University Press.

Survey (Small Arms Survey). 2001. *Profiling the Problem.* Cambridge: Cambridge University Press.

2002. *Counting the Human Cost.* Cambridge: Cambridge University Press.

2013. The Arms Trade Treaty: A Step Forward in Small Arms Control? *Research Notes* 30 (June).

Thomson, Janice. 1994. *Mercenaries, Pirates and Sovereigns: State Building and Extraterritorial Violence in Early Modern Europe.* Princeton: Princeton University Press.

Thomson, W. Scott and Donald D. Frizzell, eds. 1977. *The Lessons of Vietnam.* Brisbane: University of Queensland Press.

UNGA United Nations General Assembly. 1995. Supplement to an Agenda for Peace: Position Paper of the Secretary General on the Fiftieth Anniversary of the United Nations, A/50/60-S/1995/1, January 3.

1996. General and Complete Disarmament, A/RES/50/70, January 15.

UNWG (United Nations Working Group on the Use of Mercenaries). 2011. Report to the 66th Session of the General Assembly, GA A/66/317, August 22.

White House. 2000. *Clinton Administration Reaches Historic Agreement with Smith and Wesson.* Press Release, March 17.

2 The Bretton Woods Moment
Hierarchies, Networks, and Markets in the Long Twentieth Century

Miles Kahler

Rapid growth in global governance formats that diverge from formal, multilateral institutions has been framed as unprecedented. The labels differ – informal international law-making, private transnational regulatory organizations, private authority, new interdependence approach – but the conclusion is the same: the era of conventional intergovernmental organizations (IGOs) and the mode of governance that they represent has at best reached a plateau, and at worst faces erosion and decline.[1] These observations occur, somewhat paradoxically, during an era of globalization, an expansion of cross-border economic flows and deeper integration that was promoted by the very IGOs that are now viewed as less central to global governance.

This apparent paradox can be explained by the transitory monopoly that IGOs – and the states behind them – acquired during a particular historical moment, when hierarchies (national governments) reasserted their control over markets, internally and externally. This extension of the regulatory state was expressed internationally in the form of IGOs. Those IGOs, however, aimed to tame and constrain *both* markets and states, transferring to the global domain the regulated markets that had been built in the aftermath of war and depression and preventing the emergence of deviant forms of capitalist autarchy (and, during the Cold War, communist autarchy).

Before this mid-century Bretton Woods moment, less interventionist national governments allowed for the emergence of alternative forms of global governance. The expansion of international markets provided a challenge to both public and private actors, a challenge that was met by networks, often combining public and private actors, or by informal

---

The author thanks Kyle Evanoff and Frieder Dengler for their research assistance on this project. Lawrence Broz, Benjamin Cohen, Orfeo Fioretos, and Eric Helleiner provided valuable comments on an earlier version of this chapter.

[1] The labels applied, respectively by Pauwelyn et al. 2012; Abbott et al. 2016; Green 2013; Farrell and Newman 2014.

IGOs (IIGOs). Private governance attempted to deal with the uncertainties of markets (cartels) or the need to govern cross-border disputes (commercial arbitration) that could not be resolved through intergovernmental mechanisms. As international markets recovered in the post-1945 decades, these forms of governance resurfaced or were recreated as significant parts of global economic governance. During this latter period, however, reliance on deregulated markets as a means of constraining national governments also became part of the portfolio of global governance. With the global financial crisis of 2008–2009 and its aftermath, signs of a reversion to greater government intervention and a renewed reliance on regulation marked a further move in the cyclical influence of markets, hierarchies (both national governments and IGOs), and networks in the mix of global governance institutions.

In the first section that follows, the interwar decades (1920s and 1930s) are treated as a formative and often neglected period in global economic governance. Although economic governance was less dominated by national governments and their intergovernmental creations, governance innovations took place, and many persisted through the disruptions of depression and war. Networks and markets were important constituents of global governance. In economic domains, private and hybrid (public-private) modes of governance were significant parts of the global landscape.

Three issue areas illustrate this variety – international monetary and financial affairs, which were conducted largely by central banks (private or semi-private) and their private financial partners; cartels, through which many economic sectors governed themselves with little interference and considerable encouragement from national governments; and international commercial arbitration (ICA), which took its modern form in the decades after the First World War, offering private dispute resolution to international corporations. In the second section the Bretton Woods moment is viewed through the lens of the newly empowered regulatory state and its design of IGOs to constrain national policies and tame international markets. Finally, as the liberalization encouraged by those institutions expanded during the 1970s and 1980s, markets and networks resumed their earlier prominence in public and private global governance.

Throughout, a primary driver, which is also endogenous to this timeline of governance, is globalization – the expansion of cross-border flows of capital, goods, and labor. Globalization created the demand for governance, as well as shaping the supply, rendering IGOs less effective and alternative formats more appealing for both public and private actors. The era of dominance by hierarchies (national governments and formal

IGOs) in global governance was a moment born of particular historical circumstances (a closed world economy and triumphant regulatory states), circumstances that were inevitably undermined by the liberalization of the world economy. As the second era of globalization proceeded after 1970, the world returned to the new-old normal of economic governance: a mix of global governance institutions that reflected the IGO legacy but also awarded a greater role to networked, informal, and private modes of governance, as well as markets.

The Gold Standard and Networked Governance in International Monetary and Financial Affairs

International monetary and financial governance during the 1920s represented one model of governance among three that have competed and coexisted over the past century: a network of central banks and private finance; an institutionalized IGO model (the Bretton Woods system, at least until 1973); and less institutionalized intergovernmental bargaining (the Tripartite Agreement of the late 1930s or the G7 framework of the 1970s and 1980s). Each of these was embedded in an international economy that was more or less open to cross-border financial flows, an environmental condition that influenced both the choices of national governments and the viability of these alternative forms of governance.

Before 1914 the gold standard was based on commitments to maintain a fixed parity between currencies and gold, usually reinforced by national legislation. Formal intergovernmental agreement was unnecessary given the depth of elite commitment to the gold standard. To the degree that this system, viewed as self-regulating, required crisis management, major central banks supplied the resources and limited cooperation that were necessary, although the level and importance of that cooperation remains contested.[2] The degree of ongoing central bank cooperation hardly merited the label of networked governance, since central bank cooperation was more often tacit than explicit, limited in time, and limited in scope to a few counterpart central banks. The line between public and private blurred in the governance of central banks themselves; ownership in many cases remained in the hands of private shareholders or, as in the case of the US Federal Reserve, governance was a blend of public and private.[3] In an era of large and unrestricted cross-border financial flows, both their responsibilities and their governance gave central banks close links to the private financial sector.

---

[2] Eichengreen 1992, 8; Gallarotti 1995, 80.   [3] Broz 1997.

After the First World War, market instability awarded central banks a more central role in the restored gold standard monetary order. Reconstruction of the gold standard became a major economic priority; Peter Temin has argued that financial leaders of the period "could not even conceptualize an orderly alternative to the gold standard."[4] Central bankers understood, however, that pre-1914 institutional supports were insufficient: adherence to the gold standard and inflation-fighting credibility required reinforcement. Structural weaknesses had appeared, notably persistent surplus (United States, France) and deficit (United Kingdom) economies.[5] More importantly, the domestic political consensus that had sustained the gold standard was eroding as internationalist finance faced opposition from protectionist manufacturing sectors and the growing organizational and political power of labor and labor-based political parties.[6] Monetary policy was increasingly directed toward domestic economic ends rather than maintaining external balance and an exchange rate dictated by the gold standard.[7]

These political and structural strains in the interwar monetary system produced a gap between the domestic credibility and international cooperation required for system stability on the one hand, and their existing international and domestic supply on the other. Several institutional remedies were attempted during the 1920s; ultimately, all failed. The first was an attempted turn toward more formal hierarchy in monetary governance: explicit intergovernmental agreement on rules governing monetary and exchange rate policy, as a supplement or substitute for central bank cooperation. However, international monetary conferences after the First World War created neither formal institutions for consultation and coordination nor agreed rules to govern exchange rates.[8] Another intergovernmental vehicle, the League of Nations Financial Committee, participated, in partnership with private finance, in stabilizing individual economies during the 1920s. Its practices resembled later International Monetary Fund (IMF) conditionality with a critical difference: the loans disbursed originated with commercial lenders.[9]

Given the domestic political pressure placed on national commitments to the gold standard, shoring up the independence of central banks became a second institutional remedy for the postwar monetary system. At postwar international conferences in Brussels and Genoa participating governments approved the creation of independent central banks and monetary policies "freed from political pressure and ... conducted solely

---

[4] Temin 1989, 14.   [5] Eichengreen 1992.   [6] Simmons 1994.
[7] Eichengreen 1990, 1992; Simmons 1996.   [8] Pauly 1997; Eichengreen 1990, 1992.
[9] Pauly 1997; Jacobsson 1979.

on the lines of prudent finance."[10] This shared model of central bank governance was also diffused to the periphery in technical assistance missions to Latin America and other developing regions by the "money doctor," Princeton's Edwin M. Kemmerer.[11]

Growing independence and close ties to private finance enabled central banks to create a third governance alternative: networked cooperation that would have been difficult for their more politically constrained governments. The central bank network that emerged in the 1920s was an early example of a transgovernmental network (TGN), connecting relatively autonomous actors in national governments to each other. Although central bankers recognized that closer central bank cooperation was necessary to defend the reconstituted gold standard, collaboration was often difficult to implement. Nevertheless, cooperation in the central bank network increased during the 1920s through exchange of information, routinized provision of services, negotiating loans for stabilization, and managing German reparations.

The central bank network was also connected to private financial diplomacy, which flourished in this era. International banks played a "quasi-governmental role" in US dollar diplomacy with China and Japan.[12] Thomas W. Lamont was regarded as J.P. Morgan's "ambassador," and considerable exchange in personnel occurred between the worlds of finance and diplomacy.[13] These overseas activities of US private finance were, in turn, promoted by national legislation, which relaxed regulatory restrictions on interfirm cooperation abroad.[14] Support from a national government that was itself reluctant to engage in global economic governance indicated that networked governance by private financial consortia often served public ends.

As Stephen Clarke suggests, despite limited international collaboration, central bankers soon reverted to their roles as *national* central bankers.[15] Central bank cooperation was relatively high when measured against compliance with the rules of the gold standard game: increased central bank independence produced both more consistent adherence to the gold standard and more limited current account imbalances.[16] Central bankers embraced the view that their adherence to "agreed rules of behavior, and especially to the principle that the maintenance of exchange rate stability should take precedence over all other economic objectives, was itself a form of cooperation that normally made other forms of cooperation redundant."[17] Measured against a definition of

[10] Gregory 1955, 8.   [11] Drake 1989.   [12] Drake 1989, 175, 184–187.
[13] Pak 2013, 161.   [14] Pak 2013, 171–172.   [15] Clarke 1967.
[16] Simmons 1994, 138.   [17] Clarke 1967, 28.

cooperation as policy coordination, however, networked central bank collaboration proved inadequate to sustain the monetary order of the gold standard. As Simmons describes, greater independence meant a less cooperative stance on this measure; the narrower definition of cooperation dominated.[18]

The creation of the Bank for International Settlements (BIS) in 1930 epitomized global economic governance in monetary and financial affairs immediately before that monetary order collapsed during the Great Depression. The BIS was the first international financial organization, designed to facilitate the conversion of German reparations payments to commercial debt. The BIS was "conceived and designed by private financiers and central bankers" to reinforce Germany's commitment to payment of its international debt obligations.[19] The organization had a second role, however. Rather than embodying an institutionalized hierarchy that supported central bank cooperation, the BIS served as a critical, central node in what had been a very loose network of collaboration among the major central banks. It became – and remains – a "club of central bankers," dedicated to cooperation through "frequent meetings, visits, incessant exchange of information, common consultation and joint discussion."[20] More ambitious institutional innovations, such as the "international corporation" (a proto-World Bank) proposed by the Bank of England's Montague Norman, were rejected.

The failure of intergovernmental cooperation, in the form of the World Monetary and Economic Conference in June 1933, marked the effective end of the gold standard, although a gold bloc persisted until 1936. Central bank cooperation continued at the BIS, but the rebuilding of the international monetary regime, when it began in the 1930s, was dominated by national governments, first in the Tripartite Agreement of 1936 and later at Bretton Woods. The model of global economic governance characteristic of the gold standard – networked, with a prominent role for central banks and private financial institutions – did not disappear. It would reemerge when a new era of globalization commenced in the 1970s and 1980s.

An intergovernmental solution to international monetary and financial governance, in the form of an IGO, could not be negotiated during the 1920s and 1930s. That alternative may have required hierarchy: authority exerted by a dominant economic power or a collective of powers. The withdrawal of the US government from active participation in the League

---

[18] Simmons 1996.   [19] Simmons 1993, 364.
[20] 1935 Annual Report of the BIS, cited in Toniolo and Clement 2005, 3. Also Jacobsson 1979, 95; Auboin 1955.

of Nations made it an unlikely partner; persistent political divides among the major European powers hindered collective intergovernmental action. Two other efforts to reinforce the gold standard – enhancing central bank independence through domestic means and building cooperation through a central bank network – worked at cross-purposes: greater independence from domestic political intervention weakened any impulse for more than the narrowest form of cooperation. As the economic crisis deepened, the networked cooperation of central banks was insufficient to preserve the gold standard. Efforts at preservation also demonstrated that too much cooperation of the wrong kind – strict compliance with the monetary rules of the game – could produce disastrous economic outcomes.

International Cartels: Governance in Private Hands

Following the First World War, the limited role of national governments in both domestic political economies and global governance led to unmet demand for governance on the part of private actors. Private corporations were not devotees of untrammeled international markets. Given price volatility, particularly in commodity markets, firms in many sectors set out to tame markets through private governance in the form of cartels. As Fear describes, cartels are best considered as "voluntary, private contractual arrangements among independent enterprises to regulate the market." They are "a strategic option between markets and hierarchies," one that does not obliterate competition but can "reshape the rules of the game on which competition rests."[21] In other words, private actors attempted to make and enforce rules to sustain a form of collective self-regulation. Their success – the persistence of cooperation over time – relied on features familiar from the literature on interstate cooperation, among them prior experience with collusion (organizational learning and the buildup of trust over time) and a more specialized and complex governance structure that served to reinforce credible commitments on the part of cartel partners.[22]

International cartels existed before the First World War, but "their coverage and impact became significantly more pronounced during the interwar period."[23] The prevailing consensus among governments endorsed their stabilizing influence. For corporations operating across

---

[21] Fear 2006, 7.

[22] Storli 2014, 462; Spar 1994. See also Taylor 2007 on US domestic cartels and the positive effect of "institutionalization" for cartel success, measured by persistence.

[23] Fitzgerald 2015, 204.

national borders, they offered one of several strategies for expansion abroad; as a response to declining sales in periods of recession or depression (after the First World War and during the 1930s), cartels provided price stability and capacity rationalization through production quotas and agreed division of markets.[24] Price management was only one of their cooperative product lines, however, which could also extend to technology transfers and risk management.[25]

The international aluminum industry exemplified this form of private governance, which persisted through a series of cartels with different lifespans; the peak of intra-industry cooperation occurred in the 1930s.[26] After 1924, in the electrical equipment sector, suppliers controlled production, prices, and patents of electric lamps.[27] The diamond cartel, created by Cecil Rhodes in the nineteenth century, was strengthened by the acquisition of De Beers by Anglo-American in 1929. Other commodity sectors – tin, rubber, cocoa, coffee, sugar, tea, and bananas – were also cartelized. Most famously the 1928 Achnacarry Agreement among the world's three largest oil companies was designed to balance supply and demand through fixing market shares at existing levels.[28] By the outbreak of the Second World War it was estimated that 40 percent of world trade was governed by cartels.[29]

Governance of private cartels demonstrated varying degrees of hierarchy and institutionalization. In its most successful manifestation, the international aluminum cartel was incorporated as a holding company in Switzerland. Its regulation of the production of cartel members was sustained by the purchase of surplus stocks and enforced by "an independent audit company."[30] Governance of the electric lamp cartel included a court of arbitration to hear disputes.[31]

Cartels were also supported or undermined by the hierarchies of national governments. International commodity cartels resembled contemporary multi-stakeholder agreements, in which imperial governments and their colonies, multinational corporations, and plantation owners engaged in "complicated economic diplomacy."[32] Government enforcement rendered three of those cartels – tin, rubber, and tea – particularly effective.[33] In these cases, rather than influence through a shadow of hierarchy, national and imperial hierarchies directly supported private governance. US antitrust law and its exemptions also shaped the behavior of US corporations and their relations with international cartels.

---

[24] Fitzgerald 2015, 204; Koch 1945.   [25] Fear 2006, 1.
[26] Bertilorenzi 2016; Storli 2014, 448–451.   [27] Fitzgerald 2015, 229.
[28] Fitzgerald 2015, 229.   [29] Fear 2006, 15.   [30] Storli 2014, 450–451.
[31] Fitzgerald 2015, 299.   [32] Fear 2006, 13.   [33] Fitzgerald 2015, 229.

For example, the Achnacarry Agreement among oil majors could not apply to the United States because of US antitrust prohibitions. Alcoa could participate in the international aluminum cartel only through its Canadian subsidiary, Alcan. The 1918 Webb–Pomerene Act in the United States, on the other hand, granted antitrust immunity to export cartels. The Great Depression and the early New Deal brought an even more positive attitude toward cartels by the US government, which viewed them as a means to spur economic recovery. A domestic oil cartel, created and enforced by the National Recovery Administration (NRA) Oil Code, was later replaced by the 1935 Interstate Oil Compact, which persisted until 1972. By creating and enforcing a steel industry cartel, the NRA also "taught the steel producers how to collude."[34] Throughout the 1930s and 1940s warfare or political conflict between governments disrupted international cartels, as corporations were mobilized to support the national military effort.

At the end of the Second World War, one might have predicted that international cartels and their variant of private governance in international markets would play a prominent role in the postwar order, since "most of the world thought that cartels could bring widespread benefits and that cooperation between producers was a way to avoid the ravages of cut-throat competition."[35] Even before the Great Depression, the official attitude toward cartels recognized their benefits in regulating markets. The final report of the 1927 World Economic Conference concluded that international cartels "must be considered good or bad according to the spirit which rules the constitution and operation of the agreements." That evaluation depended on whether those directing the cartel were "actuated by a sense of the general interest."[36] International cartels might have been viewed as a foundation for international cooperation through self-regulation of industry and as important constituents of the postwar order. Instead an ideational turn coupled with US extraterritorial power would create a second Bretton Woods moment that eventually led to the slow demise of most international cartels and the private governance that they embodied.

International Commercial Arbitration: Private Governance and Its Limits

Few forms of international governance have a longer history than ICA. The medieval law merchants created a "reputation-based system of

---

[34] Baker 1989, S72.   [35] Storli 2014, 448.   [36] Cited in Koch 1945, 133.

enforcement" to govern disputes that arose from long-distance trade at a time when domestic commercial law was rudimentary and intergovernmental means of dispute resolution did not exist.[37] As national legal systems developed, together with modern banking and insurance, states asserted jurisdiction over transnational commercial activity and national courts developed the techniques of conflict of laws to deal with disputes arising from cross-border economic exchange. At the same time, the industrial revolution had produced an explosion of domestic private governance in the form of commercial arbitration in England. Trade associations and exchanges provided template contracts and arbitration for their members. Through the 1889 Arbitration Act, these arbitration clauses were made enforceable under British law in British courts. In the United States, arbitration also flourished, although it remained "outside the law" until states (New York in 1920) and finally the federal government (1925) provided for enforcement of arbitration awards in the courts.[38] Arbitration represented a form of private authority and governance. As in the case of international cartels, however, private governance was reinforced by the hierarchy of national governments in the form of enforcement in national courts.

The first era of globalization produced heightened demand for the resolution of cross-border commercial disputes. Because of earlier domestic development of commercial arbitration, two alternative paths seemed possible. ICA could "borrow" the arbitration capabilities that existed in the major commercial centers of London and New York. Because of the central position of London and Britain in the world trading system, the London Court of Arbitration provided a practical, functioning, "low-cost option, based on a large inflow of domestic legal know-how, social legitimacy and geopolitical power."[39] Another alternative, New York, provided what Jérôme Sgard labels a second "neo-imperial" project, as economic power shifted from London to New York before and after the First World War. However, traders from other European countries and the United States found London discriminatory and inflexible; smaller-scale arbitration platforms were established as alternatives in Europe.[40] Even though New York was promoted as a "novel, broad-based, generic model of dispute resolution," it did not become the dominant center and model for ICA outside the United States.[41] A second alternative to either London or New York, an international court for private disputes at the Hague, proved too ambitious for

---

[37] Stone Sweet and Grisel 2017, 38–39.
[38] Macassey 1938, 190; Sgard 2016. On the history of ICA, also Hale 2015a.
[39] Sgard 2016, 169.   [40] Sgard 2016.   [41] Sgard 2016, 167.

the times, despite support from the powerful transnational movement linking arbitration and international peace.

The center for ICA that was most successful before the Second World War was situated in an unlikely location: at the headquarters of the International Chamber of Commerce (ICC) in Paris. Although initially supported by a transatlantic network of chambers of commerce and notable private diplomats, such as Owen D. Young, American business soon lost interest in the ICC arbitration services, regarding its ICA as "catering to European continental needs."[42] The lack of connection to an international economic center (and its legal infrastructure) ultimately became a strength of the ICC, however, since it became identified as a more neutral, extraterritorial arbitration court. By limiting its work to international disputes, it was able, during the interwar years, to take the first steps toward developing a set of transnational legal principles to govern ICA. The organization of the ICC Arbitration Court was also multilateral and multinational: its most prominent practitioners were not those who carried high status from their national legal positions; instead, they displayed "multiple legal identities and cultures."[43]

Despite efforts to disentangle the ICC's International Court of Arbitration from national legal impediments, the number of arbitration settlements overseen by the court was disappointing during the 1920s and 1930s: in its first eighteen years, only seventy-seven cases were settled by award, and 120 by "conciliation." Its efforts at outreach to other arbitration commissions and services were "conspicuous failures."[44] The closure of the international economy, which reduced business demand as well as heightened interstate conflict, provides one explanation for the failure of ICA to expand rapidly during the 1930s.

Equally important was the inability of ICA to provide guaranteed enforcement of arbitration decisions through national legal systems, guarantees that had been crucial in the success of domestic arbitration. During the 1920s, international business pressed for multilateral conventions that would provide a set of "coordinating rules" to insure enforcement of arbitration awards across national boundaries.[45] Two such agreements were negotiated under the auspices of the Economic Committee of the League of Nations in 1923 and 1927, perhaps "the foremost original contribution of the League to international legislation."[46] Several important economies, including the United States, were

---

[42] Sgard 2016, 172.   [43] Grisel 2017, 801.   [44] Nussbaum 1942, 219.

[45] Sgard 2016, 156.

[46] Nussbaum 1942, 22. These were the Geneva Protocol on Arbitration Clauses (1923) and the Geneva Convention on the Execution of Foreign Arbitral Awards (1927).

not parties to these agreements, however.[47] The relationship of the ICA regime to national hierarchies during the interwar decades was complicated: it could not succeed if it were closely tied to the national legal system of one of the major economies, and it could not succeed if it were less attached to means of enforcement through national judiciaries and relied on a purely reputational system of sanctions. The resolution of this dilemma was only achieved in the post-1945 decades when growing economic integration once again increased demand for ICA from international business and national judiciaries provided support for enforcement of its awards.

Hierarchies, Networks, and Markets before 1945

The balance among hierarchies, networks, and markets in global governance during the 1920s and 1930s can be explained by three features of the global and national environments: a level of global economic openness that produced demand from business constituencies for governance arrangements; national governments that had a limited role in domestic regulation of business; and a scarcity of global intergovernmental instruments. A demand-based, functionalist explanation for this equilibrium is supported by the statements and activities of business representatives and their political allies. The restoration of the gold standard after the First World War was viewed by those elites as essential to the restoration of an open international economy and cross-border capital flows, which was essential for the reconstruction of European economies and the development of economies outside the industrialized core. Cartels could also be explained by demand for cooperation that could solve problems of coordinating international production and marketing through "the initiative, flexibility, and adaptability of trade associations rather than state direction."[48] Markets regulated by private governance were viewed as instruments for market stability and corporate security. ICA was also based on demand from international business: national courts, often unversed in the intricacies of trade in manufactures and services, could not meet the demand for "speed, expert knowledge, and smooth and inexpensive methods in the settlement of disputes."[49] Demands for international cooperation and peace, fulfilled neither by national nor intergovernmental action, led to increased support for these private and public-private alternatives. In the case of ICA, the peaceful resolution of commercial disputes was regarded as both a model for interstate

---

[47] Macassey 1938, 196.   [48] Koch 1945, 138.   [49] Nussbaum 1942, 219.

dispute resolution and a contribution to the reduction of a major cause of armed conflict.[50]

Demand-based explanations, driven by international markets and reticent national hierarchies, however, must confront the question of *whose* demand was satisfied. International business and finance, made more powerful by the partial revival of global business in the 1920s, enjoyed unmatched political influence until the Great Depression. The configuration of global governance in these economic domains reflects a particular constellation of power in domestic political economies, a configuration that was reflected in international organization. That political constellation in turn produced ideational and cognitive biases that reinforced this institutional mix of private governance and networks; the menu of plausible governance alternatives was limited by ideological presuppositions. Although challenged by brilliant gadflies such as John Maynard Keynes, the gold standard retained its hegemony in elite beliefs, viewed as an irreplaceable barrier to economic chaos. Self-regulation by cartels, sometimes with government support, was viewed as a superior means of managing international market shares and commodity markets. An international court of commercial arbitration had been quickly dismissed as an alternative to private governance through ICA. Although corporate power and self-governance persisted into the 1930s, a turn toward hierarchy as the dominant mode of global economic governance would follow the retreat from globalization and this expansion of the national regulatory state.

The Bretton Woods Moment in Monetary Affairs: Constraining Hierarchies and Regulating Markets

The Bretton Woods agreements that created the IMF and the World Bank were striking innovations in international monetary governance and a departure on all important institutional dimensions from the preceding pattern of monetary and financial governance. Bretton Woods created a legalized, multilateral arrangement among national hierarchies – contracting governments – that was not dependent on a transnational network of central banks and private finance for its operation. Alternative institutional arrangements – ad hoc bargaining among the largest economies or a return to the gold standard – remained appealing to some wartime constituencies. The choice of Bretton Woods and the eclipse of the gold standard's hybrid governance can be

---

[50] Szalai 2007, 370.

explained in part by the preferences of the American and British negotiators who dominated the negotiations that created the IMF and the World Bank. The two teams were in broad agreement on an intergovernmental institution that would permit the pursuit of national economic goals within rules that would prevent competitive depreciation of exchange rates. The constraints placed on governments were not those of international financial markets, which had disappeared during the economic depression and world war. The new system was constructed by governments, for governments, and it would be managed by national governments. Rather than a return to bargaining among the great economic powers, however, Bretton Woods endorsed multilateralism in the form of IGOs that aspired to universal membership.

The design of the Bretton Woods institutions, like the governance configuration of the interwar gold standard, reflected a changed domestic balance of power. The political cleavages revealed during the Bretton Woods ratification debates in the United States and Britain demonstrated that the political underpinnings for the gold standard had eroded as a result of depression and war. The disintegration of international capital markets and the imposition of capital controls, which were countenanced by Bretton Woods, reduced the trade-off between national policy autonomy and stable exchange rates. As a result, the Roosevelt administration was able to build a new political coalition in support of the modified internationalism represented by Bretton Woods.

Resistance centered on the weakened financial internationalists of Wall Street and their representatives at the New York Federal Reserve. Institutionally, the independence of central banks, so important to the governance of the gold standard, had been reduced across the industrialized world: public ownership, viewed with great skepticism in the 1920s, had now become the norm.[51] Opposition to the IMF from the financial internationalists did not center on fixed versus flexible exchange rates, however, but rather on the question of *whose* system of fixed exchange rates: one managed by a network of central bankers and private finance or one managed by the finance ministries of member governments. In contrast to internationally oriented banks, export industries supported a new system that promised gains from stable exchange rates and the gradual end to foreign exchange restrictions that closed markets and distorted trade. Most surprisingly, labor, a core constituency that had been critical of the adjustment costs imposed by the gold standard,

---

[51] In the early 1930s, only ten central banks were owned by their governments (including the Soviet Union). By 1951, forty-nine out of seventy-five central banks were entirely government-owned (Gregory 1955).

supported the Bretton Woods agreements. The institutional design of Bretton Woods solved the international policy dilemmas of left-wing, labor-based coalitions through its combination of capital controls, adjustable exchange rate parities, and financial support that was not dependent on the whims of bankers. Paradoxically, given its later reputation as a proponent of economic orthodoxy, the creation of the IMF represented a political moment when two labor-based coalitions, both dedicated to policies of full employment, had achieved a position of influence in the world's two leading financial powers.

Bretton Woods also reflected the emergence of a newly confident regulatory state. Rather than accepting the orthodoxy of unrestricted capital flows, capital controls were accepted as a pragmatic necessity. Governments were confident of their ability to negotiate and manage exchange rates using new instruments, such as the US Exchange Stabilization Fund. Intergovernmental agreements would extend the regulatory state to new domains, although in certain cases, such as the International Trade Organization (ITO), those initiatives would fail. The central bank network and the BIS, threatened with extinction at Bretton Woods, would persist, but their role was sharply reduced until a new era of capital mobility and a retrenchment of the regulatory state introduced a reversion to governance that awarded a larger role to networks and financial markets.

International Cartels and the Postwar Reach of the American Regulatory State

The influence of national hierarchies – particularly the United States government – on international cartels had been longstanding. US antitrust laws had shaped cartel behavior, even though the US Congress had legislated exemptions for American firms and their participation in cartels. During both world wars, the US government had also found cartels to be useful tools of wartime mobilization. Unease with international cartels had grown in the 1930s, however, when US cartel members in the chemical and petroleum industries were discovered to have agreements with German industrial giants such as I.G. Farben.[52] In part because of their involvement with the Nazi regime, international cartels came to be seen not as a form of regulated competition but rather as an expression of corporatist or totalitarian power.[53] As the demands of

---

[52] Wells 2002.   [53] Fear 2006, 15; Hillman 2010, 338.

wartime mobilization eased, international cartels were targeted, including previously exempted Webb–Pomerene associations.[54]

The renewed assault on international cartels by the United States government was given legal foundation in the 1945 *Alcoa* case.[55] As Kal Raustiala describes, the strict territoriality view of American legal jurisdiction, particularly in antitrust, had eroded over time.[56] *Alcoa* was a Bretton Woods moment for international cartels, one in which a clash of national regulatory hierarchies was resolved in favor of an effects-based interpretation of US jurisdiction. Effects-based thinking on the part of the judiciary was encouraged by a growing awareness of international interdependence and the expanding international range of American corporations. Of equal importance was the fact that the newly expanded regulatory scope of the state increased its sensitivity to actions by private actors in foreign regulatory environments.[57] The redefinition of extraterritoriality provided a useful instrument for the US government to expand its regulatory reach in domains where negotiated intergovernmental harmonization of regulations was absent or ineffective. This new and more aggressive American stance against international cartels may also have reflected the availability after 1945 of alternative public instruments for exercising American power – from foreign aid to IGOs. Cartels were no longer necessary for the pursuit of public and private economic diplomacy.

Despite the US turn toward extraterritorial pursuit of international cartels, these widespread modes of private governance did not disappear from international economic governance. Debate over the charter of the ITO, which included commodity agreements and private cartels as targets of regulation, revealed a divide between the United States and American business on the one hand, and the rest of the world on the other. US business criticized the ITO's endorsement of international commodity agreements and worried that strict US antitrust enforcement would place them at a disadvantage against private cartels elsewhere.[58]

In contrast to their support for the turn to intergovernmental solutions in monetary affairs, European governments were less enthusiastic about the new anti-cartel line of the United States. The European Coal and Steel Community, the precursor to the European Economic Community, was an intergovernmental descendant of interwar cartels. Although private cartels in sectors such as aluminum were not reestablished in the postwar

---

[54] Wells 2002, chapter 4.
[55] *United States* v. *Aluminum Co. of America*, 148 F.2d 416, 427 (2d Cir. 1945).
[56] Raustiala 2009, 101–103.   [57] Raustiala 2009, 117–119.
[58] Diebold 1952, 17–18.

period, many commodity agreements, supported by government protection, continued as less formal networks of producers under new labels, "the direct heirs of pre-war organizations."[59] The interwar tin cartel was transformed into the International Tin Council (ITC), founded in 1956, which brought together producer and consumer interests.[60] In the aluminum sector, private governance was supplemented by collaboration at an IGO, the Organisation for Economic Co-operation and Development (OECD).[61]

Informal, networked private governance in aluminum, tin, and other sectors was undermined by both national policies and markets in the 1960s and 1970s. US strategic stockpiling, which had both stabilized and destabilized efforts to manage the market in strategic minerals, ended.[62] New market entrants, such as the Soviet Union in aluminum and zinc and Japan in lead, as well as exchange rate fluctuations in the new monetary order, thwarted producer power to manage international prices.[63] The European Community (EC) reinforced the turn to the market with its more active competition policy.[64] Corporations in commodity sectors also had new, market-based instruments to deal with an uncertain environment in the form of contracts on the London Metals Exchange, an option encouraged by the EC.[65] Hierarchies (national governments and the EC) viewed "an institutional market with the key guarantees of transparency and publicity [as] the best way to fight concentration and collusive attitudes."[66] Elsewhere, cartels lingered with selective support from national governments. In Japan, cartels reached their peak during the boom years of the 1960s, and some cartels were exempted from competition policy into the 1990s.[67] In other sectors, such as shipping, American legislation continued to exempt international cartels from antitrust action.

In the developing world, government-organized cartels, often incorporating intergovernmental agreements and organizations, became part of the demand for a New International Economic Order in the 1970s. Rather than serving private corporate interests in managing markets over the long run, the new efforts at cartelization, backed by the United Nations Conference on Trade and Development (UNCTAD), aimed to transfer resources from consumers to Southern producers in the interests of development. In earlier commodity pacts, producer and

---

[59] Bertilorenzi 2016, 258.   [60] Hillman 2010, 356.   [61] Bertilorenzi 2016, 324–325.
[62] Bertilorenzi 2016, 305; Hillman 2010, 356, 363.
[63] Bertilorenzi 2016, 323; Tsokhas 2000, 268, 275; Hillman 2010, 364.
[64] Bertilorenzi 2016, 305, 323.   [65] Bertilorenzi 2016, 338–339.
[66] Bertilorenzi 2016, 339.   [67] Fear 2006.

consumer governments negotiated intergovernmental agreements, with private participation, to manage fluctuations in supply and price. Despite its ideological opposition to international cartels, the United States during the Cold War engaged in stockpiling strategic materials, which often supported private efforts to regulate market competition.[68] The International Coffee Organization (ICO), perhaps the most successful major commodity agreement, was supported by the US government because of a different Cold War logic: aligning the United States with major producing governments in the developing world. Also important to the agreement were the large corporations in the United States that dominated coffee roasting (and purchase of coffee imports) and viewed the ICO as a means of reducing competition. As Robert Bates argues, although the ICO was formally an intergovernmental agreement, it was more properly viewed as an example of complex or hybrid governance, "a coalition among bureaucrats, politicians, and firms that used the power of states to restructure markets."[69] In similar fashion and for similar reasons, the US government joined the ITC, which was supported by another international agreement that included both producers and consumers. These agreements dissolved with the end of the Cold War, the deepening of anti-cartel, pro-market ideology, and new entrants outside the agreement.[70]

Those commodity cartels based solely on producer governments, in sectors such as oil, bauxite, and copper, were less successful. As their private counterparts discovered, international markets were increasingly difficult to control as the second era of globalization accelerated. A more surprising cause for the failure of commodity cartels was the inability of producer governments to create, through intergovernmental agreement, a hierarchy that could sustain market-regulating rules. The Intergovernmental Council of Copper Exporting Countries was not governed by robust institutions or binding rules; it was unable to overcome divergent positions on copper prices among its members.[71] The most famous and long-lived of these organizations, the Organization of the Petroleum Exporting Countries (OPEC) was not, despite its reputation, a cartel.[72] Control of world oil prices resided at times with Saudi Arabia and its Gulf allies, but Saudi price leadership was not exercised as a result of collective agreement by OPEC's members. OPEC was not able to reconstruct the "supra-sovereign constraints" or "private treaties" devised by the corporate oil cartel; the "oligopoly of nation-states has not

[68] Bertilorenzi 2016, 269.   [69] Bates et al. 1998, 216.
[70] Bates et al. 1998, 227; Hillman 2010, 363.   [71] Mingst 1976, 273–275.
[72] Alhajji and Huettner 2000; Colgan 2014.

been able to duplicate those state-like efforts."[73] Market pressures introduced by oil producers that were not part of OPEC were similar to those
faced periodically by earlier corporate cartels. A more significant obstacle
to a cartel of government producers rather than multinational corporations were the political incentives against taking a long-term view of the
industry's interests. Many OPEC member states were dependent on oil
revenues for economic performance and, ultimately, political survival. As
a result, their domestic interests often diverged, and they failed to regulate supply if such steps would produce short-term political costs. For
some observers, OPEC was best defined not as a cartel, but as a "political
club," generating domestic credit and diplomatic influence for its
members.[74]

International Commercial Arbitration: Evolution beyond the Reach of the Regulatory State

If the international rise of formal intergovernmental institutions and the
domestic expansion of the regulatory state subordinated or eliminated
certain forms of private governance, ICA appeared to be an exception. As
the global economy gradually liberalized in the 1950s and 1960s, the
newly expanded regulatory state created more demand for ICA from
those who had to negotiate this complicated environment. During the
Bretton Woods moment, ICA had evolved in two directions that would
make it more attractive as a site for commercial dispute settlement. In
contrast to the ICC model of the interwar decades, which was often
implemented by businessmen rather than lawyers, ICA after 1945 was
increasingly legalized and professionalized.[75] As a result, ICA was better
able to meet international business demand for the arbitration services
required in a more complex regulatory environment.

The shadow of hierarchy was also important: national governments
provided important support for ICA through formal and informal intergovernmental initiatives. The 1958 New York Convention,[76] negotiated
and ratified after intensive lobbying by the American Arbitration
Association and the ICC, replaced the two Geneva conventions negotiated in the 1920s. The New York Convention insured that private
arbitration decisions would be enforced in the domestic courts of its
signatories. Soft law intergovernmental institutions – UNCITRAL and

---

[73] Moran 1987, 606.   [74] Colgan 2014, 616.   [75] Grisel 2017, 808.
[76] The New York Convention on the Recognition and Enforcement of Foreign
Arbitral Awards.

UNIDROIT[77] – provided technical support for ICA by offering voluntary guidelines for tribunals and model arbitration laws for states.[78] ICA had finally discovered its necessary and symbiotic relationship with national legal systems and judiciaries as its own professional cadre developed a body of transnational rules for arbitration, rules that were not dependent on the national law of any one country or group of countries. The process of professionalization worked in tandem with the New York Convention to spread ICA beyond its Atlantic core. As Hale demonstrates, ratification of the New York Convention was promoted not by national governments or domestic lobbies, but by "transnational communities of legal practice," those professionals who identified with the ICA legal order and its institutions.[79] The shadow of hierarchy in ICA – national enforcement and intergovernmental agreements – was one element in a landscape of complex governance that included both networks and hierarchies. The demand for governance was, in turn, driven by the expansion of cross-border international exchange during the Bretton Woods moment.

Networks and Markets in a New Era of Globalization

As first the Atlantic and then the global economy liberalized after the 1960s, a second era of globalization set the conditions for a reemergence of networks and markets as central constituents of global economic governance. The need to protect domestic financial systems from the consequences of cross-border lending as well as the management of international financial crises awarded renewed importance to the network of central banks with their close links to the private financial sector. Rapid growth in international trade led to an explosion in demand for ICA. The opening of international markets destabilized international cartels, however, and a hardening of pro-market ideology completed their transformation from instruments of international cooperation to symbols of abusive private collusion. A convergence among the major industrialized countries on competition policy and a deepening commitment to market-based policy solutions led to a final assault on a form of private economic governance that had once been pervasive and accepted.

---

[77] The United Nations Commission on International Trade Law and International Institute for the Unification of Private Law.
[78] Hale 2015b, 487–488.   [79] Hale 2015b, 484.

Central Banks, Private Finance, and Global Financial Governance

As cross-border financial flows grew, and new offshore markets attracted banks from the major financial centers, the regulatory role of central banks – enhanced during the Great Depression and after – led to the creation of a formal regulatory network, the Basel Committee on Banking Supervision (BCBS), headquartered at the BIS. Through its initial Concordat and subsequent revisions, the BCBS aimed to prevent financial institutions from escaping supervision in their international lending operations. Central bank coordination in banking regulation and supervision is not highly legalized, however. Apart from an agreement on capital adequacy standards (Basel I), early understandings reached in the BCBS were designed to extend national banking supervision in an agreed fashion to offshore and international financial markets. After a move toward more self-regulation by the largest international banks in Basel II, the global financial crisis of 2008–2009 produced a return to more regulatory supervision by central banks and other national regulatory authorities (Basel III).

Increased capital mobility also increased the likelihood of financial crises. The major central banks, individually and collectively, played a role in the management of those episodes of financial instability. In the largest financial crises to affect the developing world – the Latin American debt crisis of the 1980s and the Asian financial crisis of 1997–1998 – central banks were able to provide a limited amount of finance more rapidly than the IMF. Given their mandates, however, such lending was directed to preserving the stability of their domestic financial systems and the soundness of their national financial institutions. Although they might take a systemic view of the spillover effects from financial crises in the emerging economies, the major central banks bore no obligations, informal or formal, to assist the recovery of debtor economies. Far more important has been cooperation among the central bank network in managing crises in global financial markets: October 1987 (stock market crash), September–October 1998 (Long Term Capital Management's collapse), and, most importantly, the global financial crisis of 2008–2009. In these cases, central banks coordinated the provision of liquidity to the financial system at a time when confidence appeared to be collapsing.

In these domains of financial regulation and crisis management, a network of central banks and private financial actors did not supplant IGOs, particularly the IMF. In recent financial crisis management – such as the successive Greek programs during the eurozone crisis – the troika that oversaw Greece's adjustment program included the IMF, the European Central Bank, and the European Commission. The G20, an IIGO, played a central role in encouraging policy coordination during the global financial crisis. Global coordination of financial regulation is now centered on the Financial Stability Board, a TGN that includes representatives from the governments of major national economies, international financial institutions, and international standard-setting bodies.

In the new era of financial globalization, the central bank–private finance network of the 1920s has been revived and embedded in a larger system of governance that includes governments, IGOs, and representatives of private finance, such as the Institute for International Finance. As in the earlier period, independent central banks worked under economic requirements, often incorporated in their statutes, that were imposed by their domestic principals. These goals, whether inflation targets or full employment, created tension with the system-stabilizing role of central banks. In contrast to the pre-Bretton Woods years, however, the principals of central banks are never in question. No matter how independent their institutional status, central banks ultimately respond to politicians and their publics.[80] Close ties to the private financial sector remain, particularly in the case of those central banks with regulatory oversight. Private finance, however, does not act as a co-equal in governance of the international monetary and financial system, as it often did before the Great Depression. Networks have supplemented hierarchies in an era of expanded financial markets, but they have not displaced them.

International Cartels: Beleaguered but Persistent Private Governance

Few forms of governance have experienced changes in public perception and official acceptance as radical as those of international cartels. This once pervasive form of private governance has, in the words of Jeffrey Fear, witnessed "rise, boom, collapse, revitalization, gradual decline, and then criminalization."[81] American power and US willingness to extend its antitrust legislation extraterritorially signaled a more hostile international environment for international cartels after 1945. Corporate cartels continued to be created, but their members had significant incentives to conceal their existence. Only when US agencies used a new enforcement tactic and played on incentives to defect from cartels did

---

[80] On the political limits on Federal Reserve independence, Binder and Spindel 2017.
[81] Fear 2006, 18.

enforcement accelerate and gain what appeared to be a sharp uptick in success.[82] Data from these prosecutions demonstrate that international cartels continue to exist and that, counter to the beliefs of many economists, they are not "fundamentally unstable." As was the case with interwar cartels, successful cartels have displayed institutionalization: "new rules, including governance and compensation systems that raise the quality and credibility of information and better align individual firms' incentives with those of the group."[83]

The end of the Cold War and the rise of market ideology in the industrialized world led to a withdrawal of support from intergovernmental commodity agreements by consumer governments. The Reagan administration left the ITC. The International Coffee Agreement, which ceased setting export quotas in 1989, has witnessed repeated departures and reentries on the part of the United States government. Anti-cartel ideas and networks have also spread from North to South. Competition policy diffused to the developing world, targeting a resilient population of private international cartels. By 2017, nearly 140 jurisdictions had competition laws and institutions. Cooperation grew among national competition authorities, through support from the OECD and UNCTAD as well as the International Competition Network.[84] Preferential trade agreements, which proliferated in the era of globalization that began in the 1990s, also served as a means of strengthening commitments to competition policy, particularly at the regional level.[85]

The private governance of cartels has become identified in prevailing pro-market ideology with negative effects on a wider group of stakeholders. The recent history of De Beers, a central player in the long-running diamond cartel, demonstrates both the obstacles to maintaining a contemporary cartel and the ways in which new actors can change the normative complexion of a cartel. As the 1970s had for the aluminum cartel, the 1990s introduced a number of challenges to the diamond cartel: political change in South Africa; the collapse of the Soviet Union, a major diamond supplier that had supported the cartel; new entrants such as Angola; and, an antitrust case, brought by the US Justice Department, alleging price fixing in the market for industrial diamonds.

---

[82] Storli 2014; Levenstein and Suslow 2011. The new tactic was a 1993 leniency program that offered exemption from fines in exchange for cooperation by firms that were cartel members. The EU and other major economies soon followed the more aggressive US stance toward the prosecution of international cartels. The case that marked a turning point in enforcement strategy was the lysine cartel, which had Archer Daniels Midland at its center.

[83] Levenstein and Suslow 2011, 456.   [84] Horna 2017; Aydin and Büthe 2016.

[85] Horna 2017, 87.

Allegations that De Beers and others were trafficking in "conflict dia-monds" and sustaining violent civil wars in Africa appeared to deliver a final blow.

The launch of the Kimberley Process in 2002, however, demonstrated that a canny cartel could use control of supply to its advantage, while at the same time burnishing its image. This "extraordinary enterprise" created a "complex certification system for all diamonds and a commit-ment by all participants to adhere to the rules embedded in the system." Since it provided an internationally recognized reason for maintaining oversight (and restriction) of the supply of diamonds, placed De Beers in a central role, and rewarded those who could certify their supply chain (i.e., De Beers), the Kimberley Process was a positive development for the diamond cartel.[86] This alliance of "Baptists and bootleggers" also suggested a new role for international cartels if their self-interested cooperation could also be portrayed as supporting other, valued international ends.

International Commercial Arbitration in a New Era of Globalization

The new era of globalization produced increased demand for the private, networked governance of ICA. The rapid expansion of international commerce since the late 1950s has been the principal catalyst for a parallel explosion in the number of ICA centers and caseloads: a recent estimate has found 207 established international arbitration centers in 102 countries; with few exceptions, all are private entities.[87] For some observers, this archipelago of arbitration signifies a "networked set of institutions and organizations" that constitutes a "transnational system of governance for transnational business."[88] For internationally active cor-porations, this system of governance has usurped the dominance of national courts and legal regimes. Those who espouse this transnational view of the ICA regime accept a central, constitutional role for the 1958 New York Convention and its requirement for acquiescence and collaboration on the part of national judiciaries. They argue, however, that the content of the New York Convention largely matched the preferences of the ICC, not national governments, and that the convention was the "first treaty of global scope to make decisions issuing from private, transnational legal process directly effective within national legal orders."[89]

---

[86] Spar 2006, 205; 1994, 39–87.
[87] Mattli and Dietz, 2014, 2–3, figures 1.1 and 1.2; Stone Sweet and Grisel 2017, 45–58.
[88] Stone Sweet and Grisel 2017, 35.   [89] Stone Sweet and Grisel 2017, 61.

Those who emphasize the continued anchoring of ICA in national legal hierarchies point to the failure to develop transnational contract law. Most transnational contracts incorporate a choice of national law, one which typically reflects the preferences of the most powerful participants.[90] The ICA universe is also far from universal: islands of resistance remain, particularly among the emerging economies.[91]

The spread and acceptance of ICA, its institutions, and its legal framework, which does not distinguish sharply between hard and soft law, is owed in part to a growing professional community of those specializing in arbitral law. These arbitrators set the stage for the rapid growth of ICA during the decades of globalization through their judicialization of arbitration and their role as brokers between different systems of national law.[92] The expansion and acceptance of the system, with its necessary compromises of national legal sovereignty, was also owed to its highly competitive structure: hosting an arbitration center attracts valuable business. The system also reflects the power of a constituency, major multinational corporations and their home governments in North America, Europe, and Japan. Whatever its residual dependence on national legal hierarchies and their judiciaries for enforcement, ICA represents a variant of networked economic governance – a network of ICA centers supported by a network of transnational legal expertise – that has flourished because of the acceptance of major economic powers and the demand from international business for its services during an era of globalization.

Global Economic Governance in the Long Twentieth Century

Although most accounts of global governance begin with the appearance of intergovernmental economic organizations in the late nineteenth century, governance of cross-border exchange, in which private actors operating under informal rules play a central role, has an even longer history. The mix of national hierarchies and their IGO creations, networks of public and private actors, and markets has varied with the growth of international trade and capital flows during two eras of globalization and the recession of cross-border economic exchange during the middle

---

[90] Mattli and Dietz 2014, 13.
[91] Among them: China, Argentina, Indonesia, South Africa, and the Persian Gulf states (Mattli and Dietz 2014, 65).
[92] Grisel 2017, 793–794.

decades of the last century. In recent decades, that exchange itself has become more complex. The growing significance of intellectual property, services, and global value chains has contributed to heightened demand for governance that could not be supplied easily or efficiently by national governments in the form of international agreements, rules, or institutions.

A second driver of change also influenced the balance among governance formats over the course of the century. The democratization of economic governance within the industrialized states led to the inclusion of newly organized interests and stakeholders beyond those private interests engaged in cross-border exchange. The demands from these new actors produced an expansion of the scope of domestic governance in the form of the regulatory state. These changes brought the downfall of the gold standard, which had also displayed structural weaknesses, and produced the Bretton Woods moment, in which national hierarchies asserted themselves through intergovernmental regulation of domestic and international markets. The same changes began a shift in public policy toward private international cartels. Their effect on the evolving ICA regime was less profound, although the assertion of national regulatory authority probably speeded efforts to ground ICA in an international convention. Following the Bretton Woods moment, new intergovernmental agreements and organizations produced a substitution effect, supplanting earlier governance by private or hybrid networks in a world in which trade and investment had reached a low ebb.

Networked and private governance survived the Bretton Woods moment and enjoyed a revival as economic globalization accelerated in the 1980s and 1990s. In contrast to the interwar decades, however, renewed demand had to be accommodated within parameters set by national legislation and regulation. What has emerged is not a displacement of hierarchy and intergovernmentalism by markets and networked private governance, but a more complex combination of hierarchy, market, and networks. Building on longstanding links to the financial sector, the network of central banks acquired a new role coordinating banking regulation and supervision across national borders. As other regulators became engaged in regulatory coordination, central banks were embedded in a larger network centered on the Financial Stability Board, a new institution that was proclaimed, the fourth pillar of global economic governance. In the face of financial and banking crises, which grew more frequent with the increase in cross-border capital flows, central banks also retained an essential role as lenders of last resort.

Based on recent evidence, international cartels also became more widespread during the second era of globalization. Apart from those that could evade the extraterritorial reach of American antitrust law, however, cartels had to operate in the shadow of illegality, a stark contrast to their acceptance before the Bretton Woods moment. Rather than choosing to regulate cartels, as some had proposed at the end of the Second World War, the United States and other major economies chose to destroy them, assisted by the pressure of expanding international markets. For most cartels, a strategy of accommodation with the new regulatory reality was not possible. Finally, ICA managed a successful disengagement from national oversight by providing services that were highly valued by international business. By creating a species of private governance that did not collide with or adopt the legal order of any of the major economies, ICA could proclaim a transnational identity.

Although they represent networked and private governance rather than the institutionalized and legalized governance of IGOs, each of these modes of governance relied upon and was strengthened by hierarchy: the support of governments, intergovernmental agreements, and IGOs. The cooperation of central banks alone was unable to halt the Great Depression, and, despite their critical role during the recent global financial crisis, leading central bankers were insistent in asking for governments to provide fiscal expansion to support their provision of liquidity to the financial system. The transgovernmental network of central banks and other national financial regulators ultimately rested on authority delegated by national governments. Successful international cartels had relied on explicit government support or regulatory forbearance during the 1920s and 1930s; the withdrawal of that support after 1945 and its replacement with legal sanctions and policies to promote competition transformed the incentives for participation in this form of governance. The fate of intergovernmental commodity agreements underscored the requirement of support from both producer and consumer governments. Finally, during the interwar decades, ICA lacked a guarantee that the judiciaries of major economies would enforce arbitral decisions, a shortcoming that reduced its appeal and its expansion. The New York Convention added that important and essential ingredient, enabling the expansion of ICA during a new era of transnational business activity. Even when governments and IGOs were not evident in governance, hierarchy cast a long shadow.

International markets, both promoted and regulated by global economic governance, have also served as instruments of governance, deployed by governments, individually and collectively, for their individual and collective ends. Like the regulatory state, the expansion of international markets could be both an ally and a foe of other forms of governance. The conditionality of the IMF was strengthened when private financial markets supported its policy recommendations to governments (and often they did not); cross-border financial flows disrupted fixed exchange rate systems under both the gold standard and Bretton Woods. International markets disrupted carefully crafted cartels, which aimed at market regulation in the interests of their members, and later supported efforts by competition authorities to discipline private collusion. Divergent national efforts to regulate markets provided a major stimulus for the growth of ICA.

Two drivers were central in the variation of global economic governance over the long twentieth century: globalization – the ebb and flow of cross-border exchange – and the rise and evolution of the regulatory state. The United States and its public and private sectors reflected and deepened these drivers. The respective, divergent fates of these forms of complex governance depended on the mobilization of interests that lay outside their core constituencies – international finance and business – and the power wielded by those interests. Before and after the Bretton Woods moment. global economic governance often embodied the power of private business and its favored representatives. In the case of central banks, their nationalization and subordination to national economic authorities rendered their role less contentious and more secure. Nevertheless, their regulatory role and their position as guarantors of financial system stability meant that they had to maintain close ties to the financial sector and, at the same time, avoid any appearance of collusion with private finance. International cartels finally lost the contest for acceptance to a belief that their self-interested cooperation, manifest in price fixing and market sharing, operated against the public interest, whatever the other benefits provided by their cooperative arrangements. ICA remained largely outside public controversy, since its services were limited to major corporations and their private dispute settlement was not read as imposing costs on those outside the arbitration chamber. When arbitration was advanced in other domains, however, the asymmetry between large corporations and their opponents quickly sparked political conflict, whether in the widespread inclusion of arbitration clauses in consumer purchase contracts or the introduction of investor–state dispute settlement into trade agreements. In those cases, arbitration seemed weighted toward powerful economic interests and opposed to those of the wider public.

Although private power has often seemed unlimited in global governance, it is far more circumscribed today than it was in the early decades of the last century. What has disappeared with that private hegemony is the normative aura that once surrounded private or semi-private governance and, to a lesser degree, the authority of markets. Central bankers, the lords of finance, were the guardians of the gold standard, which symbolized for many a stable and unshakable international economic order. International cartels were viewed as possible building blocks for wider international cooperation. Commercial arbitration was part of a much larger movement that saw the peaceful resolution of disputes as transferable from the private domain to interstate conflict.

That normative environment is long past: governance is now viewed instrumentally, by both its proponents and its critics. The legitimacy of all forms of global governance are increasingly challenged by stakeholders whose interests have been ignored and publics that demand more accountability. Those normative challenges are likely to increase variation and experimentation in governance. The reaction to the global financial crisis of 2008–2009, the uncertain response to the 2020 global pandemic, and the rise of economies such as China, which endorse hierarchies over markets, may suggest another move away from networks and markets toward more reliance on intergovernmental or purely national hierarchies in governance design. Rather than regarding the dominance of hierarchies as the norm and other formats as novelties or sideshows, however, this account suggests that the search for alternative forms of governance is persistent, and that for some actors those alternatives are the main event.

References

Abbott, Kenneth W., Jessica F. Green, and Robert O. Keohane. 2016. Organizational Ecology and Institutional Change in Global Governance. *International Organization* 70 (2): 247–277.

Alhajji, A. F. and David Huettner. 2000. OPEC and Other Commodity Cartels: A Comparison. *Energy Policy* 28 (15): 1151–1164.

Auboin, Roger. 1955. *The Bank for International Settlements, 1930–1955*. Essays in International Finance 22. Princeton: Princeton University, International Finance Section.

Aydin, Umut and Tim Büthe. 2016. Competition Law and Policy in Developing Countries: Explaining Variations in Outcomes; Exploring Possibilities and Limits. *Law and Contemporary Problems* 79: 1–36.

Baker, Jonathan B. 1989. Identifying Cartel Policing under Uncertainty: The U.S. Steel Industry, 1933–1939. *The Journal of Law and Economics* 32 (2, part 2): S47–76.

Bates, Robert H., Avner Greif, Margaret Levi, Jean-Laurent Rosenthal, and Barry R. Weingast. 1998. *Analytic Narratives*. Princeton: Princeton University Press.

Bertilorenzi, Marco. 2016. *The International Aluminium Cartel, 1886–1978: The Business and Politics of a Cooperative Industrial Institution*. New York: Routledge.

Binder, Sarah A. and Mark Spindel. 2017. *The Myth of Independence: How Congress Governs the Federal Reserve*. Princeton: Princeton University Press.

Broz, J. Lawrence. 1997. *The International Origins of the Federal Reserve System*. Ithaca, NY: Cornell University Press.

Clarke, Stephen V. O. 1967. *Central Bank Cooperation: 1924–31*. New York: Federal Reserve Bank of New York.

Colgan, Jeff D. 2014. The Emperor Has No Clothes: The Limits of OPEC in the Global Oil Market. *International Organization* 68 (3): 599–632.

Diebold, Jr., William. 1952. *The End of the I.T.O*. Essays in International Finance 16. Princeton: Princeton University, International Finance Section.

Drake, Paul W. 1989. *The Money Doctor in the Andes: The Kemmerer Missions, 1923–1933*. Durham, NC: Duke University Press.

Eichengreen, Barry. 1990. *Elusive Stability: Essays in the History of International Finance, 1919–1939*. Cambridge and New York: Cambridge University Press.

   1992. *Golden Fetters: The Gold Standard and the Great Depression, 1919–1939*. New York: Oxford University Press.

Farrell, Henry and Abraham L. Newman. 2014. Domestic Institutions beyond the Nation-State: Charting the New Interdependence Approach. *World Politics* 66 (2): 331–363.

Fear, Jeffrey. 2006. Cartels and Competition: Neither Markets Nor Hierarchies. Harvard Business School (Working Paper 07-011).

Fitzgerald, Robert. 2015. *The Rise of the Global Company: Multinationals and the Making of the Modern World*. Cambridge: Cambridge University Press.

Gallarotti, Giulio M. 1995. *The Anatomy of an International Monetary Regime: The Classical Gold Standard, 1880–1914*. New York: Oxford University Press.

Green, Jessica F. 2013. *Rethinking Private Authority: Agents and Entrepreneurs in Global Environmental Governance*. Princeton: Princeton University Press.

Gregory, Sir Theodore. 1955. *The Present Position of Central Banks*. London: Athlone Press.

Grisel, Florian. 2017. Competition and Cooperation in International Commercial Arbitration: The Birth of a Transnational Legal Profession. *Law and Society Review* 51 (4): 790–824.

Hale, Thomas. 2015a. *Between Interests and Law: The Politics of Transnational Commercial Disputes*. Cambridge and New York: Cambridge University Press.

   2015b. The Rule of Law in the Global Economy: Explaining Intergovernmental Backing for Private Commercial Tribunals. *European Journal of International Relations* 21 (3): 483–512.

Hillman, John. 2010. *The International Tin Cartel*. London: Routledge.

Horna, Pierre M. 2017. Cartels in Latin America: A Cross-Border Competition Assessment. PhD dissertation. Geneva, Switzerland: Graduate Institute of International and Development Studies.

Jacobsson, Erin E. 1979. *A Life for Sound Money: Per Jacobsson, His Biography*. Oxford: Clarendon Press.

Koch, F.E. 1945. Cartels as Instruments of International Economic Organization: Public and Private Legal Aspects of International Cartels. *The Modern Law Review* 8 (3): 130–148.

Levenstein, Margaret C. and Valerie Y. Suslow. 2011. Breaking Up Is Hard to Do: Determinants of Cartel Duration. *The Journal of Law and Economics* 54 (2): 455–492.

Macassey, Lynden. 1938. International Commercial Arbitration: Its Origin, Development and Importance. *Transactions of the Grotius Society* 24 (Problems of Peace and War): 179–202.

Mattli, Walter and Thomas Dietz. 2014. Mapping and Assessing the Rise of International Commercial Arbitration in the Globalization Era: An Introduction. In *International Arbitration and Global Governance: Contending Theories and Evidence*, edited by Walter Mattli and Thomas Dietz, 1–24. New York: Oxford University Press.

Mingst, Karen A. 1976. Cooperation or Illusion: An Examination of the Intergovernmental Council of Copper Exporting Countries. *International Organization* 30 (2): 263–287.

Moran, Theodore H. 1987. Managing an Oligopoly of Would-Be Sovereigns: The Dynamics of Joint Control and Self-Control in the International Oil Industry Past, Present, and Future. *International Organization* 41 (4): 576–607.

Nussbaum, Arthur. 1942. Treaties on Commercial Arbitration: A Test of International Private-Law Legislation. *Harvard Law Review* 56 (2): 219–244.

Pak, Susie. 2013. *Gentlemen Bankers: The World of J.P. Morgan*. Harvard Studies in Business History 51. Cambridge, MA: Harvard University Press.

Pauly, Louis. 1997. *Who Elected the Bankers? Surveillance and Control in the World Economy*. Ithaca, NY: Cornell University Press.

Pauwelyn, Joost, Ramses A. Wessel, and Jan Wouters, eds. 2012. *Informal International Lawmaking*. New York: Oxford University Press.

Raustiala, Kal. 2009. *Does the Constitution Follow the Flag? The Evolution of Territoriality in American Law*. New York: Oxford University Press.

Sgard, Jérôme. 2016. A Tale of Three Cities: The Construction of International Commercial Arbitration. In *Contractual Knowledge: One Hundred Years of Legal Experimentation in Global Markets*, 153–184. Cambridge: Cambridge University Press.

Simmons, Beth A. 1993. Why Innovate? Founding the Bank for International Settlements. *World Politics* 45 (3): 361–405.

1994. *Who Adjusts? Domestic Sources of Foreign Economic Policy during the Interwar Years*. Princeton: Princeton University Press.

1996. Rulers of the Game: Central Bank Independence during the Interwar Years. *International Organization* 50 (3): 407–443.

Spar, Debora L. 1994. *The Cooperative Edge: The Internal Politics of International Cartels*. Ithaca, NY and London: Cornell University Press.

2006. Continuity and Change in the International Diamond Market. *Journal of Economic Perspectives* 20 (3): 195–208.

Stone Sweet, Alec and Florian Grisel. 2017. *The Evolution of International Arbitration: Judicialization, Governance, Legitimacy*. New York: Oxford University Press.

Storli, Espen. 2014. Cartel Theory and Cartel Practice: The Case of the International Aluminum Cartels, 1901–1940. *Business History Review* 88 (3): 445–467.

Szalai, Imre S. 2007. Modern Arbitration Values and the First World War. *American Journal of Legal History* 49 (4): 359–391.

Taylor, Jason E. 2007. Cartel Code Attributes and Cartel Performance: An Industry-Level Analysis of the National Industrial Recovery Act. *The Journal of Law and Economics* 50 (3): 597–624.

Temin, Peter. 1989. *Lessons from the Great Depression: The Lionel Robbins Lectures for 1989*. Cambridge, MA: MIT Press.

Toniolo, Gianni and Piet Clement. 2005. *Central Bank Cooperation at the Bank for International Settlements, 1930–1973*. New York: Cambridge University Press.

Tsokhas, Kosmas. 2000. The Rise and Decline of an International Zinc and Lead Cartel, 1945–1975. *Australian Economic History Review* 40 (3): 263–286.

Wells, Wyatt. 2002. *Antitrust and the Formation of the Postwar World*. New York: Columbia University Press.

3   Climate Change Governance
Past, Present, and (Hopefully) Future

Jessica F. Green

Introduction

The news on climate change was not good to begin with, and is getting worse. This chapter examines our collective efforts to address this increasingly grave and urgent problem. I trace the evolution of the climate regime and the shift from "old" to "new" governance. Despite its relative newness compared to other global issues, there has been a transformation in climate governance over the last two decades. Most characterize this as a transition from a traditional hierarchical model of governance, embodied by the Kyoto Protocol to a more bottom-up approach codified in the Paris Agreement. I argue that this is an overly simplified distinction. In fact, Kyoto contained both markets and networks, which were significant parts of its design. Similarly, Paris preserves an important – and indeed expanded – role for states.

Nonetheless, there is a shift in how the climate regime operates now versus "then." I detail these differences and suggest two primary drivers for the change. First, profound geopolitical changes – namely the rise of the BRICs (Brazil, Russia, India, and China) – quickly made the Kyoto Protocol politically untenable. Second, the rise of global rationalization meant that states conceived of climate change primarily as a technical problem. All the while market ideologies of governance were lurking in the background, reinforcing the notion that markets, rather than governments, could provide the necessary innovation and action to address climate change. This view papered over profound political conflicts which ultimately led to Kyoto's failure.

I suggest that the new governance, embodied by the Paris Agreement, goes further to address these problems. And while the *processes* institutionalized by Paris provide some reasons for optimism, the *outcomes* fall far short of what is needed. At present the Paris Agreement falls well short of its own stated goal of limiting warming to 1.5 degrees Celsius. "New governance" has clearly been good for building new institutions, and is a more flexible and politically realistic approach to climate change.

The bet is that this arrangement is better suited to both the realities of domestic politics and profound uncertainty surrounding climate change than the old governance model. If we are correct then we have created the enabling conditions for decarbonization. The question is: will it happen fast enough?

It is not an overstatement to say that the answer to this question is critical both for the future of the planet and the legitimacy of global governance. Climate change will likely exacerbate existing problems in world politics such as armed conflict and mass migration.[1] And the iron law of climate change is that those least responsible will be most affected, creating an ever greater need for global action. A shift to a "new" global governance architecture means little if climate change continues apace. To preserve the legitimacy of the climate regime, as well as much of the fabric of the current liberal international order (such as it is), actors will have to move more swiftly and decisively toward a fossil fuel-free world.

What Is Happening? From Kyoto to Paris

The changes in climate governance can be understood as a *proliferation* of authority rather than a shift in its locus. The Paris Agreement is best viewed as a "choose your own adventure" approach to climate govern-ance: like the children's books of old, many types of actors get to select what types of measures they will take to address climate change. This includes non-state actors, firms, and subnational actors such as cities and regions. States too, both developed and developing, get to decide what types of climate policies are optimal.

The "choose your own adventure" approach has not lessened state authority in any way; if anything it has expanded the possibility for states to exercise authority, since there are now many more opportunities to engage with and coordinate non-state and subnational rule-makers. Thus, as I have argued elsewhere, authority in the climate regime is best conceived of as positive sum rather than zero sum.[2]

To understand the proliferation of authority it is useful to juxtapose the design of the Kyoto Protocol with the Paris Agreement. The trans-formation of the climate regime illustrates that hierarchies, networks, and markets are present at both phases, though the emphasis has changed somewhat. Kyoto is typically depicted as a top-down hierarchical model, while the Paris Agreement is billed as bottom up.[3]

---

[1] Busby 2018; Mach et al. 2019.   [2] Green 2014.   [3] Green et al. 2014.

While this is true in the main, a closer examination demonstrates that both phases of the climate regime have aspects of all three modes of governance: networks, markets, and hierarchies. The transformation of the climate regime is not a change from one mode of governance to another, but is best understood at the reconfiguration of the embedded relationships among these three modes.

The Kyoto Protocol: Both Market and Hierarchy

The Kyoto Protocol is now ancient history, but is critical to understanding the current state of climate politics. Even at its moment of conception in 1997, Kyoto was a tenuous political agreement. It divided the world into two – developed and developing nations. Developed nations were required to reduce their collective emissions to 5 percent below 1990 levels by the end of 2020.[4] States recognized even then that this was a minuscule reduction in light of the science of climate change. Moreover, the 5 percent target was an average across all developed nations. Thus, leaders like Germany agreed to reduce their emissions significantly (by 21 percent) while middle-income nations were allowed to increase their emissions. This was hardly a path to decarbonization.

Importantly, in accordance with states' "common but differentiated responsibilities," Kyoto did not require developing countries to reduce their emissions. The UN Framework Convention on Climate Change (UNFCCC), which provides the legal basis for the Kyoto Protocol, notes that "that the share of global emissions originating in developing countries will grow to meet their social and development needs."[5] Common but differentiated responsibilities was, until Paris, a defining feature of the climate regime. And it proved to be the undoing of Kyoto. As a result the USA – the world's largest emitter at the time – refused to ratify. In a strong and sweeping statement to the rest of the world the US Senate adopted the Byrd–Hagel Resolution in 1997 stating that the USA should not become a signatory to the Kyoto Protocol, with a vote of 95–0.

While Kyoto can primarily be understood as hierarchical in its rule-making and implementation,[6] network and market approaches were also present. One of the main innovations of the Kyoto Protocol was the creation of an international market on carbon offsets, called the Clean

---

[4] UNFCCC 1997.   [5] UNFCCC 1992, preamble.

[6] The protocol itself is silent on the matter of enforcement. Subsequent negotiations established an enforcement branch to facilitate compliance but it had little in the way of punitive powers.

Development Mechanism (CDM).[7] The CDM allowed developed countries to offset their emissions by paying for emissions reducing projects in the developing world. Indeed, by many accounts the market mechanisms were the linchpin to securing consensus.[8] Developed countries now had a much-needed escape hatch: if domestic reductions became too politically onerous or costly then states could instead pay for mitigation activities in the developing world. Developing countries, for their part, saw the CDM as an important revenue stream in promoting sustainable development.

The creation of the CDM gave rise to a booming offset market and the proliferation of many different types of actors to support it. CDM projects required project designers, investors, monitors, verifiers, and of course implementers. A number of business and environmental NGOs created their own rules to create and commodify carbon offsets, creating a voluntary market in parallel to the CDM.[9] These were (and still are) sold to interested buyers – often firms – who seek to reduce their carbon footprint voluntarily. However, the weaknesses of offsets quickly became evident.

The climate regime has also had networked governance structures since its inception. The Global Environment Facility has served as the financial mechanism for the convention since its entry into force in 1994. It administers a variety of special funds created by states which address adaptation and the needs of least developed nations. The Green Climate Fund, another financial mechanism of the climate regime, was created in 2010 to help developing countries address climate change. Both are independent organizations whose work is closely tied to the UNFCCC. In addition the three "Rio Conventions" – signed at the Rio Conference on Environment and Development in 1992 – created the Joint Liaison Group in 2001. The three multilateral environmental agreements – on biodiversity, desertification, and climate change – have clear and substantive overlap. As rule-making and implementation of each agreement expanded the secretariats of each created the "Joint Liaison Group" as a way to coordinate their efforts. Other UN bodies, such as the UN Environment Programme and the UN Development Programme, also have climate change as major programmatic priorities.

Thus, even in its early phase, this group of international organizations had elements of networked governance, as defined by the editors of this volume in the Introduction. They worked for a common purpose

---

[7] There were two other markets created by Kyoto: one for offset initiatives conducted jointly by developed nations and one for trade in emissions allowances.
[8] Werksman 1998.   [9] See, e.g., Green 2013; Peters-Stanley and Gonzalez 2014.

through voluntary arrangements. As international organizations (IOs) they enjoy formal equality, despite varying levels of resources and authority. In the parlance of theorists of regime complexity this early instantiation of the climate regime had loosely coupled sets of rules with little in the way of formal procedures to adjudicate among them, which is further evidence of networked governance.[10]

Paris: Choose Your Own Adventure

Fast-forward fifteen years to the Paris Agreement. There are three main differences between Kyoto and the Paris Agreement. First, the nature of the commitment has changed. Second, and related to the former, the breadth of state participation has vastly expanded. Under Paris climate change is no longer the sole responsibility of the developed world; all nations must do their part, even though the extent of these contributions varies widely. Third, non-state and subnational actors now occupy a prominent role in both rule-making and implementation.[11] This shift is an explicit acknowledgment of the interdependence of many different types of actors in addressing climate change.

After a series of failures in the run-up to Paris, states committed to the "choose your own adventure" approach to climate governance. Instead of setting hard reduction targets each state submits its own "Nationally Determined Contribution" (NDCs) detailing the measures it will implement to reduce emissions, and in the case of many developing nations adapt to the effects of climate change. Although the agreement calls for limiting temperature increases to below 2 degrees Celsius below preindustrial levels, most analyses indicate that the NDCs will not achieve that goal.[12] The "choose your own adventure" approach allowed the climate regime to expand its participation. The Kyoto model, which excluded developing nations, was barely politically workable at the time of drafting, and became impossible after the rise of the BRICs. Once China had surpassed the USA as the world's largest emitter in 2007 few states could countenance giving it, or others nations with growing emissions, a complete pass on reductions. This remained true for the USA, and became true in developed nations where conservative governments had come to power, like Australia and Canada. As a result Paris replaced the principle of common but differentiated responsibility with a more verbose but politically acceptable principle: "common but differentiated responsibilities and respective capabilities in the light of

---

[10] Raustiala and Victor 2004.   [11] Hsu et al. 2015; Hale 2016; Bäckstrand et al. 2017.
[12] UNEP 2020.

different national circumstances."[13] Under Paris every state has to do *something* to address climate change, however small.

Finally, and most importantly, Paris shifted to an "all hands on deck" approach, inviting and encouraging action by non-state and subnational actors.[14] This is evidenced by the Non-State Actor Zone for Climate Action (NAZCA), which was launched in 2014 and has since expanded to play a major role in the Paris regime. Major voluntary efforts under NAZCA include RE100, a network of multinational firms that plan to source 100 percent of their energy needs from renewables.[15] In all, NAZCA provides a hub for non-state and substate actors to document their voluntary commitments, which now number over 26,000.[16]

Simultaneously, cities became a focus of transnational climate policy. Former New York City Mayor Bloomberg launched the C40 Cities initiative in 2005, which promotes information sharing and promotion of best practices among city governments around mitigation and adaptation.[17] A similar effort, the Covenant for Mayors, was launched in Europe in 2008.[18]

In addition to the NAZCA platform, the Paris Agreement establishes a set of institutions to support these activities. Specifically, it creates an annual review process so that non-state efforts can be tracked over time. It also appoints two "champions" – governmental officials to essentially be in charge of this review process. This means that non-state actors are now part of the institutional infrastructure supporting Paris. NAZCA is an explicit signal from states that climate change does in fact require commitment and action by many different types of actors – an acknowledgment of interdependence and common purpose, both hallmarks of networked governance. But more significantly it demonstrates a willingness to integrate multiple efforts – and multiple sources of authority – into the international legal framework for climate change. This is not the same as true equality, since states are firmly in control of this multilateral process. Nonetheless, the ongoing efforts to incorporate non-state actors into what had been an exclusively state-driven process signals something of a shift to networked governance.

Paris also creates a more prominent role for market approaches, which are growing features of the new climate architecture. Article 6 of the Paris Agreement calls for the voluntary use of "internationally agreed mitigation outcomes" to help states achieve the goals set forth in their national pledges. This decision lays the foundation for a new form of market

---

[13] UNFCCC 2015, article 2.2.   [14] Hale 2016; Chan et al. 2018.
[15] http://there100.org/.   [16] As of June 1, 2020. See http://climateaction.unfccc.int/.
[17] www.c40.org/.   [18] www.covenantofmayors.eu/index_en.html.

activity. It is not the same as carbon trading, since "mitigation outcomes" can include many different types of activities. States are still negotiating how, exactly, this would work. There are a variety of technical challenges to deal with, not least of which is how to standardize different carbon mitigation efforts so that they can be properly quantified and traded. Nonetheless, the logic is very much market-based: one country pays another to reduce emissions premised on the assumption that the marginal cost of reduction is lower in some jurisdictions than in others. The exchange is Pareto-improving both for the parties involved and the global climate.

Beyond the Paris Agreement carbon markets are catching on. Roughly 20 percent of global carbon emissions are now covered by a carbon price.[19] The EU has the largest regional carbon market. Others include a growing market between the state of California and Canadian provinces, and a regional market in the Northeast and Midwest of the US. In December 2017, China launched a national carbon market covering the electricity sector. There is enthusiasm among some to link these disparate markets together to create a global carbon price.[20] However, some have been wary of such an approach.[21]

In sum, the evolution of the climate regime is best understood as a *growth* in authority rather than a shift from one form to another. Though state-based rule-making was perhaps the most prominent feature of the Kyoto phase it was by no means the only mode of governance. Markets and hierarchies were also present. The Paris Agreement marks a more pronounced commitment to markets, and networks, but these are in addition to (and in some instances also subject to) the hierarchical authority of states. Many of the "new governance" approaches have now been institutionalized in the Paris Agreement – thus rendering them part of the "traditional" approach to intergovernmental cooperation.

Why Is It Happening?

Given that there are many potential explanations behind the changing constellation of modes of governance, and many are likely correlated, the task is to sift through these varied drivers to find those that are most important, in the sense of being causally prior. In explaining the shift from Kyoto to Paris I argue that there are two structural variables that "begin" the story: changes in geopolitics and the rise of global rationalization. As I explain in this section, these two factors drive the failure of

---

[19] World Bank Group 2019.   [20] Ranson and Stavins 2016.   [21] Green 2017.

the Kyoto Protocol, which then gives rise to more modular approach of the Paris Agreement. There is also an important background condition: the pervasive neoliberal emphasis on markets and trade. As with many other areas of world politics, governance through markets was a hallmark of climate politics as early as the mid-1990s. In turn, the emphasis on markets provided an important entry point for a variety of non-state actors, further accelerating the diffusion of authority.

Geopolitics

The significance of the rise of the BRICs cannot be understated in mapping out Kyoto's failure. Common but differentiated responsibility (CBDR) is a principle of international environmental law that dates back to the mid-twentieth century. A number of environmental agreements identify parts of the environment that are the "common heritage of mankind." The notion of differentiated responsibility first appears in the 1970s, and its variants are found in significant agreements like the UN Convention on the Law of the Sea. Though the phrase "common but differentiated responsibility" does not formally appear until the 1992 Rio Declaration, it has been present in various forms for most of the life of contemporary environmental law.[22]

Given the well-established history of CBDR, it was virtually unavoidable that the principle be applied to the Kyoto Protocol – especially given the fact that it was drafted in the years following the Rio Declaration. CBDR was first institutionalized in the climate regime through the Berlin Mandate of 1995, which stated that "developed countries should take the lead in combating climate change" and that no new commitments would be introduced for developing countries.[23] Thus, any subsequent agreements *would have to* be governed by CBDR. This was the first battle of many about the appropriate obligations for the developing world.

CBDR created problems from the earliest days of the climate regime. The decision not to require developing countries to reduce their emissions was the primary reason given by the George W. Bush administration for its decision not to ratify. And it made reluctant nations like Russia even more disinclined to participate. After the USA declined to ratify, Russian participation became essential; without it Kyoto would likely not have entered into force. (Entry into force required ratification by fifty-five countries, representing 55 percent of global emissions.) Russia flirted with ratification for several years. By the time it decided

---

[22] Sands et al. 2012.   [23] UNFCCC 1995.

to join, its emissions had fallen well below the baseline level, creating a windfall of "hot air" which it could then sell on the newly created Kyoto carbon markets. Indeed, although Kyoto was signed in 1997 it did not enter into force for another eight years – once it had secured ratifications from states representing 55 percent of total global emissions.

Kyoto was built on shaky political foundations. But as the BRICs and other emerging economies began their meteoric economic growth in the early 2000s that foundation became even more precarious. Asian emissions roughly doubled between 2000 and 2011.[24] And critically in 2007, just two years after the Kyoto Protocol entered into force, China overtook the United States as the world's top emitter. It was no longer politically feasible that it remain unconstrained by global rules on greenhouse gases.

The rise of the BRICs could not have occurred at a more inopportune moment for the climate regime: just as states began to negotiate the terms of the second commitment period of the Kyoto Protocol. The Protocol was divided into two periods, the first from 2008 to 2012 and the second from 2012 to 2020. The Doha Amendment, adopted in 2012, laid out a more ambitious reduction target for the second commitment period: 18 percent below 1990 levels. But a number of nations declined to sign up for another round, including Japan, New Zealand, and Russia. In addition Canada withdrew in 2011 after it became clear that it would not meet its target. The stated reason, however, was the non-participation of the USA and China.[25] Nonetheless, the USA held firm on its position not to ratify. Only the EU remained unwavering in its commitment to reductions – aiming for an ambitious 20 percent reduction below 1990 levels by 2020.

Thus, the rise of the BRICs and their emissions levels made the paradox of CBDR untenable. It was clear that any future climate regime could not be based on the Kyoto model and the principle of CBDR if it was to get continued support from the developed world. Something had to change.

The USA–China joint announcement on climate provided that much-needed change. In 2014, in the run-up to Paris, presidents Obama and Xi announced their joint commitment to climate change. The USA rolled out its Clean Power Plan, which aimed to reduce US emissions from electricity 26–28 percent below 2005 levels by 2025. At the same

---

[24] www.wri.org/blog/2014/05/history-carbon-dioxide-emissions.
[25] www.theguardian.com/environment/2011/dec/13/canada-pulls-out-kyoto-protocol.

time China committed to peaking its emissions by 2030, and to increasing its share of renewables to 20 percent by the same date.[26]

The announcement was significant for three reasons. First, it signaled that the two biggest emitters were willing to act on climate change without the commitment of other nations. Their actions demonstrated that this was no longer a free-rider problem which required consensus and commitment to avoid defection.[27] These pledges helped refocus climate politics as an issue of domestic policy. Second, though Obama had been in office since 2009, an intransigent Republican Congress had stymied federal legislation on climate change. The Clean Power Plan showed Obama's willingness to use his executive power to move climate policy forward. Similarly, President Xi's pledge demonstrated that China was ready to take on its role as an emerging economy and the concomitant responsibility to act on climate change. This was a definitive reversal from the Kyoto era, when developing countries resolutely insisted that the principle of common but differentiated responsibility exempted them from action. Finally, the joint agreement set the stage for the more variable, less rigid approach embodied by the Paris Agreement.

Global Rationalization

A second critical driver in the shift from Kyoto to Paris is the cultural shift to global rationalization. Global rationalization is a process that valorizes rational-legal authority over other types of authority. It privileges standardized approaches to governance and creates a prominent role for international experts specializing in narrow areas within the regime. These are all the hallmarks of the Kyoto Protocol, which viewed climate change as a technical problem to be managed by experts and bureaucrats at the global and national levels rather than as a fundamental problem of distribution. But ultimately this approach to climate change resulted in the creation of a political institution that was doomed to fail – both politically and in terms of outcomes. The emphasis on standardization and expertise was an attempt to paper over profound political differences.

But, as others have pointed out, climate change is not simply a technical problem. It is not only – or for some states, even primarily – a question of emissions mitigation.[28] It is also a problem of adapting to a changing climate, intra and intergenerational equity, social justice, and

---

[26] https://obamawhitehouse.archives.gov/the-press-office/2014/11/11/fact-sheet-us-china-joint-announcement-climate-change-and-clean-energy-c.
[27] Colgan et al. 2020.   [28] Roberts and Parks 2006.

"deep decarbonization."[29] Yet, the dominance of global rationalization framed climate change as a first-world problem of emissions reductions, and made the politics of cooperation particularly contentious for three reasons.

First, global rationalization suggested that a standardized approach to climate change was appropriate. All countries would commit to a target – a specified level of emissions reductions.[30] This would be politically negotiated, but the assumption was that once states agreed the hard problem of overcoming free riding was solved.[31] Then addressing climate change was "simply" a question of ensuring that states met their targets. But, in terms of domestic politics, these commitments were much more complicated than just agreeing on a number. Many countries committed to goals that were incompatible with domestic interests and politics.[32] Once translated into national policies these targets created hard political questions about winners and losers. By the logic of the two-level game, then, the Kyoto Protocol should never have come into existence, since states overpromised on what they could reasonably deliver politically.[33]

Although global rationalism has hardly disappeared from the climate regime, it looks different in the "new" governance of the Paris Agreement. In contrast to the "targets and timetables" approach espoused by Kyoto, Paris rejects a standardized approach. Instead it allows countries to propose policies most in line with their own needs and compatible with the domestic constraints. As a result the NDCs are incredibly varied. So, while the EU focuses on an ambitious emission reductions goal (40 percent reduction in all greenhouse gas emissions below 1990 levels by 2030), Brazil emphasizes adaptation as a fundamental part of its commitment. India is focused on scaling up renewable energy.

Second, and related to the first, global rationalization suggests that the "best" institutional solution to collective action problems is one that enhances efficiency. Thus, the concern surrounding climate change was to create institutions that deter free riding.[34] Yet, the contentious nature of the political debate meant that an enforcement mechanism for Kyoto was nearly impossible. Indeed, states studiously avoided the

---

[29] Bernstein and Hoffmann 2015.
[30] Since the Kyoto Protocol required that all developed (or Annex I) nations achieve a *global average* reduction of 5 percent below 1990 levels, some nations were actually allowed to increase their emissions. Others set more ambitious targets, well below the global average, to offset these permitted increases.
[31] Barrett 2003.   [32] Victor 2011.   [33] Putnam 1988.
[34] See, e.g., Aldy and Stavins 2007; Keohane and Victor 2016.

question of enforcement in drafting the Protocol, postponing discussion about it until after entry into force. They then created a weak oversight mechanism that has been little used, and even then primarily in its "facilitative" capacity – to help states that want to comply but lack the capacity to do so. Thus, while efficiency was a central preoccupation as mandated by the logic of global rationalization, politically an "efficient" institutional design was infeasible.

The view of climate change as a collective action problem was further cemented by the success of the Montreal Protocol to address the depletion of the ozone layer. The Montreal Protocol provided the template for Kyoto. The ozone regime began with a framework convention – a soft law instrument in which states declared their intention to address the problem with greater ambition in the future. Like Kyoto, the Montreal Protocol divided the world into developed and developing nations. Developed nations had to begin phasing out the production of ozone-depleting chlorofluorocarbons (CFCs) almost immediately. Developing nations, by contrast, got a pass. They would *eventually* have to phase out production, but had at least a decade before they had to address the issue. The same playbook was replicated in Kyoto – which began with a framework convention and was then followed by a legally binding protocol, which distinguished among developed and developing country commitments.

It is beyond the scope of this chapter to provide an in-depth analysis of the Montreal Protocol.[35] However, Montreal's success is not only, or even principally, due to its institutional design. Compared to climate change, ozone depletion was an easy technological fix (though ironically the main substitutes for CFCs, called hydrofluorocarbons, are extremely powerful greenhouse gases). The biggest producer, the United States, backed the treaty, and indeed, as Barrett shows, would even have benefited hugely from unilateral action.[36] Thus, the assumption that the Montreal model could be readily exported to the problem of climate change was a miscalculation of epic proportions. Unsurprisingly, when large emitters pulled out of Kyoto (or failed to ratify in the first place) collective action quickly unraveled. A logic of global rationalization indicated that there was an "optimal" institutional design for global environmental problems. However, the empirical record demonstrates the flaws in this thinking.

Finally, global rationalization was the driving factor behind the creation of carbon markets in the Kyoto Protocol. An army of international

---

[35] Benedick 1991.   [36] Barrett 2003, chapter 8.

bureaucrats and expert nongovernmental organizations (NGOs) understood that carbon markets could provide some flexibility in how states met their targets; again, this served the purpose of lessening political conflict. They also recognized that markets could become a mainstay of their own activities, creating a potential influx of resources. Yet, carbon markets – particularly offset markets – have been widely criticized. Rather than create actual emissions reductions, critics argue that they simply create a new commodity to be bought and sold. Indeed, thus far there is evidence that existing markets have contributed relatively little to emissions reductions.[37] Prices are far too low to produce the needed changes in behavior, much less a viable pathway to decarbonization. By contrast there is ample evidence that carbon markets are a politically palatable approach to mitigation, even if the outcomes are less than robust.[38] Markets provided some of the political momentum that allowed Kyoto to totter along, as well as the questionable results that prompted a rethinking of climate governance.

These two drivers set climate policy on a course for failure. The change in geopolitics and the rise in global rationalization allowed states to strike a deal they shouldn't have. It quickly began to unravel. Political momentum slowed, and gridlock ensued.[39]

New Actors, New Ideologies of Governance

Thus far I have argued that geopolitical shifts and the imprint of global rationalization set in motion a tenuous agreement which was unlikely to be viable in the long term. In addition to these key causal factors, additional elements influenced the shift from "old" to "new" governance. In particular the presence of non-state actors and the emergence of "liberal environmentalism" as an ideology of governance are important to understanding the evolution of the climate change regime.

Environmental issues have typically been viewed as "low politics" and therefore more permeable to non-state actors.[40] NGOs in particular have been active in international climate politics from the outset. As early as 1992 major international environmental NGOs including Greenpeace, the World Wildlife Fund, and Friends of the Earth organized into a transnational advocacy network.[41] In the early days of the climate regime they were typically "leader" international NGOs – with lots of resources and mainstream views and a technocratic approach to climate change.[42]

---

[37] Cullenward and Victor 2020.   [38] Wara 2014.   [39] Victor 2011.
[40] Betsill and Corell 2008.   [41] Hadden 2015, chapter 2.   [42] Stroup and Wong 2017.

As the regime shifted the number and types of non-state actors also grew, many becoming integral to the implementation of the Paris Agreement.

At the same time liberal environmentalism became an important norm in global environmental politics.[43] Liberal environmentalism conveniently viewed free markets as entirely compatible with environmental protection. Thus, policies focused on market-based mechanisms, business partnerships, and open markets. As Bernstein notes, "norms of liberal environmentalism predicate international environmental protection on the promotion and maintenance of a liberal economic order."[44]

Liberal environmentalism first emerged in the early 1990s and became more pronounced over time. The enthusiasm for markets provided a logical entrée for more non-state actors. Beyond just NGOs, firms, subnational actors, and transnational networks increasingly became part of the institutional landscape.[45] Using market-based and expert authority, new non-state actors were able to find niches in an ever-expanding governance landscape.[46]

In response to the gridlock of the intergovernmental process, and the increasing urgency coming from the scientific community, non-state actors became regulators in their own right.[47] Non-state actors had already mobilized around the intergovernmental process; acting independently of this process was the next logical step. Firms began to realize that climate change was a risk management issue – for their reputations and their supply chains.[48] And subnational governments began to see climate change as a local issue about air pollution, extreme weather, land use change, and any number of other topics. This pluralization of actors resulted in shifting new policy activity on climate *outside* the intergovernmental rule-making process.

The explosion of transnational climate governance in the late 2000s and early 2010s provided much-needed momentum for a flagging intergovernmental process. Through a mutual process of pushing from non-state actors and leadership from inside the intergovernmental arena[49] this transnational activity was gradually integrated into the climate regime. In 2014 states created NAZCA. NAZCA provides a platform within the UNFCCC for sharing information about non-state and substate climate activities.

---

[43] Bernstein 2001.   [44] Bernstein 2002, 1.   [45] See, e.g., Bulkeley et al. 2014.
[46] Abbott et al. 2016.   [47] Green 2018.   [48] Dauvergne and Lister 2013; Green 2014.
[49] See, e.g., Galvanizing the Groundswell for Climate Action, which seeks to build and expand an institutional framework for non-state action within the UNFCCC. http://www .climategroundswell.org/.

The Paris Agreement simply institutionalized NAZCA through a process of annual reviews and designated officials to direct the review process. From a political perspective this institutionalization is important. Non-state actors are now formally part of the institutional infrastructure supporting Paris.

Hindsight, of course, is 20–20, but in this retelling it seems clear that Kyoto could not have been a successful model. Because of the age-old practice of CBDR in international environmental law developing countries could not be drafted into the fight against climate change. The rise of the BRICs and concomitant increase in emissions made this division politically untenable. Political differences were further papered over by the trend toward rationalization, which emphasized technocratic approaches to what are fundamentally distributional problems. As non-state actors proliferated, due in part to the privileging of market-based logics, the structure of the climate regime was turned on its head.

How Does It Matter?

Though political scientists may be interested in explaining how we got here, the most important question, in terms of the future of our planet, is what this shift in governance arrangements means for our collective ability to produce sound climate policies or the political processes that lead to those policies. By sound climate policies I mean moving quickly toward deep decarbonization and implementing adaptation and resilience policies to protect societies from the impacts of climate change that are already underway, particularly the most vulnerable. The latest United Nations Environment Programme emissions report estimates that in order to achieve Paris's goal of limiting warming to 2 degrees Celsius we must approach net zero emissions by mid-century.[50] In short, we want to know whether Paris will produce processes and outcomes that Kyoto could not.

Of course, it is early days to make assessments about outcomes. As such, I start by looking at the processes that the Paris approach has put in place. And here there are reasons to be cautiously optimistic.

First, the Paris Agreement has provided much-needed momentum to the intergovernmental process. After it became clear that many major emitters would not sign on to the second commitment period of Kyoto

[50] UNEP 2020.

there was genuine concern about whether a successor agreement was politically possible. This was further compounded by the view that the 2009 climate negotiations in Copenhagen were a failure. By comparison, the elation in Paris showed not only that an agreement was possible, but also that it could include the developing world. In turn, this development lessened the importance of free riding as a political obstacle to cooperation. Paris has demonstrated that climate cooperation is possible without the "you first" logic built into the Kyoto Protocol.[51] It is noteworthy that the commitment to action persisted, despite the Trump administration's nonsensical withdrawal from the agreement.

Second, the Paris approach has made significant progress in institutionalizing processes for learning. While climate change is at base a political problem, there are technical issues involved, and "new governance" can help address this subset of issues. This argument is captured by work on experimentalist governance, where "actors facing uncertainty can jointly explore practical ways to realize their goals."[52] This approach is particularly useful when there is "thin consensus" – agreement that there is a problem that requires action but no clear sense of how to proceed.[53] Experimentalist governance is essentially structured, institutionalized trial and error, with additional information informing future plans. In the case of some of the more technical aspects of climate mitigation it may prove to be helpful.[54] Some have gone further, arguing that experiments are not merely improving rationalist approaches to policy-making but can give rise to normative shifts and transformational changes.[55]

Third, the Paris process can potentially catalyze larger political and normative changes. Hale has recently suggested that climate change is not an n-person prisoner's dilemma, as rational institutionalists maintain, but rather is best conceived of as a "tipping point problem." In this view, "catalytic" institutions help early movers act; over time these early actors lower costs to action, thus incentivizing the more recalcitrant to follow suit.[56]

Bernstein and Hoffman similarly argue that pathways to decarbonization can lock in transformational changes.[57] The question, then, is not how to "deepen commitments" but how to make the necessary energy transformation both inevitable and irreversible. Seen through this lens the Paris pledges are not "shallow" but rather the first steps in changing

[51] Aklin and Mildenberger 2020; Colgan et al. 2020; Hale 2020.
[52] Sabel and Victor 2017, 18.   [53] Sabel and Victor 2017.   [54] Sabel and Victor 2017.
[55] Hoffmann 2011.   [56] Hale 2020.   [57] Bernstein and Hoffmann 2018.

others' incentives to act. The only question becomes whether incentives can be shifted quickly enough to avoid catastrophic climate change.

While there are reasons to believe that the Paris approach can set us collectively on a path toward better climate policies, it would be remiss not to discuss the shortcomings of the new governance model.

First, the pledges are not enough. The most recent models state that the Paris pledges only get about one-third of the way to the 2 degree target.[58] This suggests that the "choose your own adventure approach" may produce optimism about the *process* of cooperation but ultimately lead to outcomes that are insufficient to avoid dangerous climate change – at least thus far.

Second, the Paris Agreement does not explicitly address the problem of obstructionism from those industries, states, and firms that stand to lose out from climate policy. A growing body of literature identifies obstructionism as the key obstacle to climate action, rather than free riding.[59] But the voluntarism of the Paris pledges is particularly vulnerable to obstructionists.

Third, we have little way of assessing the aggregate effects of the NAZCA initiatives. The efforts of subnational and non-state actors are numerous and diverse. We know a lot about what these pledges look like[60] but relatively little about how they have performed. There are serious challenges to assessing NAZCA's impacts. It is difficult to compare – let alone add – apples (states' actions) and oranges (transnational activities). Even parsing transnational activities from state pledges is a challenging undertaking.[61]

There are a number of initiatives underway to help evaluate the impacts of transnational activities. The Greenhouse Gas Protocol, created by two NGOs, is a series of tools to measure and report greenhouse gas emissions and reductions.[62] It has vastly expanded since its creation in 2010 and is now creating new tools precisely for the purpose of evaluating national pledges and non-state activity to implement Paris.[63] In the age of global rationalization measurement has become a key form of governance.[64] But right now the necessary measurement tools are only in their earliest stages. Without them it will be difficult to assess progress.

Fourth, the continued reliance on carbon markets is worrisome. The evidence on their effectiveness at reducing emissions is mixed, and it is

[58] http://web.unep.org/emissionsgap/.   [59] Colgan et al. 2020; Stokes 2020.
[60] http://visuals.datadriven.yale.edu/climateaction/.   [61] Hsu et al. 2018.
[62] Green 2014, chapter 6.   [63] Green forthcoming.   [64] Kelley and Simmons 2015.

clear that other types of mitigation policies are much more effective.[65] Yet the Paris Agreement creates a prominent role for carbon markets to continue into the future – despite the fact that negotiations remain contentious and unresolved.

Finally, there will undoubtedly be interactive effects among the governance activities of this diversity of actors. New governance is complex: there are lots of actors with many connections between them.[66] Complex systems behave in non-linear ways, producing unexpected outcomes and interactions among policies. For instance, despite its ambitious climate policies the European Union's cap and trade scheme performed inconsistently. Since its creation in 2005 it has struggled to establish a strong price signal. Much ink has been spilled to deconstruct the shortcomings of the EU market. But one piece of the explanation stems from the interactive effects of other climate policies. The EU has committed to generating 20 percent of its energy from renewables by the year 2020. This has resulted in a huge increase in the amount of installed capacity of renewables, particularly wind.[67] The growth in renewables has reduced the demand for carbon allowances in the cap and trade market, further depressing prices. Thus, while both policies are working toward the same goal – a reduction in greenhouse gas emissions – the interactive effect has produced some unintended and unwanted outcomes.[68] These perverse and unanticipated effects will become more prominent as complex governance grows – presenting new challenges for policy design and management.

Conclusion

In the end it seems that in the realm of climate politics "new governance" has been good for building new institutions, and has provided a more flexible and politically realistic approach to climate change. The bet is that this arrangement is better suited to both the realities of domestic politics and profound uncertainty surrounding climate change than the old governance model. If we are correct then we have created the enabling conditions for decarbonization, though obstructionism remains a challenge. The question is: will it happen fast enough?

The timeline is incredibly tight. The Intergovernmental Panel on Climate Change states that the globe must have "net zero" emissions

---

[65] Wara 2014. See also, Green 2021.   [66] Kahler 2016.   [67] Vaughan 2017.
[68] Green 2017.

by 2050 in order to limit warming to 1.5 degrees Celsius. And the difference between 1.5 degrees and 2 degrees is immense in terms of impacts, so every bit of avoided warming is critical. In this view, governance processes to facilitate change are not enough. What is needed is immediate and drastic action.

References

Abbott, Kenneth W., Jessica F. Green, and Robert O. Keohane. 2016. Organizational Ecology and Institutional Change in Global Governance. *International Organization* 70 (2): 247–277.

Aklin, Michaël and Matto Mildenberger. 2020. Prisoners of the Wrong Dilemma: Why Distributive Conflict, Not Collective Action, Characterizes the Politics of Climate Change. *Global Environmental Politics* 20 (4): 4–27.

Aldy, Joseph E. and Robert N. Stavins, eds. 2007. *Architectures for Agreement: Addressing Global Climate Change in the Post-Kyoto World.* Cambridge: Cambridge University Press.

Bäckstrand, Karin, Jonathan W. Kuyper, Björn-Ola Linnér, and Eva Lövbrand. 2017. Non-state Actors in Global Climate Governance: From Copenhagen to Paris and Beyond. *Environmental Politics* 26 (4): 561–579.

Barrett, Scott. 2003. *Environment and Statecraft.* Oxford: Oxford University Press.

Benedick, Richard. 1991. *Ozone Diplomacy: New Directions in Safeguarding the Planet.* Cambridge, MA: Harvard University Press.

Bernstein, Steven. 2001. *The Compromise of Liberal Environmentalism.* New York: Columbia University Press.

2002. Liberal Environmentalism and Global Environmental Governance. *Global Environmental Politics* 2 (3): 1–16.

Bernstein, Steven and Matthew Hoffmann. 2015. *The Politics of Decarbonization: A Framework and Method.* SSRN Scholarly Paper. Rochester, NY: Social Science Research Network. https://papers.ssrn .com/abstract=2619322.

2018. The Politics of Decarbonization and the Catalytic Impact of Subnational Climate Experiments. *Policy Sciences* 51 (2): 189–211.

Betsill, Michele Merrill and Elisabeth Corell, eds. 2008. *NGO Diplomacy: The Influence of Nongovernmental Organizations in International Environmental Negotiations.* Cambridge, MA: MIT Press.

Bulkeley, Harriet, Liliana B. Andonova, Michele M. Betsill, Daniel Compagnon, Thomas Hale, Matthew J. Hoffmann, Peter Newell, Matthew Paterson, Charles Roger, and Stacy D. VanDeveer. 2014. *Transnational Climate Change Governance.* Cambridge: Cambridge University Press.

Busby, Joshua William. 2018. Warming World: Why Climate Change Matters More than Anything Else. *Foreign Affairs* 97 (4): 49–55.

Chan, Sander, Robert Falkner, Matthew Goldberg, and Harro van Asselt. 2018. Effective and Geographically Balanced? An Output-Based Assessment of Non-state Climate Actions. *Climate Policy* 18 (1): 24–35.

Colgan, Jeff D., Jessica F. Green, and Thomas N Hale. 2020. Asset Revaluation and the Existential Politics of Climate Change. *International Organization.* First View. https://doi.org/10.1017/S0020818320000296.

Cullenward, Danny and David G. Victor. 2020. *Making Climate Policy Work.* Cambridge: Polity.

Dauvergne, Peter and Jane Lister. 2013. *Eco-Business: A Big-Brand Takeover of Sustainability.* Cambridge, MA: MIT Press.

Green, Jessica F. 2013. Order out of Chaos: Public and Private Rules for Managing Carbon. *Global Environmental Politics* 13 (2): 1–25.

    2014. *Rethinking Private Authority: Agents and Entrepreneurs in Global Environmental Governance.* Princeton: Princeton University Press.

    2017. Don't Link Carbon Markets. *Nature News* 543 (7646): 484.

    2018. From Green to REDD: Protean Power and the Politics of Carbon Sinks. In *Power in Uncertainty: Exploring the Unexpected in World Politics,* 246–263. Cambridge: Cambridge University Press.

    2021. Does Carbon Pricing Reduce Emissions? A Meta-analysis. *Environmental Research Letters.* First View. https://doi.org/10.1088/1748-9326/abdae9.

    Forthcoming. Greenhouse Gas Accounting and the Dynamics of Global Administrative Law. In *Global Hybrid and Private Governance: Standard-Setting, Market Regulation, and Institutional Design,* edited by Benedict Kingsbury and Richard Stewart. Oxford: Oxford University Press.

Green, Jessica F., Thomas Sterner, and Gernot Wagner. 2014. A Balance of Bottom-Up and Top-Down in Linking Climate Policies. *Nature Climate Change* 4 (12): 1064–1067.

Hadden, Jennifer. 2015. *Networks in Contention: The Divisive Politics of Climate Change.* New York: Cambridge University Press.

Hale, Thomas. 2016. "All Hands on Deck": The Paris Agreement and Nonstate Climate Action. *Global Environmental Politics* 16 (3): 12–22.

    2020. Catalytic Cooperation. *Global Environmental Politics* 20 (4):73–98.

Hoffmann, Matthew J. 2011. *Climate Governance at the Crossroads.* Oxford: Oxford University Press.

Hsu, Angel, Andrew S. Moffat, Amy J. Weinfurter, and Jason D. Schwartz. 2015. Towards a New Climate Diplomacy. *Nature Climate Change* 5: 501–503.

Hsu, Angel, Oscar Widerberg, Amy Weinfurter, Sander Chan, and Fatemah Bakhtiari. 2018. *Bridging the Emissions Gap: The Role of Non-state and Subnational Actors.* Nairobi: United Nations Environment Programme.

Kahler, Miles. 2016. Complex Governance and the New Interdependence Approach (NIA). *Review of International Political Economy* 23 (5): 825–839.

Kelley, Judith G. and Beth A. Simmons. 2015. Politics by Number: Indicators as Social Pressure in International Relations. *American Journal of Political Science* 59 (1): 55–70.

Keohane, Robert O. and David G. Victor. 2016. Cooperation and Discord in Global Climate Policy. *Nature Climate Change* 6 (6): 570–575.

Mach, Katharine J. et al. 2019. Climate as a Risk Factor for Armed Conflict. *Nature* 571 (7764): 193–197.

Peters-Stanley, Molly and Gloria Gonzalez. 2014. *Sharing the Stage: State of the Voluntary Carbon Markets 2014*. Washington, DC: Forest Trends' Ecosystem Marketplace.

Putnam, Robert. 1988. Diplomacy and Domestic Politics: The Logic of Two-Level Games. *International Organization* 42 (3): 427–460.

Ranson, Matthew and Robert N. Stavins. 2016. Linkage of Greenhouse Gas Emissions Trading Systems: Learning from Experience. *Climate Policy* 16 (3): 284–300.

Raustiala, Kal, and David G. Victor. 2004. The Regime Complex for Plant Genetic Resources. *International Organization* 58: 277–309.

Roberts, J. Timmons and Bradley Parks. 2006. *A Climate of Injustice: Global Inequality, North–South Politics, and Climate Policy*. Cambridge, MA: MIT Press.

Sabel, Charles F. and David G. Victor. 2017. Governing Global Problems under Uncertainty: Making Bottom-Up Climate Policy Work. *Climatic Change* 144 (1): 15–27.

Sands, Philippe, Jacqueline Peel, Adriana Fabra, and Ruth MacKenzie. 2012. *Principles of International Environmental Law*, 3rd edition. Cambridge and New York: Cambridge University Press.

Stokes, Leah C. 2020. *Short Circuiting Policy: Interest Groups and the Battle Over Clean Energy and Climate Policy in the American States*. Studies in Postwar American Political Development. Oxford and New York: Oxford University Press.

Stroup, Sarah S. and Wendy H. Wong. 2017. *The Authority Trap: Strategic Choices of International NGOs*. Ithaca, NY: Cornell University Press.

UNEP. 2020. *Emissions Gap Report 2020*. Nairobi, Kenya: UNEP. www.unep .org/emissions-gap-report-2020.

UNFCCC. 1992. United Nations Framework Convention on Climate Change. https://unfccc.int/resource/docs/convkp/conveng.pdf.

1995. The Berlin Mandate. FCCC/CP/1995/7/Add.1. Decision 1/CP.1.

1997. Kyoto Protocol. FCCC/CP/1997/L.7/Add.1.

2015. The Paris Agreement. FCCC/CP/2015/10/Add.1. https://unfccc.int/ sites/default/files/english_paris_agreement.pdf.

Vaughan, Adam. 2017. Almost 90% of New Power in Europe from Renewable Resources in 2016. *The Guardian*. www.theguardian.com/environment/ 2017/feb/09/new-energy-europe-renewable-sources-2016.

Victor, David G. 2011. *Global Warming Gridlock: Creating More Effective Strategies for Protecting the Planet*. Cambridge: Cambridge University Press.

Wara, Michael W. 2014. California's Energy and Climate Policy: A Full Plate, but Perhaps Not a Model Policy. *Bulletin of the Atomic Scientists* 70 (5): 26–34.

Werksman, Jacob. 1998. The Clean Development Mechanism: Unwrapping the Kyoto Surprise. *Review of European Community and International Environmental Law* 7 (2): 147–158.

World Bank Group. 2019. *State and Trends of Carbon Pricing 2019*. Washington, DC: World Bank. https://openknowledge.worldbank.org/handle/10986/ 31755/.

4   A Shadow of Its Former Self
Hierarchy and Global Trade

Susanne Mueller and Jon C. W. Pevehouse

Global trade has expanded rapidly since the end of the Second World War. The global institutions that have guided and supported that growth are often held up as shining examples of successful global governance in the postwar world. Credit is often given to the architecture of the trade regimes' rules: "The GATT/WTO's [General Agreement on Tariffs and Trade/World Trade Organization] unique structure and rules proved exceptionally successful in promoting trade."[1] Yet, those rules have been subject to challenges and changes in the past seventy-plus years.

In the nomenclature of Barnett, Pevehouse, and Raustiala (BPR), we contend the multilateral trade regime that emerged in the postwar period was, and remains, hierarchical. We reach this conclusion by examining rule creation as our focal process of global governance. Yet, challenges have begun to chip away at the hierarchical nature of the global trade regime. We identify two central changes and challenges. First, we argue that while global trade rules are hierarchical, rule-based constructs, it is now a multilevel hierarchy thanks to growing regionalism. We argue that to date regional arrangements have largely nested into the global trade regime, but there is no guarantee this will continue. If one sees regionalism as a substitute for multilateralism, the multilateral trade regime is in growing danger.

Second, while multilateral rule-making power remains exclusively with states, non-state actors have elbowed their way into the process due to the expansion of regionalism, the changing nature of global trading relationships, and the growing emphasis on non-trade issues as central to trade agreements. This has allowed networks of actors, including firms and nongovernmental organizations (NGOs), to influence the rules of the trade regime, even though they have no formal "seat at the table" in Geneva.

---

[1] Baldwin 2014, 261.

This chapter proceeds as follows. First, we establish that rule-making in global trade governance is hierarchical. Second, we note changes in rule-making over the years. Some of this change resulted from a key mechanism identified by BPR: shifting geopolitical power – which has slowed multilateral negotiations and spurred regionalism. Yet, the origins of regionalism are the global trade rules themselves – the desire for regional exceptions in the GATT were exploited first by colonial powers, then by developing countries. Third, we argue that non-state actors are playing a growing role in rule creation. This is both a cause and consequence of the increasing number of non-trade issues taking center stage in trade negotiations. In short, the trade regime has become increasingly about more than trade – agreements now cover other issues ranging from intellectual property to labor rights to environmental regulation. This is due to systemic factors, such as the changing nature of trade, but also because of state strategy at the international and domestic level. As the scope of trade agreements has grown, the ability of non-state actors to influence content has grown. As a result, networks have become involved in aspects of non-trade rule creation as well as enforcement.

The Global Trade Regime as Hierarchy

In most areas of global governance the presence of a large, universal international organization designed by large states with consistent compliance would be sufficient to conclude that a hierarchical arrangement ruled the day. And for most of the post-Second World War era that would be a safe conclusion. Yet, it is worth reviewing how we come to this conclusion in the area of trade governance. After all, the GATT's enforcement mechanism was very diffuse (rather than centralized) and the GATT itself was not meant to be a large, universal international organization (IO) at its conception.[2] Despite these caveats the case for the GATT as a hierarchical governance structure is straightforward. Its development of a rule-based system has its origins in politics and the structure of international trade. In the wake of the Second World War and an earlier wave of global protectionism following the Smoot–Hawley tariff of 1930, the Allied nations pushed for the development of a multilateral trade organization. But while the Bretton Woods system successfully implemented an international arrangement for monetary policy, the proposed International Trade Organization (ITO) never came to fruition.

---

[2] Irwin 1995.

Instead the GATT, which began as a provisional agreement, created a rule-based system centered on the ideas of reciprocity and nondiscrimination through the most favored nation rule. It was agreed upon while negotiations for the more powerful ITO were also taking place. Eventually the United States blocked the creation of the ITO because it perceived its provisions as too far-reaching, placing too many restrictions on domestic economic policy. With the failure of the ITO, the GATT became the de facto governance institution for international trade.[3]

Although any state committing to GATT or WTO rules has been allowed to join, it was really the "big four" that wrote the rules themselves. The United States, the EU, Japan, and Canada have historically been the drivers of the multilateral governance process.[4] Barton et al. go so far as to argue that "the United States must be considered the most dominant state shaping GATT and WTO institutions over their history."[5]

How exclusive to large, powerful states was the rule-making in the GATT? According to Hoekman and Kostecki many developing countries did not even bother to send delegates to several of the GATT negotiation rounds of the 1960s and 1970s.[6] Moreover, as more developing states began to arrive and, in some cases, objected to new agreements proposed by wealthy states, the latter moved to adopt "codes" in areas such as anti-dumping, government procurement, and customs evaluations. These codes required only agreement among like-minded states and were not subject to the two-thirds majority vote of the GATT.[7] And while developing countries could join these side agreements in trade-related policies they had little input on their form. Barton and co-authors, reflecting on rule-making and formal institutions within the GATT and WTO, conclude that "the change in (global) power structure has not been accompanied by change in the GATT/WTO's fundamental constitutions rules or practices. Moreover, changes in rules and practices ... do not seem directly related to power shifts."[8]

Why would less powerful states agree to this arrangement? As emphasized by Baldwin, the bargain was to allow nonbinding rules for developing countries in exchange for their membership and an implicit promise to not object.[9] Under the principle of special and differentiated treatment developing countries who joined the GATT (and later the WTO) were granted access to developed country markets without needing to cut their

---

[3] For a history of the GATT and failed ITO, see Goldstein and Gowa 2002; Drache 2000.
[4] Baldwin 2014.   [5] Barton et al. 2006.   [6] Hoekman and Kostecki 2009.
[7] Hoekman and Kostecki 2009, 104.   [8] Barton et al. 2006, 13.   [9] Baldwin 2014.

own tariffs. In response, developing states played little role in rule development: as Baldwin labels the dynamic – "don't-obey-don't-object."[10]

In terms of content of rules of the multilateral trade system, governance within the GATT and the WTO was centered around specific reciprocity: those deviating from the rules to fairly apply tariff rates could be punished by aggrieved parties. Both the GATT and the WTO could hear disputes over the application of those punishments, which meant it had control over when negative reciprocity, the cornerstone of the agreement, was allowed. A dispute panel system was created to hear cases of alleged noncompliance. In theory countries could block the formation of panels or ignore their reports, yet few did.[11] While a sizable literature has now analyzed the reasons for disputes and their outcomes[12] most scholars agree that the panel system under the GATT worked surprisingly well, mimicking a domestic court system in many ways. The WTO's enforcement mechanism is stronger and more legalistic than the GATT's.[13] These quasi-judicial institutions are an important aspect of a hierarchical governance architecture. In our view both the GATT and WTO fit perfectly into BPR's definition of hierarchy regulating what "relations between relatively dependent actors and enforce the rules through command and force."[14] It is worth noting why the other two models are not applicable. Is trade governance about market mechanisms? One could imagine that, on its own, the reciprocity system could be described as market-based since it is relatively decentralized and there are no requirements to respond to all violations, leaving state members (as actors in the market) to decide their course of action. Yet, the dispute settlement system of the GATT and WTO governs the use of retaliation through reciprocity. So while there is no requirement to punish transgressions, and disputes may resolve themselves without the command of a hierarchical body like a court, there are rules governing this process.

This hierarchical (versus market-based) design choice for a trade regime is not surprising given the interwar period, where more diffuse cooperation mechanisms failed to contain a ruinous trade competition. Indeed, states vacillated between market and nonmarket trade-relevant policies in the interwar period, most prominently with the gold standard.[15] State intervention in markets became a political strategy spurred by political rivalry and geopolitical maneuvering, making a centralized agreement during this period unlikely. Yet, the lesson taken from the

---

[10] Baldwin 2014, 268.   [11] Hoekman and Kostecki 2009, 74; Hudec 2000.
[12] Busch 2000; Busch and Reinhardt 2003.   [13] Bello 1996; Steinberg 2004.
[14] See Introduction.   [15] See Chapter 2.

interwar period was that the antidote to beggar-thy-neighbor was a strong, cooperative, rule-based system.

It would be hard to claim that the interwar period was network-like. As Great Britain tied down its main trade partners in a series of bilateral trade deals, other powerful states followed suit.[16] The result was a web of trade (and currency) blocs. Yet it is a stretch to describe the relationships within these blocs or between them as network-like. There was no coordination between the blocs – they were explicitly in competition with one another and the larger states within them (especially Germany) used them to augment their economic and military power.[17] Each bloc was dominated by a great power that exerted strong control over (materially weaker) members. None of the core elements of the BPR definition of networks: "interdependent equal actors," "voluntary negotiat[ion]," "bargaining and persuasion," nor enforcement through "trust" are present in the interwar trade governance system. Rather, it resembled a highly fragmented hierarchy – a point we return to in the Conclusion.

After the war, not wanting to rely strictly on market-based mechanisms again, nor encourage exclusionary networks of agreements, states moved to centralize and coordinate state governance, eschewing the market mechanism in both trade and finance.[18] And while countries could operate outside the GATT's hierarchy (as the communist bloc did during the Cold War), the fact that the global trade regime was cheap to join and brought few significant demands on smaller and developing states paved the way for most states to accede to the GATT.

We argue in sections two and three, however, that the hierarchical nature of the multilateral regime is under threat. First, from regionalism and second, from the increasing scope of trade agreements. And while the exact nature of what could replace the hierarchy is not clear, it will likely involve regional agreements that are expansive in their governance ambitions.

Finally, it is worth noting what is different about the issue area of international trade that might help explain the state-centric nature of governance. At a basic level the collection of tariffs is a state function. Historically it is one of the most important functions of a state. Even in an era when tariffs no longer provide a large percentage of state income for developed economies, central governments have every incentive to oversee and control this process. For both economic and security reasons, regulation on the flow of goods across borders is traditionally a state prerogative.

[16] Gowa and Hicks 2013.   [17] Hirschman 1945.   [18] See Chapter 2.

Add to this the political economy insight that externalities from trade also drive incentives. Classically, we believe that the coordination of trade policies is much like a prisoner's dilemma: states have incentives to defect in the face of cooperation.[19] Specifically, states have incentives to impose unilateral import tariffs in order to improve their own terms of trade. In short, trade agreements are a cooperation game, not a coordination game. By establishing rules for mutual cooperation, monitoring, and punishing defections, a hierarchical trade organization can help states overcome this prisoner's dilemma. Governments thus keep a close eye (and a tight hold) on trade policy.

Challenges to Multilateral Rule-Making? The Rise of Regionalism

If economists and political scientists have expressed consternation about the postwar global trade regime, it has centered on one issue: regionalism. One of the major threats to the trade governance regime and its hierarchy is the proliferation of regional trade agreements.[20] This threatens to turn (or according to some has turned) a system dominated by a single, global IO to one governed by an irregular patchwork of regional treaties and organizations. This new world begins to look much more like a network of smaller hierarchies.

From where does this threat to the multilateral trade regime arise? We note two main factors – one of which is closely tied to a mechanism identified in the Introduction. First, the changing geopolitical distribution of power brought developing nations to the negotiating table for the first significant WTO round of talks in the 1990s. This changing balance of power slowed multilateral negotiations. Relatedly, these new developing states felt pressures to lead at the regional level (e.g., Brazil). Second, the GATT itself sowed the seeds of discord by granting a back door to regionalism. We discuss each of these factors in turn.

Geopolitics and Shifting Power

A vigorous literature has examined the causes of the expanding number of regional trade institutions. That expansion has been rapid and has continued rapidly since the mid-1990s.[21] Between 1950 and 1990 the number of Preferential Trading Arrangements (PTAs) rose from around a dozen to nearly fifty. Between 1991 and 2000, however, that number

---

[19] Bagwell and Staiger 1999.   [20] Bhagwati 1992.   [21] Mueller 2019.

skyrocketed to 200.[22] Some scholars point to the expanding number of democratic governments as an important factor;[23] others point to domestic veto players as a key determinant.[24] Others suggest a decline in American power and leadership is at work.[25] Still others suggest that contagion and demonstration effects play a significant role[26] as well as political–military relationships.[27] Economic factors, of course, play a role as well, whether it be the business cycle[28] or trade levels.[29]

Yet there is near consensus on the importance of one factor: fear of the collapse of the multilateral trading system. Regional arrangements serve as a backstop in the face of a declining global trade regime. Should negotiations to expand the coverage and rules of the WTO fail, trading partners can lock in trade deals with a regional pact.

The Uruguay round of GATT negotiations, which begat the WTO, lasted for eight years and involved 123 parties. By the close of those negotiations a "grand bargain" had been reached: wealthy states would drop barriers to goods from developing countries (mostly textiles and clothes) in exchange for the inclusion of provisions on intellectual property and trade in services.[30] Thus, the core states were able to push the agreement across the finish line, convincing developing countries that the agreement would be in their interests.

Beginning with the Seattle ministerial meeting in 1999, however, progress in WTO negotiations ground to a halt. Although some side agreements were reached in the early 2000s, the Doha Development Round of negotiations, launched in 2001, moved slowly, eventually stalling. Indeed, by 2015 many states were openly calling for an end to the Doha Round. The *Financial Times* declared in December 2015: "the Doha Round has finally died a merciful death."[31]

And while thousands of protesters in the streets of Seattle and the image of global citizens standing up to make their voices heard make a compelling narrative to explain the struggles of international trade negotiations, the core issues that have undermined the Doha Round involve tensions between the developed and the developing countries, including expanding intellectual property protections and cutting agricultural subsidies.[32]

Many observers blame American, Japanese, and EU insistence on keeping agricultural subsidies as a key stumbling block.[33] On one level

---

[22] Mansfield and Milner 2012.   [23] Mansfield et al. 2002.
[24] Mansfield et al. 2007; Mansfield and Milner 2012.   [25] Mansfield 1998.
[26] Yarbrough and Yarbrough 1992.   [27] Gowa 1994.   [28] Mattli 1999.
[29] Nye 1988.   [30] Odell 2006.   [31] *Financial Times*, December 21, 2015.
[32] Gallagher 2008.   [33] Wolfe 2015.

the wealthy countries attempted to convince the developing countries to trade better access to wealthy country markets in exchange for leaving some subsidies in place and setting binding tariffs for the developing world (thus ending the "don't-obey" part of the original deal). Yet, the newly powerful China, India, and Brazil led the charge against this bargain. Although these states had benefited from the GATT and WTO provisions they were not willing to allow binding tariffs while allowing the continued protection of wealthy state markets. Nor would they continue to accept wealthy country preferences concerning service sector rules.

Some have also pointed out that the intellectual property protections developing nations previously granted the developed economies had more detrimental effects than anticipated, including their ability to provide affordable drugs and combat health epidemics. Having learned their lesson from not asserting themselves on these issues, developing countries refused to allow wealthy countries to write the rules to which they would be bound without their input. As summarized by Wolfe: "the WTO, in common with most multilateral organizations, has not caught up with the shifting centre of gravity in global governance. The trading system is no longer a transatlantic bargain."[34]

Why were the developing countries able to assert more control in the Doha Round than the Uruguay Round? First and foremost they were much more economically powerful – in part because they played a much larger role in global trade in the early days of the WTO. Trade between developing economies has increased rapidly since the mid-1990s. China, in particular, was not at the table during the Uruguay Round, famously joining the WTO in 2001. China's, Brazil's, and India's trade fortunes improved dramatically after the creation of the WTO. Indeed, some scholars blame the political backlash over trade to China's entry into the multilateral trading system.[35] In this way the geopolitical power shifts led to tougher negotiations for the deepening of the global trade regime.

How did these negotiating dynamics matter for regionalism? First, as negotiations began to intensify in the Uruguay Round developing states gambled that they would fare better in groups than on their own. Indeed, regionally powerful states such as Brazil, Nigeria, South Africa, and India have all attempted to create regional trading systems to solidify their own power on top of a regional hierarchy while providing power in numbers to developing states versus wealthy states in multilateral trade negotiations. For example, as Brazil finished MERCOSUR negotiations with

[34] Wolfe 2015, 7.   [35] Autor et al. 2016.

its neighbors, a Brazilian official remarked: "Dealing directly with the U.S. on international trade issues is like getting into a cage with a tiger. Only if we have others in with us do we stand a better chance of getting some satisfactory results."[36] By aggregating their market power (and potentially trade expertise) developing countries use regional blocs as a tool of multilateral negotiations.[37]

This strategy has been pursued most aggressively by China. In fact, China's active pursuit of bilateral and regional trade agreements has been one of the key drivers of regionalism in recent years.[38] Since its WTO accession China has entered into more than fifteen trade agreements with both developed and developing economies. While some of these agreements are cross-regional, China's key focus has been on strengthening trade cooperation in the Asia-Pacific region. This is motivated largely by geopolitical concerns, with China seeking to take the lead in building regional cooperation in Asia as well as cementing its global position as a major power.[39]

Rising powers, especially China, realize that the WTO has been shaped by primarily by the US, EU, Japan, and Canada. While these emerging powers seek a place at the table of multilateral trade negotiations, they also realize that their influence in established trade organizations is limited. China's WTO accession conditions were more stringent than those of other developing economies. As a result, some Chinese officials have expressed frustration over the contrast between their economic power and their bargaining leverage within the WTO.[40] In regional trade forums, China's role as the dominant economic power allows it to shape institutional rules in accordance with its own preferences. Thus, by building regional cooperation in Asia, China is creating "alternative bargaining forums for Chinese trade diplomacy."[41] These preferences differ in many respects from those of the USA and EU. Notably, Chinese trade agreements tend to lack formal dispute settlement provisions, or environmental or labor provisions, and tend to favor flexible arrangements over strong legal commitments.[42]

Again, one consequence of this is the emergence of more coherent regional trade blocs that have similar within-group trade preferences and can ultimately bargain more effectively in multilateral trade forums.[43] As a number of authors have pointed out, China thus "aims to accelerate the emergence of a tripartite world between NAFTA [North

---

[36] Mansfield and Reinhardt 2003, 836.   [37] Lawrence 1996.   [38] JiangYu 2011.
[39] Kaczmarski 2017.   [40] Zeng 2010.   [41] Zeng 2010.
[42] Antkiewicz and Whalley 2005.   [43] Cheng-Chwee 2005.

American Free Trade Agreement], EU, and East Asian groups."[44] With China pursuing this strategy successfully, regionalism now has champions in the developed and developing world. The bad news for trade cooperation is that with this increasing global divergence in trade preferences, finding common ground in multilateral trade negotiations will likely be more difficult in the future.

Fear of rising Chinese economic and political influence may also push developed economies to be more cautious about further multilateral negotiations. The rising backlash against globalization in the United States and some European countries has been driven to a large degree by fears of Chinese economic dominance. This is heightened by China's status as an authoritarian regime that lacks transparency in the eyes of many Western economies.[45]

Second, regionalism provides a safety net in the case of failed multilateral trade negotiations[46] or in the case of weak enforcement at the multilateral level.[47] Should the multilateral trade regime falter, and there is global defection, the independent regional arrangements serve as a backstop to a collapse of key trading partnerships. This has been true not only for developing countries,[48] but the United States as well. During the Uruguay round of negotiations, for example, US Trade Representative Mickey Kantor suggested that growing American interest in regional trade agreements served as a market access strategy in case that round failed.[49]

Mansfield and Reinhardt outline both arguments, suggesting that "periodic multilateral trade negotiations (MTNs) sponsored by GATT/WTO can prompt members to enter PTAs as a means of guaranteeing they will not be left behind if the MTN stalls and of boosting their bargaining position in the multilateral talks."[50] Regionalism thus serves as an insurance policy against the failure of multilateralism. That failure materialized because of shifting power in the trade issue area. Moreover, regional agreements served as a tool for the developing world to aggregate their power, enhancing their bargaining leverage while simultaneously creating alternatives to multilateralism.

Institutional Design

A second factor contributing to regionalism has been discussed extensively in the economics literature: the permissive rules of the GATT in

---

[44] Cheng-Chwee 2005, 118.   [45] Chen et al. 2019.   [46] Whalley 1998.
[47] Bagwell and Staiger 2001.   [48] Perroni and Whalley 2000.
[49] Mansfield and Reinhardt 2003, 835.   [50] Mansfield and Reinhardt 2003, 830.

allowing the existence of regional arrangements. This factor does not fit neatly into the BPR list of causal mechanisms and indeed may only be relevant to the global trade regime. In short, what we have referred to as the core states in the GATT wanted to have their cake and eat it too. They desired a comprehensive multilateral trade agreement, yet they left a gaping hole: Article XXIV, which allows for regional customs union, free trade areas, and provisional regional arrangements.

Why did the founders of the multilateral trading system allow this loophole? Three theories are suggested in the literature. First, some believe that Article XXIV was a nod to developing countries to allow them to create their own regional trade systems.[51] If developing countries could not fully benefit from the GATT, perhaps they could become members while writing a set of their own rules. Because their markets were generally small compared to Europe, Japan, and the US, the threat from even discriminatory regional arrangements was small. A similar logic followed the adoption of the "enabling clause" in the 1979 Decision on Differential and More Favorable Treatment of Developing Countries. The enabling clause allows developing states to form regional trade agreements even if they violate Article XXIV.[52] Obviously, the nature of the economic "threat" from regional arrangement would change in the future.

In addition, recall that the GATT was supposed to be a temporary agreement – the main goal of the core states was passage of the Havana Charter to create the ITO. Core states expected more developing country resistance to the ITO as it contained stronger rules on trade and proposed to create an international currency. Ironically, however, the Havana Charter went unratified by the United States (in part because of its stronger regulatory rules and currency proposals).

Second, some scholars argue that desires for European integration motivated the inclusion of Article XXIV.[53] The emerging idea of the US Marshall Plan was to encourage postwar regional integration as a tool of both relief and war prevention. Indeed, some saw the eventual language of the plan as conditional on European efforts at economic integration. To have this policy goal consistent with the new global trade regime an exception had to be made – thus Article XXIV took shape.

Finally, Kerry Chase has dismissed both of these claims in favor of an argument that the United States designed Article XXIV to facilitate a significant trade agreement between the United States and Canada.[54] As Chase argues, Canada desired a non-customs union agreement with the

---

[51] Goldstein and Gowa 2002.   [52] Hoekman and Kostecki 2001, 355.
[53] Odell and Eichengreen 1998; Bhagwati 1991, 65.   [54] Chase 2006.

United States (so as not to threaten their position in the Commonwealth). But such tariff reduction agreements that did not include provisions concerning third parties, and were not part of the GATT or Havana Charter discussions. Thus, the US State Department "wished to adjust trade rules for preferential arrangements."[55] Ironically, the proposed US–Canada agreement never came to fruition and it would be nearly forty years until a bilateral agreement was reached between those two countries.

It is worth noting that, under the provisions of Article XXIV, the GATT (now WTO) has a right to pass judgment on any regional agreement. In theory, not any regional trade agreement is acceptable – the article demands that any non-multilateral arrangements significantly decrease tariffs between members while not discriminating against non-members.[56] Of course, of the hundreds of regional agreements notified to the GATT and the WTO only one arrangement has been officially condoned: the Czech–Slovak Customs Union which was created after those two countries emerged from Czechoslovakia.

This institutional design argument is important to explain the emergence of regionalism. Even if all of the pressures discussed in the subsection "Geopolitics" had gathered to push a regional trade agenda, in the absence of Article XXIV and the Enabling Clause to what end would those pressures have built? The desire for a backstop and more negotiating capacity provide the will; the institutional design provides the way.

These regional arrangements are themselves a form of hierarchy. While there are vast differences in design, effectiveness, and legalism among them,[57] all are state-centric, rule-based orders. The resulting governance system in global trade looks a bit like a many peaked tent, with the GATT/WTO forming the center, highest peak. Yet, that peak is surrounded by smaller peaks of regional arrangements. The ultimate question becomes: how much of a threat are these regional trade arrangements? Is the postwar global trade hierarchy under pressure?

A vigorous debate exists on this question in the trade and trade regimes literature. Some scholars see the multitude of regional arrangements as "building blocks" for advancing the multilateral trading system. Under this logic, regional arrangements and the liberalization they provide help tame the domestic interests and forces that would push against similar cuts in multilateral negotiations. If regional arrangements serve to lock in a state's best trading partners, extending tariff cuts to those partners who are less important should be straightforward.[58] Yet, many

---

[55] Chase 2006, 16.   [56] Hoekman and Kostecki 2001, 352.   [57] Dür et al. 2014.
[58] E.g. Estevadeordal et al. 2008.

do not see these regional arrangements as propitious for multilateralism, but rather view them as "stumbling blocks."[59] If states have their best partners locked in, say the critics, what incentive do they have to make any further cuts to minor partners? And because many of these regional agreements do allow discrimination against third parties, reducing those tariffs will be especially difficult. Finally, if regional arrangements were supposed to assist the multilateral process, why did the Doha Round die a long, quiet death after the explosion of regional agreements in the 1990s and 2000s?

Our reading of the literature is that the stumbling blocks argument has carried the day (especially against the empirical reality of the growing failure of multilateralism), although significant controversy remains. In short, the difficulty is establishing the counterfactual of what trade patterns would look like in the absence of regional trade agreements, especially flows with third parties. Trade agreements nearly always increase trade among participants, but the core question is whether they divert trade from nonmembers by raising tariffs on those goods. Scholars now tend to analyze this question on an agreement-by-agreement or country-by-country basis. In a widely cited study,[60] Limão shows that American free trade agreements (FTAs) have led to less generous multilateral tariffs on goods that are heavily imported under the FTAs. Moreover,[61] Limão contends that agreements with non-trade provisions, which we discuss in the next section, are particularly large stumbling blocks to multilateralism. And while this evidence is not uniform across countries or agreements, there is significant evidence that regionalism has been a substitute for multilateralism. We return to this question in the context of mega-FTAs in the Conclusion.

Challenges to Rule-Making: Non-trade Governance and Non-state Actors

Much to the chagrin of NGOs the GATT and WTO have remained largely closed to inputs from non-state actors. This has closed off the rule-making process from direct inputs into the multilateral process. Yet this conclusion seems to run afoul of the received wisdom that tariff-setting and trade deals are consistently influenced by firms and other non-state actors. Has the rise in the number of international actors, as identified by BPR, played no role in trade governance?

---

[59] Limão 2006; Bhagwati 1991; 2008.   [60] Limão 2006.   [61] Limão 2007.

We argue that at the level of the state and the regional agreement (versus multilateral governance), firms and NGOs can and do play a role in trade policy. Both economists and political scientists have generated significant theory and evidence to this end – usually under the heading of endogenous protection.[62] This has certainly influenced the goals and positions of states as they approach multilateral trade negotiations. Moreover, state leaders must be cognizant of the need for domestic ratification to approve any trade agreement.[63]

We argue there are two mechanisms that have led to the growing influence of non-state actors in trade governance: the changing nature of international trade and the use of trade agreements to address non-trade issues. The former is a partial, but incomplete, explanation of the latter, which also encompasses domestic political prerogatives.

In truth, non-trade provisions in trade agreements are not new – some pushed for these even in the early phases of trade liberalization after the Second World War. But these early attempts almost uniformly failed. The ITO itself failed partly because its advocates pushed for the inclusion of labor and employment standards that were thought to go too far beyond core trade issues.[64] While the GATT avoided these problems, it developed in the context of the Cold War and its evolution was shaped by security concerns.[65] Nonetheless, although trade agreements were never solely about trade liberalization, the main focus of early trade agreements was reciprocal tariff reduction.

The Changing Nature of International Trade

The changing nature of international trade itself is opening new opportunities for more network-oriented structures within international trade governance. Manufacturing has become more complex and regionally dispersed, with different production stages occurring in different countries or even regions. Typically, global production now uses technology from developed economies and cheaper labor from developing economies. Economists have pointed out that such an increase in "global value chains" or "supply chain trade" positively affects trade volume even if there is no change in tariffs.[66] For some this is evidence that traditional multilateral trade governance through the WTO is "eroding and will continue to erode."[67]

---

[62] Grossman and Helpman 1994; Gawande and Bandyopadhyay 2000.
[63] Mansfield et al. 2007.   [64] Drache 2000.   [65] Vogel 2013.   [66] Vogel 2013.
[67] Baldwin 2014, 281.

There are several implications of the expansion of global supply chains for trade governance. First, large multilateral corporations now have some of the highest stakes in trade negotiations and play a key role in lobbying.[68] Indeed, the current "favorite" economic model of international trade, new-new trade theory,[69] suggests that large firms are the driving force and beneficiary of trade liberalization. Most firms do not trade internationally, but for those that do access to supply chain linkages are vitally important. This comes at the expense of smaller, more local producers that do not benefit from economies of scale and political connections in multiple countries, forcing them into niche markets or driving them out of business.

Second, these large firms tend to be less concerned with tariff levels and more concerned with non-tariff regulatory issues such as labor standards, property rights, and dispute settlement procedures. Concerns about regulatory expropriation are of particular importance.[70]

As a result the rise of global value chains is associated with trade agreements that focus more frequently on non-trade issues. Supply chain trade integration requires significant domestic policy commitments by developing countries. Global firms are concerned with ensuring that these are implemented in the long run. Baldwin[71] argues that this leads to a "hold-up problem": developing countries have incentives to reverse commitments and expropriate foreign firms, especially stealing intellectual property, once these have made costly investments in their economies.[72] Fear of such expropriation then causes firms to underinvest in developing economies. How can firms, along with their home and host governments, solve this dilemma?

Baldwin suggests that this hold-up problem can best be solved through formal multilateral agreements.[73] But as previously discussed, developing countries have been hesitant to make multilateral commitments in the Doha Round. Thus, the home governments of large firms press bilateral and regional agreements, further eroding momentum toward multilateral liberalization.

The agreements are chock full of provisions with different goals, ranging from standard-setting, harmonization, and establishing regulatory norms,[74] to integrating different areas of liberalization such as services and financial liberalization.[75] As a result there is now much more issue linkage in trade agreements. Moreover, these non-trade provisions are mostly not covered by WTO rules, further robbing momentum of

---

[68] Osgood 2018.   [69] Melitz 2003.   [70] Hoekman and Nelson 2018.
[71] Baldwin 2014, 274.   [72] See also Carnegie 2014.   [73] Baldwin 2014.
[74] Hoekman and Nelson 2018.   [75] Milewicz et al. 2016.

multilateral negotiations. As a result trade negotiations have become centered around more complex, non-trade issues. This provides increased opportunities for non-state actors to coordinate, often through transnational networks, opening up opportunities for less hierarchical, more network-based trade governance. And while these firms and production networks may not have a formal seat at the WTO table, they can exert more influence in smaller, regional negotiations.[76] Coordination and standard-setting, property rights guarantees, and integration of trade, services, and movement of capital and investment have been key to recent agreements, more so than traditional reciprocal trade liberalization. The "new NAFTA," the United States–Mexico–Canada Agreement signed in 2018, is a case in point. What held up negotiations was not tariff levels but regulatory issues (intellectual property and labor rights guarantees) and dispute settlement procedures.

Thus the rise of global value chains has contributed to the decline of multilateral trade governance. Non-state actors in the form of large multinational corporations play a key role in the development of new types of trade networks. These are less hierarchical and potentially more network-based. In fact, the construction of global supply chain networks has given rise to trade relations among firms that most closely appropriate network-oriented structures in the area of trade. And while states still set the rules as sovereign equals within regional arrangements, their demands and constraints are directly shaped by these networked actors. This is all because global value chains have created a new form of global interdependence.[77]

Other Non-trade Issues in Trade Negotiations

Yet, the explosion of non-trade issues covered in trade agreements is not only a result from the changing nature of trade and the pressures from large multinational firms. Security concerns, human rights, labor rights, and the environment are not often the concerns of multinational firms negotiating trade deals. Non-trade issues of human rights and environmental protection in particular are driven by EU and US interests. States themselves bring many of these issues to the negotiating table – at times due to concerns over these issues, but also to help secure domestic ratification of any agreement that is reached.

What then explains the more recent success of non-trade provisions in trade agreements? The answer depends somewhat on the issue in

---

[76] Chase 2004.   [77] Farrell and Newman 2014.

question. For example, the spread of security cooperation linked to trade has followed somewhat different paths from that of human rights and environmental linkages.[78] Nevertheless, a number of general observations can be made about these rising linkages.

One obvious cause of the spread of non-trade provisions in trade agreements, as noted by Milewicz et al.,[79] is that prior trade agreements between states lower the cost of additional agreements with more far-reaching, non-trade provisions. Similarly, the inclusion of environmental or labor regulations in trade agreements paves the way for additional provisions in future agreements. This applies both to existing trade partners and to new partners seeking to enter into similar agreements.[80] Research suggests that trade agreements often copy or imitate the clauses and frameworks of existing trade agreements, especially those signed by the USA and the EU.[81] In other words, once non-tariff issues are included in an agreement it becomes highly likely that they will get adopted by other agreements signed by similar parties.

Relatedly, the inclusion of non-tariff issues subsequently lowers the cost of collective action for non-state actors, such as environmental or labor rights activists, who have a stake in trade negotiations. Recent years have seen a rising number of domestic actors with a stake in trade liberalization and more diverse interests represented in regional and bilateral trade negotiations. The inclusion of non-trade issues provides new opportunities for NGOs and other domestic groups to participate in the negotiation and monitoring of these agreements. Similarly, non-state actors can observe and learn from previous successes and consequently make their own activism more impactful.

One agreement that illustrates these dynamics and laid the foundation for the spread of non-trade issues in trade agreements was NAFTA, which was one of the first to include both labor provisions and environmental protection clauses. These provisions were shaped to a significant extent by non-state actors, such as environmental NGOs.[82]

At the same time, increasingly complex trade relations between states have also increased the need for better coordination across issue areas. States have learned lessons about the consequences of not coordinating over non-tariff issues. For instance, Hafner-Burton notes that the European Community struggled to find an appropriate response to the conflict in Yugoslavia in 1991. Since its existing trade agreement lacked human rights provisions, "the Community faced its neighbor's crisis with

---

[78] Powers 2004.   [79] Milewicz et al. 2016   [80] Milewicz et al. 2016, 749.
[81] Baccini et al. 2015.   [82] Aggarwal 2013; Vogel 2013.

no standard legal recourse to pull out from its obligations."[83] This experience contributed to the inclusion of human rights clauses in subsequent treaties involving the EU.

Similarly, controversial GATT disputes have sometimes been a motivator for environmental activism. For instance, in 1991 the USA tried to protect dolphins being killed by tuna fishing nets by banning tuna originating from Mexico where a particularly harmful fishing technique was common, but GATT subsequently found the United States to be in violation of GATT rules by imposing this ban. This controversial decision led to increased collective action on trade issues by environmental groups.[84] In their attempts to influence trade policy, activist groups frequently ally with other lobby groups. Environmental groups in particular have been known to join forces with importers.[85] From the point of view of economists, this leads to increased protectionist pressures, which is why economists tend to view trade agreements with environmental provisions as stumbling blocks for multilateral trade cooperation.[86] Finally, non-trade provisions are often included in trade agreements to ensure domestic ratification. By buying off potential veto players (e.g., labor or environmental NGOs) states include these provisions to convince key domestic actors to support (or at least not object to) agreements at the domestic level.[87]

What, then, have been the overall effects of the rise of non-trade issues on trade governance? The effects have been somewhat conflicting. Theoretically issue linkage potentially facilitates cooperation by increasing the bargaining space, making an agreement more likely. This issue linkage effect was no doubt the motivation of wealthy states using trade agreements in an attempt to influence domestic governance in trading partners. Given the clear ability of states to withhold the benefits of trade agreements in cases of violation of governance standards in areas such as human rights, this bundling of trade and non-trade issues gave wealthy states leverage.[88] The evolving, more complex nature of trade relations between states also necessitates increased issue linkage. Non-trade issues have opened avenues for activism for a greater number of actors – NGOs, firms, labor unions, etc. This allows for a wider range of actors to be involved in trade negotiations, and potentially opens room for less hierarchical, more network-based trade governance.

Yet there are also reasons to believe that the proliferation of non-trade issues can be a stumbling block to multilateral trade governance.

---

[83] E.g. Hafner-Burton 2009a, 35.   [84] Vogel 1999.   [85] E.g. Lechner 2016.
[86] Limão 2006.   [87] Mansfield and Milner 2012.   [88] Hafner-Burton 2009b.

Non-tariff issues are mostly addressed in bilateral and regional agreements, much less in multilateral institutions. As is widely recognized, some of these provisions, such as environmental protection and labor rights, can provide effective trade barriers and increase protectionism. On the other hand, trade and security linkages could motivate increased trade integration.

Finally, non-trade issues are not promoted equally by all states. As in other areas of trade integration, the development of non-trade clauses was driven primarily by the United States and the EU. Provisions often involve the Global North driving non-tariff issues to effect changes in the Global South.[89] One possible effect is that regions may be drifting further apart in their trade liberalization if some states prefer to stay away from some types of provisions, for example human rights. Moreover, recent studies provide evidence that groups of developing states have supported one another in multilateral trade negotiations against developed states on efforts to resist environmental provisions.[90] Thus the inclusion of security provisions is quite common in Asian PTAs but they contain far fewer environmental and human rights provisions.[91]

Implications and Conclusions

Many other chapters in this volume describe how various areas of global governance have already changed due to the mechanisms identified by BPR. In the area of global trade those changes have been slow and uneven. The hierarchical multilateral trade regime is under siege – from newly powerful state actors, from changing patterns of international trade, and from aggressive non-state actors. Will the multilateral system continue its slow death? And if so, will regional agreements take its place?

One could imagine, in the absence of progress on a hierarchical, multilateral agreement, reversion to something akin to the interwar architecture dominated by a combination of market mechanisms and networks. After all, prisoner's dilemmas can be overcome even in the absence of formal enforcement mechanisms if states interact repeatedly and care sufficiently about the future.[92] As countries become more integrated it may become more difficult for them to "defect" by imposing short-term barriers to trade. Moreover, countries today are relying less on tariff revenue. This potentially opens up avenues for more market-based trade governance.

---

[89] Aggarwal 2013.   [90] Johnson and Urpelainen 2020.   [91] Dür et al. 2014.
[92] E.g. Grossman 2017.

That said, there are reasons to believe that hierarchical organization will persist in the multilateral setting. First, the increasing complexity of trade relations makes coordination over the exact form that trade cooperation should take more important. Second, information provision is another function that a multilateral trade organization can play that cannot easily be met by purely market-based mechanisms. And lastly, participation in the WTO provides commitment mechanisms that allows states to credibly tie their hands with respect to domestic groups.

Some of these functions can no doubt be fulfilled by smaller, hierarchical regional trade agreements. And as we have emphasized, this may be the biggest source of concern for the multilateral trading system. Even in the era of growing nationalist economic policies, regionalism has momentum over multilateralism. To wit, the advent of mega-regional arrangements. Proposal such as the Transatlantic Trade and Investment Partnership (TTIP) and the Trans-Pacific Partnership (TPP) promise to link some of the largest economies in the world. Central to these mega-regional agreements are non-trade provisions, including regulatory coordination. In short, these agreements become vehicles for like-minded groups to move beyond tariff reductions on issues that do not get traction within the WTO. And even though the Trump administration moved away from these particular arrangements, they appear to be moving ahead with other states at the helm. And of course, these regionally based arrangements are hierarchical by nature.

Central to our argument is that these regional hierarchies are comparatively more likely to develop cracks for networks to open. The move to incorporate non-trade-related provisions in the trade regime has occurred at the regional level. Attempts to incorporate non-trade provisions at the WTO have largely foundered or are moving at a glacial pace. Thus, where networks are engaged in trade governance it is within the context of non-trade issues in regional agreements.

We would be remiss not to note that the decline of multilateralism has a come at a cost: some developing economies are left out, and are falling further behind states that can successfully leverage their position in supply chain trade. And while large international firms have gained a voice in trade governance, this voice is uneven, concentrated on firms located in the USA, EU, and Japan. Thus, these new emerging networks of actors still lack an important aspect of network-oriented governance structures: equality.

We have largely ignored the topic *du jure* among trade scholars: the rise of so-called populist nationalism and growing public opposition to multilateral and regional trade agreements. Signified by the election of Donald Trump, the passage of the Brexit referendum, and growing objections to the liberal order in Western nations, this is yet another factor that challenges the multilateral regime and regional trade arrangements.[93]

We would argue that the threats from regionalism and the influence of the changing structure of trade are far more important factors in predicting the future of trade governance. While public opposition to any trade agreement can make reaching an agreement more difficult, we would note that despite his protests to the contrary, even Donald Trump renegotiated one of the largest trade agreements in the USMCA. And while he pulled the United States out of the TPP, TTIP is still on the table. Moreover, if populism disappeared from the global scene, multilateral trade negotiations would still be a long slog. The changing distribution of global economic power, the changing nature of trade, and the proliferation of actors demanding input on rule-making will still exist. As would the challenge of regionalism.

References

Aggarwal, Vinod 2013. U.S. Free Trade Agreements and Linkages. *International Negotiation* 18: 89–110.

Antkiewicz, A. and J. Whalley. 2005. China's New Regional Trade Agreements. *World Economy* 28 (10): 1539–1557.

Autor, D.H., D. Dorn, and G.H. Hanson. 2016. The China Shock: Learning from Labor Market Adjustment to Large Changes in Trade. *Annual Review of Economics* 8: 205–240.

Baccini, Leonardo, Andreas Dür, and Yoram Z. Haftel. 2015. Imitation and Innovation in International Governance: The Diffusion of Trade Agreement Design. In *Trade Cooperation: The Purpose, Design and Effects of Preferential Trade Agreements*, edited by Andreas. Dür and M. Elsig, 167–194. Cambridge: Cambridge University Press.

Bagwell, Kyle and R.W. Staiger. 1999. An Economic Theory of GATT. *American Economic Review* 89 (1): 215–248.

   2001. Reciprocity, Non-discrimination, and Preferential Agreements in the Multilateral Trading System. *European Journal of Political Economy* 17 (2): 281–325.

Baldwin, Richard. 2014. WTO 2.0: Governance of 21st Century Trade. *The Review of International Organizations* 9 (2): 261–283.

Barton, John H., Judith L. Goldstein, Timothy E. Josling, and Richard Steinberg. 2006. *The Evolution of the Trade Regime: Politics, Law and Economics of the GATT and the WTO*. Princeton and Oxford: Princeton University Press.

Bello, Judith Hippler. 1996. The WTO Dispute Settlement Understanding: Less Is More. *The American Journal of International Law* 90 (3): 416–418.

Bhagwati, Jagdish. 1991. *The World Trading System Is at Risk*. Princeton: Princeton University Press.

---

[93] Copelovitch and Pevehouse 2019.

1992. Regionalism versus Multilateralism. *World Economy* 15 (5): 535–556.

2008. *Termites in the Trading System: How Preferential Agreements Undermine Free Trade*. Oxford: Oxford University Press.

Busch, Marc. 2000. Democracy, Consultation, and the Paneling of Disputes under GATT. *Journal of Conflict Resolution* 44 (4): 425–446.

Busch, M.L. and Eric Reinhardt. 2003. Developing Countries and GATT/WTO Dispute Settlement. *Journal of World Trade* 37 (4): 719–735.

Carnegie, Allison. 2014. States Held Hostage: Political Hold-Up Problems and the Effects of International Institutions. *American Political Science Review* 108 (1): 54–70.

Chase, Kerry A. 2004. From Protectionism to Regionalism: Multinational Firms and Trade-Related Investment Measures. *Business and Politics* 6 (2): 1–36.

Chase, Kerry. 2006. Multilateralism Compromised: The Mysterious Origins of GATT Article XXIV. *World Trade Review* 5 (1): 1–30.

Chen, Frederick R., Jon C.W. Pevehouse, and Ryan M. Powers. 2019. *Democracy and International Trade Policy Preferences*. Manuscript, University of Wisconsin.

Cheng-Chwee, Kuik. 2005. Multilateralism in China's ASEAN Policy: Its Evolution, Characteristics, and Aspiration. *Contemporary Southeast Asia: A Journal of International and Strategic Affairs* 27 (1): 102–122.

Copelovitch, Mark S. and Jon C.W. Pevehouse. 2019. International Organizations in a New Era of Populist Nationalism. *Review of International Organizations*.

Drache, Daniel. 2000. The Short but Significant Life of the International Trade Organization: Lessons for Our Time. Working Paper 62. Centre for the Study of Globalisation and Regionalisation, University of Warwick.

Dür, Andreas, Leonardo Baccini, and Manfred Elsig. 2014. The Design of International Trade Agreements: Introducing a New Dataset. *The Review of International Organizations* 9 (3): 353–375.

Estevadeordal, Antoni, Caroline Freund, and Emanuel Ornelas. 2008. Does Regionalism Promote External Trade Liberalization toward Nonmembers? *Quarterly Journal of Economics* 123 (4): 1531–1575.

Farrell, Henry and Abraham L. Newman. 2014. Domestic Institutions beyond the Nation-State: Charting the New Interdependence Approach. *World Politics* 66 (2): 331–363.

Gallagher, Kevin P. 2008. Understanding Developing Country Resistance to the Doha Round. *Review of International Political Economy* 15 (1): 62–85.

Gawande, Kishore and Usree Bandyopadhyay. 2000. Is Protection for Sale? A Test of the Grossman-Helpman Theory of Endogenous Protection. *Review of Economics and Statistics* 89: 139–152.

Goldstein, Judith and Joanne Gowa. 2002. US National Power and the Post War Trade Regime. *World Trade Review* 1 (2): 153–170.

Gowa, Joanne. 1994. *Allies, Adversaries, and International Trade*. Princeton: Princeton University Press.

Gowa, Joanne and Raymond Hicks. 2013. Politics, Institutions, and Trade: Lessons of the Interwar Era. *International Organization* 67 (3): 439–467.

Grossman, Gene. M. 2017. The Purpose of Trade Agreements. In *The Handbook of Commercial Policy*, edited by K. Bagwell and R.W. Staiger, 379–434. Amsterdam: North Holland.

Grossman, Gene M. and Elhanan Helpman. 1994. Protection for Sale. *American Economic Review* 84 (4): 833–850.

Hafner-Burton, Emilie M. 2009a. The Power Politics of Regime Complexity: Human Rights Conditionality in Europe. *Perspectives on Politics* 7 (1): 33–38.

2009b. *Forced to be Good: Why Trade Agreements Boost Human Rights.* Ithaca, NY and London: Cornell University Press.

Hirschman, Albert O. 1945. *National Power and the Structure of Foreign Trade.* Berkeley and Los Angeles: University of California Press.

Hoekman, Bernard and Douglas Nelson. 2018. Twenty-First-Century Trade Agreements and the Owl of Minerva. *Annual Review of Resource Economics* 10: 161–183.

Hoekman, Bernard and Michel Kostecki. 2009. *The Political Economy of the World Trading System,* 3rd edition. Oxford: Oxford University Press.

Hoekman, Bernard M. and Michel Kostecki. 2001. *The Political Economy of the World Trading System: WTO and Beyond,* 2nd edition. Oxford and New York: Oxford University Press.

Hudec, Robert E. 2000. *Essays on the Nature of International Trade Law.* London: Cameron May.

Irwin, Douglas A. 1995. The GATT in Historical Perspective. *The American Economic Review* 85 (2): 323–328.

JiangYu, Wang. 2011. China and East Asian Regionalism. *European Law Journal* 17, (5): 611–629.

Johnson, Tana and Johannes Urpelainen. 2020. The More Things Change, the More They Stay the Same? Developing Countries' Unity at the Nexus of Trade and Environmental Policy. *Review of International Organizations* 15: 445–473.

Kaczmarski, Marcin. 2017. Non-Western Visions of Regionalism: China's New Silk Road and Russia's Eurasian Economic Union. *International Affairs* 93 (6): 1357–1376.

Lawrence, Robert Z. 1996. *Regionalism, Multilateralism, and Deeper Integration.* Washington, DC: Brookings Institution.

Lechner, Lisa. 2016. The Domestic Battle over the Design of Non-trade Issues in Preferential Trade Agreements. *Review of International Political Economy* 23 (5): 840–871.

Limão, Nuno. 2006. Preferential Trade Agreements as Stumbling Blocks for Multilateral Trade Liberalization: Evidence for the U.S. *American Economic Review* 96 (3): 896–914.

2007. Are Preferential Trade Agreements with Non-trade Objectives a Stumbling Block for Multilateral Liberalization? *Review of Economic Studies* 74 (3): 821–855.

Mansfield, Edward D. 1998. The Proliferation of Preferential Trade Agreements. *Journal of Conflict Resolution* 42 (5): 523–543.

Mansfield, Edward D. and Eric Reinhardt. 2003. Multilateral Determinants of Regionalism: The Effects of GATT/WTO on The Formation of Preferential Trading Agreements. *International Organization* 57 (4): 829–862.

Mansfield, Edward D. and Helen V. Milner. 2012. *Votes, Vetoes, and the Political Economy of International Trade Agreements*. Princeton: Princeton University Press.

Mansfield, Edward D., Helen V. Milner, and Jon C.W. Pevehouse. 2007. Vetoing Cooperation: The Impact of Veto Players on Preferential Trading Agreements. *British Journal of Political Science* 37 (3): 403–432.

Mansfield, Edward D., Helen V. Milner, and B. Peter Rosendorff. 2002. Why Democracies Cooperate More: Electoral Control and International Trade Agreements. *International Organization* 56 (3): 477–513.

Mattli, Walter. 1999. *The Logic of Regional Integration*. Cambridge: Cambridge University Press.

Melitz, Marc J. 2003. The Impact of Trade on Intra-industry Reallocations and Aggregate Industry Productivity. *Econometrica* 71 (6): 1695–1725.

Milewicz, Karolina, James Hollway, Claire Peacock, and Duncan Snidal. 2016. Beyond Trade: The Expanding Scope of the Nontrade Agenda in Trade Agreements. *Journal of Conflict Resolution* 62 (4): 743–773.

Mueller, Susanne. 2019. *Authoritarian Politics and Trade Policy*. PhD dissertation, University of Wisconsin-Madison.

Nye, Joseph S. 1988. Neorealism and Neoliberalism. *World Politics* 40 (2): 235–251.

Odell, John S. 2006. *Negotiating Trade: Developing Countries in the WTO and NAFTA*. New York: Cambridge University Press.

Odell, John S. and Barry Eichengreen. 1998. The United States, the ITO, and the WTO: Exit Options, Agent Slack, and Presidential Leadership. In *The WTO as an International Organization*, edited by Anne O. Kruger, 181–209. Chicago and London: University of Chicago Press.

Osgood, Iain. 2018. Globalizing the Supply Chain: Firm and Industrial Support for US Trade Agreements. *International Organization* 72 (2): 455.

Perroni, Carlo and John Whalley. 2000. The New Regionalism: Trade Liberalization or Insurance? *Canadian Journal of Economics* 33 (1): 1–24.

Powers, Kathy L. 2004. Regional Trade Agreements as Military Alliances. *International Interactions* 30 (4): 373–395.

Steinberg, Ron H. 2004. Judicial Lawmaking at the WTO: Discursive, Constitutional, and Political Constraints. *The American Journal of International Law* 98 (2): 247.

Vogel, David. 1999. *The Politics of Trade and Environment in the United States*. Working Paper 94. Berkeley: Berkeley Roundtable on the International Economy, University of California, Berkeley.

——— 2013. Global Trade Linkages: National Security and Human Security. In *Linking Trade and Security: Evolving Institutions and Strategies in Asia, Europe, and the United States*, edited by Vinod K. Aggarwal and Kristi Govella, 23–48. New York: Springer Verlag.

Whalley, John. 1998. Why Do Countries Seek Regional Trade Agreements? In *The Regionalization of the World Economy*, edited by Jeffrey A. Frankel, 63–90. Chicago and London: University of Chicago Press.

Wolfe, Robert. 2015. First Diagnose, then Treat: What Ails the Doha Round? *World Trade Review* 14 (1): 7–28.

Yarbrough, Beth V. and Robert M. Yarbrough. 1992. *Cooperation and Governance in International Trade: The Strategic Organizational Approach*. Princeton: Princeton University Press.

Zeng, Ka. 2010. Multilateral versus Bilateral and Regional Trade Liberalization: Explaining China's Pursuit of Free Trade Agreements (FTAs). *Journal of Contemporary China* 19 (66): 635–652.

5 The Humanitarian Club
Hierarchy, Networks, and Exclusion

Michael N. Barnett

Does humanitarian governance resemble a hierarchy, market, or network mode of governance? Many of the most enduring and endearing descriptions of humanitarianism map onto a network approach.[1] This is a humanitarian community whose members aspire to save as many lives as possible. Idealized network characteristics are functional for the situations they confront and their principled commitments. Networks are superior to markets and hierarchies when addressing complex, fluid problems – which give complex emergencies their very name – because they facilitate nimble, flexible collective action. Networks also aspire to principles of democracy, egalitarianism, and equality, which match humanitarian principles. Other perspectives, though, use market metaphors and mechanisms to understand humanitarian governance.[2] Importantly, these writings tend to emphasize how markets introduce perverse incentives to aid agencies and drive ineffective and dysfunctional outcomes. In this view, aid agencies are like firms that care about their bottom line, compete for scarce resources, and respond to a contracting environment that generates incentives that can shift the organization's interests from the survival of those in need to its own survival.[3] Humanitarianism is also not a market with lots of firms competing against each other, but rather an oligopoly with a few states, UN agencies, and international nongovernmental organizations (INGOs) at the top.[4] And as an oligopoly, it resembles a hierarchy. An additional perspective on hierarchy is provided by a critical literature that traces humanitarianism's origins and workings to colonialism and paternalism, with Western actors doing what they can and Southern NGOs and affected populations accepting what they must.[5]

This chapter argues that contemporary humanitarian governance is best understood as a club that combines features of both networks and

---

[1] Ramalingam 2014; Collinson 2016, 4; Currion 2018; UN OCHA 2012.
[2] Gottwald 2010; Bennett 2018; and Carbonnier 2015.   [3] Cooley and Ron 2002.
[4] Weiss 2013; Minear and Smilie 2004.   [5] Barnett 2011.

hierarchy. Most applications of the club concept to governance derive from a political economy perspective, and are akin to Miles Kahler's chapter on cartels (Chapter 2), highlighting the benefits to individual actors when a small group of states produce a collective good for themselves or regulate a global problem.[6] In contrast, I develop a sociological alternative. Four overlapping concepts are central to this exercise: field, elite, capital, and durable inequality. The field is a collection of actors that have a common understanding of the field's shared purpose, its rules, and basic practices. It is often created by a selective group that becomes the elite. Elites not only control the preponderance of resources but they also have the "right stuff" that qualifies them to be part of the elite and exclusive clubs. Following Bourdieu and others, this "right stuff" is capital, which has four forms: economic (money), symbolic (identity), social (trust), and cultural (knowledge). Capital in the right kinds and the right amounts provides entrée into the right clubs, and the right clubs also confers status on its members. There is stratification in the club, as there are even in those communities that aspire to egalitarian principles, but they nevertheless have the characteristics of a network. But the club distinguishes insiders from outsiders and has considerable authority to set the rules in its area of governance and consumes most of the resources, leaving outsiders often in the cold. The forms of capital and the mechanisms of inclusion and exclusion help to explain the considerable durable inequality that exists within a sphere of governance. Club governance is something of a double entendre: it is "clubby" for its members but can be a force against outsiders.

I apply this argument to humanitarian governance as follows. The first section provides a brief sketch of humanitarianism prior to the 1990s, best characterized as a largely local effort with growing involvement by undertrained international actors that marched to the beat of their own drum. The second section examines the post-Cold War evolution of a club that has the characteristics of a network on the inside and hierarchy on the outside. The primary driver of the change is the rising incidence of and attention to humanitarian emergencies by Western states and the UN. A handful of Western states, UN agencies, and leading Western-based INGOs began to form an exclusive elite that helped to set the rules and build the infrastructure of the humanitarian sector. This elite formed a Humanitarian Club with network-like characteristics, and members had the right kind of capital in the right amount. Although the Club

---

[6] For great power club: Carranza 2017; Larson 2018. For nuclear club: Bell 2015. For G7 and G20: Brandi 2019. For financial club: Tsingou 2015. For climate club: Nordhaus 2015; Falkner 2016. For trade club: Lamp 2016.

professed that the humanitarian sector was a community and operated on egalitarianism principles in the spirit of partnership, in practice relations between the Club and outsiders resembles a hierarchy. The much more numerous, Southern agencies became rule-takers and subcontractors, and received a pittance of the resources even though they are the first responders to emergencies and do the bulk of the work that affect their communities. Even worse, when the Western agencies come to town they often smother and displace local efforts.[7] This West casts a giant "shadow of hierarchy."

The third section explores the resilience of the Humanitarian Club and the durable inequality in the humanitarian field. For the last two decades there have been periodic field-wide efforts to change patterns of inclusion and exclusion and shift authority from the West to the South. These efforts are often prompted by claims, from both inside and outside the Club, that humanitarianism is not as effective and legitimate as it might be because of the concentration of power in the hands of a small number of Western-based actors. But they have largely come to naught. One reason for the resilience of the Club is the individual and collective self-interest of its members. Yet a closer look at capital illuminates the structural forces that work to reproduce the status quo but that cannot be traced back to the intentions of privileged actors. Interests are entangled with cultural beliefs that warn against shifting authority to the South for various reasons, including the fear that Southern actors do not have the capacity to act in the best interests of the victims. The Conclusion considers several factors that might push for greater inclusion and the possible that its appearance might mask the continued existence of hierarchy.

The Rise of the Humanitarian Club

Contemporary humanitarian governance arose from three relatively independent historical origins: abolitionism, missionary activity, and colonialism (saving lives and societies); nineteenth-century European wars and the First and Second World Wars (saving soldiers and civilians); and decolonization and the rise of development (moving from relief to reconstruction and welfare).[8] After the Second World War they began to integrate into a humanitarianism that had four defining elements. Humanitarianism was generically defined as providing relief to distant strangers, but relief provision came from the West and went to

---

[7] Christian Aid, Save the Children, and Humanitarian Accountability Partnership 2013.

[8] For a review of the history of humanitarianism see Barnett 2011.

the South. This growing activity sometimes supplemented local practices of relief, but often they ran roughshod over them, much to their detriment and to that of the local moral economy.[9] Whereas once humanitarianism was largely dominated by private, voluntary organizations, after the Second World War it became supplanted by the United Nations, Western donors, and Western-funded INGOs. Lastly, aid agencies went from one emergency to another, reinventing the wheel as they did. There were no standard operating procedures, codes of conduct, or formal or informal rules that created a template for action. Many volunteers were trained in emergency medicine and public health, but many others had little or no experience, jumping into the fray believing that all they needed was a can-do attitude and good intentions. INGOs rarely coordinated their activities with each other or with local and national institutions.[10]

The end of the Cold War can be read as either the transformation or the beginning of humanitarian sector: this was the moment when the rather unorganized and motley set of aid agencies began to develop some coherence, coordination, and sets of rules to improve their effectiveness. Various factors produced more demand for and supply of humanitarian governance. The hope was that the end of the Cold War would produce a kinder, gentler world order. For some it did. For others, though, it unleashed once relatively contained and submerged conflicts, producing "new" wars that were creating mass refugee flights, killing, and suffering. With more emergencies than ever before there was a greater demand for emergency relief, leading to more kinds of interventions by more kinds of actors. An increasingly active UN Security Council, working with an expanded notion of international peace and security, began authorizing others to intervene and doing so itself on an unprecedented scale. In response to many actions without structures, in December 1991 the UN passed UNGA/RES/46/182, which put into place many of the crossbeams for the humanitarian sector. States began to pour more money into humanitarian operations, which were funneled through increasingly well-funded international organizations (IOs) and nongovernmental organizations (NGOs). Sometimes states provided more than money, as they used their militaries to move mountains of aid and protect aid workers on the ground. Many existing NGOs got bigger, and a growing number of emergencies and an expanding level of resources grew the population of aid agencies. This rapid and impressive growth, though, meant that there were more actors descending on an emergency than

---

[9] Boateng 2018.   [10] Boateng 2018; Juma and Suhrke 2002.

ever before, creating more confusion than effective action on the ground. More was not better. In response, a handful of the leading states, UN agencies, and NGOs began to try and develop coordination mechanisms, common rules, standards, codes of conduct, and other regulatory guidelines.[11]

Humanitarianism began to develop the qualities of a field: "a collection of actors that interact with one another on the basis of shared (which is not to say consensual) understanding about the boundaries and purpose of the field, relationships to others in the field, and the rules governing legitimate action."[12] Before discussing the elements, it bears emphasizing that the boundaries and rules of the field are openly and continuously contested, fueled by principled differences and self-interest, for the winning side can gain resources and status.[13] Nevertheless, fields have several defining qualities.

First, members of the field have a shared understanding of its purpose and what is at stake.[14] For those in the humanitarian field it is a humanitarian imperative – action should be taken to prevent or alleviate human suffering arising out of disaster or conflict, and nothing should override this principle.[15] In other words, at stake are lives and humanity itself. The humanitarian imperative is intertwined with principles that shape how humanitarianism is supposed to be done. Four principles have become central.[16] Humanity, which commands attention to all people. Impartiality, which requires that assistance be based on need and not discriminate on the basis of nationality, race, religion, gender, or political opinion. Neutrality, which demands that humanitarian organizations refrain from taking part in hostilities or from any action that either benefits or disadvantages the parties to the conflict. And independence, which means that financial and other forms of assistance should not be connected to any of the parties directly involved in armed conflicts or who have a vested interest in the outcome. These principles are both constitutive and regulative. They help to define what humanitarian *is*. They also helped aid agencies get access to victims. If combatants and others with authority and arms perceive aid agencies as helping victims alone, then they are more likely to get access. The moment they are perceived as having ulterior motives they risk losing their humanitarian space and become suspects and targets.

---

[11] Barnett 2005; Kennedy 2019; Krause 2013; Roth 2016.
[12] Fligstein and McAdam 2012, 9.
[13] Fligstein and McAdam 2012, 10, 15; Emirbayer and Johnston 2008, 6; Kauppi and Madsen 2014.
[14] Bourdieu and Wacquant 1992; Jenkins 1992, 84.   [15] Sphere Project 2018, 28.
[16] Sphere Project 2018, 6; Pictet 1979; Weiss 1999.

Second, and related, fields have rules to define what counts as legitimate and effective action. These rules can evolve without a guiding hand, but often leading actors gather in formal settings to debate, define, and revise what counts as competent and legitimate action. In response to their own desire to improve their effectiveness and pressure from donors, INGOs played a leading role in establishing the rules governing relief, including voluntary minimum standards of care and accountability to affected populations. Their debates and decisions fed into sector-wide discussions, often occurring at the UN, between states, UN agencies, and a handful of INGOs, resulting in the adoption and revision of new rules and reform initiatives such as the Humanitarian Response Review in 1995 and the "transformational agenda" in 2005.[17] The process of creating rules for legitimate action led to a growing rationalization of the field, which has several dimensions. It includes developing methodologies for calculating results, abstract rules to guide standardized responses, and procedures to improve efficiency in identifying the best means to achieve specified ends. It includes bureaucratization, with growing specialization, spheres of competence, and standardization to drive means–ends calculations. And it includes professionalization, with a growing demand for expertise both in individual fields of intervention such as sanitation and in humanitarianism more generally.[18] The concerted effort to rationalize the field began in the mid-1990s, and because of two major factors. Aid workers began to confront soul-shaking failures in places like Rwanda, leading them to question their professionalism and knowledge. From then on aid agencies began to chant the mantra "do no harm" and acknowledge that emergency relief was no place for amateurs. Donors also began to insist on specialized knowledge and to know that their money was being well spent with evidence to prove it – or risk their funding.

Third, a field can, and usually does, consist of actors of different kinds – firms, states, NGOs, and so on. States, IOs, and INGOs have dominated the humanitarian field. Over the last fifteen years other kinds of actors have become more involved, including corporations, philanthropies and foundations, faith-based organizations, local NGOs, and diaspora networks. But states and their IOs, and INGOs, continue to dominate the field. Not all actors, moreover, necessarily play the same role; that is, there can be differentiation. For instance, states and their militaries have their role, such as funding, delivery, and protection; IOs have their role, such as legitimation and coordination; and NGOs have

---

[17] Walker and Maxwell 2008; Maxwell and Gelsdorf 2019.
[18] Barnett 2005; Kennedy 2019; Krause 2013.

their role, such as the delivery of assistance. These actors do not always agree on the limits of their role and the boundaries between them. Such friction has been most manifest in the relationship between aid agencies and military forces. Militaries sometimes take it upon themselves to provide aid for various reasons – because they can, because there is a need, and because they want to win hearts and minds. Aid agencies, though, worry that such relief and development activities will complicate their ability to deliver relief, because they will be perceived as sharing the military's concern with winning wars.

The relatively exclusive group of states, IOs, and INGOs that were creating a field also were becoming an elite. Fields almost always have elites, whose signature characteristic is the "vastly disproportionate control over or access to a resource … that advantage them."[19] Because of their advantages and privileges, elites often become a ruling or dominant class with a common outlook and interest in preserving the status quo. Moreover, these elites often interact, network, and circulate in overlapping and interlocking institutions that reflect and reinforce their exclusive standing and serve their common interests.[20]

The humanitarian elite includes three kinds of actors: states, UN agencies, and INGOs. A few donors provide the bulk of the official assistance. The top three – the U.S., the European Community, and the United Kingdom – provide almost 50 percent of all aid, and the inclusion of other Western donors brings the total to 87 percent. The remaining 13 percent is divided between Turkey (the second largest donor and largely because of the Syrian crisis), the Gulf states, China, Brazil, and a few other countries; these are often referred to as "new" or "nontraditional" donors. At least for the moment the Gulf countries and China have not participated in these sector-wide associations. Money does not just buy membership – it also buys influence. Many of the rules of the humanitarian sector, especially those dealing with funding and financial accountability, are dictated by states. A handful of UN agencies are part of all discussions pertaining to humanitarian action, and they are members of the highly influential Inter-Agency Standing Committee (IASC): it is chaired by the head of the Office of the Coordinator of Humanitarian Affairs (OCHA) and includes the World Food Program, United Nations High Commissioner for Refugees and five other specialized UN agencies. Standing invitees include the World Bank, International Committee of the Red Cross, the International

---

[19] Khan 2012, 362. Also see Mills 2000; Therborn 2008; Domhoff 1994; Mosca 1939; Bell 1958; Pakulski 2012; Farazmand 1999.
[20] Collinson 2016, 1.

Federation of the Red Cross, the International Council of Voluntary Agencies, and the Office of the High Commissioner of Human Rights. There are thousands of INGOs, but the major INGOs can be counted on two hands. Five – Doctors without Borders, World Vision International, International Rescue Committee, Oxfam, and Save the Children – collect about one-third of the available aid. The top-ten agencies, including Mercy Corps, Christian Aid, Action in Aid, Norwegian Refugee Council, and International Rescue Committee, bring the total to over 70 percent. Other Western-based agencies scoop up nearly all the rest. Local NGOs receive below 2 percent of all direct aid (and less than 1 percent according to some sources). Or, according to another figure, of the $20 billion available in 2016, local organizations received a minuscule $129 million.[21]

Elites are distinguished by their preponderant control over resources, which can be understood as capital. It takes capital to become a member of an exclusive club. Bourdieu and others have proposed four forms of capital.[22] Economic capital includes wealth, income, and property. For aid agencies this is primarily about funding. Symbolic capital concerns being held in esteem and conferred honor. In the aid world, organizations and individuals often achieve such recognition for claiming fealty to the fundamental principles of humanitarianism and serving nobly in the field, and especially in the major, landmark emergencies (even in operations that are subsequently labeled a "failure"). Social capital derives from relations of acquaintance and familiarity. Friendships and "bands of brothers" are formed between aid workers in emergencies, which can be strengthened in their ongoing sector-wide meetings and debates about humanitarian governance. Western aid workers often have comparable experiences and reference points, speak English and the jargon, and generally have a comfort level with each other that is not easily achieved between Western and Southern aid workers.

Cultural capital refers to educational achievement and credentials.[23] A rationalized world produces specialized knowledge and the category of the "expert," an actor who is perceived to possess specialized skill and knowledge about an area of life. Although expertise can be achieved through experience and practice, in modern society the emphasis is on formal education, training, and credentials.[24] Specialized knowledge is

---

[21] These numbers are drawn from various sources, including Humanitarian Outcomes; Development Initiatives; the Global Public Policy Institute; OCHA; Els and Carstensen 2015; Mowjee et al. 2017.

[22] Bourdieu 2011; Jenkins 1992; Pouliot 2016; Swartz 2012.   [23] Brint 1996.

[24] Brint 1996; Collins and Evans 2007; Boswell 2009, 23–24.

not esoteric or ideographic. Instead it is generalizable knowledge – it can travel from one case to another because of the systematic consideration and structured comparison across different contexts. Such knowledge has the added advantage of being more objective and less prone to subjective judgments, mistaken analogies, or personal experience. Although humanitarianism has stressed the importance of volunteerism, which sometimes translates into amateurism, humanitarianism has always benefited from expertise in the fields of medicine, public health, and the health sciences. Over the last two decades the field has become more specialized with a greater demand for expertise in a range of domains, including logistics, human resources, information technology, engineering, policy analysis, grant writing, evaluation, and security.[25] As Sending perceptively observes, "humanitarian relief is already made up of a range of specialized professional actors … What unites these different specialties is the distinct attributes of a humanitarian situation in which these different professionals work, in particular the stress on working in difficult, often extreme, situations to save lives."[26] In addition, humanitarianism has become a profession unto itself, defined by the kinds of demands imposed by the specifics of a humanitarian setting.[27] There are now stand-alone master's programs, web-based certificates, and other outlets for specialized and credentialed training in humanitarian action.

The concept of capital introduces four additional claims that are relevant for understanding relations within the group and with outsiders. Capital is not a thing but rather is a social relation and thus helps generate hierarchy, patterns of inclusion and exclusion, and positions of superiority and inferiority. Second, the value of capital can change depending on the underlying field and social structure. In other words, the field assigns value to the capital. For instance, modern society is a "credentialed" society, in which knowledge and expertise has become more highly valued relative to two centuries ago.[28] Symbolic capital, to the extent that it is constituted by honor and esteem, might be less valuable today than a century ago. In an article written four decades ago on the concept of honor, the eminent sociologist Peter Berger opened by comparing it to chastity in terms of its "unambiguously outdated status."[29] Third, because a changing field can produce changing values of capital, the exchange rate between forms of capital can shift. Honor might be less valuable than specialized knowledge in the modern economy. Fourth, capital is central to the struggle for

---

[25] Krause 2013.   [26] Sending 2017, 67.   [27] Walker and Russ 2009.
[28] Collins 1979.   [29] Berger 1970, 339.

dominance, status, and authority. And, in fact, what forms of capital are most valuable will itself be a site of struggle.[30]

Elites and those with capital and status often form clubs. Clubs, generically speaking, are an association of actors with shared interests. There are rugby clubs, garden clubs, literary clubs, knitting clubs, service clubs, swimming clubs, country clubs, officers' clubs, metropolitan clubs, and on and on. But, as this list suggests, not all clubs are the same, differing in purpose, relationship to outsiders, barriers to entry, and other assorted matters. The sorts of clubs that most interest students of global governance are those that govern not just themselves but also others, limit membership to those with the right stuff, and enjoy private benefits, even for clubs whose purpose is to serve others.

A political economy approach dominates the literature on global governance. Economists define a club as "a voluntary group deriving mutual benefits from sharing one or more of the following: production costs, the members' characteristics, or a good characterized by excludible benefits."[31] In this perspective, clubs are formed by actors to generate "club" benefits – that is, benefits that could not be generated individually. These benefits can be individual welfare, satisfaction, well-being, or wealth. The political economy perspective also emphasizes how membership is usually limited to ensure club benefits. Said otherwise, clubs provide benefits that cannot be achieved individually, but there comes a point of saturation, diminishing returns, and increasing costs. Swim clubs have this characteristic, which is why they cap how many families can belong and why families often pay high fees to join rather than go to much less expensive public pools. But other sorts of clubs generate private and quasi-public goods. These are the sorts of clubs that most concern students of global governance because they act like a quasi-governor.[32] Members of international trade and financial clubs, for instance, will establish rules to regulate non-members to create collective goods that typically generate benefits that favor them.[33] Some of the proposed climate clubs represent a form of minilateralism as a select group of states to establish rules that are intended to regulate a quasi-public good.

Whereas the political economy approach starts and ends with *homo economicus*, the sociological approach weaves a normative dimension into group life.[34] Before identifying the differences, I want to stress three shared claims: actors are often motivated to form and join clubs for

---

[30] Emirbayer and Johnston 2008, 6.
[31] Sandler 2013, 267; Buchanan 1965. Also see Prakash and Gugerty 2010.
[32] Keohane and Nye 2002.   [33] Tsingou 2015.
[34] Tsingou 2015, 225–256; Emirbayer and Johnson, 2008, 6.

self-interested reasons and to achieve benefits and produce collective outcomes that they could not achieve on their own; clubs create mechanisms of exclusion, and often do so to protect their stream of benefits; and clubs establish rules that regulate not just the actions of their members but also the wider community.

The sociological approach, though, adds several features that are quite familiar to anyone who has ever tried to gain admission or belonged to an exclusive club. Whereas the political economy approach limits motives to material interests, the sociological approach includes nonpecuniary, charitable, and philanthropic reasons for joining. Many service clubs have this attribute, as do many international groupings and associations that are designed to help others, including the Humanitarian Club. Of course, self-interest is present in everything actors do, and this includes the desire to join even the most altruistic clubs whose explicit goal is to serve others. Whereas the political economy approach emphasizes that being admitted to the club is based primarily on the ability to contribute to the collective good, a sociological approach allows for other criteria. New members must have the "right stuff." Sometimes it is money, but it can also include the right breeding and background, culture, gender, racial, religion, or educational credentials.[35] In other words, it includes all four forms of capital.[36] Whereas the political economy approach tends to presume group solidarity is maintained by selective incentives, the sociological approach recognizes how a club contains social relations that produce a club identity and mutual belonging that can become the ties that bind.[37] These integrative processes are particularly evident in socializing mechanisms that are responsible for assimilating new members, producing a common culture, and creating a high degree of trust.[38] They often are "Good Old Boy Networks" in the truest sense of the phrase.[39] This common culture produces common outlooks and even "inside" humor; see, for instance, the website "Stuff Expat Aid Workers Like."[40] Moreover, this common culture can produce a shared outlook and policy cohesion, which is particularly evident when the club is confronted by ambiguities and uncertainties; it will often react to events that distinguish it from non-members.[41] Lastly, members of the club are more likely to be open to persuasion from other members than they are from non-members.[42] Clubs, like all groups, will have internal

---

[35] Fligstein and McAdam 2012, 88; Tsingou 2015, 261; Kendall 2008.
[36] Kendall 2008, 51–54.   [37] Kendall 2008, 29.
[38] Bond 2012, 615; Harrington and Fine 2000; Kendall 2008, 3.   [39] Kendall 2008, 8.
[40] https://stuffexpataidworkerslike.com/.   [41] Swartz 2012, 100.
[42] Domhoff 1994, 18.

disagreements and pecking orders, but these occur in the context of a sense of distinction between the members of the club and outsiders.[43]

The sociological approach to boundaries emphasizes their material and symbolic character, and how, in turn, they create distinctions and differences. While distinctions need not translate into feelings of superiority, they often do, especially for those clubs formed by elites. Clubs in colonial societies are a vivid example of such dynamics.[44] Leonard Wolff observed that they were "the centre and symbol of British imperialism ... with its cult of exclusiveness, superiority, and isolation."[45] Club members might deny their elitism, but outsiders certainly feel it, which is one reason why they want to be admitted. As C. Wright Mills astutely observed: "To the outsider the club to which the upper class man or woman belongs is a badge of certification of his status; to the insider the club proves a more intimate or clan-like set of exclusive groupings which places and characterizes the man."[46]

Humanitarian governance has the characteristics of a club, but there is no literal Humanitarian Club. Like many exclusive clubs, the Humanitarian Club is not brick-and-mortar but rather wall-less, often having formal and informal bodies with rotating locations or interacting through variable arrangements and gatherings. Much like other clubs in global governance there is no authorized list. Instead there are the "usual suspects" that play a dominant role in the humanitarian sector and are active participants across the various standard-setting, coordinating, and rule-making bodies. Some are limited to states, such as the Development Assistance Committee and UN meetings, and others, such as the IASC, include the International Committee of the Red Cross and several INGO bodies. There is a slew of INGO-led and dominated associations, including: SPHERE, ALNAP, and the Humanitarian Accountability Project. There are umbrella organizations for NGOs, such as Interaction in the United States and the International Committee of Voluntary Agencies in Geneva.

In addition to playing a dominant role in humanitarian governance institutions, the Club also directs action on the ground and at field level. In the major crisis countries of Somalia, Sudan, and Democratic Republic of Congo, the Club members controlled 85 percent of the UN's pooled funds.[47] The Club tends to relegate non-members such as local NGOs to the role of subcontractors and implementing

---

[43] Pouliot 2016.   [44] Kendall 2008, 29.
[45] Sinha 2001, 490; Cohen 2009; Batzell 1998.   [46] Mills 2000, 61.
[47] CAFOD 2013, 40.

partners.[48] As bemoaned by former USAID administrator, Andrew Natsios, the major aid agencies have translated partnerships into subcontracts and delivery.[49] In 2005, in the hope of improving efficiency, effectiveness, and accountability, the UN created "clusters," which divided humanitarian action into different categories, such as sanitation, reconstruction, livelihoods, and education. Different organizations were deputized as having lead responsibilities – and they all came from the UN and leading Western aid agencies. The Southern agencies continue to be marginalized. English is often the lingua franca in the field and at these meetings another barrier to local community participation.[50] An extraordinary moment occurred at a cluster meeting during the Philippine typhoon response in 2018 – the cluster meeting was held in the local language, which one UNHCR official said was the first to her knowledge.

The Resilience of the Humanitarian Club

Humanitarian governance has become increasingly institutionalized, the Humanitarian Club has maintained its centrality, and patterns of inclusion and exclusion have continued. These patterns resemble what Charles Tilly called durable inequality: "those that last from one social interaction to the next, with special attention to those that persist over whole careers, lifetimes, and organizational histories."[51] These durable inequalities can become established for various reasons, including perceptions of competence, and then maintained through processes of social closure.[52] Although these inequalities and closures can be attributed to strategic and instrumental action, this is not the case for all of them; there are "diverse practices ... which are practically organized toward this end, without in any way being explicitly conceived and posed in reference to it."[53] Forms of capital reproduce because of structural and agentic dynamics that cannot be reduced to interests.

The Humanitarian Club plays a central role in producing and reproducing the durable inequalities in the humanitarian sector. And these inequalities have led to two major critiques of humanitarian governance and the demand for widening patterns of inclusion. The first is the lack of effectiveness. There were many explanations for its shortcomings, but a growing theme was that it was due to its overly centralized and top-down

[48] Humanitarian Exchange Network 2011; Gingrich and Cohen 2015, 30–31.
[49] Natsios 2010.   [50] Knox and Campbell 2015; Humphries 2013.   [51] Tilly 1997, 6.
[52] Weber 1968, 1, 43–46, 341–338; Parkin 1979; Murphy 1988; Naylor 2019; Keene 2012.
[53] Wacquant 1993, 31; quote is from Bourdieu.

governance structure that marginalized local actors – the very ones who are the first responders, do the bulk of the work, can more easily mobilize local resources, and have the necessary local knowledge. The other is a lack of legitimacy because of the Humanitarian Club's arbitrary power, failure to incorporate those affected by its actions, and absence of accountability.[54] It is a "pathology," observed a veteran observer, because the "people most affected by the crisis have the least involvement in the international relief system."[55]

The obvious remedy to these maladies was to increase the authority and voice of local actors, and the periodic reform efforts almost always included a push to increase participation, partnership, accountability, and other adjustments that would limit the arbitrary power of the Club and alter patterns of exclusion and inclusion. "Localization" is the most recent and substantial effort to reform the system and shift power and authority from the "international" to the "local." Inaugurated at the World Humanitarian Summit in 2016, localization has attracted sector-side support, including from the Humanitarian Club, but all this lip service and activity has had little tangible effect. The humanitarian sector with the Club at the center is nothing if not durable.[56]

What accounts for the durable inequality and the resilience of humanitarian governance's hierarchy? The simplest answer is self-interest – those with power rarely want to yield it.[57] Western aid agencies might advocate reform, but when faced with the choice of maintaining or yielding power they behave just like all organizations. As explained by one critic of the sector, the elite is unable to put "egos and logos aside."[58] A Self-interest certainly plays a part, but not all practices can be traced back to self-interest. Interests are entangled with judgments about whether Southern actors can act in ways that are in the best interests of victims and saving lives at risk. In short, if Western actors have their reservations about inclusion, it is partly due to the often unstated belief that they are better than local actors at saving lives. In other words, inclusivity will translate into lives lost.

---

[54] Humanitarian Leadership Academy and British Red Cross 2015; Zyck with Krebs 2015; Gingrich and Cohen 2015; Humanitarian Policy Group 2016b.

[55] Bennett 2018, 12.

[56] Barnett and Walker 2015; Hough 2018; Gingrich and Cohen 2015; Bennett and Foley 2016; Humanitarian Policy Group 2016a, 2016b; Aly 2016; Steets et al. 2016; Barbalet and Wake 2020; Humanitarian Aid International 2017; Patel 2021.

[57] Barbalet 2018, 10; CAFOD 2013; Bennett and Foley 2016; Collinson 2016; Featherstone 2017.

[58] Parker 2017, 2; Singh 2016.

Economic Capital

If Southern NGOs have one chief complaint it is that they are excluded from humanitarian financing. Those outside the Humanitarian Club get a pittance of the available funds. Because they exist subcontract-to-subcontract, if at all, this means that they are unable to retain quality staff or develop the capacity and infrastructure they need to be an attractive recipient to potential donors. Why are they reduced to this threadbare existence? One answer is that those who receive the bulk of the funds will view any decrease as a threat. Simply put, they view humanitarian financing in zero-sum terms: an increase in funding for local actors means a decrease for international agencies.[59] This has been the case when there is more money flowing into the sector, and it is particularly pronounced when it is constant or declines.

Major donors and INGOs explain and justify this inequality in various ways, but all reinforce the message that it would be unwise to increase funding to local aid agencies.[60] Western donors have developed a fair degree of trust and comfort with the major INGOs, which has reinforced the belief that Western organizations are more effective, efficient, and accountable. Moreover, major donors have imposed heavy reporting demands on recipients, expecting them to provide detailed records of their spending to ensure upward accountability and transparency. And Western donors have much less confidence in Southern agencies, worried that their contributions will be mismanaged, be poorly spent and on the wrong things, be pocketed by corrupt local actors, and lead to rampant fraud. Additionally there is the post-9/11 fear that Southern NGOs might be fronts for terrorist or radical organizations; such fears are amplified by the fact that most aid flows to Muslim-majority countries and many local agencies have a Muslim identity. These reporting requirements create a heavy administrative and bureaucratic burden that even the largest NGOs have difficulty meeting.[61] Southern agencies have requested financial support from Western donors to build the necessary administrative capacity, but for various reasons donors are reluctant to do so.[62]

Many INGOs offer a public-spirited reason for their own lack of enthusiasm. Humanitarian emergences are exactly that – emergencies. They require urgent action. It is well known what victims need medicine, shelter, food, clean water, sanitation, and other life-saving assistance.

---

[59] Redvers 2017; Pantuliano 2016, 4.   [60] Poole 2013.
[61] Humanitarian Policy Group 2016b, 60. Redvers 2015.
[62] Troicare 2017; CAFOD 2013.

And the very reason why international actors must provide such services is because of an absence of local capacity.[63] But if Western agencies shift scarce funds into the hands of local NGOs during an emergency, it will cost lives.[64] As put by someone from a large INGO, "To do capacity building, INGOs have to tolerate failure."[65]

Yet even if Southern agencies received a bigger slice of the funding pie it would not necessarily increase their autonomy or influence. Western donors have tightened control over recipient agencies over the last two decades, allowing for less discretion and demanding more oversight, monitoring, and reporting documents. In fact, more money has resulted in diminished autonomy for Western agencies.[66] Relatedly, it has produced upward rather than downward accountability – that is, accountability to the donors at the expense of the recipients. And they focus on what donors want, which includes financial accountability.[67] The reasonable inference is that if Western donors increased funding to Southern NGOs, donors would still demand control and responsiveness to their interests. In short, direct funding might "transform local NGOs into auxiliaries of the North."[68] As summarized by the Indian-based Humanitarian Aid International: despite all these initiatives to localize aid, "there is a fear that existing power structures and complex dynamics within the humanitarian fraternity may not help in realizing the vision of empowering local organizations through higher resource allocation."[69]

Symbolic Capital

Another source of resistance to widening inclusion is the fear that local actors will not or cannot honor the core principles of humanitarianism, neutrality, impartiality, and independence.[70] As Paul Currion observes regarding the difference between "genuine" humanitarian actors and others such as the private sector that also provide assistance: it is not the kinds of work they do but rather the principles they use.[71] It must be noted, though, that Western actors are not paragons of principles. Humanitarian actors rely on large donors, who have a large say over

---

[63] Wall and Hedlund 2016, 18–20.   [64] Obrecht et al. 2015, 16–17.
[65] Quoted from Gingrich and Cohen 2015, 32.
[66] Barnett 2005; Humanitarian Accountability Partnership 2013, 31; Turk and Eyster 2010, 168.
[67] Humanitarian Accountability Partnership 2013, 19, 61; Deloffre 2016.
[68] Dubois, 2016, 4. Also see Banks et al. 2014.   [69] Singh 2016.
[70] Schenkenberg 2016, 12, 14–17.   [71] Currion 2018, 2.

where and what kind of aid is delivered; in this respect they often are heavily instrumentalized.[72] Moreover, aid agencies must consistently adapt these principles to circumstances on the ground. Improvisation is the name of the game.[73] In that respect these principles are aspirational. But the central concern is not whether local actors fall short of complying with these principles in practice, but whether they even see them as integral to the humanitarian identity.

Club members raise several concerns regarding the ability and willingness of local actors to follow these fundamental principles. Local agencies might not interpret the principles as Western agencies do or even find value in them.[74] Because of pressures and interests, local and national actors might "twist or manipulate the localization agenda to their advantage."[75] Other local actors might even "redefine 'humanitarianism' to their liking in a particular crisis situation."[76] They are more likely to have a stake in the outcome. Because local actors are local they are much more likely to depart from needs-based principles and help those with whom they have cultural proximity. And even if they wanted to help those on the "other side," it might be harder for them to do so because of pressures from friends, families, and local combatants to demonstrate loyalty to one's own. And these pressures can be violent; local aid workers have had their families threatened if they refuse to demonstrate favoritism.

From the perspective of the Humanitarian Club, the inability or unwillingness of local agencies to embrace these principles might hollow out the meaning and practice of humanitarianism – and increase risks to Western actors. Western aid agencies believe that these humanitarian principles help to establish a space that both protects aid workers from attack and provides access to vulnerable populations. If these principles disappear, or the commitment by aid agencies to them is questioned by local authorities and combatants, then all aid agencies will become targets and aiding victims will become hazardous to their health. In this regard, the fear that local actors will not pledge allegiance to humanitarian principles provides Western actors with lots of reasons to keep their distance.[77]

---

[72] Donini 2012.   [73] Humanitarian Policy Group 2016a, chapter 3.
[74] Schenkenberg 2016, 12, 14; Troicare 2017; Stoddard 2004; Wall and Hedlund 2016.
[75] Schenkenberg 2016, 24.
[76] Campbell and Hoffman 2015, 194; cited from Boateng 2018, 63. Also see European Parliament 2015; Humanitarian Policy Group 2016a, 53; Troicare 2017.
[77] Barbalet 2018, 23.

Social Capital

The heart of social capital is the intense and continuous interaction between individuals that leads to the formation of solidarity, emotional bonds, and trust. Members of the Club enjoy social capital for two major reasons. One is that they have had shared experiences forged in the heat of emergencies. There are several waves of aid workers that have immediate identification with each other because they worked in the same emergency; Cambodia, Sudan, Darfur, Iraq, Somalia, Bosnia, Kosovo, and Rwanda have all provided common experiences and weak ties between aid workers. Another source of social capital are the many associations, meetings, and gatherings that are intended to help forge and distribute rules of humanitarianism. Although these are no longer monopolized by Westerners, my interviews with various participants from the Global South suggest a feeling that they are not trusted in the same way that Westerners are and are often there because of tokenism.

Trust is at the heart of social capital, and the insinuation of the previous paragraph is that, *ceteris paribus*, the distinctions between Western and Southern aid agencies and workers would erode with more opportunities for interaction. But is there something else that hinders interactions or dulls the trust that might otherwise emerge between those from the West with the same history? One possibility is race. In my interviews with staff from Southern agencies, race was a frequent topic of conversation for explaining the unwillingness of Western agencies to relinquish power to Southern agencies.[78] According to Adia Benton, African expatriates working in other parts of Africa are frequently positioned on a "lower rung of the humanitarian professional hierarchy."[79] African aid workers were assumed to be less competent, and even when they demonstrated they had the skills white aid workers would still question their competency.[80] African aid workers constantly felt as if they were having to prove themselves and were never quite treated as an equal member. The Black Lives Matter protests have produced considerable introspection in many Western aid agencies, with many organizations looking around the room and discovering few people of color in leadership positions and wondering why.

Cultural Capital

Humanitarianism used to be staffed predominantly by volunteers. Indeed, volunteerism is a principle of humanitarianism. For decades a

---

[78] Barnett 2020.   [79] Benton 2016, 268.   [80] Benton 2016, 270.

good heart could seem to matter more than experience or competence. As discussed in the first section, beginning in the late 1990s the humanitarian field became increasingly bureaucratized, rationalized, and professionalized, increasing the salience of credentials and specialized knowledge. Lived and local experience still counted, but increasingly ranked below credentials and objective, specialized knowledge that could be generalized across cases. As one staff member of a Southern agency observed, Western agencies rhetorically recognized the importance of local knowledge but international "expert" knowledge remained privileged.[81]

A perceived advantage of credentialed and expert knowledge is that it is available to all. In other words, it is egalitarian and democratic. This is more accurate in theory than in practice. Most of the knowledge-producing and training institutions are in the West, which are more accessible to those in the West than those from the Global South. Not only are the major centers for specialization located there, but Western-based humanitarian agencies and institutions are the critical producers of knowledge. When Southern agencies and actors participate in the process of knowledge production it is almost always as a subcontractor, translator, or informant.[82] The world of knowledge production has the same hierarchical patterns as everything else in humanitarian governance.

Durable inequality is produced and reproduced by economic, social, symbolic, and cultural capital. These patterns that maintain inequality are arguably to the advantage of Western actors, but it is difficult to reduce these patterns to self-interest. Partly this is because capital cannot be reduced to economic logics, and partly this is because these patterns are often defended or justified not on the grounds of self-interest but rather in the interests of others. Any substantial reform that shifted authority and resources from the West to the South would certainly cost Western aid agencies dearly, but, respond many in the Club, would it save more lives? And even if Western aid agencies were willing to take the risk, Western donors are not prepared to gamble with house money.

Conclusion

I have painted a picture of humanitarian governance that is a highly durable club – in which the members of the Club have a network-like

---

[81] Urvashi 2016, 8. Also see Redvers 2015; Schenkenberg 2016, 21.
[82] Domhoff 1994, 18.

association and the Club members enjoy considerable authority over non-members. The critiques leveled at the Club, including its lack of legitimacy and effectiveness, continue, and the proposed solutions remain the same – more inclusion. As I have suggested, those in the Club do not duck the criticism and are broadly sympathetic that a humanitarianism that lived its principles would be more inclusive than it currently is.

In 2020 two dramatic events have raised the question of effectiveness and legitimacy with greater urgency. The first is Black Lives Matter. Many of the largest aid agencies either came out of colonialism or stepped into the shoes of the departing colonialists. Humanitarianism has largely been about white people doing things for non-white people. Many from the Global South attribute the unwillingness of Western aid agencies to relinquish power as a product of racism, though masked through the language of competence and capacity building. The Black Lives Matter movement has not only provided a jolt to these feelings, it has also caused most of the largest aid agencies to question whether and how race works in and through their agency. Will this moment of introspection lead to tangible change and greater inclusion, or will it become the most recent challenge to the Club's attempt to maintain its legitimacy?

The second event is Covid-19. The humanitarian sector is no better positioned to respond to the considerable suffering caused by the virus than are much better resourced states. And just like Moon describes in Chapter 8, so too is humanitarian governance attempting to fix a tattered architecture on the fly. An additional challenge is that Western workers are having difficulty getting access to those in need because they are concerned about their own risk of infection and worried about spreading the infection to others. Such developments have left many Western aid agencies with little choice but to shift authority and power to local actors. This development builds on previous pressures to remove western staff from the field because of security concerns. Because of security considerations and attacks on aid workers, many INGOs have shifted greater responsibility to local actors as they retreat behind barricades and to distant capitals.

But does this foreshadow a change in the mode of governance? Will there be more inclusion and less hierarchy? Will the shadow retreat? Possibly, but there are three reasons to suggest that the Club will adapt. The first is that any substantial change will require a dramatic shift in the financing of humanitarian action, and there is no indication that the donors are prepared to do anything radical. Nor is there any evidence that the "nontraditional" donors are prepared to provide an alternative pool of resources without conditions. Second, those instances in which the Club has admitted new members might give the appearance of growing diversity without the substance. New members are expected to exhibit decorum and accept the rules of the Club. It can have all the characteristics of tokenism, especially since being admitted to the Club does not mean that their voices are truly welcome. Moreover, while such selective inclusion provides opportunities for upward mobility and greater inclusion and diversity, it might also help to preserve the Club's power because it potentially works against forms of solidarity and protest among Southern agencies and networks.[83] Third, and related, the literature on multistakeholderism suggests that there might be more actors around the table, but the critical decisions are made by the same elite before they enter the room.[84] For these and other reasons, the Club is well set up to continue to operate in the shadows.

References

Aly, Heba. 2016. The Humanitarian System: A Mammoth Machinery Losing Track of What It Is for. *The Guardian*, May 22. www.theguardian.com/global-development-professionals-network/2016/may/22/humanitarian-aid-system-power-concentrated-hands-of-few-losing-track.

Banks, Nicola, David Hulme, and Michael Edwards. 2014. NGOs, States, and Donors Revisited: Still Too Close for Comfort? *World Development*, 66: 707–718.

Barbalet, Vanessa. 2018. *As Local as Possible, as International as Necessary: Understanding Capacity and Complementary in Humanitarian Action*. HPG Working Paper. London: ODI.

Barbalet, Vanessa and Caitlin Wake. 2020. *Inclusion and Exclusion in Humanitarian Action: The State of Play*. London: Overseas Development Institute. https://odi.org/en/publications/inclusion-and-exclusion-in-humanitarian-action-the-state-of-play/.

Barnett, Michael. 2005. Humanitarianism Transformed. *Perspectives on Politics*, 3: 723–740.

2011. *Empire of Humanity: A History of Humanitarianism*. Ithaca, NY: Cornell University Press.

2020. The Humanitarian Global Colour Line. ALNAP. www.alnap.org/blogs/the-humanitarian-global-colour-line.

Barnett, Michael and Peter Walker. 2015. Regime Change for Humanitarian Aid: How to Make Relief More Accountable. *Foreign Affairs* 94 (4): 130–141.

Batzell, Norman. 1998. *Imperiled Innocents*. Princeton: Princeton University Press.

---

[83] Naylor 2019, 4–5.   [84] Wade 2011; Wade 2013; Saffer et al. 2018.

Bell, Daniel. 1958. The Power Elite Reconsidered. *American Journal of Sociology* 64 (3): 238–250.

Bell, Mark. 2015. Beyond Emboldenment: How Acquiring Nuclear Weapons Can Change Foreign Policy. *International Security* 40 (1): 87–119.

Bennett, Christine. 2018. Constructive Deconstruction: Imagining Alternative Humanitarian Action. HPG Working Paper, Humanitarian Policy Group, May.

Bennett, Christine and Matt Foley. 2016. *Time to Let Go: Remaking Humanitarian Action for the Modern Era.* Humanitarian Policy Group. April. www.odi.org/sites/odi.org.uk/files/resource-documents/10422.pdf.

Benton, Aida. 2016. African Expatriates and Race in the Anthropology of Humanitarianism. *Critical African Studies* 8 (3): 266–277.

Berger, Peter. 1970. On the Obsolescence of the Concept of Honor. *European Journal of Sociology* 11 (2): 339–347.

Boateng, Oheneba Agyenim. 2018. *Localising Humanitarian Governance: The Organization of the Africa Unity/African Union Since 1963.* Phd dissertation, Freie Universität Berlin, December.

Bond, Matthew, 2012. The Bases of Elite Social Behavior: Patterns of Club Affiliation among Members of the House of Lords, *Sociology*, 46: 4.

Boswell, C. 2009. *The Political Uses of Expert Knowledge: Immigration Policy and Social Research.* New York: Cambridge University Press.

Bourdieu, Pierre, 2011. The Forms of Capital. *Cultural Theory: An Anthology* 1: 81–93.

Bourdieu, Pierre and Louis Wacquant. 1992. *An Invitation to Reflexive Sociology.* Chicago: University of Chicago Press.

Brandi, Clara. 2019. Club Governance and Legitimacy: The Perspective of Old and Rising Powers on the G7 and the G20. *South African Journal of International Affairs* 26 (4): 685–702.

Brint, Stephen. 1996. *In an Age of Experts: The Changing Role of Professionals in Politics and Public Life.* Princeton: Princeton University Press.

Buchanan, Alan. 1965. An Economic Theory of Clubs. *Economica* 32: 1–14.

CAFOD. 2013. *Funding at the Sharp End.* London: CAFOD, July. http://cafod.org.uk/content/download/24369/175018/file/Funding%20at%20the%20 20sharp%20end.pdf.

Campbell, Susanna and Stephanie Hoffman. 2015. Regional Humanitarian Organizations. In *The Routledge Companion to Humanitarian Action,* edited by Roger McGinty and Jenny Peterson, 195–203. London: Routlege.

Carbonnier, Gilles. 2015. *Humanitarian Economics: War, Disaster, and the Global Aid Market.* London: Hurst.

Carranza, Mario. 2017. Rising Powers and International Order: Comparing Brazil and India's Strategies for Admission to the Great Power Club. *Contemporary Security Policy* 2 (September): 491–498.

Christian Aid, Save the Children, and Humanitarian Accountability Partnership. 2013. Improving Impact: Do Accountability Mechanisms Deliver Results? June. www.christianaid.org.uk/images/accountability-impact-report-2013.pdf.

Cohen, Benjamin. 2009. Networks of Sociability: Women's Clubs in Colonial and Postcolonial India. *Frontiers: A Journal of Women Studies* 30 (3): 169–195.

Collins, H. and R. Evans. 2007. *Rethinking Expertise*. Chicago: University of Chicago Press.

Collins, Randall. 1979. *The Credential Society: A Historical Sociology of Education and Stratification*. New York: Academic Press.

Collinson, Sara. 2016. *Constructive Deconstruction: Making Sense of the International Humanitarian System*. HPG Working Paper, July. London: Overseas Development Institute.

Cooley, Alex and James Ron, 2002. The NGO Scramble. *International Security* 27 (1): 5–39.

Currion, Paul. 2018. *Network Humanitarianism*. HPG Working Paper, May. London: ODI.

Deloffre, Maryam. 2016. Global Accountability Communities: NGO Self-regulation in the Humanitarian Sector. *Review of International Studies* 42 (4): 724–747.

Domhoff, G. William. 1994. Social Clubs, Policy-Planning Groups, and Corporations: A Network Study of Ruling-Class Cohesiveness. *Bulletin of Sociological Methodology*, 2 (April): 17–29.

Donini, Antonio, ed. 2012. *The Golden Fleece: Manipulation and Independence in Humanitarian Action*. Sterling, VA: Kumarian Press.

Dubois, Marc. 2016. Be Careful What You Wish for. August 8. www.irinnews .org/opinion/2016/08/08/be-careful-what-you-wish.

Els, Christian and Nils Carstensen. 2015. The Humanitarian Economy: Where Is All the Money Going? July 1. IRIN. http://newirin.irinnews.org/the-humanitarian-economy.

Emirbayer, Mustafa and Victoria Johnston. 2008. Bourdieu and Organizational Analysis. *Theory and Society* 37 (1): 1–44.

European Parliament. 2015. *Toward More Effective Global Humanitarian Action: How the EU Can Contribute*. Director-General for External Policies, Policy Department.

Falkner, Robert. 2016. A Minilateral Solution for Global Climate Change? On Bargaining, Efficiency, Club Benefits, and International Legitimacy. *Perspectives on Politics* 14 (1): 87–101.

Farazmand, Ali. 1999. The Elite Question: Toward a Normative Elite Theory of Organization. *Administration and Society* 31 (3): 321–360.

Featherstone, A. 2017. *Time to Move On: National Perspectives on Transforming Surge Capacity*. AFOD, Christian Aid, Tearfund, and Islamic Relief Worldwide. www.alnap.org/help-library/time-to-move-on-national-perspectives-on-transforming-surge-capacity.

Fligstein, Neil and Doug McAdam. 2012. *A Theory of Fields*. New York: Oxford University Press.

Gingrich, Tara and Marc Cohen. 2015. *Turning the Humanitarian System on Its Head*. Oxfam Research Reports, July.

Gottwald, Martin. 2010. *Competing in the Humanitarian Marketplace: UNHCR's Organizational Culture and Decision-Making Processes*. Geneva: UNHCR, Policy Development and Evaluation Service.

Harrington, Brooke and Gary Fine. 2000. Opening the "Black Box": Small Groups and Twenty-First Century Sociology. *Social Psychology Quarterly* 63 (4): 312–323.

Hough, Victoria Metcalfe. 2018. *Grand Bargain Annual Independent Report*. HPG Commissioned Report, Humanitarian Policy Group, Overseas Development Institute, London, June.

Humanitarian Accountability Partnership. 2013. *Humanitarian Accountability Partnership Annual Report*. Geneva: HAP. https://reliefweb.int/sites/ reliefweb.int/files/resources/2013-har.pdf.

Humanitarian Aid International. 2017. Toward a Localized Humanitarian Response in India. New Delhi, India. www.alnap.org/system/files/content/ resource/files/main/hai-position-paper-localisation.pdf.

Humanitarian Exchange Network. 2011. Humanitarian Partnerships. *Humanitarian Exchange Magazine*, May. https://odihpn.org/magazine/ humanitarian-partnerships/.

Humanitarian Leadership Academy and British Red Cross. 2015. *Local Humanitarian Action in Practice: Case Studies and Reflections of Local Humanitarian Actors*. London. https://reliefweb.int/sites/reliefweb.int/files/ resources/Academy-Red-Cross-Case-Studies-Final-Med-Res-Spreads.pdf.

Humanitarian Policy Group. 2016a. *Planning for the Future*. London: Overseas Development Initiative. https://fic.tufts.edu/wp-content/uploads/pff_report_ uk.pdf.

   2016b. *Time to Let Go: Rethinking Humanitarian Action for the Modern Era*. London: Overseas Development Institute.

Humphries, Vanessa. 2013. Improving Humanitarian Coordination. *Journal of Humanitarian Assistance* (May 29). http://sites.tufts.edu/jha/archives/1976.

Jenkins, Richard. 1992. *Pierre Bourdieu*. London: Routledge.

Juma, Kathina and Astri Suhrke, eds. 2002. *Eroding Local Capacity: International Humanitarian Action in Africa*. Uppsala: Nordiska Africaninstitut.

Kauppi, Nillo and Mikael Madsen. 2014. Fields of Global Governance: How Transnational Power Elites Can Make Global Governance Intelligible. *International Political Sociology* 8 (3): 324–330.

Keene, Edward. 2012. Social Status, Social Closure and the Idea of Europe as a "Normative Power." *European Journal of International Relations* 19 (4): 939–956.

Kendall, Diana. 2008. *Elite Clubs and the Process of Exclusion*. Lanham, MD: Rowman & Littlefield.

Kennedy, Dennis. 2019. Humanitarianism Governed: Rules, Identity, and Exclusion in Relief Work. *Humanity* 10 (2): 207–237.

Keohane, Robert and Joseph S. Nye Jr. 2002. The Club Model of Multilateral Cooperation and Problems of Democratic Legitimacy. In *Power and Governance in a Partially Globalized World*, edited by Robert Keohane. New York: Routledge.

Khan, Shamuis Rahman. 2012. The Sociology of Elites. *Annual Review of Sociology* 38: 361–377.

Knox, Paul and Leah Campbell. 2015. *Exploring Coordination in Humanitarian Clusters*. London: ALNAP.

Krause, Monica. 2013. *The Good Project: Humanitarian NGOs and the Fragmentation of Reason*. Chicago: University of Chicago Press.

Lamp, Nicolas. 2016. The Club Approach to Multilateral Trade Making. *Vanderbilt Journal of Transnational Law* 49 (1): 7–55.

Larson, Deborah. 2018. New Perspectives on Rising Powers and Global Governance: Status and Clubs. *International Studies Review* 20: 247–254.

Maxwell, Dan and Kirsten Gelsdorf. 2019. *Understanding the Humanitarian World*. New York: Routledge.

Mills, C. Wright. 2000. *The Power Elite*. New York: Oxford University Press.

Minear, Larry and Ian Smilie, 2004. *The Charity of Nations*. Bloomfield, CT: Kumarian Press.

Mosca, Gaetano. 1939. *The Ruling Class*. New York: McGraw-Hill.

Mowjee, Tasneem, Lydia Poole, and Barnaby Willitts-King. 2017. *From Grand Bargain to Beneficiary: An Analysis of Funding Flows through the Humanitarian System*. HPG Commissioned Report. London: ODI.

Murphy, Raymond. 1988. *Social Closure*. New York: Oxford University Press.

Natsios, Andrew. 2010. *The Clash of the Counter-Bureaucracy and Development*. Washington, DC: Center for Global Development.

Naylor, Tristen. 2019. *Social Closure and International Society: Status Groups from the Family of Civilised Nations to the G20* New York: Routledge.

Nordhaus, William. 2015. Climate Clubs: Overcoming Free-Riding in International Climate Policy. *American Economic Review* 105 (4): 1339–1370.

Obrecht, Alice, et al. 2015. WHS Effectiveness Theme Focus, Paper 5: Accountability. London: ALNAP.

Pakulski, Jan. 2012. The Weberian Foundations of Modern Elite Theory and Democratic Elitism. *Historical Social Research* 37 (1): 38–56.

Pantuliano, Sara. 2016. How Do We Create a Humanitarian System Fit for Today – and Tomorrow? May 20. www.weforum.org/agenda/2016/05/how-can-we-fix-a-broken-humanitarian-system/.

Parker, Ben. 2017. Aid Reform: Cash, World Bank Stand Out as Localization Stalls. *The New Humanitarian*, July 3. www.thenewhumanitarian.org/feature/2017/07/03/aid-reform-cash-world-bank-stand-out-localisation-stalls.

Parkin, Frank. 1979. *Marxism and Class Theory: A Bourgeoise Critique*. New York: Columbia University Press.

Patel, Shmuti. 2021. Cultivating Change in the Humanitarian Sector. Global Mentoring Initiative, Geneva Switzerland. January 2. www.linkedin.com/pulse/cultivating-change-aid-sector-smruti-patel/?trackingId=%2F3bCOH%2FWRNC3hl%2BWqZJEfA%3D%3D.

Pictet, Jean. 1979. *The Fundamental Principles of the Red Cross*. Geneva: Henry Dunant Institute.

Poole, Lydia. 2013. *Funding at the Sharp End: Investing in National NGO Response Capacity*. CAFOD. www.caritas.org/wordpress/wp-content/uploads/2017/05/FundingAtSharpEnd.pdf.

Pouliot, Vincent. 2016. *International Pecking Orders: The Politics and Practice of Multilateral Diplomacy*. New York: Cambridge University Press.

Prakash, Aseem and Mary Kay Gugerty, eds. 2010. *Advocacy Organizations and Collective Action*. New York: Cambridge University Press.

Ramalingam, Ben. 2014. *Aid on the Edge of Chaos*. Oxford University Press.

Redvers, Louise. 2015. NGOs: Bridging the North–South Divide. IRIN, June 8. www.irinnews.org/analysis/2015/06/08/ngos-bridging-north-south-divide.

2017. Local Aid Agencies: Still Waiting for a Bigger Share of the Funding Cake. March 27. www.irinnews.org/analysis/2017/03/27/local-aid-agencies-still-waiting-bigger-share-funding-cake.

Roth, Silke. 2016. *The Paradox of Aid Work: Passionate Professionals*. London: Routledge.

Saffer, Adfam, Aimei Yang, and Maureen Taylor. 2018. Reconsidering Power in Multistakeholder Relationship Management. *Management Communication Quarterly* 32 (1): 121–139.

Sandler, Todd. 2013. Buchanan Clubs. *Constitutional Political Economy* 24: 265–284.

Schenkenberg, Ed. 2016. *The Challenges of Localized Humanitarian Aid in Conflict*. Emergency Gap Series. Barcelona: MSF. https://arhp.msf.es/sites/default/files/MSF_EGS03_The%20challenges%20of%20localised%20humanitarian%20aid%20in%20armed%20conflict_november%202016_0_0.pdf.

Sending, Ole Jacob. 2017. Contested Professionalization in a Weak Transnational Field, in *Professional Networks in Transnational Governance*, edited by Leonard Seabrooke and Lasse Folke Henrickson. New York: Cambridge University Press.

Singh, Sudhanshu. 2016. As Local as Possible as International as Necessary. December 16. https://charter4change.org/2016/12/16/as-local-as-possible-as-international-as-necessary-humanitarian-aid-internationals-position-on-localisation/.

Sinha, Mrinalini. 2001. Britishness, Clubability and the Colonial Public Sphere: The Genealogy of an Imperial Institution in Colonial India. *Journal of British Studies* 40 (4): 490.

Sphere Project. 2018. Humanitarian Charter. www.spherehandbook.org/en/the-humanitarian-charter/.

Steets, Julia, Andrea Binder, Andras Derzsi-Horvath, Susanna Krüger, and Lotte Ruppert. 2016. *Drivers and Inhibitors of Change in the Humanitarian System*. Berlin: Global Public Policy Institute.

Stoddard, Abby. 2004. You Say You Want a Devolution: Prospects for Remodeling Humanitarian Assistance. *Journal of Humanitarian Assistance*. www.jha.ac/articles/a154.pdf.

Swartz, David. 2012. *Culture and Power: The Sociology of Pierre Bourdieu*. Chicago: University of Chicago Press.

Therborn, Goran. 2008. *What Does the Ruling Class Do When It Rules?* New York: Verso.

Tilly, Charles. 1997. *Durable Inequality*. Berkeley: University of California Press.

Troicare. 2017. More than the Money: Localisation in Practice. July. www.trocaire.org/sites/default/files/resources/policy/more-than-the-money-full-report.pdf.

Tsingou, Eleni. 2015. Club Governance and the Making of Financial Rules. *Review of International Political Economy* 22 (2): 225–256.

Turk, Volker and Elizabeth Eyster. 2010. Strengthening Accountability in UNHCR. *International Journal of Refugee Law* 22 (2): 168.

UN OCHA. 2012. *Humanitarianism in the Network Age.* New York: UN Publications.

Urvashi, Anija. 2016. *Bold Reform or Empty Rhetoric? A Critique of the World Humanitarian Summit.* New Delhi: Observer Research Foundation. www .orfonline.org/research/bold-reform-or-empty-rhetoric-a-critique-of-the-world-humanitarian-summit/.

Wacquant, Loïc. 1993. From Ruling Class to Field of Power: An Interview with Pierre Bourdieu on *La noblesse d'État. Theory, Culture, and Society* 10: 19–44.

Wade, Robert. 2011. Emerging World Order: From Multipolarity to Multilateralism in the G20, the World Bank, and the IMF. *Politics and Society* 39 (3): 347–378.

2013. The Art of Power Maintenance: How Western States Keep the Lead in Global Organizations. *Challenge* 56 (1): 5–39.

Walker, Peter and Catherine Russ. 2009. *Professionalizing the Humanitarian Sector: A Scoping Study.* London: Enhancing Learning and Research for Humanitarian Assistance.

Walker, Peter and Dan Maxwell. 2008. *Shaping the Humanitarian World.* New York: Routledge.

Wall, Imogen with Karren Hedlund. 2016. Localisation and Locally-Led Crisis Response: A Literature Review. Local to Global Protection. www .local2global.info/wp-content/uploads/L2GP_SDC_Lit_Review_ LocallyLed_June_2016_revisedJan_2017_online.pdf.

Weber, Max. 1968. *Economy and Society.* Berkeley: University of California Press.

Weiss, Tom. 2013. *Humanitarian Business.* New York: Polity.

Weiss, Thomas. 1999. Principles, Politics, and Humanitarian Action. *Ethics and International Affairs* 13: 1–22.

Zyck, Stephen with Hannah Krebs. 2015. *Localising Humanitarianism: Improving Effectiveness through Inclusive Action.* July. London: Overseas Development Institute. www.odi.org/publications/9695-local-humanitarian-localisation-red-cross-aid.

6 The Supply of Informal International Governance

Hierarchy plus Networks in Global Governance

Michael W. Manulak and Duncan Snidal

States increasingly favor informal forms of international cooperation. International actors are weaving intricate transgovernmental networks (TGNs), permeating and penetrating more formal state interactions, as well as creating higher-level informal intergovernmental organizations (IIGOs). Since 1990 the number of IIGOs has grown dramatically (from 27 to over 140) whereas the number of formal intergovernmental organizations (FIGOs) has increased only slightly (from 320 to 340) before plateauing in the new millennium.[1] Informal networks and institutions do not entail legally binding agreements or bureaucratic structures, such as secretariats or organizational headquarters. Informal commitments are typically "soft" and political in nature, and rely on voluntary implementation. But informal governance nevertheless creates shared and consistent practices that structure ongoing relations among participants. This makes them very different from purely ad hoc policy coordination.

Existing accounts explain this phenomenon by focusing on the demand for informal governance. In periods of accelerating global change and high uncertainty, states wish to avoid the sovereignty costs entailed in binding legal obligations and delegation to independent international agents. While these accounts make a persuasive case about the demand for informal arrangements, they have devoted comparatively little attention to factors that have changed the supply conditions for informal governance. This chapter fills that gap by showing that the emergence and adoption of new communication technologies increased the feasibility and lowered the cost of informal governance. This has

We thank Michael Barnett, David Hagebölling, Anne Holthoefer, Walter Mattli, Jon C.W. Pevehouse, Felicity Vabulas, Kal Raustiala, and David Welch and participants at the Balsillie School of International Affairs IR Workshop, the Hertie School of Governance, the Oxford IR Colloquium, and participants in this project, for their valuable comments.
[1] See the Introduction. For a comparison of the definitions and growth of IIGOs versus FIGOs see Vabulas and Snidal 2020.

strongly shaped the choice and design of global governance arrangements which are now based increasingly on informal governance.

The Hierarchy plus Networks (HpN) model explains how the interconnection between IIGOs and TGNs is emerging as an important nexus of global governance. We build on key elements in the Introduction to show how the hierarchical relations between IIGOs and TGNs, combined with the network properties of TGNs, provides a new and important combination of global governance. Technological change, specifically the emergence of new possibilities for long-distance communication and their falling costs over time, have served as the main driver of this new form of governance.[2] This shift explains the relative decline in the role of FIGOs and their secretariats. While they continue to serve a vital function within the international system, FIGOs are increasingly being complemented – and in a few places supplanted – by the HpN combination of IIGOs and TGNs. However, this is not a shift from hierarchy to networks, but a complementary recombination of hierarchy *through* networks.[3] Rather than undercutting states, moreover, these informal institutional arrangements provide new opportunities for states (at least powerful ones) to increase their control over international policy. This has further implications in strengthening the foreign policy-making role of "central" executive agencies and of domestically oriented "line" departments within states. It explains the relative decline of foreign ministries (FMs) and generalist diplomats as "middle-men" gatekeepers, both domestically and abroad. Thus our analysis points toward profound changes in modes of global governance at both the global and national levels.

We begin by situating our contribution within the growing literature on informal governance. Following a historical analysis of the impact of transportation and communication technology on the design of FIGOs and the structures of multilateral diplomacy, we show how, just as the

---

[2] See the Introduction on "drivers" of change. While we focus on technological change here, the increasing complexity of global problems provides a complementary reason for the emergence of HpN governance.

[3] We adopt the conceptions of hierarchy and networks advanced in the Introduction. Hierarchy is a top-down, centralized organizational form; heads of government use IIGOs to centralize coordinated top-down delegation to their respective departments, or to centrally orchestrate TGN activities. Networks are interdependent relations that entail decentralized collaboration. While hierarchically orchestrated by IIGOs, TGNs engage in decentralized, horizontal collaboration in their areas of technical expertise. Interestingly, although they are a source of hierarchy in our model, IIGOs themselves are organized through networked interaction among high-level actors. FIGOs, in contrast, rely on legalized and hub-based delegation arrangements to produce a high degree of centralized hierarchy.

advent of the telegraph and improvements in transportation enabled the rise of multilateral organizations, so internet and internet-enabled technologies are enabling new patterns of international cooperation. By lowering the costs of interaction and facilitating more decentralized modes of governance, technological change has opened up possibilities for a conjunction between high-level head of government (HOG) interactions and TGNs among lower-level national officials.

Information, and how it is communicated, is central to our analysis and we distinguish two broad categories of information. One is *technical information* about how the world works and how to implement specific policies – the sort of information handled well by experts and bureaucrats;[4] the other is *political information* generated in deciding what is to be done – the sort of information that is created by political leaders. Where issues are well-defined, meetings among top political leaders can provide the large-scale agreement necessary to guide lower-level implementation. Where issues are not well-defined, high-level meetings can provide a way to share worldviews and identify common (and conflicting) interests and values, as well as set agendas. Jennifer Mitzen argues for a "forum effect" of such meetings whereby leaders establish collective goals that guide states in governing together even for the most difficult problems.[5] Face-to-face diplomacy allows leaders to understand each other's intentions and assuage uncertainties that make it hard to cooperate;[6] in the extreme, direct meetings might allow state leaders to "bond" and achieve the high levels of trust necessary to generate collective intentions and cooperation on the most difficult issues.[7]

FIGOs traditionally brought these two types of information together by combining political decisions agreed by national political representatives (diplomats) with technical directives to be implemented by the international bureaucracy or passed through foreign ministries to national bureaucracies (which, if they lack capacity, are often supported by the international secretariats). By contrast, we argue that a new HpN arrangement is emerging whereby political decisions are determined

---

[4] Although the political takes precedence over the technical (in the world and in our model), technical management is enormously consequential not just for implementing politically determined policies but also because of the autonomy and power that it can create for bureaucracies. An interesting question that we do not explore here is whether TGN networks are subject to tighter control by the political process than are FIGOs.

[5] Mitzen 2013, 46–61. In many cases, HOG agreement on collective goals depends on extensive preparatory work by "sherpas" working with TGNs, but only high-level HOGs can solidify expectations.

[6] Holmes 2018.   [7] Wheeler 2018.

through the direct interactions of HOGs[8] within IIGOs and implemented by direct interactions among networked national line departments.[9] Arguably this combination is even more powerful than traditional FIGO-based governance because it brings together the very top leadership to forge common understandings while institutionalizing those agreements through highly integrated transgovernmental networks that directly connect the implementing domestic agencies.

Our HpN model bridges hierarchy and networks. World leaders use the increasing number of available IIGOs to interact directly in order to identify priorities, agree on objectives, and steer key aspects of international life. HOGs exercise a growing agenda-setting power, relying more on their close political advisors than delegation to their foreign ministry. While HOGs use their authority to shape overall policy directions, they rely on networked collaborations through TGNs among line departments to implement their decisions and pursue the objectives identified through IIGOs. Although they formally oversee the officials interacting within TGNs, HOGs cannot track TGN interactions closely. The need for frequent high-level political approvals would, moreover, stifle the free-flowing and technical quality of information exchange that make these networks effective. Thus, elements of hierarchy remain but TGN interactions produce a strong horizontal networked quality to international cooperation.

After briefly discussing the increased demand for informal governance, we show how advances in communication technologies enable informal institutions with their accompanying reductions in management and sovereignty costs. We then represent the hierarchical interactions between high-level intergovernmental forums (IIGOs) and operational-level domestic agencies connected through TGNs in terms of a simple HpN model. We illustrate this mode of governance by analyzing the design and development of the Proliferation Security Initiative (PSI), an informal intergovernmental institution created to counter the illicit trafficking of weapons of mass destruction. We conclude with a

---

[8] We use HOGs in an expansive way to refer not only to the top executive position (president, prime minister, etc.) in a given state, but also to other high-level offices with authority to make major political commitments on behalf of a state in the international setting. Plenipotentiary ambassadors historically had this capacity, as do high state officials more generally. Operationally, we follow the measurement criteria for IIGOs that defines "high-level" meetings involving actors at or above the ministerial or ambassadorial level (Vabulas and Snidal 2020).

[9] "Line departments" refers to issue-specific ministries, such as "health" or "transportation," as well as to specialized agencies within them, such as (in the US case) the Food and Drug Administration or the Federal Aviation Administration.

discussion of the implications of our analysis for international cooperation and for the exercise of power within global institutions.

The Demand for Informal Governance

States are increasingly utilizing less formal modes of international cooperation. In contrast with earlier periods of institution building, when states created dozens of formal, legally binding international agreements and organizational structures, governments are increasingly opting for an "adaptable multilateral sprawl that delivers a partial measure of international cooperation through a welter of informal arrangements and piecemeal approaches."[10] In counter-proliferation, for instance, states have supplemented formal treaty commitments, such as the Nuclear Non-Proliferation Treaty, with informal organizational arrangements, including the Proliferation Security Initiative and the Global Partnership Against the Spread of Weapons and Materials of Mass Destruction.

Informal modes of governance are more than a waystation to formal institutions and have shown significant staying power.[11] Felicity Vabulas and Duncan Snidal find that the prevalence of IIGOs, such as the G7 and G20, has increased rapidly in recent decades vis-à-vis FIGOs. They argue that IIGOs have advantages including providing flexibility and speed while minimizing bureaucracy and protecting sovereignty.[12]

Anne-Marie Slaughter has analyzed the parallel growth of TGNs of national regulators, legislators, and judges, who have become "the new diplomats," often supplanting foreign ministries in consequential international forums.[13] TGNs represent "a prime form of global governance, equivalent in importance and effectiveness to traditional international organizations."[14] The demand for TGNs has been fueled by "complex interdependence" and the increasingly transnational quality of many issues faced by states.[15]

This phenomenon has also been noted by analysts with a more prescriptive outlook. Richard N. Haass advocates convening informal "posses" to advance US global leadership.[16] These voluntary coalitions allow states to adopt flexible nationally determined contributions as a part of a wider international effort.[17] Similarly, Stewart Patrick has highlighted the declining importance of formal legal and organizational arrangements, despite an increased demand for international

---

[10] Patrick 2014.   [11] Vabulas and Snidal 2020.   [12] Vabulas and Snidal 2013, 2020.
[13] Slaughter 2004, 2017.   [14] Slaughter 2004, 230.   [15] Slaughter 2004, 39–40.
[16] Haass 2001.   [17] Haass 2017.

cooperation. States are instead opting for less bureaucratic venues.[18] For Haass and Patrick, the demand for informal governance is a consequence of states' desire to move swiftly and preserve flexibility in an uncertain and dynamic global context.

While these treatments document the growing importance of informal governance and explain the demand for these forms of cooperation, they have not analyzed the factors that have influenced the recent expansion in the supply of informal governance. Given the importance of information flows to transnational coordination, the impact of the "information revolution" should not be underestimated. The freefalling costs of creating, processing, transmitting, and searching for information are having a transformative effect on international organization. The internet era, Joseph Nye argues, has contributed to a diffusion of power to a wide array of international actors and fueled the rise of loosely structured global networks with minimal bureaucratization.[19] Taylor Owen goes further, arguing that new communications technologies have the potential to undermine large hierarchical organizations, replacing them with networked structures that are decentralized, collaborative, and resilient.[20]

Communications Technology and the Design of Multilateral Diplomacy

The possibility and design of international institutions depends on communications technologies. In a world where diplomatic dispatches were delivered via diplomatic couriers traveling on horseback or slow transatlantic vessels, messages could take months to reach their intended recipient. During Benjamin Franklin's tenure as US ambassador to France, for example, diplomatic dispatches could take six months to reach their mark.[21] As a result, before the telegraph diplomats had a very high degree of autonomy in their international engagements. The sheer difficulty of assembling top officials and decision-makers at international meetings necessitated the delegation of significant, even plenipotentiary, powers to diplomatic representatives. Diplomats were laws unto themselves, exercising sovereign authority on behalf of governments.

The widespread adoption of telegraphy altered this situation, greatly accelerating the speed of communications by disentangling it from that of long-distance transportation. Capitals could exercise closer control over

---

[18] Patrick 2014.   [19] Nye 2011, 116–120.   [20] Owen 2015, 30–32.
[21] Aharoni 2015.

diplomatic interactions and even bypass resident missions altogether.[22] The impact of this enhanced capacity to communicate between national capitals was not instantaneous, however, and the full impact of these changes occurred only as the cost of telegraphy declined over a long period. A 780-word transatlantic telegraph from the USA to France in November 1866, for instance, cost an astonishing $19,540.50, over $300,000 in current dollars, a sum triple the annual salary of its sender, US Secretary of State William H. Seward.[23] While the telegraph was used as a means of diplomatic communications by all major FMs by the First World War, costs still limited direct interactions between national capitals.[24] Even in the late 1940s, George Kennan was chided for the high cost of sending his 5,000-word "long telegram."[25] Multilateral messages (i.e., sent to multiple international capitals) only compounded difficulties and costs. These means of communication were, furthermore, unreliable, with messages frequently garbled in transmission or lost. The high risk of interception, furthermore, required extensive cryptography, which slowed telegraphic communications and further increased costs. Given the high costs and difficulty of sending diplomatic cables, documents or analyses of any substantial length were still carried by diplomatic pouch late into the twentieth century. Even the most detailed instructions, moreover, could not anticipate all the issues that might arise. This meant that details of negotiations were necessarily left to local diplomats. While advances in telephonics in the second half of the twentieth century deepened contacts between national capitals, the costs of secure teleconferencing remained high at the century's end.[26]

The costliness and unreliability of communications shaped the design of many existing intergovernmental institutions. These institutions are predicated on a hub-and-spokes structure, connecting FMs (FM$_A$, FM$_B$, etc.) through diplomatic hubs (FIGOs), as depicted in Figure 6.1. Traditional diplomatic hubs are organized around international secretariats with permanent state diplomatic representatives serving in

---

[22] Berridge 2002, 90–91. The growing capacity to communicate with resident missions abroad also helped precipitate the creation of FMs. Berridge 2002, 5.

[23] Nickles 2003, 181.   [24] Nickles 2003, 8.   [25] Keating 2010.

[26] Telephones took a long time to become a regular instrument of governance. President Rutherford B. Hayes was an early adopter in getting a telephone into the White House telegraph room in 1877, only fourteen months after Alexander Graham Bell's famous first call. Rutherford was able to get a good number (1) but his only outside connection was to the Treasury Department. Only in 1929 did President Hoover have a telephone installed in the Oval Office. The Soviet–American "hotline" (which transmitted only text so was neither a telephone nor red) was installed in 1963 after delays in delivering diplomatic messages complicated negotiations during the Cuban Missile Crisis.

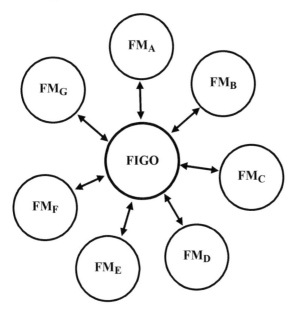

Figure 6.1 FIGOs as diplomatic hubs.

permanent missions at organizational headquarters.[27] In a world of costly communications the hub-and-spokes structure provided the best available means of multilateral diplomacy. This system was characterized by four key features.

First, states delegated authority to international organizations to provide forums and managerial capability to facilitate interstate relations. Technical expertise was concentrated within secretariats to provide advice on cooperation issues. Although states' collective technical capacity usually exceeded that housed within secretariats, this combined national capacity was dispersed and not well connected.[28] The cost of

---

[27] We define diplomatic hubs in terms of traditional geographically based arrangements. Increasingly, the possibility of "virtual diplomatic hubs" is emerging, but our following discussion regarding IIGOs suggests the continued importance of personal face-to-face meetings as part of diplomacy in combination with virtual diplomacy at the intergovernmental level. Virtual diplomacy is increasing the overall scope of international relationships and will likely occupy an increasing proportion of consequential interactions, particularly as the post-Covid-19 world takes shape. But our argument does not imply that face-to-face diplomacy will fade into obsolescence.

[28] Capacity also is unequally distributed. Large and developed countries sometimes have greater capacity than the FIGO, whereas small countries are often reliant on the FIGO or other countries to provide technical assistance. International organizations may have the advantage of providing less biased information to smaller countries and serve an

direct communication, informational exchange, and policy coordination among national technocrats at multiple locations remained prohibitive through much of the twentieth century, so physical proximity of technical specialists and state representatives to handle quotidian decisions on an ongoing basis mattered greatly.

Second, because of the high costs of communications states delegated a wide and diverse array of functions to a relatively small number of international organizations with broad scope. There were scale economies to be realized when capitalizing on established communication channels between diplomatic hubs and national capitals. Maintaining government control over distant representatives was easier when organized in a more centralized manner with a smaller number of high-level national officials abroad. Even "specialized" agencies were embedded in conglomerate international organizations with broad remit, such as the UN or World Bank systems. As new cooperation problems arose, it was usually quicker, cheaper, and easier to assign new tasks to established organizations than to launch new ones.[29] Further economies of scale were achieved by locating FIGOs primarily in a few locations, especially New York and Geneva.

Third, to enhance information flow between the diplomatic hub and national capitals, states created permanent missions to international organizations.[30] Given the diverse functions addressed at hubs, top diplomats had to be generalists, able to move seamlessly across issues. Information – political and technical – was channeled back to the capital from permanent missions through foreign ministries. This system of diplomatic hubs allowed states to economize on communication costs. Large quantities of information on a range of issues could be carried by one diplomatic courier, expensive telegraphs could cover multiple subjects, and delegations from national capitals could address several priorities in one trip. While the most important decisions had to be ratified back home, efficiency required that permanent missions wield substantial autonomy on more routine decisions and in setting the agenda for items to be referred home for concurrence. To enable cooperation, therefore, the hub-and-spokes system integrates political and technical information. However, diplomatic hubs lack the authority necessary to make the highest-level decisions which depend on state membership approval where important decisions and agreements require ratification in national capitals.

---

important role in bringing together national information to create a collective picture that no state has by itself.
[29] Jupille et al. 2013, chapter 2.   [30] Tobin 1933; Potter 1931.

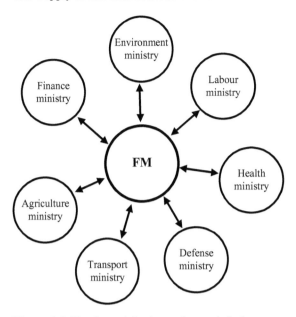

Figure 6.2 Foreign ministries as domestic hubs.

Fourth, FMs served as national hubs for the (indirect) interactions of line departments with international forums, as shown in Figure 6.2. Given the broad scope of issues addressed at diplomatic hubs, the entrenched role of FM officials in those hubs, and the high costs of communicating, FMs were gatekeepers for national engagements in international forums. Gatekeeping within national governments, and control over communications going out via costly telegraph or diplomatic pouch, allowed FMs to establish priorities – reinforcing centralization and hierarchy among and within government departments.[31] In addition, FMs controlled the amount and quality of information sent back from diplomatic hubs and managed its distribution among national government departments. With early advances in telephone communications, FMs acquired a switchboard function, regulating international calls on behalf of national government officials and departments.[32] Thus, FMs were intermediaries among government departments housing the national technical experts of member states that provided the necessary inputs for negotiation and implementation of agreements.

[31] Nickles 2003, 34–35, 49.   [32] Berridge 2002, 14–15.

The hub-and-spokes system crystallized under the auspices of the League of Nations and became the template for modern FIGOs. An independent international civil service was established within the League of Nations in the 1920s by its secretary-general, Eric Drummond.[33] Prior to this secretariat functions had been provided mainly by temporarily detached national officials that remained partial to their own governments. As the benefits of an independent and impartial secretariat became clear, governments created permanent delegations in Geneva to facilitate communications back to capitals and maintain "a watching brief" over the secretariat.[34] Indeed, their enhanced ability to exercise control over distant agents made states more willing to delegate to international organizations. Permanent delegations were particularly prevalent among states situated far from Geneva. European countries, which faced fewer obstacles to travel from their capitals, were slower to adopt this practice.[35]

The hub-and-spokes structure ensured that detailed negotiations and technical work occurred primarily at diplomatic hubs, with technocrats within secretariats producing reports that would be discussed among state representatives and fed, as appropriate, through permanent missions and FMs back to HOGs and technical experts in capitals for input, concurrence, or implementation.[36] The reluctance of governments to concentrate too much authority at the hub – either within intergovernmental organizations' secretariats or by delegation to their own permanent representatives – limited the activities that could be undertaken at the international level. This system also limited the flow and production of political information, since interaction among HOGs was generally infrequent and mediated by FMs. This system created lengthy delegation chains, high sovereignty and management costs, and the potential for opportunism among agents. Nevertheless, it constituted the most advanced institutional technology available throughout the twentieth century to facilitate international cooperation. The alternative of direct interactions among HOGs and the involvement of national decision-makers were simply too costly, slow, and unreliable.

Improved Communications and the Design of International Institutions

Here we develop an alternative HpN model, based on HOGs agreeing in IIGOs on hierarchical directions to be carried out by TGNs among

---

[33] Walters 1965, 75–80.   [34] Walters 1965, 197–199.   [35] Appathurai 1985, 95.
[36] The hub-and-spokes system, therefore, served as a mechanism for reinforcing centralization. Often this system entailed delegation to secretariats and legal-underpinnings.

national line departments. We begin by explaining how advances in communication technologies have enhanced the possibilities for informal international cooperation, resulting in an increase in the number and importance of IIGOs and TGNs. These informal international institutions have important complementarities for the management of international cooperation and limiting sovereignty costs. HOGs reach political agreements in IIGOs that can be implemented by direct TGN interactions among their respective (technical) line departments. FMs and FIGOs no longer need be central actors, although they can play important supporting roles in organizing and facilitating IIGO–TGN interactions. This system combines political and technical information in a new way, allowing them to be managed within separate spheres.

The HpN Model

The arrival of the internet, and the slate of technologies enabled by it, has fundamentally expanded the organizational possibilities available to states. The ability to transmit large quantities of data across borders quickly, cheaply, and reliably, to multiple recipients, simultaneously, has had great implications for international affairs. The telegraph and the telephone accelerated the speed of communication and progressively lowered its cost; the internet has rendered the transmission of even large amounts of information instantaneous and virtually costless; and the continuing drop in the cost and, the increased speed and – over the longer run – falling costs of international travel, has increased the frequency, quality, and scope of interpersonal international interactions.

The ease with which international information exchange and collective action can be organized utilizing new communication technologies has thus reduced the transaction costs of intergovernmental organization.[37] Correspondingly, the bureaucratic infrastructure necessary at the international level for achieving a given measure of cooperation has fallen. Dispersed technical experts can now share information and communicate on an ongoing basis without ever coming together. Video-teleconferencing and email facilitate rapid coordination with actors around the world, enabling "just in time and in place operational effectiveness."[38] Never before has physical distance been so surmountable a barrier to international engagements.[39] Following the Covid-19

---

[37] Shirky 2008, 45–48.   [38] Smith 1997.

[39] This expansion of communication has had many other impacts. Notably important at the international level has been the rise of international nongovernmental organizations (INGOs) as consequential actors. We do not discuss them here, although their

pandemic, states and other international actors have stepped up their use of new communication technologies, realizing policy coordination through online platforms.[40]

New communication technologies have increased international connectivity among national officials and opened up new avenues for transnational knowledge-sharing and persuasion, facilitating international collaborations that would have been infeasible in the past.[41] Effective "self-regulation" by transnational networks of regulators creates new possibilities for regulatory innovation.[42] Professional norms and standards of practice, shared across borders among government experts, provide a vehicle for adaptable modes of governance that do not rely on formal treaties and legalization. The benefits of an independent secretariat (to provide expertise on international issues) and organizational centralization (to coordinate policies across states), two principal motivations for acting through formal international organizations, have diminished.[43]

These informal patterns of cooperation also emerge in combination with FIGOs and formal international legal measures.[44] But the proliferation of voluntary agreements, soft legalization, and TGNs has shown the growing importance of nonbinding cooperative mechanisms in supplementing legalization. These developments have a lasting effect by diminishing the expectation among states that substantive international cooperation requires FIGOs in association with international treaties.[45] Networked TGN interactions can also make it easier to informally engage non-state actors in cooperative forums. For example, less formalized rules concerning membership and participation, as well as more flexible communications, allow non-state actors to become active players within TGNs. Improved communications allow a looser and more varied

increased participation in FIGOs has been one of the important parallel changes in international governance. Ironically, the rise of IIGOs may in part be a means to limit the role of INGOs in interstate diplomacy (Vabulas and Snidal 2013).

[40] The G20 held its first virtual leaders conference on March 26, 2020 to address the pandemic; virtual G20 ministerial and working group meetings have also emerged.

[41] Manulak 2019a; Slaughter 2016   [42] Majone 1997.

[43] On the role of centralization and independence in motivating the use of FIGOs, see Abbott and Snidal 1998.

[44] Raustiala 2002, 84–88.

[45] The rapid growth of informal modes of governance reduces the proportion of consequential activity governed by international treaties. Raustiala argues that TGNs are most likely to substitute for legally binding agreements when regulatory power is moderately asymmetric, when regulatory differences among states are of moderate diversity, and when states are somewhat reluctant to compromise their domestic structures. Raustiala 2002, 16, 89.

constellation of players to interact, potentially opening up multiple centers of institutional activity and increasing flexibility.

Improvements in transportation and communication also make it dramatically easier for HOGs to interact directly through IIGOs and set international agendas. For example, in 1906 Theodore Roosevelt was the first US president to travel abroad (to Panama). Woodrow Wilson made two trips to Europe in the aftermath of the First World War and spent nearly seven months there. Going back and forth more frequently would have taken too much time, since Wilson's trips took nine days each way by ocean liner. By contrast, with the advent of jets, Dwight Eisenhower's eight European trips took about nine hours each way. In 1990 the presidential plane (Air Force One) became a modified Boeing 747 replete with a presidential bedroom, shower, secure communications, and 4,000 square feet of office space. It is hardly surprising that frequent international summitry, and the era of IIGOs, only really began in the 1970s and has since taken off.[46,47]

The speed of international travel allows HOGs to attend international meetings and expeditiously return to their capitals. The low cost and increased feasibility of international communication, moreover, have lowered the threshold point at which international leaders interact directly from their respective capitals.[48] Breaking with traditional diplomatic protocol, for example, some HOGs favor interacting on an almost impromptu basis. This can even involve direct calls over cellular phone[49] or private sidebars at conference dinners.[50] These interactions are very different from the formal, highly scripted interactions of past decades, typically coordinated with substantial FM mediation.

Improved communication technologies enable IIGOs to convene high-level political leaders from different states to provide political guidance for, and orchestrate transnational interactions among, technocrats within national line departments. The Nuclear Security Summit process exemplifies this conjunction where a high-level IIGO established the parameters of an action agenda to be implemented by lower-level informal TGNs, such as the Global Initiative to Combat

---

[46] See: https://en.wikipedia.org/wiki/List_of_international_trips_made_by_the_President_of_the_United_States.

[47] Only 13 of the 149 IIGOs identified by Vabulas and Snidal (2020) were created before 1970 and six of those were regional (mainly intra-European) and therefore more feasible even without modern communication.

[48] Berridge 2002, 91–96. Better communication allows leaders to manage domestic issues while abroad.

[49] PBS News Hour 2017.

[50] Famously, Donald Trump and Vladimir Putin had an (initially) secret conversation at the 2017 G20 conference dinner in Germany. BBC News 2018.

Nuclear Terrorism. Frequently, IIGO leadership takes less direct forms. Instead of calling on particular TGNs to act, high-level forums can set broad priorities that shape the incentive structures that guide lower-level national officials. Thus, even when the role of HOGs is indirect, the shadow of hierarchy can spur TGN collaboration. This arrangement provides a means through which IIGOs, which lack any independent bureaucratic capacity, reach the targets of their regulatory agenda. The lower-level networks are, in turn, enhanced through acting under the authority and legitimacy of the higher-level bodies.

While IIGOs can also orchestrate FIGOs, as the G7/G20 has done vis-à-vis international financial institutions, working through TGNs is often more advantageous from the HOG perspective. First, FIGOs may have a different membership than the IIGO that seeks to orchestrate their activities. As a result, other FIGO members may question the legitimacy of decisions taken in HOG forums in which they lack representation. Second, even for countries represented within the relevant IIGO, FIGO membership typically involves the delegation of decision authority to specific national government departments. Although HOGs ultimately exercise oversight over these delegation relationships, the relevant domestic offices typically guard their operational and decision-making autonomy jealously, even from HOGs. In contrast, the lack of formal organizational arrangements avoids these additional layers of bureaucratic infighting and enhances HOG control. Third, TGNs are flexible and have fluid membership configurations, even involving non-state actors in their deliberations. Rather than requiring consensus, furthermore, TGNs facilitate implementation through whichever domestic agencies support IIGO-sponsored activities. Finally, since informal institutions are not predicated on an international treaty they do not normally require domestic legislation to implement their (voluntary) provisions. The absence of domestic legislation means that the lead department or agency need not be legally specified and can, therefore, more easily shift as operational imperatives change.[51] In short, IIGO–TGN arrangements provide a flexible way for the HOG to control key policies and shape the activities of global technical networks. At the same time the lack of legalization and formalization can maximize the discretion and freedom of maneuver for line departments to implement the agenda.

Advances in communication technologies facilitate synergism between IIGOs and TGNs. The proliferation in the number and scope of IIGO and TGN activities in recent decades has increased the likelihood of

---

[51] For a related argument that IIGOs help the executive branch circumvent domestic legislative constraints, see Vabulas and Snidal 2017.

complementary agendas and institutional aims. As HOGs consider potential cooperative opportunities, the available vehicles for realizing such international collaboration are many. Perhaps more importantly, by enabling the spread of political and technical information about the state of the world, the internet has empowered actors that would have otherwise relied on classified diplomatic dispatches or the reports of international secretariats. These actors can now engage from capitals with minimal involvement by intermediaries based at diplomatic hubs. By cutting out multiple levels of delegation between dispersed national officials responsible for implementing international agreements, states dramatically reduce the management costs of policy coordination and regulatory alignment. This means that a growing proportion of consequential international governance occurs in a more decentralized format, outside of the formally established hubs that have been the center of intergovernmental relations for a century.[52] This potent combination addresses some of the principal defects of both highly scripted, leader-driven interactions and more substantive, yet less legitimate, informal meetings of lower-level officials.[53]

Improving communication and transportation is much more than a matter of lowering costs; it is a matter of creating new possibilities for global governance. Frequent, low-cost interactions among subject matter experts allow HOGs to avoid the sovereignty costs of delegating to FIGOs, a key "demand side" explanation for the rise of IIGOs.[54] As we discuss later in this section, IIGO–TGN relations further strengthen central executive authority within states, allowing HOGs to bypass FMs and directly engage global networks of subject matter experts.

We summarize and stylize these changes in terms of the HpN model in Figure 6.3, which depicts two layers of interaction among and within

---

[52] Our analysis focuses on high-level interactions among HOGs at IIGOs. Ultimately the scope of these interactions is limited by the capacities, priorities, and attention span of the HOG. Even though we include other top-level decision-makers within that category (i.e., those who can make commitments on behalf of a state, including ministers and ambassadors), and even with the expansion of the HOGs' immediate executive apparatus – such as the US National Security Council, the German Chancellery, or the Canadian Privy Council Office, – this capacity is limited. So our analysis does not include as broad a range of networked TGNs as in Anne Marie Slaughter's work, especially TGN networks focused on coordinating technical issues on relatively settled issues that operate directly between national departments.

[53] Pouliot 2016, 185–186.

[54] Vabulas and Snidal, 2013. Sovereignty and policy costs are often much more important than material costs. While many IIGOs are relatively inexpensive, others are more expensive. A striking example is the 2010 Canadian G8/G20 summits costing more than twice the Organisation for Economic Co-operation and Development annual budget. We thank David Hagebölling for this point.

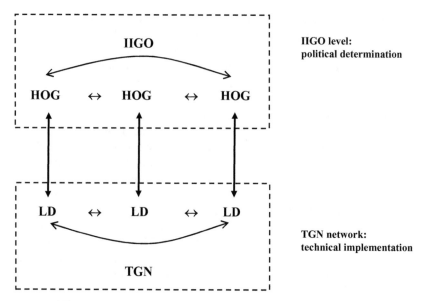

Figure 6.3 The HpN model: IIGOs governing the TGN network.

three states – although the figure could be extended to include many more states. The top IIGO layer consists of *political* interactions among HOGs and top officials from different states (HOG↔HOG) setting broad agendas, striking political bargains, and making interstate commitments. The outcome of IIGO meetings is to send directions "down" to specialized national agencies to interact with their counterparts in other states to develop and implement agreements in terms of specific policies. The lower level of Figure 6.3 represents a TGN of international *technical* interactions among national-level line departments and agencies (LD↔LD). This network operates by sharing information and expertise across national borders and negotiating details of implementation, including developing proposals to send "up" to HOGs for further commitments. But TGNs are limited to technical decisions and cannot make political commitments (although these blur into one another). Line departments also contribute to setting the agenda for HOGs at IIGOs, sometimes mediated by FMs (LD↔FM↔HOG), which we do not depict here.

Like every model, HpN offers a highly stylized depiction designed to highlight its essential differences from the diplomatic hub-and-spokes model of Figure 6.1. As noted, FMs could be included in Figure 6.3 both to show their important role in contributing to IIGO agendas and sometimes in gatekeeping among line departments. By not including those connections we emphasize the shift whereby HOGs assume more direct control of setting international policy and TGNs exercise greater influence over the implementation of cooperation. We also do not include nongovernmental organizations (NGOs), or firms, which sometimes play a role through participation within broadened TGN networks. Similarly, we have not depicted FIGOs in Figure 6.3. Most significantly, IIGOs sometimes deal directly through FIGOs – as the G20 does by orchestrating the International Monetary Fund and other financial institutions.[55] These FIGOs, in turn, often provide information and advice to national line departments, thereby blending Figure 6.3 with the more traditional models of Figures 6.1 and 6.2. Such models provide useful benchmarks for understanding the wide variety of arrangements that have opened up in this period of more efficient communication.

Choosing HpN over Hub-and-Spokes

The ability of national experts in line departments and government agencies to communicate directly on an ongoing basis from national capitals presents an alternative to concentrating technical expertise and managerial capacity in international secretariats. While independent secretariats continue to provide important benefits in many contexts, many IIGOs and other cooperative forums without secretariats have been established in recent decades. Furthermore, the role of existing secretariats is changing. The United Nations Secretariat, for example, has seen its administrative and coordinative role decline relative to operational activities.[56] Similarly, with the increased capacity of technical experts and lower-level officials to communicate directly with their international counterparts, the representational role of diplomatic generalists with limited subject matter expertise has been lessened. Consequently, new communications technologies have eroded the logic of diplomatic hubs.[57]

The coordinative role of FMs is also undermined in a world of decentralized international communications among line departments. Costless and reliable communications diminish the gatekeeping power obtained from rationing space in costly telegraphs or diplomatic pouches. In addition, as the cost of transmitting information has fallen knowledge

---

[55] Viola 2015.
[56] United Nations General Assembly, "Investing in the United Nations: For a Stronger Organization Worldwide: Report by the Secretary-General," A/60/692, March 7, 2006.
[57] For a general discussion of the internet's disintermediating effect on social relations see. Rothkopf 1998, 335.

of important international developments has become much more wide-spread. This has decreased the reliance of both line departments and HOGs on information provided by diplomats through the FM. With cheap international telephone and internet calls, the past insistence by many FMs that they play the role of switchboard or "international operator" among government departments is similarly undermined.[58] The result has been a diffusion of diplomatic functions to heads of state and other government departments, thereby diminishing the role of FMs both from "above" and, in a sense, from "below."[59]

National agencies and HOGs now participate directly in global talks on a much more frequent basis.[60] Indeed, the possibility of ongoing, decentralized interactions may be stretching the definition of "inter-national talks." This has led many line departments to establish their own international bureaus and secure their own representation within embassies abroad.[61] The diffusion of diplomatic functions across gov-ernment departments and agencies has necessitated a strengthening of the role of central executive agencies – such as the US National Security Council, Canada's Privy Council Office, the German Chancellery and the United Kingdom's Cabinet Office – in coordinating whole-of-gov-ernment international policy-making.[62] The transformation of national foreign policy-making has also affected the bureaucratic design of FMs. In order to compete with these new alternatives, FMs have expanded their subject matter expertise in recent decades, for example through a proliferation of functional bureaus within FMs covering issues such as non-proliferation, human rights, or environmental affairs.[63] This changing operational context has contributed to ongoing efforts to imple-ment major reforms within FMs. In the international affairs of the internet era, the importance of FM "middle-men" is shrinking.[64]

---

[58] Berridge 2002, 14–15.   [59] Hamilton and Langhorne 2011.

[60] Copeland 2009, 152.

[61] Take the Canadian Mission to the European Union, for example. In addition to Foreign Ministry representatives, the embassy includes representatives from Agriculture and Agri-Foods Canada, the Canadian Border Services Agency, the Canadian Food Inspection Agency, Immigration, Refugees and Citizenship Canada, and the Department of Justice. See: GAC 2018.

[62] Hamilton and Langhorne 2011, 259–263.

[63] Hamilton and Langhorne 2011, 233. A comparison of the organizational charts of foreign ministries in recent decades with those of the 1940s, for example, illustrates the dramatic growth of functional bureaus. While not disappearing, geographical bureaus have remained roughly constant in number and have declined in relative prestige.

[64] Disintermediation in the international space is manifested mainly in a changing role for actors relative to their past functions. In the internet era, functions that rely mainly on physical proximity to bring value will be limited over time. See Copeland 2009, 156.

Rapid and cheap communications allow states to incur fewer sovereignty costs by minimizing the delegation of decision authority to secretariats; internally other domestic agencies are not beholden to enterprising permanent missions controlled by their FM. Thus, the availability of direct modes of governance creates opportunities for states to economize on the costs of international cooperation and provides opportunities for other departments and even HOGs to get out of the shadow of their foreign offices.

The extensive international bureaucratization of many FIGOs, which are characterized by formal decision structures and legalization, is increasingly regarded as cumbersome and unwieldy.[65] Informal arrangements can bring a degree of flexibility and adaptability to cooperative relations that complement legally binding formal structures. Orchestration points to further possibilities for voluntary collaboration, whereby high-level bodies enlist "intermediaries," such as other intergovernmental organizations, NGOs, or private regulatory bodies, in advancing regulatory aims.[66] Institutions, such as the G20, utilize their flexibility, collaborative set-up, and legitimacy to further cooperation through intermediary institutions with requisite national and international legal authorities. Orchestration can obviate the need for introducing new regulatory powers and avoid drawbacks of establishing new formal international machinery.

Opportunities for adaptation and innovation made possible by new communication technologies facilitate ongoing course corrections by regulators and decision-makers. In this environment states can flexibly move back and forth between the formulation and implementation of international agreements, adapting at more frequent intervals to changing circumstances and emerging best practices. These experiences can be shared among national government officials and HOGs, providing quick adaptation and enhancements of policies. Such "real time" international collaboration would have been infeasible or prohibitively costly before the adoption of new communication technologies into multilateral relations. This stands in stark contrast to formal legal arrangements, which require extensive negotiation, typically take years to ratify and implement, and therefore promote institutional stasis. By contrast, informal agreements can be focused on the progressive strengthening of national policies within a defined issue area. While binding legal agreements will continue to provide a key foundation for the international

---

[65] Slaughter 2004, 181; Majone 1997, 267.   [66] Abbott et al. 2015.

system, informal arrangements add considerable value when flexibility is required or when binding agreements prove elusive.

Of course, FIGOs are also adopting new communication technologies, utilizing nonbinding agreements and thinning bureaucratization, but their capacity to do so is limited by their locked-in formality. The hub-and-spokes model exists uneasily alongside an informal IIGO–TGN nexus because the viability of hubs rests on ensuring that the bulk of consequential interactions occur at the hub. Formal rules and procedures enforce this system, creating a context that is inherently inimical to the development of the multiple centers of consequential institutional activity that are characteristic of decentralized networks. The established role of secretariats, permanent missions, and FMs within these institutions means that key actors have a stake in preserving the central role of formally established hubs. But it has become increasingly difficult for them to maintain a predominance that was predicated to a large extent on the costliness and infeasibility of frequent transnational interactions among national officials.

States have created informal intergovernmental structures outside the auspices of existing formal institutions for two main reasons. First, the start-up costs of launching new institutional frameworks have dropped precipitously in recent decades. Improved communications make it easier to locate like-minded actors, identify areas for agreement, and develop a cooperative response. New tools of social interaction have greatly eased coordination among actors at a distance, including, as we have seen, for HOGs and TGNs. This is the same dynamic that has lowered the barriers to entry into world political actorhood for a range of players, facilitating a diffusion of power within the international system.[67] Given low levels of bureaucratization and legalization, furthermore, informal governance structures can be established rapidly and cheaply, lowering ex ante transaction costs.[68] While falling start-up costs lower the threshold at which states create new structures, it is nevertheless normally easier to add additional functions on to an existing international organization than to launch new ones.[69] Though eased greatly by new communication technologies, efforts to coordinate participation and establish shared expectations around new structures remain resource-intensive and increase transaction costs. Thus, lower start-up costs only provide a partial explanation for the increased resort to informal governance.

The second reason for the rise of informal governance is that it dramatically reduces the ongoing costs of international organization.

---

[67] Naím 2013, 44.   [68] Vabulas and Snidal 2013, 211.   [69] Jupille et al. 2013.

Limited bureaucratization of informal governance structures helps to explain the appeal of informal institutions relative to FIGOs. The absence of an organizational headquarters and, in many cases, annual budgets allows countries to limit the monetary commitments associated with their participation. The participatory and self-organizing quality of informal governance reduces the organizational and administrative burden of international cooperation, allowing activity levels to ebb and flow as required. Informal modes of governance also generally entail minimal sovereignty costs, allowing states to maximize their freedom of maneuver and flexibility. Moreover, since informal governance mechanisms do not feature binding legalization or formal organizational structures the participation of a wide array of actors with varying levels of commitment can be enabled. As the circle of involved actors widens these institutional structures can benefit from network effects.

The growing view that hub-and-spokes-style cooperation is unnecessarily costly and inefficient is thus partly a response to the increased supply of less bureaucratic institutional design alternatives. Existing, hub-and-spokes-style organizations have a bureaucratic stake in preserving the status quo that makes them change-resistant so that the most significant changes in institutional choice and design are seen in the proliferation of alternative, informal forums, such as IIGOs and TGNs. These are occupying a growing proportion of substantive international activity and contribute to changing expectations concerning the size and role of international bureaucracy. In contexts where limiting international delegation and bureaucracy is feasible, the ability to economize on management and sovereignty costs motivates states to opt for less formal modes of cooperation.

Informal Governance in the Communications Era

The preceding discussion leads to two conjectures concerning the increasing tendency for states to favor informal cooperation through IIGOs and TGNs. First, new communication possibilities make IIGOs and TGNs possible; and their low costs promote growth of informal governance mechanisms. The view that existing structures are excessively bureaucratic and that formal decision mechanisms are unnecessarily cumbersome is a key motivating factor for informality. An expressed desire among leading actors to avoid excessive formalization and bureaucratization would be an observable implication of this institutional design imperative. States also wish to minimize sovereignty costs, retaining full decision authority over cooperative efforts. Given our emphasis on the role of technology in enhancing the supply conditions for informal governance, one would expect to observe a key role for new technologies in making informal governance arrangements possible.

Second, changes in communications technology fuel a conjunction between the high-level political activities of IIGOs and lower-level TGNs. This conjunction may be top down, with IIGOs calling on TGNs to advance priorities identified in high-level forums. Or it may be bottom up through TGN initiatives that identify a favorable political opportunity structure brought about by IIGO activities and work within these broad parameters to advance their technical or operational agenda. What distinguishes this form of cooperation from traditional hub-and-spokes interactions are: (1) a limited role for bureaucratic intermediaries, such as FMs and international secretariats; (2) the deliberate decoupling of technical and political decision-making fora; and (3) a more direct role for HOGs and line departments in international cooperation.[70] Observable implications would be interactivity between the activities of IIGOs and TGNs, such as through IIGOs statements calling on lower-level institutions to implement IIGO priorities, or the explicit invocation of IIGO decisions as a rationale for TGN activities.

The Institutional Design of the Proliferation Security Initiative

We illustrate the impact of technology on institutional design and activities through a case study of international efforts to combat the illicit trafficking of weapons of mass destruction (WMD). The creation of the PSI in 2003 constitutes a "least likely" case of institutional design for an assessment of the impact of informal governance structures. The ongoing, detailed exchange of policy information characteristic of TGNs and most informal forms of governance is unlikely to occur in issue areas with serious national security implications. Indeed, the exchange of intelligence is one of the most carefully guarded and sensitive areas of international cooperation. Moreover, while efforts to counter the trafficking of WMD have technical aspects, most of these issues have significant political implications that would make world leaders read "technical" reports with greater care and less deference.

Subsequent to the discovery of Scud missiles being transferred to Yemen on an unmarked North Korean freighter, US president George

---

[70] We are drawing the extreme case here. In practice, for example, FMs may play an important role in the preparation of IIGO meetings, although with line ministers directly involved there is no FM monopoly. FIGOs may similarly play a role in facilitating TGN networks.

W. Bush proposed a PSI in a May 2003 speech; the PSI was established among eleven countries in Madrid two weeks later. Its initial design was strongly shaped by US leadership and eschewed formal bureaucratization or legally binding arrangements. Indeed, a PSI is "an activity, not an organization."[71] The PSI's foundational document, its *Statement of Interdiction Principles*, requires a political commitment by participating states to cooperate in the interdiction of shipments of WMD between "actors of proliferation concern." States join the PSI effort through unilateral endorsement of the *Statement*, which is a nonbinding pledge with no international legal standing.[72] There are no PSI "members" per se, just "endorsing" or "participating" states. The PSI has no organizational headquarters, no secretariat, and no permanent missions accredited to it.[73] All meetings are hosted on a voluntary basis by participating states.

Despite this light institutional footprint, PSI states have established shared expectations concerning key institutional design features, including criteria for participation and the scope of institutional activities. The PSI's twenty-one-country Operational Experts Group (OEG) is a TGN that meets on an annual basis and serves a steering function. High-Level Political Meetings occur on a quinquennial basis supplemented by Mid-Level Political Meetings – usually convened at the assistant secretary level – that serve the IIGO function of establishing a flexible and voluntary set of action items for endorsing states to pursue both individually and collectively. These are typically contained within "Joint Statements" adopted by endorsing states.[74]

PSI states cooperate on the interdiction of WMD, as well as in related areas, such as the enhancement of national export control and customs enforcement mechanisms. The high-level political commitments contained within the *Statement of Interdiction Principles* are coordinated at the international level while individual states implement these principles according to their specific national circumstances and legal authorities. With an OEG providing the most active forum for collaboration, the PSI enables networked cooperation among military, intelligence, customs, legal, and diplomatic officials with national operational

---

[71] Durkalec 2012, 1. See also Belcher 2011.
[72] The *Statement of Interdiction Principles* proposes to make use of states' domestic legal authorities and relevant international law. Thus, it makes no claim to constitute international law.
[73] Durkalec 2012, 2. Note how closely this fits the Vabulas and Snidal's (2013, 2020) definition of IIGO
[74] Dunne 2013, 6.

responsibilities.[75] These transgovernmental connections are encouraged by the OEG but are not centrally organized. Endorsing states simply organize relevant events and attribute them to the PSI. No state or small group of states has a veto over these activities.

The PSI is a clear example of the informal HpN governance that has proliferated in recent decades. Though built upon a nonbinding, political commitment with no formal organizational foundation, TGN interactions are too structured and regularized to be regarded as purely ad hoc coordination. HOG-level interactions through an IIGO provide a political foundation for operation-level interactions.

Supply-Side Drivers

The PSI's design was shaped significantly by changed supply conditions for informal governance, allowing for a minimization of management or sovereignty costs. Consistent with our argument, informality is enabled by the technological viability of using TGN and IIGO alternatives to the hub-and-spokes system. Moreover, the adaptability and flexibility of TGNs and IIGOs allow for quick interstate cooperation to govern rapidly evolving circumstances where states would be unwilling to delegate requisite authority to FIGOs.

Endorsing states established a strong operational focus for PSI, cutting out certain diplomatic intermediaries in shaping the initiative. Controversially, diplomatic players that contributed no operational capabilities were marginalized in early discussions, ensuring that "PSI would be the real thing, not just chitchat."[76] The strong operational and expert orientation of early meetings was enhanced through joint exercises and military engagements. Intelligence and law enforcement sessions were added shortly thereafter.[77] When the OEG emerged as the institutional successor of the "core group," the PSI's technical and operational orientation was reinforced. Delegations to OEG meetings, which include representation from multiple government departments and agencies, are frequently led by defense ministries or operational agencies rather than FMs.[78] Other government organizations participating at PSI

---

[75] See Manulak (2019b) for a detailed discussion of transgovernmental linkages in the context of the PSI.

[76] Bolton 2007, 122–124.   [77] Koch 2012, 20–21.

[78] Koch 2012, 20. Because PSI objectives are relatively stable there is no need for ongoing high-level intervention as there is in areas such as financial management where circumstances change more rapidly requiring that, for example, the G7 and G20 meet on a more regular basis. Were a proliferation crisis to require it, the PSI could provide the organizational framework within which to provide such leadership.

meetings frequently include customs and border services and police agencies, as well as justice, health, finance, and transport departments. These actors weave transgovernmental linkages that interact on an ongoing, intersessional basis, furthering implementation of the *Statement of Interdiction Principles* and associated national legal authorities. Linkages among OEG countries are complemented by ongoing capacity-building work.

PSI states put a premium on the development of transgovernmental linkages among operational agencies of endorsing countries. No central international coordinating machinery, such as a secretariat or permanent missions, was established to provide a basis for a hub-and-spokes structure. Interestingly, this networked set-up has proved congenial for non-state actors, such as think tanks and transnational corporations. At the 2016 OEG meeting, for example, representatives from the Royal United Services Institute and international shipping firms enjoyed almost unfettered access to the discussions. The viability of this dispersed network of officials is predicated on the availability of email and reliable telephone networks to facilitate cooperation in the interdiction of WMD shipments. A password-protected PSI website, maintained by the German government, facilitates the communication and coordination of PSI activities and promotes the sharing of best practices among national officials.[79] Such a lean cooperative endeavor would not have been feasible in a world of expensive, slow, or unreliable communication. The minimal central coordination machinery erected would have been a recipe for inaction and confusion.

This informal institutional set-up was a deliberate effort among endorsing states to make the PSI as bureaucratically lean as possible.[80] The statements and recollections of those involved in its institutional design suggest that this choice was motivated by a distaste for the longer-term costs and heavy bureaucracy characteristic of FIGOs.[81] States built a cooperative infrastructure that minimized the role of diplomatic intermediaries operating at a hub, instead weaving multiple linkages across government agencies to facilitate interdiction operations on a broad international basis.

IIGO–TGN Conjunctures

In addition to flourishing transgovernmental linkages, the PSI's cooperative agenda has been shaped by HOG engagement and linkages with

---

[79] Dunne 2013, 41–42.   [80] Bolton testimony, 175.   [81] Bolton 2007, 122–124.

IIGOs. Endorsement of the *Statement of Interdiction Principles* constitutes a HOG pledge to implement the principles contained within it. This overarching political commitment provides an authoritative basis for ongoing activities of TGNs operating through PSI forums. National recommitments to the *Statement* have been frequent, most recently at the 2018 PSI High-Level Political Meeting and the 2016 Mid-Level Political Meeting.

PSI's early development relied heavily on direct HOG engagement. Its status as a US presidential initiative immediately afforded those seeking to expand participation in the PSI with access to the highest levels of decision-making within other capitals. As one participant in the PSI's early negotiations recalls, HOG-level support meant that conversations with other governments were akin to "knocking on an open door." High-level support enabled those involved in the PSI to quickly bring line department TGNs into the PSI fold. Domestically, the PSI's status as a presidential initiative and the necessity of ensuring coordination across multiple government agencies privileged the position of the National Security Council vis-à-vis other US players.

Ongoing HOG guidance and direction has been provided at regular intervals through G7/G8 statements on nonproliferation and disarmament, including in 2008, 2009, 2012, and 2016.[82] G7/G8 statements have voiced continued support for and prioritized the PSI among competing forums and in relation to other activities underway in the non-proliferation space. Further HOG support for the PSI has been provided through other HOG statements, most notably by the US president, and through ministerial statements such as the 2016 Port of Spain Declaration of the Conference of the Defense Ministers of the Americas.[83]

The PSI advances the G7/G8 nonproliferation and disarmament agenda, providing a ready vehicle to give effect to the political agenda of HOGs. The fact that all G7/G8 members are leading participants in the PSI's OEG further reinforces this IIGO–TGN conjunction. Tight linkages forged through the PSI among national militaries, customs services, intelligence agencies, and export control bureaus complement the high-level political attributes of the G7/G8 processes. Symbiosis between political and technical forums is a defining feature of the HpN relationship. Rather than have their messaging filtered through formal diplomatic channels, HOGs call on TGNs of domestic agencies with strong operational foundations to advance this broader international political agenda.

---

[82] See, G8 2008, 2009, 2012; G7 2016.
[83] Obama 2009, 2016; Conference of Defense Ministers of the Americas 2016.

TGN actors within the PSI, furthermore, benefit from the political authority and high agenda status provided by IIGO statements that reinforce and legitimize their working-level interactions. The PSI *Statement of Interdiction Principles*, for example, points to the consistency of the principles with recent G8 statements.[84] In turn the consistency of the PSI with the agenda of leading HOG forums underpins the high political status that the PSI enjoys within national government activities in the counter-proliferation realm. G7/G8 backing demonstrates that the PSI remains a high priority at the HOG level and helps to ensure that domestic government agencies continue to resource their participation in PSI exercises and activities. Within the PSI the shadow of hierarchy works in an indirect though potent manner.

There is, therefore, a strong and symbiotic relationship between the broader political agenda of the G7/G8 in the non-proliferation and disarmament space and the operational interactions of PSI-endorsing states. The G7/G8 benefits from the networked operational linkages of the PSI; conversely, the PSI, which plays host to flourishing transgovernmental linkages, benefits from the political authority of the G7/G8, and from the endorsement of the *Statement of Interdiction Principles* by HOGs. Finally, this discussion points out that the HpN model itself is flexible: just as the PSI guides multiple TGNs in different technical areas, so other IIGOs such as the G7/G8 provide political support and guidance for those TGNs.

Conclusion

This chapter has shown how technological change enables informal modes of international cooperation and motivates states to use them. In the post-Covid-19 world, where states have been forced to increase their use of communication technologies as a means of policy coordination, these trends are likely to accelerate. While traditional FIGOs have been organized around a hub-and-spokes system, improvements in communication and transportation have fundamentally altered the cooperative landscape. Whereas FMs have been traditional gatekeepers for national diplomacy and operated heavily through FIGOs in their multilateral relations, national line departments and agencies increasingly operate independently of both FMs and FIGOs. Higher-level political guidance and authorization on broad policy issues can be provided by HOGs and their central executive through periodic IIGO interactions.

---

[84] Proliferation Security Initiative 2003.

Line departments and agencies then refine and implement decisions in a rapid, reliable, and low-cost manner through TGN arrangements. Both the role of FMs in managing individual states' multilateral policy and the value-added of high levels of delegation to intergovernmental organizations – key characteristics of the hub-and-spokes system – have diminished as a result. While FIGOs will continue to occupy a prominent place in the international landscape, the proportion of consequential international activities occurring within their remit is likely to continue to shrink as states increasingly embrace informal modes of governance.

Our analysis of the institutional design of the PSI explored the impact of technological change on the design and interaction of informal international institutions. The decentralized institutional form avoids high management costs associated with utilizing existing formal intergovernmental structures, which are cumbersome and excessively bureaucratic. Nonbinding commitments allow states to adapt the pace and scale of implementation to national conditions, minimizing sovereignty costs. The PSI case further highlights how high-level engagement can provide an agenda-setting and convening mechanism for a range of TGNs.

The increasingly informal design of international institutions has important implications for the exercise of power in the international system. Within the hub-and-spokes system, smaller states could concentrate diplomatic capacity at hubs and benefit from the technical expertise of secretariats. A world where policy coordination occurs increasingly through TGNs of national officials engaging on an ongoing basis from capitals further advantages states with greater national bureaucratic capacity. It has thus become more difficult for small states to use a limited number of diplomats, reinforced by the technical capacity within secretariats, to "punch above their weight" in intergovernmental organizations. States with capacity to organize operational exercises and workshops, and promote export of their regulatory models, can amplify their influence through TGNs.[85] When IIGOs orchestrate the activities of TGNs, furthermore, states that have representation in these forums are further advantaged. G7 states, for example, may be able to augment their influence in these types of arrangements.

Digital diplomacy and "webcraft" are vital tools of international influence going forward and states that continue to emphasize more traditional modes of diplomacy may be outmaneuvered by nimble international players that recognize the importance of positioning themselves in nodal positions among actors. Finally, non-state actors such as

---

[85] Raustiala 2002.

firms and NGOs may gain better access through connections with domestic partners in TGN networks but have weaker access to IIGOs than to (some) FIGOs to which they are increasingly being accredited.

The preceding discussion highlights the importance of conjunctures among high-level IIGOs and TGNs, with the former authorizing, legitimizing, and convening the activities of the latter. TGNs, in turn, extend the reach of HOGs, allowing these bodies to regulate national actors. This complementary activity strengthens both forms of informal governance. In this world the value-added of the hub-and-spokes system – predicated on delegation to FMs and international secretariats – is reduced. Furthermore, flexibility and collaborative quality are major advantages of informal governance. This emerging mode of HpN governance represents a potentially fundamental shift in patterns of international cooperation.

References

Abbott, Kenneth W. and Duncan Snidal. 1998. Why States Act through Formal International Organizations. *The Journal of Conflict Resolution* 42 (1): 9–23.

Abbott, Kenneth W., Philipp Genschel, Duncan Snidal, and Bernhard Zangl, eds. 2015, *International Organizations as Orchestrators*. Cambridge: Cambridge University Press.

Aharoni, Ido. 2015. How Technology Has Revolutionized Diplomacy. *Time*, September 8, 2015. http://time.com/4015667/how-technology-has-revolutionized-diplomacy/.

Appathurai, Edward R. 1985. Permanent Missions in New York. In *Diplomacy at the UN*, edited by Geoff Berridge and Anthony Jennings, 94–108. Houndmills: Macmillan.

BBC News. 2018. Trump and Putin Had Another, Undisclosed Conversation at G20. www.bbc.co.uk/news/world-us-canada-40651502.

Belcher, Emma. 2011. The Proliferation Security Initiative: Lessons for Using Nonbinding Agreements. Working Paper, Council on Foreign Relations, International Institutions and Global Governance Program, July.

Berridge, Geoff. 2002. *Diplomacy: Theory and Practice*, 2nd edition. London: Palgrave.

Bolton, John. 2007. *Surrender Is Not an Option: Defending America at the United Nations and Abroad*. New York: Threshold Editions.

Conference of Defense Ministers of the Americas. 2016. Port of Spain Declaration. Twelfth Conference of the CDMA, October 10–12, 2016, Port of Spain, Trinidad and Tobago. http://scm.oas.org/pdfs/2016/CP36917E.pdf

Copeland, Daryl. 2009. *Guerilla Diplomacy: Rethinking International Relations*. Boulder, CO: Lynne Rienner.

Dunne, Aaron. 2013. *The Proliferation Security Initiative: Legal Considerations and operational Realities*. Policy paper 36. Solna: Stockholm International Peace Research Institute.

Durkalec, Jacek. 2012. The Proliferation Security Initiative: Evolution and Future Prospects. *EU Non-Proliferation Papers*, June 16.

G7. 2016. G7 Statement on Non-proliferation and Disarmament . Hiroshima, Japan, April 11, 2016. www.g7.utoronto.ca/foreign/formin160411-nonproliferation.html.

G8. 2008. G8 Declaration on Political Issues. Hokkaido, Tokyo, Japan, July 6–9, 2008. https://georgewbush-whitehouse.archives.gov/news/releases/2008/07/20080708-10.html.

2009. L'Aquila Statement on Non-Proliferation. L'Aquila, Italy, July 9, 2009. www.g8.utoronto.ca/summit/2009laquila/2009-nonproliferation.html.

2012. Group of Eight Declaration on Nonproliferation and Disarmament for 2012. Camp David, Maryland, USA, May 21, 2012. www.g8.utoronto.ca/summit/2012campdavid/g8-npt.html; www.g8.utoronto.ca/foreign/ for min160411-nonproliferation.html.

Haass, Richard N. 2001. *The Reluctant Sheriff: The United States After the Cold War*. New York: Council on Foreign Relations.

2017. *A World in Disarray: American Foreign Policy and the Crisis of the Old Order*. New York: Penguin.

Hamilton, Keith and Richard Langhorne. 2011. *The Practice of Diplomacy: Its Evolution, Theory and Administration*, 2nd edition. London: Routledge.

Holmes, Marcus. 2018. *Face-to-Face Diplomacy: Social Neuroscience and International Relations*. Cambridge: Cambridge University Press.

Jupille, Joseph, Walter Mattli, and Duncan Snidal. 2013. *Institutional Choice and Global Commerce*. Cambridge: Cambridge University Press.

Keating, Joshua E. Why Do Diplomats Still Send Cables? To Keep a Record and Advance Their Careers. *Foreign Policy*, November 30, 2010. http://foreignpolicy.com/2010/11/30/why-do-diplomats-still-send-cables/.

Koch, Susan. 2012. *Proliferation Security Initiative: Origins and Evolution*. Occasional Paper No. 9. Washington: National Defense University Press.

Majone, Giandomenico. 1997. The New European Agencies: Regulation by Information. *Journal of European Public Policy*, 4 (2): 262–275.

Manulak, Michael W. 2019a. Why and How to Succeed at Network Diplomacy. *The Washington Quarterly* 42 (1): 171–181.

2019b. Turning up the Heat on North Korea. *The National Interest*, April 23. https://nationalinterest.org/blog/korea-watch/turning-heat-north-korea-53922.

Mitzen, Jennifer. 2013. *Power in Concert: The Nineteenth-Century Origins of Global Governance*. Chicago: University of Chicago Press.

Naím, Moisés. 2013. *The End of Power: From Boardrooms to Battlefields and Churches to States, Why Being in Charge Isn't What It Used to Be*. New York: Basic Books.

Nickles, David Paull. 2003. *Under the Wire: How the Telegraph Changed Diplomacy*. Cambridge, MA: Harvard University Press.

Nye, Joseph S. 2011. *The Future of Power*. New York: Perseus.

Obama, Barack. 2009. Remarks by President Barak Obama in Prague as Delivered. April 5, 2009. https://obamawhitehouse.archives.gov/the-press-office/remarks-president-barack-obama-prague-delivered.

2016. Statement to the PSI 2016 Mid-Level Political Meeting. January 20, 2016. https://2009-2017.state.gov/documents/organization/252009.pdf.

Owen, Taylor. 2015. *Disruptive Power: The Crisis of the State in the Digital Age.* Oxford: Oxford University Press.

Patrick, Stewart. 2014. The Unruled World: The Case for Good Enough Global Governance. *Foreign Affairs* (January/February): 58–73.

PBS News Hour. 2017. AP Report: Trump Has Urged World Leaders to Call His Cell Phone. May 30, 2017. www.pbs.org/newshour/nation/ap-report-trump-urged-world-leaders-call-cell-phone.

Potter, Pitman B. 1931 Permanent Delegations to the League of Nations. *American Political Science Review* 25 (1): 21–44.

Pouliot, Vincent. 2016. *International Pecking Orders: The Politics and Practice of Multilateral Diplomacy.* Cambridge: Cambridge University Press.

Proliferation Security Initiative. 2003. *Statement of Interdiction Principles.* www.psi-online.info/Vertretung/psi/en/07-statement/Interdiction-Principes.html.

Raustiala, Kal. 2002. The Architecture of International Cooperation: Transgovernmental Networks and the Future of International Law. *Virginia Journal of International Law* 43: 1–92.

Rothkopf, David J. 1998. Cyberpolitik: The Changing Nature of Power in the Information Age. *Journal of International Affairs* 51 (2): 325–359.

Shirky, Clay. 2008. *Here Comes Everybody: The Power of Organizing without Organizations.* London: Penguin.

Slaughter, Anne-Marie. 2004. *A New World Order.* Princeton: Princeton University Press.

2016. Global Complexity: Intersection of Chessboard and Web Trends. *Notes Internacionales* 147 (May): 1–6.

2017. *The Chessboard and the Web: Strategies of Connection in a Networked World.* New Haven, CT: Yale University Press.

Smith, Gordon. 1997. *The Challenge of Virtual Diplomacy.* United States Institute of Peace. www.usip.org/sites/default/files/challenge_virtual_diplomacy_vdi.pdf.

Tobin, Harold. 1933. The Problem of Permanent Representation at the League of Nations. *Political Science Quarterly* 48 (4): 481–512.

Vabulas, Felicity and Duncan Snidal. 2013. Organization without Delegation: Informal Intergovernmental Organizations and the Spectrum of Intergovernmental Arrangements. *Review of International Organizations* 8 (2): 193–220.

2017. Bypassing Domestic Political Constraints through Informal Intergovernmental Organizations. Presented at the International Studies Association Meetings, Baltimore, February.

2020. Cooperation under Autonomy: Building and Analysing the Informal Intergovernmental Organizations 2.0 Data Set. *Journal of Peace Research:* 1–11. https://doi.org/10.1177/0022343320943920.

Viola, Lora Anne. 2015. Orchestration by Design: The G20 in International Financial Regulation. In *International Organizations as Orchestrators*, edited by Kenneth W. Abbott, Philipp Genschel, Duncan Snidal, and Bernhard Zangl, 88–113. Cambridge: Cambridge University Press.

Walters, Francis Paul. 1965. *A History of the League of Nations.* London: Oxford University Press.

Wheeler, Nicholas. 2018. *Trusting Enemies: Interpersonal Relationships in International Conflict.* Oxford: Oxford University Press.

7   Global Governance, Expert Networks, and "Fragile States"

Leonard Seabrooke and Ole Jacob Sending

The first wave of global governance studies was premised on the notion that the very term signaled a significant transformation of world politics in terms of the plurality of types of actors.[1] In the Introduction, the editors of this volume move beyond this to ask whether, why, and to what end we are seeing a change in the architecture of global governance. In so doing the question is not primarily about the relative power of state and non-state actors, but about the modes of governance – different configurations of hierarchies, markets, and networks – that characterize different issue areas. Our focus is on changes in modes of governance around so-called "fragile states," which is of particular interest for analyses of transformations in global governance due to the heterogeneity of actors involved – states, international organizations (IOs), nongovernmental organizations (NGOs), and firms – and the different expertise and governance activity it involves, including military, development, and humanitarian work. We provide evidence that the architecture for governance in this area has indeed changed, in terms of which types of actors are important, the interfaces between them, and the resulting modes of governance that prevails.

We seek to explain how these changes in governance architecture have occurred, acknowledging the range of factors identified in the Introduction, such as geopolitical and ideological changes. We also zoom in on an important and often overlooked vehicle of change, namely issue-specific professional networks. We treat networks in keeping with the Introduction's definition as actors being linked by interdependence, rather than dependence (hierarchy) or independence (markets), but we look more specifically at professional networks that not only share an interest in particular issues (human rights, climate, conflict, health, etc.),

Research for this chapter was supported by the Research Council of Norway (RCN) "The Market for Anarchy", project number #274740.
[1] See, for example, Mathews 1997.

but also compete to control them.[2] Actors in these professional networks formulate, tinker with, and diffuse ideas about how to define and act on particular problems and link these to operational tasks.[3] Their operations may, at times, resemble those of epistemic communities, claiming expert authority and a shared policy objective, but they also have access to – and seek to foreground – different policy tools, such as military troops, support for institutional reforms, or legal instruments.[4] These networks have been with us for a long time, but they are now more central to global governance, not least because the role and functioning of IOs are also changing.[5]

IOs were established to forge a new institutional framework for world politics after the Second World War. That project rested on a three-legged stool: leg one was the commitment to multilateralism; leg two the pooling of resources to address common problems; and leg three the establishment of an international bureaucratic machinery to manage it all on behalf of states.[6] Over the last two decades, states have systematically reduced their core funding to many of these IOs, forcing these organizations to adjust their operating models to cater to different state interests. At the same time, broader changes in ideas about what constitutes effective management have occurred, where performance assessment, risk management, and competition have replaced ideas about the virtues of the bureaucratic form of global governance.[7] Taken together these trends have produced a system where global governance is an "open system"[8] – where entrepreneurial authority[9] is increasingly important and where IOs are less important as sites of hierarchically based fixing of policy. The result, as we explore here, is that the substantive contents of governance may exhibit tendencies toward differentiation and fragmentation, as different groups or actors advance ever more specific problem-definitions and attendant solutions within and through IOs.

As we explore in the third section, the military operations in Afghanistan and Iraq introduced a new set of actors and new governance tools with regard to fragile states, key among which were military and intelligence actors whose views on how to act on, and in, fragile states were different than those found within IOs such as the UN and the World Bank. This development clearly indicates the importance of hierarchy where powerful states, and international bodies such as the UN Security Council (UNSC), set the terms for other actors' modes of

---

[2] Abbott 1988; Hoffman 1999; Sending 2015a; Seabrooke and Henriksen 2017.
[3] Haas 1992; Kortendiek 2021.   [4] Seabrooke 2015.   [5] Abbott et al. 2016.
[6] Mazover 2013; Schlesinger 2003.   [7] Seabrooke and Sending 2020.
[8] Scott 2015.   [9] Green 2014.

operation. But grasping its effects necessitates a look at the professional networks that have a stake in, and competence on, fragile states.[10] We can detect a change from "peacebuilding," focused on building institutions to support the rule of law and democracy, with development actors in a key role, to "stabilization" and counterterrorism, which entails support for whatever regime is in place to help in fighting insurgents and conduct anti-terrorism operations. This development runs parallel to another transformation, whereby the focus on societal change and institution building has been replaced by an overarching focus on the protection of civilians, with human rights organizations and humanitarian organizations – while different[11] – assuming more prominent roles.

International Organizations and the Differentiation of Governance Tasks

There is no novelty in the role of non-state or private actors in the waging of war or the management of violent conflicts. Charles Tilly's observation that states are essentially protection rackets captures this historical fact: the appropriation or enrolment of private actors and resources have historically been central for the waging of war and the management of polities.[12] The historiography on empire is similarly replete with examples of the intermingling of public and private actors in the establishment and management of imperial rule. As Max Weber noted, the process of state formation entailed the progressive enrolling of private soldiers into the evolving machinery of the state. Weber writes, for example, that the agents of private capitalism were heavily involved in the bureaucratization of armies, with the soldier owning his own weapons and horses and providing his services for a fee.[13] Weber's observation also applies today, as the literature on private military contractors testifies.[14] In this historical perspective it is not surprising that efforts to prevent and manage violent conflicts involves a range of non-state actors. The absence of non-state actors in settling conflicts is the historical anomaly rather than the other way around.

Nonetheless, the architecture of global governance that was established with the UN and Bretton Woods institutions had one distinguishing feature: states not only negotiated rules, as they had done in the past, but they also set up a bureaucratic machinery to monitor, interpret, and

---

[10] Heritier and Lehmkhul 2008.   [11] Barnett 2018.   [12] Tilly and Besteman 1985.
[13] Weber 1978, 981–982.
[14] Avant 2005; Abrahamsen and Williams 2009; Leander 2005.

help enforce these rules.[15] While quite a few humanitarian NGOs predate both the League of Nations and the founding of the UN, a global network of largely Western-based NGOs emerged which advanced goals similar to those embedded in organizations such as the UN. In time, this global network grew considerably, especially from the mid-1970s onwards, and its members served both as implementers and advocates of the work of IOs.[16] In ideal-typical terms this was a hierarchical system, with member states and rule-governed IOs at the top and NGOs playing a supporting role. Over the last two decades, however, this system has been changing gradually. At the very moment when the UN reached its full potential with the end of the Cold War, the system for conflict prevention, post-conflict reconstruction, and mediation efforts started to change. It did so because UN member states launched ever more ambitious mandates to both prevent and manage violent conflicts, but provided insufficient funding for these new tasks.[17] In part to alleviate the gap between goals and resources, but also to tap into the expertise and networks of non-state actors, the UN and other IOs increasingly came to rely on voluntary funding and outside actors[18] to implement conflict-reducing measures.[19] As we discuss in the second section, this has produced a new configuration of global governance with certain hier-archical features (such as the UNSC being important for mandates) coexisting with clear network features, where different IOs (such as the United Nations Development Programme (UNDP) and the World Bank) cooperate and compete with one another but also with NGOs and firms in designing and performing tasks relating to conflict preven-tion and management.

To capture this evolution in governance systems it is useful to ask how IOs exert control over issues. Extant theories vary considerably in how they answer this question. Theories organized around organizational design[20] or principal-agent theory[21] focus on authority chains, treating IOs as having a set of core attributes but only qua an agent to which states, as principals, delegate authority. For this reason an IO is defined as an actor that is distinct from principals, but an actor that is operating under very distinct constraints, defined by the set-up of the principal–actor (P–A) model. As Hawkins et al. argue, IOs are "bureaucracies that … can be more or less controlled by their political masters."[22] Most importantly, IOs are here seen as actors that are created by states,

---

[15] Barnett and Finnemore 2004; Mazover 2013; Orford 2011, Sending 2014.
[16] Barnett 2012; Hopgood 2006.   [17] Graham 2017; Mir 2019.   [18] Andonova 2017.
[19] Bantekas et al. 2013.   [20] Koremenos et al. 2001.   [21] Hawkins et al. 2006.
[22] Hawkins et al. 2006, 5.

but actors nonetheless, since P–A models assume that agents have independent and possibly divergent interests from the principal. Barnett and Finnemore's seminal work took the description of IOs populated by experts in a bureaucratic system as their theoretical point of departure.[23] They draw on a broad interpretation of Weber's discussions of bureaucracy to argue that the nature of bureaucratic organization establishes a level of autonomy from the environment, which means that there is potential for IOs to also be authoritative through their expertise,[24] which helps them legitimately claim control over professional tasks for particular issues.

The most significant difference between these theories have mostly to do with the fact that rationalist theories tend to explain IO behavior by looking at the dynamic *between* states and IOs, whereas constructivist and institutional theories borrow more heavily from insights about the bureaucratic characteristics of IOs to make claims about their authority, thereby locating the explanatory thrust primarily with the IO itself. This also holds for more recent work on IOs as "orchestrators," where a key point is to show how IOs may shape states not directly through commands, nor indirectly through delegation, but through soft and indirect forms of governance where IOs enroll and govern through intermediate actors.[25] While this focus on orchestration is more open to the relationships between IOs and its environment, the assumption – it seems to us – is that whereas the mode of how IOs govern may change, their identities as bureaucratic entities remain stable. Following Abbott et al., we would not expect to see changes *within* IOs in terms of how they are managed and organized as a result of the prevalence of "orchestration" as a mode of governance.

We adopt a view of IOs as "open systems"[26] to draw attention to how factors such as ideological change and actor pluralization can come to shape the boundaries, organizational form, and mode of operating of IOs. In particular, treating IOs as open systems draws attention to the shifting institutional registers that the professionals that populate IOs draw on in their work. Students of global governance have, in the main, been concerned to identify and explain the variety of actors involved, their sources of authority, and the relations between the two. They have – as a consequence – been less well equipped to capture how global governance entails a system where different actors use different types of

---

[23] Barnett and Finnemore 2004.

[24] And then train policy-makers in member states to agree with them, see Broome and Seabrooke 2015.

[25] Abbott et al. 2016.   [26] Scott 2015.

resources, as they both cooperate with one another and also compete over funding and control over specific agendas.[27] In many cases the capacity to act on an issue – such as human rights protection, conflict mediation, or climate change – is distributed across a range of different actors, such as IOs, states, firms, and NGOs. This suggests that many of the activities of global governance – making rules, enforcing rules – operate in issue-specific recursive cycles where the actors involved primarily share an interest in the issue at hand, which define their outlook and behavior.[28] Actors within these environments may be able to exploit differences in knowledge and try to dominate issues and/or switch identities in different social networks to make sure they are represented among different groups.[29]

Particularly important here is that professional groups compete and coordinate to link issues and define how they are treated, as well as to draw boundaries over who is best equipped to address the issue.[30] This means that organizations, including IOs, do not control issues solely via mandates but also through professional expansion and/or coordination. It is difficult to capture changes in the governance of fragile states without considering the operations of both the UN peacekeeping machinery (Department of Peacekeeping Operations) and its humanitarian operations (Office for the Coordination of Humanitarian Affairs) as well as the UNDP and the World Bank, in addition to different NGOs engaged in humanitarian and development work. For sure, the shadow of hierarchy is noticeable. For example, it was the USA that took the lead to encourage allies to chip in to assist in fighting terrorists and insurgents via UN peacekeeping.[31] But so is the coordination – and competition – between professionals engaged in peacekeeping, intelligence, development, and humanitarian work who became involved in discussing how to use UN peacekeeping to stabilize states where terrorist groups and insurgents are operating, as in Mali and neighboring countries, while at the same time providing development assistance and humanitarian relief.[32] Adopting such a "thin" conception of the culture of IOs – not as that which explains the changing content of modes of governance, but

---

[27] Seabrooke and Henriksen 2017.
[28] Quack 2007; Halliday and Carruthers 2007; Block-Lieb and Halliday 2017; Sending 2015a.
[29] Seabrooke 2014; Sending 2017.   [30] Abbott 2005; Liu 2017.   [31] Karlsrud 2019.
[32] Karlsrud 2015; Sending 2015b. The dynamic here is similar to that found in studies of epistemic communities, but with the important difference that it is not based on claims regarding expertise alone, but on access to and control over policy tools – intelligence, strategic, and tactical experience – that emerge as central to policy debates. Cf. Haas 1992.

as structuring environment for different actors[33] – retains core insights from the institutional approach.[34] But it shifts emphasis to the original formulation as found in the works of DiMaggio and Powell,[35] where organizations are seen to be structured by their environment but in a differentiated and open-ended way depending on the particular interface of an organization with its environment.[36] It therefore matters what kind of interface an IO has with its relevant others: professional networks that cut across IOs may be as important, if not more so, in identifying and accounting for where new practices of governance may be forged between distinct groups.

The Governance of Fragile States

Armed with the analytical tools discussed in the first section, we seek to demonstrate some of its purchase by discussing the case of conflict management and in particular the types of governance arrangements that have emerged around the category of "fragile states." This category is instructive for several reasons. First, the category of fragile states is a relatively new one, but is now a central "issue" or what the sociology of professions often calls a "jurisdiction" over which different IOs both cooperate and compete.[37] For example, the World Bank and the UN recently published a joint "flagship report" on conflict prevention and state fragility, reflecting a longstanding concern within the UN and the World Bank that the two organizations should seek to cooperate more, and better, in fragile states.[38] Second, we see that fragile states is an issue that not only different IOs, but also NGOs and firms, claim competence on.

The concept of fragile states emerged as a central description for the challenge of operating in and producing development in countries plagued by violent conflict, persistent poverty, and weak governing institutions. In 2000 there were no organizational units within any of the major IOs that focused on what we today call "fragile states." In 2001 the UNDP established the Bureau for Crisis Prevention and Recovery in an effort to secure its position as a relevant IO in natural disasters, which was later expanded to include man-made disasters. Also in 2001, the World Bank established a task force and subsequently a funding mechanism for "low income country under stress," with direct reference to debates about

---

[33] Kentikelenis and Seabrooke 2017; Seabrooke and Nilsson 2015; Sending and Neumann 2011.
[34] Barnett and Finnemore 2004.
[35] DiMaggio and Powell 1983; DiMaggio and Powell 1991.   [36] Liu and Halliday 2019.
[37] Abbott 1988.   [38] United Nations and World Bank 2018.

"fragile states." In 2002 the OECD's Development Assistance Committee (DAC) initiated a process on "Cooperation in difficult partnerships," and in the following year the DAC and the World Bank co-chaired a Learning and Advisory Process on fragile states. After these initial discussions at the UNDP, Organisation for Economic Co-operation and Development (OECD), and the World Bank on the same issue, 2004–2005 can be seen as a threshold where IOs invested more significantly in developing policies on the issue. In 2004, the World Bank, UNDP, and United Nations Development Group co-authored "Multilateral Needs Assessments in Post-Conflict Situations." Also in 2004, the World Bank and OECD produced a report on "Alignment and Harmonization in Fragile States." Moreover, the UN High-Level Panel recommended the establishment of a Peacebuilding Commission in 2004, and the General Assembly in 2005 voted to establish an intergovernmental "Peacebuilding Commission" under the auspices of the General Assembly, Security Council, and "Peacebuilding Support Office" in the UN Secretariat, which included specific reference to state fragility. In the same year, the Department for International Development, Swedish International Development Cooperation Agency, Canadian International Development Agency, and United States Agency for International Development all established strategies for engaging with fragile states.

If we jump to 2011, the World Bank launched its *World Development Report* on fragile states, with major policy proposals that include moving bank staff from the headquarters to field offices in fragile states, seeking closer cooperation with the UN, and suggesting that the bank, and other actors, should move toward a "best fit" approach and be more pragmatic in demanding conformity with their standards. At the same time there is marked proliferation of both non-profit and for-profit actors that enter the debate about fragile states and seek to make their mark on how it is defined and acted upon. Oxfam launched its fragile states program, designed to deliver governance projects without going through state authorities. KPMG established a permanent office in Hargeisa, Somaliland, to offer services categorized as fragile states. Other KPMG offices also offered "thought leadership" on how to cope with the politicization of aid going to fragile states, as well as how to improve matching NGO designs to local fragile state capacities.[39]

As the editors note in the Introduction, ideological shifts are important drivers of this evolution in the pluralization of actors. So-called "new

---

[39] KPMG International 2011; KPMG Kenya 2012.

public management" thinking began to take hold in IOs as a result of donors wanting more bang for their buck. This resulted, inter alia, in the outsourcing of key tasks to non-state actors, especially in the field of development and humanitarian relief.[40] One result of this change was that bureaucratic models, based on a hierarchy of rules, defined mandates, and recognized expertise began to change and opened up space for non-state actors, especially NGOs that specialize in advocacy, resource mobilization, and project management.[41] The new actors included not only the likes of Oxfam and Human Rights Watch, but also – over time – a string of firms that specialize in providing conflict expertise and implementation of conflict-reducing measures. Examples include both for-profit consultancies like Oxcon and more established non-profit organizations like the International Crisis Group,[42] which provides country-specific assessments and policy advice, and G4S, a private security company.[43]

This development in the types of actors with claim to competence and expertise on fragile states has effects on how conflicts are understood and acted upon. First, we can observe a change in the complexity of mandates, and we think that this complexity in mandates cannot solely be attributed to a change in the reality of conflict dynamics. Rather, this complexity in mandates reflects a more general trend where "security" and "conflict" are increasingly differentiated into distinct subareas or themes (cybersecurity, insurgencies, terrorism, peacebuilding, humanitarian protection) that are always advanced by distinct groups inside and outside IOs.[44] Second, there is ongoing competition for jurisdictional control between these groups that feature state actors, international civil servants, and a string of non-state actors. These non-state actors have become more important as IOs – such as the UN – have come to rely more on earmarked funding, and on the services provided by NGOs and firms to implement specific projects. As we describe in the next section, the result has been that IOs are less important as authoritative sites for fixing the contents of governance, which helps explain a tendency toward fragmentation of governance around fragile states.

Evolution of Approaches to Fragile States: From Peacebuilding to "State" and "Individual"

The start of the UN's venture into peace operations is typically dated to 1956, when the United Nations Emergency Force (UNEF) was

---

[40] Seabrooke and Sending 2020.   [41] Hopgood 2006; Karlsrud 2015.
[42] Bliesemann de Guevara 2014; Bøås 2014.   [43] Leander 2005.
[44] Neumann and Sending 2018.

established. The establishment of UNEF is a good illustration of the "old" model for global governance: a crisis emerges, the UNSC meets to decide on the issue, and the UN machinery is mobilized to act on it. Here, the UN – via the UNSC and key member states – formulates rules, and the UN Secretariat monitors and enforces them. UNEF was organized and justified explicitly to protect a tense political situation. Peacekeepers were here solely focused on acting as a buffer between the parties to the conflict. The Congo operation (Opération des Nations Unies au Congo – ONUC), established in 1960, was markedly different from UNEF in that it was designed to uphold law and order and facilitate the orderly withdrawal of Belgian troops following Congo's declaration of independence. With ONUC, the protection of civilians becomes a defined task, specified as such, but there is a clear hierarchy: the mandate from the UNSC clearly states that the main objective is that the newly formed government is able to "meet fully their tasks" – and thus to be a fully functional state.[45] During the 1990s, by contrast, liberal ideas about human rights and the rule of law came to define the substance of what peacekeepers were supposed to be doing. The *mode of governance* initially remained the same, however: the UNSC formulated a mandate, and UN peacekeepers, now increasingly cooperating with UN civilian staff to rebuild and transforms key state institutions and advance human rights norms, were tasked with the interpretation, specification, and implementation of the rules (or mandates) provided by the UNSC. This was the case in a string of missions – in Sierra Leone, in Liberia, and in the Democratic Republic of Congo. The publication of UN Secretary-General Boutros Boutros-Ghali's *An Agenda for Peace* in 1992 reflects this initial conceptualization of what conflict management should be about. The report argued that peacebuilding must include "advancing efforts to protect human rights" – indeed, it was held that a "requirement for solutions to these problems lies in commitment to human rights" and that "the time of absolute and exclusive sovereignty has passed."[46] The report signals a focus on building particular *types of states* as a means to produce peace: the protection of civilians and the protection of human rights are conceptualized *within* a focus on state-building in terms of rebuilding and transforming institutions and engaging in capacity building.

Over time, however, there has been a change not only in the tasks specified in UNSC mandates, but also a subtle yet significant transformation in the very justification for why these specified tasks are seen as important. And this proliferation of tasks and the attendant shifts in the

---

[45] Simmonds 1968.   [46] United Nations 1992, 17–18.

Table 7.1 *Evolution from peacebuilding to rights protection and anti-terror operations*

Period	Goal	Object of governance	Role of individual
1990s	Building peace through liberal-oriented state-building	Societal transformation	Bearer of rights, to be protected by new state structures
2000s	Building peace while also protecting civilians	Societal transformation + protection of civilians	Bearer of rights deserving explicit protection by peacekeepers
2010s	Protecting civilians and combating insurgents	Protection of civilians + protection of human rights + anti-terrorism operations	Primary justification for role of UN in conflict settings

register for justifying peacebuilding is, we argue, integral to the broader changes in the types of actors involved, and in the form of governance associated with it. One expression of this evolution is the genesis of "protection" as an integral part of UN peace operations, as it has evolved in large measure as a result of distinct jurisdictional tactics advanced by actors both inside and outside the UN system to advance a specific interpretation of what "protection" entails, and how it is to be defined as part of UN peace operations.[47]

There are rules about the treatment of civilians during war, as formulated in international humanitarian law. As set out in the Introduction, these rules may be interpreted, implemented and enforced by different types of actors. But these rules are also resources for different actors to seek to change, or add to, an established policy agenda.[48] The general trend in Table 7.1 shows an evolution from peacebuilding as a master frame with a focus on state institutions, with the individual seen as a bearer of rights to be upheld by the state, toward the rights-bearing individual becoming progressively more important as the singular justification for engaging in fragile states.

It was the UN's Office for the Coordination of Humanitarian Affairs (OCHA) that initially pushed for peace operations to include the protection of civilians as a separate task. It did so on the basis of criticisms that the UN had not sufficiently focused on the plight of civilians, but also – and importantly – as part of a move to position OCHA vis-à-vis the

---

[47] Crossley 2018; Curran and Holtom 2015; Curran and Hunt 2020.
[48] Feldman 2010.

UNSC. In doing so OCHA was operating together with a string of NGOs to push for the establishment of a "culture of protection" within UN peace operations. At the same time, the very same principles – or rules – of protection were interpreted differently by both the United Nations High Commissioner for Refugees and the Office of the High Commisioner for Human Rights, both of which preferred a more conventional, legal approach to protection (of civilians, and of human rights, respectively).[49] The establishment of protection as a separate task within peace operations also meant that new types of actors established new roles within UN peace operations: UN military staff had to be trained, and had to increasingly coordinate with the United Nations High Commissioner for Refugees and other humanitarian organizations about the meaning and implementation of "protection" in the context of peace operations.

Over the course of the 2000s the task of protection became an integral part of UN peace operations. This was done through commissioned reports and specialized training programs for UN staff, as well as the development of new modes of interacting between military and humanitarian staff.[50] In due course, in no small measure through the advocacy by humanitarian NGOs and a change in the justification of peace operations as conveyed by UN leaders, "protection" became a stand-alone objective, alongside that of transforming society in conflict-ridden countries.

An additional shift took place toward the end of the 2000s, triggered by the UN's internal review of UN operations during the Sri Lankan civil war. It concluded that the UN had not done enough to report on, and seek to stop, human rights violations. In response the UN secretary-general established the "Human Rights Up Front Initiative," the purpose of which is to "ensure the UN system takes early and executive action" to "prevent or respond to large-scale violations of human rights or international humanitarian law." This was to be done through "realizing a cultural change within the UN system, so that human rights and the protection of civilians are seen as a system-wide core responsibility."[51] This was a new framing of protection of civilians, where it became a dominant register for assessing the relevance and credibility of the UN as such, and not just its peace operations. This development, which entails a distinct emphasis on protecting human rights more than protecting civilians per se, had a different register and also different sets of actors involved. Human rights organizations and UN Secretariat staff were at

---

[49] Stensland and Sending 2011.   [50] Stensland and Sending 2011.
[51] www.un.org/sg/humanrightsupfront/.

the forefront of developing this agenda, with humanitarian organizations being more marginal. As it has developed as an integral part of the UN's approach in conflict settings, it has placed the protection of human rights as central to the credibility of UN peace operations.[52]

While UN peacekeeping evolved to foreground the rights-bearing individual as both the means and ends of its operations, it also became involved in countering extremism and fighting terrorist groups. This process was de facto headed by the USA, aided by NATO allies and others, and also came to shape also the UN's approach to fragile states. For example, the UN Secretary-General Ban Ki-moon issued a "Plan of Action to Prevent Violent Extremism," which reportedly drew inspiration from the Bush administration's earlier efforts to rename its approach to prevent and counter violent extremism (PCVE). This is a case of hierarchical relations being manifested in how the UN is being retooled and partly transformed in an effort to shift focus to stabilization and preventing violent extremism. This is also evident in funding patterns from key Western donors, who have channeled significant funds to PCVE programs within the UN system. The UNDP, for example, recategorized some of their programs to make them fit the PCVE category to attract more funding. Moreover, the UN established, partly through a large donation from Saudi Arabia, the UN Counter-Terrorism Centre within the UN Secretariat. And European donors were significant contributors to the establishment of the Geneva-based NGO called the Community Engagement and Resilience Fund, whose key mission is to engage in preventing violent extremism. This trend is also reflected in how the OECD-DAC changed the rules for eligible development assistance to accommodate funding linked to stabilization operations.[53]

These developments within the UN system, with an increased focus on anti-terrorism operations and stabilization operations, built on experiences and expertise developed outside the UN system, notably through the military operations in Afghanistan. As Karlsrud notes, "the lessons from more than a decade of war-fighting in Afghanistan have over time permeated into the doctrinal thinking of Western forces and their approach to conflicts in international fora, including the UN Security Council."[54] Similarly, Knight argues that "Modern day concepts of Stabilisation originate from national stabilisation doctrines of the

---

[52] Lie and de Carvalho 2010.
[53] www.saferworld.org.uk/resources/news-and-analysis/post/185-redefining-oda-what-does-it-mean-for-peace.
[54] Karlsrud 2015, 49. See also Farrell 2020 on organizational convergence between combatants in military operations in Afghanistan.

'P3' – France, the UK and the USA – predominantly to deal with cross-governmental approaches to counterinsurgency operations conducted throughout the 2000s."[55] These changes within the UN concern not only the substance of the problem definition – to fight terrorists and help stabilize the security capacity of the central government – but also in the *mode* of governance. While there is a clear hierarchy in terms of which states have been pushing for this change, as well as in the fact that these operations are mandated by the UNSC, we can also observe a different trend that is associated with network governance, where governance is done through intermediaries, and where distinct resources are brought to bear on the problem from a variety of professional groups. Karlsrud argues, for example, that there is "a trend of decentralising authority, feeding intelligence into operations on local levels, using a combination of human and signal intelligence sources such as drones, and including special forces to support more conventional forces."[56]

This decentralization – or trend toward network governance – is also on display in the emerging relationship between UN peacekeeping troops, on the one hand, and other troops operating in the same area. Traditionally, UN peacekeepers have operated independently and specifically not been "party to the conflict." This has been the bedrock of the UN's role of remaining impartial. Now, however, the UN mission in Mali – MINUSMA – is closely coordinating with the French military operation Barkhane, a 3,000-strong counterinsurgency operation.[57] As reported by the *Washington Post*, "The French military continues to conduct its own counterterrorism mission across northwest Africa, including in Mali. The United Nations shares information with the French if it is deemed useful for protecting the lives of troops."[58] This decentralization is best seen as operating within a framework of hierarchy, or perhaps a shadow of hierarchy. Mandates are set by the UNSC, and by the P-5 – China, France, Russia, the UK, and the USA – in particular. But there is a high level of uncertainty, and hence also leeway, in how to interpret and operationalize mandates by those operating in particular conflict settings. A study from the Stimson Center noted, for example, that:

The various ways in which stabilization has been referenced in the four missions' mandates show that the Security Council does not apply a consistent meaning of the term. The mandates reveal sometimes incompatible interpretations – for example, the view expressed in several MONUSCO mandates is that

---

[55] Knight 2016.   [56] Karlsrud 2015, 44.   [57] Bøås 2015.
[58] www.washingtonpost.com/sf/world/2017/02/17/the-worlds-deadliest-u-n-peacekeeping-mission/?utm_term=.0558f66c043e.

stabilization is an objective distinct from the protection of civilians, in contrast with the view expressed in the most recent MINUSMA mandate that the protection of civilians is a component of stabilization.[59]

At the same time, this development toward more assertive and robust peace operations runs parallel to one where the focus on human rights, and protecting civilians, is becoming ever more prominent as the *sine qua non* of the UN. This represents a bifurcation inasmuch as the former approach focuses on fighting insurgents and helping regimes in fragile states build capacity to control their territory from terrorist groups, and the latter focuses on protecting civilians and their human rights. In contrast to earlier conceptualizations of fragile states within the broader paradigm of liberal peacebuilding, the governance object "society" has disappeared. Or rather, a version of the peacebuilding paradigm is still there, but it is one that is no longer linked to the military component as expressed in UN peace operations. Rather, the broader socio-economic and political focus on peacebuilding and state-building operate in parallel to the focus on insurgents, and on protecting civilians.

While hierarchies persist in terms of relations between actors, we can observe a paradoxical change in terms of the modes of governance. On the one hand, we have the emergence of more "robust" military deployment to stabilize and keep the peace, most notably in Chad, Mali, and the Democratic Republic of Congo, where the UN is now mandated to hunt down and kill insurgents.[60] This is an expression of a hierarchical and militarized mode of governance that is first and foremost focused on the *state* as the object of governance. It is focused on upholding and strengthening the state in question to identify and fight insurgents and terrorist groups. At the same time we see another development in the direction of an increased focus on *individuals* – on the protection of civilians as the foundational justification for UN conflict management, which is partly hierarchical, involving the use of force based on UNSC mandates, but also increasingly networked, relying on professionals from humanitarian NGOs and firms. This represents a significant shift in governance object, where the focus on societal reconstruction that characterized the UN's investment in "peacebuilding" in the 1990s and early 2000s in Africa and elsewhere is replaced with a focus on the *individual* civilian in need of protection, within a broader focus on stabilization that is focused on beefing up security arrangements to fight insurgents.

---

[59] Gorur 2016, 11.   [60] Karlsrud 2019.

Conclusion

What do these substantive changes in attempts to act on and govern "fragile states" tell us about broader trends in global governance? Are the developments we have described necessarily part of, or caused by, changes in *modes* of governance? At one level these changes reflect responses to events that have shaped the international system, key among them the terrorist attacks of 9/11 and the subsequent war in Afghanistan. One of the virtues of focusing on governance, however, is that changes in the content of policy can be analyzed in light of the governance modalities that are being used. These events and decisions do not determine policy responses and the trajectory of governance. Rather, the architecture of governance and the mode of governance matter for how problems are defined and acted upon. Put differently, governance content is not independent of governance mode.

In our interpretation the developments we have analyzed in this chapter indicate a trend toward issue-specific *differentiation*, or fragmentation, within specialized issue areas and niche competencies: humanitarian relief and human rights, both of which are focused on "protection," where those professionals that are engaged in doing it use their respective legal tools and expertise to advance its prominence within and outside the UN. This includes the articulation of development as focused on conflict prevention and societal transformation through institutional reform and capacity building, where those that work within, say, the World Bank, the UNDP, or the UN Peacebuilding Support Office seek to make their policy tools relevant to the task of preventing conflict and rebuilding countries emerging from violent conflict. It also includes the articulation of peacekeeping, with an increasingly strong presence of military professionals with experience from operations in Afghanistan and Iraq, focused chiefly on identifying and fighting insurgents. This is the new institutional register in which work on fragile states operates.

Hierarchies have not disappeared, however. What characterizes contemporary global governance is that hierarchies take different forms and shape other forms of governance more indirectly – via the shadow of hierarchy – where both market and network features are integral parts of governance arrangements or modes of governance. One important aspect of these arrangements is that by virtue of the relative increase in openness between organizations, professional groups of different stripes cooperate and compete more independently of their respective organizational homes as they strategize over how to define and act on different aspects of the same issue or problem. The differentiation and attendant niche strategies advanced by different subgroups is at one level an indication of decentralization and of more "networked" governance. Nonetheless, these features of the system should not detract attention from the hierarchies involved. Indeed, the differentiation that we can observe can be traced to how different professional groups within and around IOs seek recognition and funding in the eyes of more powerful actors, be they powerful member states or collective decision-making bodies like the UNSC. There is thus by now a differentiated system of governance of fragile states, where new tasks and justifications have emerged so that one is now hard-pressed to identify an overarching policy or unified approach to "fragile states."

References

Abbott, Andrew. 1988. *The System of Profession*. Chicago: University of Chicago Press.
    2005. Linked Ecologies: States and Universities as Environments for Professions. *Sociological Theory* 23 (3): 245–274.
Abbott, Kenneth W., Jessica F. Green, and Robert O. Keohane, 2016. Organizational Ecology and Institutional Change in Global Governance. *International Organization* 70 (2): 247–277.
Abrahamsen, Rita and Michael C. Williams. 2009. *Security Beyond the State: Private Security in International Politics*. Cambridge: Cambridge University Press.
Andonova, Liliana B. 2017. *Governance Entrepreneurs: International Organizations and the Rise of Global Public–Private Partnerships*. Cambridge: Cambridge University Press.
Avant, Deborah. 2005. *The Market for Force: The Consequences of Privatizing Security*. Cambridge: Cambridge University Press.
Bantekas, Ilias, Christos Kypraios, and Kebreab Isaac 2013. Outsourcing Law Reform in Developing Countries to Private Contractors: A Human Rights Perspective. *International Human Rights Law Review* 2 (1): 1–16.
Barnett, Michael. 2012. *Empire of Humanity*. Ithaca, NY: Cornell University Press.
    2018. Human Rights, Humanitarianism, and the Practices of Humanity. *International Theory* 10 (3): 314–349.
Barnett, Michael and Martha Finnemore. 2004. *Rules for the World*. Ithaca, NY: Cornell University Press.
Bliesemann de Guevara, B. 2014. On Methodology and Myths: Exploring the International Crisis Group's Organisational Culture. *Third World Quarterly* 35 (4): 616–633.
Block-Lieb, Susan and Terrence C. Halliday. 2017. *Global Lawmakers: International Organizations in the Crafting of World Markets*. Cambridge: Cambridge University Press.
Broome, André and Leonard Seabrooke. 2015. Shaping Policy Curves: Cognitive Authority in Transnational Capacity Building. *Public Administration* 93 (4): 956–972.

Bøås, Morten. 2014. "Hunting Ghosts of a Difficult Past": The International Crisis Group and the Production of "Crisis Knowledge" in the Mano River Basin Wars. *Third World Quarterly* 35 (4): 652–668.

Bøås, Morten. 2015. Crime, Coping, and Resistance in the Mali-Sahel Periphery. *African Security* 8: 299–319.

Crossley, N. 2018. Is R2P Still Controversial? Continuity and Change in the Debate on "Humanitarian Intervention." *Cambridge Review of International Affairs* 31 (5): 415–436.

Curran, David and Charles T. Hunt. 2020. Stabilization at the Expense of Peacebuilding in UN Peacekeeping Operations. *Global Governance: A Review of Multilateralism and International Organizations* 26 (1): 46–88.

Curran, David and Paul Holtom. 2015. Resonating, Rejecting, Reinterpreting: Mapping the Stabilization Discourse in the United Nations Security Council, 2000–14. *Stability: International Journal of Security & Development* 4: 1–18.

DiMaggio, Paul and Walter W. Powell. 1983. The Iron Cage Revisited. *American Sociological Review* 47 (2): 147–160.

DiMaggio, Paul and Walter W. Powell, eds. 1991. *The New Institutionalism in Organizational Analysis*, Vol. 17. Chicago: University of Chicago Press.

Farrell, Theo. 2020. Military Adaptation and Organisational Convergence in War: Insurgents and International Forces in Afghanistan. *Journal of Strategic Studies*. https://doi.org/10.1080/01402390.2020.1768371.

Feldman, Ilana. 2010. Ad Hoc Humanity: UN Peacekeeping and the Limits of International Community in Gaza. *American Anthropologist* 112 (3): 416–429.

Gorur, A. 2016. *Defining the Boundaries of UN Stabilization Missions*. Washington, DC: Stimson Center.

Graham, Erin. 2017. Follow the Money: How Trends in Financing Are Changing Governance at International Organizations. *Global Policy* 8: 15–25.

Green, Jessica. 2014. *Rethinking Private Authority: Agents and Entrepreneurs in Global Environmental Governance*. Princeton: Princeton University Press.

Haas, Peter M. 1992. Introduction: Epistemic Communities and International Policy Coordination. *International Organization* 46 (1): 1–35.

Halliday, Terrance C. and Bruce G. Carruthers. 2007. The Recursivity of Law: Global Norm Making and National Lawmaking in the Globalization of Corporate Insolvency Regime. *American Journal of Sociology* 112 (4): 1135–1202.

Hawkins, Darren G., David A. Lake, Daniel L. Nielson, and Michael J. Tierney, eds. 2006. *Delegation and Agency in International Organizations*. Cambridge: Cambridge University Press.

Héritier, Adrienne and Dirk Lehmkhul. 2008. Introduction: The Shadow of Hierarchy and New Modes of Governance. *Journal of Public Policy* 28 (1): 1–17.

Hoffman, Andrew J. 1999. Institutional Evolution and Change: Environmentalism and the U.S. Chemical Industry. *Academy of Management Journal* 42 (4): 351–371.

Hopgood, Stephen. 2006. *Keepers of the Flame*. Ithaca, NY: Cornell University Press.

Karlsrud, John. 2015. The UN at War: Examining the Consequences of Peace-Enforcement Mandates for the UN Peacekeeping Operations in the CAR, the DRC and Mali. *Third World Quarterly* 36 (1): 40–54.

Karlsrud, John. 2019. From Liberal Peacebuilding to Stabilization and Counterterrorism. *International Peacekeeping* 26 (1): 1–21.

Kentikelenis, Alexander E. and Leonard Seabrooke. 2017. The Politics of World Polity: Script-Writing in International Organizations. *American Sociological Review* 82 (5): 1065–1092.

Knight, Mark. 2016. Reversing the Stabilisation Paradigm: Towards an Alternative Approach. *Stability: International Journal of Security and Development* 5 (1): 1–10.

Koremenos, Barbara, Charles Lipson, and Duncan Snidal. 2001. The Rational Design of International Institutions. *International Organization* 55 (4): 761–799.

Kortendiek, Nele. 2021. How to Govern Mixed Migration in Europe: Transnational Expert Networks and Knowledge Creation in International Organizations. *Global Networks* 21 (2): 320–338.

KPMG International. 2011. Aid Effectiveness: Improving Accountability and Introducing New Initiatives. *Issue Monitor* (November). https://home.kpmg/content/dam/kpmg/pdf/2015/12/issues-monitor-aid-effectiveness.pdf.

KPMG Kenya. 2012. Accountability in Fragile States. Africa Impact Paper 7, March. International Development Advisory Services.

Leander, Anna. 2005. The Market for Force and the Public Security. *Journal of Peace Research* 42 (5): 605–622.

Lie, Jon Harald Sande and Benjamin de Carvalho. 2010. Between Culture and Concept: The Protection of Civilians in Sudan (UNMIS). *Journal of International Peacekeeping* 14 (1–2): 60–85.

Liu, Sida. 2017. Overlapping Ecologies: Professions and Development in the Rise of Legal Services in China. *Sociology of Development* 3 (3): 212–231.

Liu, Sida and Terrence C. Halliday. 2019. The Ecology of Activism: Professional Mobilization as a Spatial Process. *Canadian Review of Sociology/Revue canadienne de sociologie* 56 (4): 452–471.

Mathews, Jessica. 1997. Power Shift. *Foreign Affairs* 76 (1): 50–66.

Mazover, Mark. 2013. *Governing the World: The History of an Idea, 1815 to the Present*. New York. Penguin Group.

Mir, Wasim. 2019. *Financing UN Peacekeeping: Avoiding Another Crisis*. New York: International Peace Institute.

Neumann, Iver B. and Ole Jacob Sending. 2018. Expertise and Practice: The Evolving Relationship between Study and Practice of Security. In *The Oxford Handbook on International Security*, edited by Alexandra Gheciu and William H. Wohlforth, 29–40. Oxford: Oxford University Press.

Orford, Ann. 2011. *International Authority and the Responsibility to Protect*. Cambridge: Cambridge University Press.

Quack, Sigrid. 2007. Legal Professionals and Transnational Law-Making: A Case of Distributed Agency. *Organization* 14 (5): 643–666.

Schlesinger, Stephen C. 2003. *Act of Creation: The Founding of the United Nations – A Story of Superpowers, Secret Agents, Wartime Allies and Enemies, and Their Quest for a Peaceful World*. Boulder, CO: Westview Press.

Scott, W. Richard. 2015. *Organizations and Organizing: Rational, Natural and Open Systems Perspectives*. London: Routledge.

Seabrooke, Leonard. 2014. Identity Switching and Transnational Professionals. *International Political Sociology* 8 (3): 335–337.

2015. Diplomacy as Economic Consultancy. In *Diplomacy and the Making of World Politics*, edited by Ole Jacob Sending, Vincent Pouliot, and Iver B. Neumann, 195–219. Cambridge: Cambridge University Press.

Seabrooke, Leonard and Emilie R. Nilsson. 2015. Professional Skills in International Financial Surveillance: Assessing Change in IMF Policy Teams. *Governance* 28 (2): 237–254.

Seabrooke, Leonard and Lasse Folke Henriksen, eds. 2017. *Professional Networks in Transnational Governance*. Cambridge: Cambridge University Press.

Seabrooke, Leonard and Ole Jacob Sending. 2020. Contracting Development: Managerialism and Consultants in Intergovernmental Organizations. *Review of International Political Economy* 27 (4): 802–827.

Sending, Ole Jacob. 2014. The International Civil Servant. *International Political Sociology* 8 (3): 338–340.

2015a. *The Politics of Expertise: Competing for Authority in Global Governance*. Ann Arbor: University of Michigan Press.

2015b. Diplomats and Humanitarians in Crisis Governance. In *Diplomacy and the Making of World Politics*, edited by Ole Jacob Sending, Vincent Pouliot, and Iver B. Neumann, 256–283. Cambridge: Cambridge University Press.

2017. Contested Professionalization in a Weak Transnational Field. In *Professional Networks in Transnational Governance*, edited by Leonard Seabrooke and Lasse Folke Henriksen, 67–81. Cambridge: Cambridge University Press.

Sending, Ole Jacob and Iver B. Neumann. 2011. Banking On power: How Some Practices in an International Organization Anchor Others. In *International Practices*, edited by Emmanuel Adler and Vincent Pouliot, 231–254. Cambridge: Cambridge University Press.

Simmonds, R. 1968. The Functions of ONUC. In *Legal Problems Arising from the United Nations Military Operations in the Congo*, by R. Simmonds, 79–95. Dordrecht: Springer.

Stensland, Andreas Øien and Ole Jacob Sending. 2011. Unpacking the Culture of Protection: A Political Economy Analysis of OCHA and the Protection of Civilians. NUPI Report, 2.

Tilly, Charles and Catherine Besteman 1985. War Making and State Making as Organized Crime. In *Violence: A Reader*, edited by Catherine Besteman, 35–60. New York: New York University Press.

United Nations. 1992. *An Agenda for Peace*. New York: United Nations.

United Nations and World Bank. 2018. *Pathways for Peace*. Washington, DC and New York: United Nations and World Bank.

Weber, Max. 1978. *Economy and Society: Outline of an Interpretative Sociology*. Berkeley: University of California Press.

8   Global Health
A Centralized Network Searching (in Vain) for Hierarchy

Suerie Moon

Introduction: Global Governance and Health

The health of individuals and nations can be protected, promoted, or harmed by the increasing interdependence resulting from globalization. The Covid-19 pandemic that began in 2019 has illustrated how quickly pathogens can wreak havoc on a regional or global scale. Other infections, such as tuberculosis (TB), continue to cause immense suffering and impede human development. Beyond infectious disease are numerous health threats requiring effective cross-border governance – obesity, antimicrobial resistance (AMR), chemical and biological weapons, tobacco use, opioid abuse, environmental degradation, and lack of access to healthcare – yet the arrangements to do so are weak or absent. At the same time, global governance processes taking place outside the health sphere (such as those addressing security, trade, investment, intellectual property (IP), and migration) can have profound health effects.

What does the future of global governance imply for the enduring challenge of protecting health?

Some conceptual clarification is merited before diving in. "Global health" is often used in the media and academic literature as shorthand for the health challenges of developing countries. But the concept is evolving, and I use "global health" more broadly in this chapter to refer to "the health of the global population, with a focus on the dense relationships of interdependence across nations and sectors that have arisen with globalization."[1] Health can be understood in at least three ways: as an intrinsic societal goal, as a necessary input for human and

I am grateful to Kal Raustiala, Jon C.W. Pevehouse, Michael Barnett, Ayelet Berman, Dario Piselli, and Mara Pillinger for comments received on earlier versions of the chapter, as well as from three anonymous peer reviewers. I also thank participants at two workshops organized by the volume editors and supported by the Social Trends Institute in Barcelona, December 2016, and co-organized with Liliana B. Andonova and Joost Pauwelyn of the Graduate Institute in Geneva, February 2018, for the rich discussions and comments on the ideas presented here.
[1] Frenk et al. 2014.

economic development, and as an indicator of the state of a society.[2] The health challenges affecting industrialized and developing countries are increasingly converging, as demonstrated by Covid-19 and non-communicable diseases (NCDs) that pose a growing burden worldwide. The threats and opportunities linked to globalization are a third type of health challenge. These are spread through the cross-border movement of: elements of the environment (e.g., air and water pollution); people (e.g., travel); production of goods and services (e.g., global manufacturing supply chains); consumption of goods and services (e.g., food, narcotics, healthcare); information, knowledge, and culture (e.g., medical knowledge, consumption habits); and rules (formal and informal norms, rules, laws).[3]

Furthermore, health is deeply connected to the economy. Health crises can trigger economic crises, as Covid-19 has done. And healthcare is big business. Health spending has increased dramatically worldwide, more than doubling per capita from $475 in 2000 to $1,061 in 2017, now comprising one-tenth of the global economy and expected to continue rising.[4]

How can we conceptualize the relationship between global governance and health?

The terminology in the literature is fluid.[5] The term "global health governance" (GHG) usually refers to governance of the global health system – the constellation of actors and institutions whose *primary intent* is to protect health – or the health sector. "Global health architecture" is also widely used,[6] but implies more rigidity and intentional design than "system." I use GHG here as it underscores the fluidity and interconnection that often emerges in unplanned ways, and more accurately reflects the empirical reality.[7] This chapter uses GHG to refer to governance of the global health system; and simply "global governance" when discussing health-impacting governance processes outside the health sector.

With respect to this volume's conceptual framework (see Introduction), contemporary GHG can best be characterized as a network, in which independent purposive actors negotiate the rules that will regulate their relations, rather than a hierarchy or market. Hundreds, if not thousands, of new actors have begun engaging in GHG over the past several decades, influencing agendas, rule-making, implementation, monitoring, and enforcement. These actors are connected through

---

[2] Rio+20 UN Conference on Sustainable Development 2012, 20.   [3] Frenk et al. 2014.
[4] Author's calculations using World Bank World Development Indicators database.
[5] Lee and Kamradt-Scott 2014.   [6] Frenk et al. 2014.   [7] Szlezak et al. 2010.

complex networks of funding relationships, expert communities, and formal and informal governance arrangements.[8] The global health system is more centralized than many other areas of global governance such as environment or investment, with the World Health Organization (WHO) the central node. But this centralization should not be confused with hierarchy. While the 1948 WHO constitution envisioned that the organization would become the "directing and co-ordinating authority on international health work,"[9] in practice the agency has been more technical, advisory, and focused on a few issue areas where states provided the funding and political backing to act. And while the constitution granted WHO the legal mandate "to propose conventions, agreements and regulations, and make recommendations with respect to international health matters" – more expansive rule-making authority than many other intergovernmental organizations (IGOs) – this power has seldom been exercised.[10] The remainder of this chapter covers the historical evolution of GHG, offers an explanation for drivers of change over the past several decades, analyzes why these changes matter, and concludes with reflections for the future.

What Has Been Happening? Four Periods of GHG

The ways in which the world governs cross-border health issues have evolved considerably since the mid-nineteenth century. This evolution can be divided into four periods:

The Birth of International Health Cooperation (~1850–1945)

In the first era, from about the mid-nineteenth to mid-twentieth centuries, disease came to be understood as a transnational threat that required some degree of international cooperation. In 1851 the first International Sanitary Conference was held in Paris, convening European powers to establish arrangements to minimize the spread of certain infectious diseases and their potential harm to travel and trade. By the time the first treaty came into force, the 1892 International Sanitary Conventions, governments had agreed to notify each other if any of six diseases[11] was detected in their territories, and committed to refrain from implementing measures restricting travel or trade without scientific or public health grounds. Notably, the main objective was to protect the economies of the cooperating parties and to limit the spread of infectious disease, not to

---

[8] Hoffman et al. 2015.   [9] United Nations 1946.   [10] Moon 2018.
[11] Cholera, plague, yellow fever, smallpox, typhus. and relapsing fever.

protect population health in outbreak-affected countries. During this period international disease control efforts that reached behind borders were driven by colonial interests, for example, protecting soldiers and settlers from infections or improving the economic productivity of colonies by protecting workers.[12]

At the start of the twentieth century the Pan-American Sanitary Bureau and Office Internationale d'Hygiène Publique were established as the first permanent international organizations to facilitate health cooperation, followed after the First World War by the International Health Organization of the League of Nations. These organizations laid the groundwork for the creation of the WHO, but in comparison had quite limited mandates. In terms of non-state actors (NSAs), perhaps most significant was the Rockefeller Foundation, which in 1913 established its International Health Commission and launched a range of international health projects; the foundation set a precedent that endures to this day of autonomous NSAs playing an influential role in global health.[13] In the century that followed the 1851 conference the fields of medicine and biology advanced dramatically and the field of public health was invented – yet the international law of disease control barely changed.[14] This background makes the ideational and institutional shift that took place after the Second World War all the more remarkable.

The Birth of WHO and Heyday of "International" Health (1945–~1990)

The 1948 creation of the WHO, and the UN system more broadly, marks the beginning of a second era that established a far more ambitious vision for what international cooperation should achieve for health. The rather progressive WHO constitution, signed by participating governments in 1946, defined health broadly as "a state of complete physical, mental and social well-being and not merely the absence of disease or infirmity." It declared that "enjoyment of the highest attainable standard of health is one of the fundamental rights of every human being, without distinction of race, religion, political belief, economic or social condition." And it placed health among the highest priorities for international relations, asserting that "the health of all peoples is fundamental to the attainment of peace and security and is dependent upon the fullest cooperation by individuals and states."[15]

---

[12] Packard 2016.   [13] Packard 2016; Youde 2013.   [14] Fidler 2005.
[15] United Nations 1946.

WHO's mandate was expansive, covering all of public health, and its founders envisioned a hierarchical organization able to direct and coordinate others. In the ensuing decades WHO would launch ambitious programs that successfully eradicated smallpox, eliminated (at least temporarily) malaria in some regions, conducted research on tropical diseases, and launched a campaign to extend primary healthcare to all. It issued guidelines on commercially sensitive topics such as essential medicines and the marketing of breast milk substitutes, and on socially sensitive topics such as sex and reproduction. WHO wore many hats: running operations in countries, issuing technical normative guidelines that carried great weight (particularly in developing countries), advocating on health policies, and acting as a political arena for international debates through its bi-annual gatherings of member states (the Executive Board and World Health Assembly). NSAs such as religious groups, non-governmental organizations (NGOs), professional bodies, companies, and foundations were all active in this period but were relatively few in number.

Although often characterized as a technical agency, WHO was not isolated from its political context. The growing numbers of its governing body, as decolonization swelled the ranks of member states, produced strong North–South tensions.[16] The Cold War's competition over ideas and influence also enveloped WHO, as reflected in debates over whether WHO should focus narrowly on controlling particular diseases (as backed by the USA) or get involved in expanding access to healthcare (supported by the Soviet Union).[17] Not by coincidence, in the 1970s the USA began supporting increased involvement in health by the World Bank, where its influence was more concentrated.[18] These dynamics contributed to WHO's paralysis and decline through the 1980s. By the 1990s WHO had hit a low point, with weak leadership, wide criticism from the public health community,[19] and a freeze on its core budget driven by anti-UN sentiment in the USA.[20] The search for alternatives to WHO – and the state-centered, multilateral model of global governance it represented – began in earnest.

The Millennium Development Goals Era and the Birth of "Global" Health (~1990–~2015)

Beginning in the 1990s, recognition of health as an important development, economic, and security issue began to grow outside the health

---

[16] Chorev 2012.   [17] Chorev 2012; Cueto et al. 2019.
[18] Sridhar et al. 2017; Cueto et al. 2019.
[19] Godlee 1997; Smith 1995; Walt 1993; Yamey 2002.   [20] Mackey and Novotny 2012.

community. This ideational evolution was both reflected in and advanced by the World Bank's seminal 1993 *World Development Report*, "Investing in Health," which laid out the evidence and arguments for why health – and therefore health spending – was an important precondition for economic growth, as well as a worthy goal in its own right.[21] Reportedly, this analysis piqued Microsoft billionaire Bill Gates' interest in health.[22] In the years to follow the Bill and Melinda Gates Foundation (BMGF) would become one of the largest funders of global health projects (outspending many governments)[23] and an influential political voice.[24]

The rapid spread of HIV/AIDS and its unprecedented consequences for development also began to cause alarm in the 1990s. The 1996 creation of the Joint UN Programme on HIV/AIDS (UNAIDS) as a new UN entity reflected both recognition that HIV was not merely a health threat and a loss of confidence in WHO's ability to lead the global response.[25] This same loss of confidence informed the creation of the Global Alliance for Vaccines and Immunization (Gavi) in 2000 and the Global Fund to Fight HIV/AIDS, Tuberculosis and Malaria in 2002 as self-described "public-private partnerships" intended to be more tightly focused, results-oriented, and efficient than the WHO.[26] Also in 1996 the International AIDS Vaccine Initiative was founded as a non-profit organization and "public-private product development partnership (PDP)" to accelerate vaccine R&D efforts by coordinating with funders, researchers, and the pharmaceutical industry, presaging the creation of over two dozen analogous entities to mobilize R&D into neglected diseases in the ensuing decade.[27] A unifying theme underlying all these developments was a shift away from purely state-based approaches to addressing health problems.

With the agreement of the eight Millennium Development Goals (MDGs) in 2002, three of which directly targeted health,[28] health became central to the global development agenda. The term "global health" also began to overtake "international health" in usage, reflecting both a cosmopolitan concern with "the health needs of the people of the whole planet above the concerns of particular nations" and the growing influence of NSAs.[29] The dollars backed up this semantic transition. The amount of development aid allocated to health tripled over a "golden" decade, from about $11.6 billion in 2000 to $33.9 billion in 2010, with

---

[21] Musgrove 1993.   [22] World Bank 2014.   [23] Dieleman et al. 2016.
[24] McGoey 2015; Harman 2016; Youde 2013.   [25] Knight 2008; Cueto et al. 2019.
[26] Szlezak 2008.   [27] Ziemba 2005.
[28] MDGs 4, 5, and 6 on child mortality, maternal health, and HIV/AIDs, malaria, and other diseases, respectively.
[29] Brown et al. 2006.

growth leveling out subsequently.[30] Health aid grew faster than official development assistance (ODA) overall, which grew only 77 percent from 2000 to 2014; the proportion of health spending within total ODA grew from less than 2 percent in 1990 to 8 percent in 2000 to 17 percent in 2014.[31] Governments remained the largest source of development assistance for health at 73 percent in 2014, but the proportion from foundations, NGOs, and corporations increased significantly from 6.0 percent in 1990 to 16.5 percent in 2000 to 17.3 percent in 2014, with the BMGF the single largest private contributor. While aid flows are important, by 2017 significant economic growth meant that DAH accounted for only 2 percent of total public spending on health in low- and middle-income countries (LMICs).[32]

This era can be characterized by four interrelated governance features. First, rapid growth in the numbers and types of actors working in health contributed to what Fidler called an "unstructured plurality" and "anarchy" in GHG.[33] In a mapping of 200 major actors in the global health system, Hoffman et al. concluded that half had been founded between 1990 and 2010.[34] Second, both a cause and result of this population explosion was persistent questioning of the role of WHO. WHO frequently had to compete with the newer global health actors for funding and influence. That said, as a trusted source of technical normative guidance to countries and an arena for agenda-setting, negotiation, and rule-making it retained a central position. Third, this era focused on a handful of health challenges, foremost among them HIV/AIDS. This disease focus was coupled with a strong emphasis on technological interventions delivered through vertical, donor-supported programs, such as child vaccinations through Gavi and treatment for HIV and malaria with new medicines financed by the Global Fund. These investments yielded impressive and important achievements – record declines in childhood and maternal mortality, twenty-one million people on HIV treatment, decreases in malaria and TB cases, and reinvigorated pipelines of drugs and vaccines for previously neglected diseases.[35] However, these specific accomplishments did not necessarily build strong health systems that served everyone's needs, nor systems prepared for outbreaks. Finally, the MDG era saw continuing dominance by states and NSAs from the Global North as reflected in funding, leadership, and ideational influence, and continuing North–South conflicts over matters

---

[30] Institute for Health Metrics and Evaluation (IHME) 2016.
[31] Moon and Omole 2017.
[32] Author's calculations using World Bank World Development Indicators database.
[33] Fidler 2007.   [34] Hoffman et al. 2015.   [35] Ottersen et al. 2014.

such as IP and health worker migration. Nevertheless, rising powers from the South such as Brazil, India, Indonesia, South Africa, and Thailand exerted considerable political influence, as did middle powers in the North such as Norway or Switzerland.

This period also witnessed an increasing appreciation among health practitioners and scholars of the many social, economic, and political determinants of health operating outside the national health sector. The highest-profile example was the impact of globalized IP rules negotiated into trade agreements in the 1990s, which required many developing countries to grant patents on medicines for the first time and thereby enable monopoly pricing of life-saving drugs. This issue was starkly illustrated by conflicts over access to low-cost generic HIV medicines in the developing countries that were hardest hit by the epidemic: effective HIV treatment had been developed in the mid-1990s at essentially the same time that the World Trade Organization's Agreement on Trade-Related Aspects of Intellectual Property came into force. The sharp political conflicts, largely between the patent-holding pharmaceutical industry and their home governments in the North versus governments and HIV groups in the South (working with international NGOs), illustrated at least two larger governance phenomena: the profound potential health impacts of global governance processes in non-health sectors, and the complex networks and political alliances between states and NSAs wielding different types of power to influence governance outcomes.[36] These phenomena existed prior to the MDG era but intensified during this time, alongside broader global governance trends such as the rise of influential NSAs and densification of global rule-making.

The Sustainable Development Goals and Covid-19 Era: A Return to WHO and Multilateral Institutions? (~2015–Future)

The 2015 agreement of the Sustainable Development Goals (SDGs) signaled a sea change for global health. The broad scope of SDG 3, "ensure healthy lives and promote wellbeing for all at all ages," reflected a major shift away from the disease-focused MDGs toward a renewed emphasis on health systems and a much more ambitious vision. The list of health challenges on the global agenda was long and broad, including the "unfinished MDG agenda" (HIV, TB, malaria, maternal and child health), AMR, outbreaks, NCDs, aging societies, mental health, accidents, rising medicines prices, genomics, personalized medicine,

---

[36] Hein and Moon 2013.

unsustainable growth in healthcare spending, and the health impacts of climate change. One implication of this much broader agenda was continued pluralism as many more actors engaged in governance processes.

At the same time, it also implied renewed emphasis on WHO as the world's main arena for convening, priority-setting, negotiation, consensus building, and rule-making on a broad range of health matters. The large global health initiatives created during the MDG era each had tightly focused, narrow mandates: Gavi supported immunization in the poorest seventy countries; the Global Fund and UNITAID focused on HIV, TB, and malaria in developing countries. In addition the key instrument of each was funding, which was declining in relative importance with economic growth in LMICs. In 2017, external resources accounted for only 0.2 percent of health spending in upper-middle-income countries and 3.4 percent in lower-middle-income countries, on average.[37] In contrast the demand for governance – for example priority-setting, guidelines, norms and rules, monitoring, and accountability – in the face of proliferating actors and a vastly broadened agenda, was growing. Hence there was a renewed recognition of the importance of WHO.

This "return" to WHO was not inevitable. The 2014 West African Ebola crisis –particularly WHO's slowness in recognizing the severity of the outbreak, putting boots on the ground, sounding the alarm, and mobilizing an international response – spurred widespread criticism and an identity crisis.[38] A core conclusion of the seven major post-crises analyses was that WHO had indeed failed.[39] But its role as trusted interlocutor with governments, potential hub of global expertise, and arbiter of the severity of outbreaks was also recognized as irreplaceable.[40] The key question was, could WHO be reformed to fulfill these roles?

Kickbusch and Reddy called the Ebola outbreak a cosmopolitan moment for the global health community, akin to the HIV/AIDS crisis.[41] Yet the path the global community took at this crossroads was, in some senses, the opposite of HIV. Rather than create a raft of new organizations, energy was dedicated to reforming WHO. At an organizational level this focused on rebuilding the operational capacity on outbreaks that had been dismantled at the agency. At a more constitutive level, member states sent a clear message that managing outbreaks was a high priority and ought to be considered a core function.

---

[37] Author's calculations using World Bank World Development Indicators database.
[38] Moon et al. 2015.   [39] Moon, Leigh, et al. 2017.   [40] Gostin et al. 2016.
[41] Kickbusch and Reddy 2015.

Other significant WHO reforms ensued. In 2016 governments finalized a Framework of Engagement with Non-State Actors (FENSA),
which specified in unprecedented detail how WHO could engage with
private firms, academia, civil society, foundations, and other NSAs. It
was an effort to structure (at least WHO's interaction with) the unstructured plurality. To date this is the only major UN agency to have such a
framework, though engagement with NSAs is now common across the
UN system. In addition, in a first for WHO – and unprecedented for any
UN agency – in 2017 the director-general (DG) of the organization was
elected with each member state wielding one vote, a departure from
previous elections in which negotiations among a small number of countries produced a winner. In contrast, the 2016–2017 election process was
more open, involving proactive campaigning by the field of candidates,
webcast candidate forums with public participation, active press coverage, and a lively debate on the leadership profile needed at WHO.[42]
Notably, the BMGF began the millennium as the driving force behind
Gavi, seen as a workaround to WHO; but by 2014 it had become the
second largest funder of WHO – reflecting recognition of the agency's
importance and normative influence, as well as an effort to influence it.[43]

When Covid-19 struck WHO had undergone significant reform to
reprioritize outbreaks, and its leader had broad political support. The
pandemic put WHO in the global public spotlight as never before.
Seemingly overnight, starting in January 2020, the world paid close
attention to WHO. Whether WHO deemed the epidemic an official
Public Health Emergency of International Concern (PHEIC), or characterized it as a "pandemic," or recommended widespread public use of
masks, became the subject of global media coverage and heated debate.
WHO's political and technical decisions wielded global influence on
state responses to the pandemic and on individual behavior, even if its
guidance was far from universally respected.

At the same time, some ascribed to the agency far more power and
authority than it had. The US Trump administration accused WHO of
hiding information about the virus and delaying its emergency declaration, ultimately announcing US withdrawal from the organization.[44]
But investigative reporting found, rather, that the Chinese authorities
had delayed sharing information with WHO; the agency quickly shared
the information it could obtain with the international community, but
had little leverage over the Chinese government.[45] Some appeared to
believe WHO could conduct independent investigations within the

[42] Kickbusch et al. 2017.   [43] Harman 2016; Youde 2013.
[44] BBC Reality Check Team 2020.   [45] AP 2020.

sovereign territory of any nation state, which it had neither the legal nor political authority to do. In short, they believed the world had a hierarchical system of governance to address the serious threat of outbreaks, when in reality all we had was a loose, flat network.

Discussion

Several observations flow from this overview of the trajectory of GHG. First, there has been a clear move away from a primarily state-based system to one in which NSAs wield significant influence; yet this influence is often exerted in coalitions with like-minded states, or through them via domestic politics or direct lobbying of governments in international arenas. The system also remains centered around WHO. What we observe in health is a "Westphalia-plus" system in which NSAs wield influence alongside states, rather than a post-Westphalian system per se. Covid-19 – with its state-enforced lockdowns, travel bans, citizen surveillance, and economic rescue packages – has illustrated as seldom before the enduring centrality of the state: and as long as governments matter for health, WHO will matter for health. Indeed, protecting public health – which requires public goods provision, law enforcement, and collective action – demands a functioning, capable state.

Second, the beginnings of a shift to a multipolar world is certainly evident in global health politics, but dominance by the traditional powers in the North remains a key feature of the system. Money provides one indicator. High-income countries (HICs) remain the principal funders of the major global health organizations.[46] The top-five funders of WHO (USA, BMGF, Gavi, UK, Germany) accounted for half its $6 billion budget in the 2018–2019 biennium.[47] National health spending in HICs still dwarfs that of LMICs: HICs accounted for only 16 percent of the global population in 2017, but over 80 percent of total health expenditure – spending on average about twenty-two times as much per capita as the LMICs. That said, health spending in LMICs grew at a much faster pace: from 2000 to 2017 LMIC health spending increased by over 400 percent from $309 billion to $1.567 trillion, compared to 145 percent in HICs.[48] The system remains today "great powers-plus," and is only slowly becoming more multipolar.

Third, the global health system is expanding in scope and becoming more dense and complex. The increased number of health challenges

---

[46] Dieleman et al. 2016.
[47] WHO Contributors, https://open.who.int/2018-19/contributors/contributor.
[48] Author's calculations using World Bank World Development Indicators database.

understood to have transnational dimensions is prompting the engage-ment and/or creation of many new actors. As noted earlier, among the three ideal types of governance modes (hierarchy, markets, networks), contemporary GHG most closely resembles a network. In the past, the global health system exhibited more features of hierarchy. The US gov-ernment and US-based Rockefeller Foundation were dominant players in international health throughout the twentieth century,[49] and the USA and BMGF were the two largest funders of WHO at the start of the twenty-first.[50] Scholars have also highlighted the power of the World Bank, where US leadership and policy approaches have been dominant, to shape national health policies through its lending and policy advice.[51] The shadow of hierarchy cast by US global hegemony, either directly or through IGOs, covered the health sector.

But if we conceptualize global health as an issue area extending beyond development aid the picture is less clear. WHO was the site of long-standing political conflict between East and West during the Cold War, and continued through the 1990s and 2000s to be an arena for conflicts between North and South.[52] The North and the West, respectively, held dominant positions but did not always win these political contests. For example, the push for universal access to primary health care launched under the banner of "health for all by the year 2000" in 1978 at a WHO conference in Alma Ata – then part of the Soviet Union – was not welcomed by the USA but became an enduring objective in global health.[53] The goal was not achieved and was even undermined by the widespread implementation of World Bank-supported user fees under structural adjustment programs in the 1980s–1990s.[54] Yet its lasting legacy is reflected in the focus on universal health coverage in the SDGs and its central place in WHO's 2018–2023 workplan. WHO's efforts to limit infant formula and promote access to essential medicines was also hotly contested between North and South but ultimately sus-tained.[55] There were heavyweights and significant power disparities in the system but these did not add up to a clear hierarchy.

In terms of modes of governance, "markets" are even less applicable to global health. Unlike in environment, where certification schemes and harnessing consumer preferences have been prominent tools of global governance, these have not been widely used in health. This may be because health-related goods and services are more often consumed on the principle of need than consumer choice. And at national level, public

[49] Youde 2013.   [50] Clift 2014.   [51] Abbasi 1999; Sridhar et al. 2017.
[52] Chorev 2012; Cueto et al. 2019; Packard 2016.   [53] Rohde et al. 2008.
[54] Maciocco 2008.   [55] Maciocco 2008.

health is usually undergirded by laws (e.g., on air and water quality, food safety, nutrition labeling, smoking restrictions, road safety, and health insurance requirements), often collectively financed through taxation (e.g., public health insurance or care systems), and enforced through the coercive power of the state (e.g., quarantines, bans on food additives, and closure of non-compliant businesses). Involvement of market actors and market-based policy tools are certainly present in global health, but markets are far from being a primary mode of governance.

Networked governance is the most applicable of the three. One manifestation of the relevance of networks is the proliferation of multi-stakeholder partnerships as an organizational structure and governing principle in global health.[56] Informal policy networks also loosely linked together like-minded NGOs, government representatives, IGO staff, industry executives, academic experts, and journalists, such as on issues relating to medicines prices and IP.[57] Whereas WHO used to be the dominant node in the network, we observe today an expanded, diversified network with an increased density of connections between the actors and nodes. WHO remains the central node, but other major nodes now operate as well.[58]

Yet the networks observable in global health are not characterized by "equality" between actors. Rather, as Faul has argued, networks reflect and can exacerbate power disparities between constituent actors, belying the surface-level discourse of partnerships or equal standing in formal decision-making processes.[59] Furthermore, the concept of networks fails to capture the way interactions between various parts of the system collectively produce certain outcomes, such as controlling a yellow fever outbreak, developing a new vaccine for meningitis, or reducing tobacco use in children.

For this reason, I argue that "system" is a more appropriate concept than hierarchy, market, or even network to describe what we see in global health. Global health actors exhibit characteristics of a complex adaptive system in which many autonomous actors interact across multiple scales (local, national, regional, global), across time, countries, and sectors (complex); learn from previous interactions and adopt new strategies, making behavior difficult to predict (adaptive); and interact in ways that shape each other's thinking, choices, decisions, and actions (system).[60] Thus, "system" – and "complex adaptive system" in particular – offers a more apt analogy for GHG.

---

[56] Andonova 2017.   [57] Hein and Moon 2013.   [58] Hoffman et al. 2015.
[59] Faul 2016.   [60] Hill 2011.

Health has witnessed a shift from "old" (large international bureaucracies, multilateral arrangements, grand plans and designs) to "new" models of governance (smaller and nimbler organizations, club arrangements, and incremental, piecemeal, pragmatic action). But what may distinguish health from other global governance arenas is the persistent centrality of the large international bureaucracy that is the WHO. It is the largest UN specialized agency, with about 150 country offices and six regional offices, 8,000 total staff, and most recently an annual budget of about $3 billion.[61] Its scope of work and budget has increased every biennium over the past two decades. The younger organizations that were to be nimble and lean are now also bureaucracies – UNAIDS (700 staff spanning 79 countries)[62] and the Global Fund (700 staff in Geneva).[63] In addition, formal multilateral rule-making still matters, such as the International Health Regulations (IHRs), a binding set of international rules on how countries should prepare for and respond to disease outbreaks.[64] Revising the IHRs is likely to be a major post-Covid-19 effort.

Alongside the old is the new. In contrast to other sectors, there are very few treaties – only three – dedicated to health, but no shortage of guidelines, codes, technical norms and standards, frameworks, global action plans, resolutions, financial flows, and other tools that shape actor behavior. The rise of private authority from foundations, industries, and NGOs is omnipresent,[65] and hybrid formal governance arrangements (e.g., boards) combining representatives of public and private actors are the norm for new global health initiatives.[66] Yet at the WHO, where most normative instruments are negotiated, agreed, and legitimated, states have jealously guarded their decision-making authority. FENSA reinforced the principle that NSAs may contribute, participate, and collaborate with WHO, but it remains states who decide. Indeed, in her study of multi-stakeholder partnerships (many in global health) Andonova found that establishing norms and rules was a governance function rarely delegated to partnerships.[67]

Finally, the era of grand plans is not yet over. The ambition of the SDGs remains vast. The negotiation of global strategies and plans remains an oft-used tool for coordinating actors across a pluralist landscape. UN High-Level Meetings engaging heads of state on health are no longer unusual, having now been held on HIV, NCDs, AMR, TB, and universal health coverage (UHC). Covid-19 will prompt more. Massive global conferences, big ambitions, and master plans remain – but the

[61] Burci 2019.   [62] UNAIDS 2018.   [63] GFATM n.d.   [64] Fidler 2005.
[65] Hall and Biersteker 2003.   [66] Gleckman 2018.   [67] Andonova 2017.

implementation is more piecemeal and farmed out to all types of states and NSAs, from small to large, for-profit, non-profit, and in-between. In general the new has not replaced the old but rather has grown up around it – sometimes complementing, sometimes competing, but not yet overtaking it.

Why Is This Happening? Health as a Microcosm and a Unique Field

Many of the forces driving broader changes in global governance have also affected the health sector, particularly a globalizing economy, the demographic transition, neoliberal and cosmopolitan ideation, and technological change. Key features of the contemporary governance system also owe much to the particularities of the HIV/AIDS pandemic. These factors have interacted in complex ways to produce the system we see today.

In terms of material factors, a globalizing economy produced a new set of health challenges linked to the production (e.g., environmental health impacts of underregulated factories) and consumption (e.g., substandard medicines, processed foods, tobacco) of traded goods and services. It also both spurred (and was spurred by) the emergence of transnational rules seeking to govern that economy; as the health implications of these rules (e.g., IP, investment, trade in goods and services) became clearer, so did the impetus for health actors to engage in broader global governance processes. Globalized trade and travel patterns also facilitated the spread of infectious disease, moving the Covid-19 pathogen from China across Asia to Europe and the Americas in weeks, shutting down societies and economies. In addition, economic growth in middle-income countries generated both the wealth to increase domestic spending on health and transformed previously poor countries into attractive markets for multinational firms. This shift raised the prospects of heightened conflict between governments and firms on issues such as health technology pricing and regulation of goods and services.

Alongside these economic developments were important changes in population structures. Much of the world began the demographic transition over the past several decades, with populations transitioning from high to low birth rates, with a greater proportion surviving through childhood and infectious disease to face a rising tide of chronic NCDs, resulting in an overall aging of population structures. These population shifts increased demand for healthcare, prompted investment in developing an ever more sophisticated and costly suite of health technologies, and increased political and financial pressures on governments to ensure access to healthcare. They also broadened the global health agenda to examine the underlying causes of NCDs, which frequently involves a broader set of commercial actors (e.g., agriculture, tobacco, processed food, beverage, alcohol, pharmaceuticals) than the previous infectious disease agenda (primarily pharmaceuticals). The demographic transition has contributed to making health a major sector of the global economy and a hotly contested political issue.

In terms of ideational factors, as noted in the earlier subsection on "The Millennium Development Goals Era," an important shift in how health was conceived took place in the early 1990s, and caught the attention of well-resourced decision-makers – not least of whom Bill Gates. Perhaps there was also a certain fatigue with the vagaries and outright failures of development aid,[68] and that combating disease seemed (on the surface) seductively simple: few aspects of the human experience are as obsessively measured, counted, or studied as health. Technology also seemed to provide a silver bullet.[69] This appealing combination – a measurable problem and the availability of tools to solve it – may explain why health enjoyed its moment in the MDG limelight.

Furthermore, growing attention to health coincided with the post-Cold War ascendance of neoliberalism and the "new public management," which asserted that the private sector was fundamentally more capable, efficient, or effective than the public sector.[70] A frequently heard argument was that public problems could not be solved without private sector engagement, and therefore that business should "have a seat at the table."[71] The allocation of private sector seats on the boards of Gavi and the Global Fund were justified on these grounds, and this ideology is also reflected in the creation of PDPs. However, fierce debates have continued regarding what a "seat at the table" exactly means, and in particular where the line between private and public authority should be drawn.

Alongside neoliberalism, cosmopolitanism also deeply informed GHG. From Alma Ata's call for "health for all" to the BMGF's motto that "every life has equal value,"[72] global health is suffused with the idea that health is both a universal concern and responsibility of humanity. Neoliberalism and cosmopolitanism often coexisted, with broad agreement on universalist goals but strong disagreement on the appropriate roles of states and markets in reaching them.

Technological change also remains an important driver. The ever-expanding arsenal of health technologies prompted hope among patients, launched political movements for global access to medicines, strained

[68] Easterly 2006.   [69] Birn 2005.   [70] Labonte and Schrecker 2007.
[71] Ooms and Hammonds 2009.   [72] Bill and Melinda Gates Foundation n.d.

budgets, and sparked political conflicts between governments and firms.[73] Information and communication technology has also been transformative. It could rapidly translate the life experience of a malnourished child to a global public, motivating a social response. It could enable smaller, weaker states and NSAs to build cooperative networks and joint strategies. It amplified the microphones of activists and advocates. It could transmit information regarding suspicious outbreaks of infectious disease instantly from local media in one part of the world to public health agencies in another. And technology enabled man-made health threats such as chemical and biological weapons, requiring new efforts to govern and prevent large-scale disasters. Artificial intelligence and other digital technologies will bring more changes still. In sum, technology provided potential solutions to disease and bound the world more tightly together, while also creating a whole host of new challenges for governance.

With respect to the above-mentioned factors, health was a microcosm of broader global changes. But GHG was also profoundly shaped by the particular experience of HIV/AIDS, highlighting the importance of path dependence. "AIDS invented global health," as historian Allan Brandt argued.[74] AIDS was an unprecedented global health and development emergency. AIDS activists built the transnational networks that enabled worldwide social mobilization for the creation of the Global Fund (initially conceived only for HIV) and an interpretation of global IP rules that cleared the way for widespread access to generic HIV medicines.[75] By insisting that no decisions should be taken "about us, without us," AIDS activists also created the norm of community representation,[76] later replicated in other areas. The Global Fund board includes a seat for communities and two seats for NGOs, and UNITAID's board allocates two seats for communities and NGOs, for example. AIDS also galvanized unprecedented levels of development assistance, through the Global Fund, the US President's Emergency Plan for AIDS Relief, the World Bank, and numerous other initiatives. Brandt concluded that HIV/AIDS established a "new global health" that "recognizes the essential supranational character of problems of disease and their amelioration and the fact that no individual country can adequately address diseases in the face of the movement of people, trade, microbes, and risks."[77] While the growth of transnational health challenges at the start of the twenty-first century would have prompted new efforts to govern them, it was the HIV/AIDS pandemic and the remarkable political savvy of AIDS

[73] 't Hoen et al. 2011.   [74] Brandt 2013.   [75] 't Hoen et al. 2011.
[76] Smith and Siplon 2006.   [77] Brandt 2013.

activists that shaped the character of contemporary global governance institutions in health.

Kingdon's insight that change does not occur gradually, but in patterns of punctuated equilibrium, is well illustrated in global health.[78] Like HIV/AIDS the Covid-19 pandemic will surely be such a watershed moment, ushering in changes to global governance in health and far beyond. And as with HIV/AIDS, the characteristics of this new order are likely to be shaped not only by deep underlying determinants but also by the leaders and political strategies they adopt to shape it.

How Does It Matter? Implications for Governance

Global health's pluralistic, polycentric, and interconnected landscape of states and NSAs has significant implications for who has power and legitimacy in governance, and ultimately how effective GHG is.

Power

The complexity of contemporary global governance suggests that power should be conceptualized broadly, as the ability to shape the thinking and/or actions of others. An implication of considering power in this way is that many actors wield power in global governance and that power takes different forms. Elsewhere, using empirical examples from global health, I have argued for the utility of considering eight different types of power: physical, economic, structural, institutional, moral, expert, discursive, and network. (See Table 8.1 for examples).[79] Following Bourdieu's concept of power as capital,[80] I argue that these types of power are fungible, such that one type of power may readily be transformed into another. For example, economic power can be transformed through research grants into expert power, as when funders support academic research that is likely to protect their interests or uphold their world views.

Three important implications arise from this typology. First is that many more actors wield power in the global system than is widely recognized. This includes actors that international relations scholars have traditionally considered "weak" such as developing countries, moral leaders, or social influencers on Twitter. The increase and diversification of actors in GHG suggests that the distribution of power has become more diffuse. At the same time, this diffusion does not necessarily correct

---

[78] Kingdon 1995.   [79] Moon 2019.   [80] Hanefeld and Walt 2015.

Table 8.1 *Types of power in global governance, with examples from health*

Type of power	Examples of actors wielding such power	Health-related examples of uses of such power
Physical	Militaries, militia, mercenaries, peacekeeping forces, police	Cordon sanitaire, quarantine
Economic	Wealthy governments, firms, foundations, individuals	Shaping WHO priorities through funding
Structural	Governments, traditional leaders	Governments levying taxes on tobacco sales
Institutional	Depends on institution: often governments, increasingly also firms and NGOs	Civil society delegation to Global Fund board voting on grantmaking policies
Moral	Religious leaders, social movement leaders, moral authorities	Speech by Nelson Mandela on destigmatizing HIV
Expertise	Academics, scientists, lawyers	Evidence on link between alcohol and cancer leading to changes in alcohol regulation
Discursive	Media, politicians, activists, public intellectuals	Contraception as sexual and reproductive right
Network	Any well-networked individual or group of individuals	Garnering invitations to prestigious committees or conference speaking roles

major power imbalances in the system. The second implication is that different types of power can reinforce each other to widen or entrench power disparities. But not always. If we accept the premise that GHG is a complex adaptive system, then the outcome of thousands of interconnected actors wielding different types of power pursuing their interests can be unpredictable. A small exercise of power in one part of the system can have butterfly effects elsewhere. The overall implication, then, of a more pluralistic and polycentric global governance system is a far broader distribution of power (even if lumpy) with increased unpredictability of outcomes.

Legitimacy

We also observe that a broader set of actors has gained acceptance as legitimate voices in governance, but their bases for legitimacy differ. Stakeholders in GHG are now regularly defined to include: those who are directly affected by decisions (e.g., patients, community groups), those who contribute funds (e.g., foundations, billionaires, donor countries), those who have capacity to contribute (e.g., industry), those who bring evidence and expertise (e.g., academics, scientific experts), and those who simply care deeply about a topic (e.g., advocates, activists). The two largest new global health initiatives to be launched in a decade, the Global Financing Facility for Women and Children's Health in 2015 and Coalition for Epidemic Preparedness Innovations (CEPI) in 2016, were created with governing bodies consisting of all these groups. Some actors bank on normative claims to input legitimacy ("we should be at the table as democratic representatives of the governed" – governments and civil society) and others on instrumental claims to output legitimacy ("we should be at the table because the decision will be better and more likely to be implemented if we are" – experts, funders, industry, advocates). In a networked system with little hierarchy perhaps this widespread conferral of legitimacy is to be expected.

However, whether all these voices should play the same roles, and whether their underlying bases for legitimacy are equal, has remained strongly contested. These questions were central to the debate over FENSA: whereas WHO had previously considered all NSAs as a single category for establishing official relations, FENSA created four distinct groups (NGOs, the private sector, foundations, and academic institutions) with rules of engagement tailored to each. Whether the policies for engaging with commercial actors were adequate to safeguard WHO from undue influence or conflicts of interest is an unresolved debate as FENSA has moved from negotiation to implementation.[81]

And while NSAs have become widespread as stakeholders and governors it has also prompted pushback. Whereas NSAs frequently have decision-making roles in the governance of specific initiatives (e.g., the Global Fund, CEPI) that usually fund or implement programs, states have not conceded such authority in the WHO and broader UN arenas where norms and rules are decided, as noted. This is reflected in the FENSA decision, the SDG process, the election of the WHO DG, and other issues on which states made the final decisions.

For some the rise of "multi-stakeholderism" was seen as a Trojan horse for industries and foundations not only to exert more control over global health initiatives,[82] but also to counteract the numerical advantage that developing countries had in the WHO. From this perspective the shift away from WHO at the turn of the millennium could be seen, not as

---

[81] Buse and Hawkes 2016.   [82] Sridhar and Woods 2013.

a rejection of bureaucratic inefficiency, but as a shift to create new organizations where Northern actors would have more sway.

Effectiveness

The implications of these governance arrangements for effectiveness are mixed. As noted in the "Discussion" subsection, impressive achievements have been made in reducing deaths from high-burden infections. Alongside governments of LMICs, major contributions came from NGOs, foundations, and companies that were largely absent from the global health system of the 1990s. Yet these achievements are incomplete and under threat: an estimated 1.7 million new HIV infections still occur annually, a trend that has not appreciably changed in a decade;[83] malaria is developing resistance to previously effective drugs and insecticides, and cases could resurge;[84] TB cases have been declining very slowly while multi-drug resistant forms of the disease spread.[85] For health issues lower down the global agenda in the MDG era, such as mental health or obesity, the "new" global health system has not proven itself more effective than the old. This point was forcefully made by the 2014 West African Ebola crisis, which highlighted persistent vulnerability to health emergencies despite record-breaking global health spending the previous two decades. Some have argued that the potent advocacy of NGOs and foundations for their specific issues of interest – whether HIV, polio, or any other cause – allowed for a dangerous neglect of health systems. The pendulum has swung back to health systems again in the SDGs, though it remains to be seen whether in rhetoric only or in practice.

At a scale far greater than Ebola, the devastation wrought by Covid-19 has exposed, again, the fault lines in the global system. One issue that has been laid bare is that the global health system has largely been constructed to address health in LMICs. Many of the governance functions that all countries rely upon, such as the negotiation and enforcement of rules, have been neglected. For example, in contrast to security or trade, enforcement arrangements for the IHR (2005) amount to naming and shaming, with WHO often constrained from even doing that.

Overall health is a sector in which the effectiveness of global governance arrangements is relatively feasible to assess due to conceptual clarity on what "success" looks like – the control of disease, the decline of morbidity and mortality. The picture is a mix of significant achievements and many unaddressed problems.

---

[83] UNAIDS 2020.   [84] WHO 2019b.   [85] WHO 2019a.

Reflections for the Future: What Should GHG Do and What Is the Role of WHO?

There is no shortage of health challenges on the horizon: the risk of outbreaks of infectious disease linked to urbanization, meat consumption, travel, and trade; persistently high maternal mortality in the poorest countries; declining efficacy of existing antimicrobials; pressure on health systems to care for aging populations with an increasingly costly armamentarium of health technologies; and the as-yet poorly understood health effects of climate change, to name just a few. The current context of dense relationships of interdependence is likely to intensify, as is the governance system that evolves in response.

Can GHG effectively protect, restore, and maintain public health? With a plurality of actors, subsequent proliferation of interests and agendas, and significant power disparities, is effective governance feasible? What must the system achieve in order to do so? As argued elsewhere, effective governance of the global health system requires that it collectively perform four functions: managing externalities, providing global public goods, mobilizing solidarity, and stewardship.[86]

The first function, managing externalities, is the ability to address situations in which actions in one country produce significant health-related impacts in another, such as the cross-border spread of infectious disease or environmental pollution. Such externalities are expected to increase with intensifying interdependence. For example, the increasing transborder movement of goods, people, and elements of the natural environment is expected to raise the risk of infectious disease outbreaks. These threats were the original impetus for international health cooperation 150 years ago, and touch on the "high-politics" issues of economic and national security. Unsurprisingly they have largely been managed through interstate negotiations. While NSAs play an important role in providing information, implementing programs, and conducting advocacy, states have retained the central decision-making roles in policy-making and financing. Growing multipolarity is likely to make effective agreements more difficult to achieve, however, as illustrated by USA–China conflict over the causes and consequences of Covid-19.[87] A central issue for the future is whether global health actors can find ways through the "gridlock" that may result, and effectively address such threats.[88] The experience of the past two decades suggests that global

---

[86] Frenk and Moon 2013.   [87] Hale et al. 2013.   [88] Hale et al. 2013.

health has been a field of significant experimentation and innovation in governance, offering some reasons for optimism.[89]

The second function is the provision of global public goods. At national level, responsibility for provision of public goods, such as security or knowledge, generally falls to national governments (whether governments directly provide such goods or create policies that ensure private actors do so).[90] Without a global government this task falls to the global health system at large. Many global public goods for health (e.g., disease surveillance systems, scientific research, R&D for health technologies) have been financed primarily by wealthy countries, either through development aid, foreign affairs, or defense budgets.[91] Emerging powers have been increasingly called upon to share this burden and the willingness of HIC publics to do so may decline. Such trends have already characterized global policy debates on financing R&D. However, emerging powers continue to play a very limited role in financing – it is growing but very slowly.[92] A major question remains whether and how quickly[93] emerging powers will fill the gap that major powers are likely to leave in global public goods provision.

The third function is broadly conceptualized as mobilizing solidarity, and includes development assistance, technical cooperation, humanitarian aid in emergencies, and advocacy for those whose own states have failed to protect them. After a decade of rapid growth DAH reached a plateau from 2010.[94] DAH has also shifted out of middle-income countries and concentrated in the lowest-income countries where it comprises on average one-quarter of health spending.[95] However, with the majority of the world's poor living in middle-income countries, a key question is whether this DAH transition can be achieved in a manner sensitive to health inequalities such countries, as well as whether it can better address extreme deprivation and rising needs in the lowest-income countries. The rise of emerging powers as new donors – illustrated most clearly by China's large and growing role in health aid in sub-Saharan Africa[96] – may counteract the decline from traditional donor countries, though the modalities of these new aid flows is likely to differ.[97]

Similar questions arise regarding humanitarian assistance, which has been financed and delivered predominantly by the wealthy countries but where emerging powers – again, particularly China – play a growing role.[98] In the face of growing security threats and the erosion of norms

[89] Held et al. 2019.   [90] Barrett 2007.   [91] Moon, Røttingen, et al. 2017.
[92] Policy Cures Research 2017.   [93] Kahler 2013.   [94] Dieleman et al. 2016.
[95] Chatham House Centre on Health Security, Working Group on Health Financing 2014.
[96] Shajalal et al. 2017.   [97] Shajalal et al. 2017; Fan et al. 2014.   [98] Hirono 2018.

protecting humanitarian assistance, record levels of forced displacement,[99] and other humanitarian emergencies, a central question is whether these geopolitical shifts will enable the humanitarian aid system to provide adequate relief for emergencies in the decades to come.

The last subfunction under mobilizing solidarity is agency for the dispossessed, which is concerned with the extent to which outsiders can protect the right to health of people whose rights are violated by their own governments. Despite the emergence of the "responsibility to protect" doctrine, the resurgence of nationalism and efforts to weaken international institutions suggest this function will become increasingly difficult. Blatant disregard in Syria for well-established norms banning the use of chemical weapons, for example, highlight this challenge. Graphic media coverage and vocal advocacy by NGOs was inadequate to convince governments to refrain from violating long-held international norms.

Finally, the fourth function is stewardship, which refers to providing overall strategic direction so that all other functions can be performed. It includes convening for negotiation and consensus building, setting priorities, establishing rules, evaluation for accountability, and advocating for health in global governance processes beyond the health sector (e.g., trade, investment, migration). The sheer breadth of health issues requiring effective global governance and the proliferation of actors has highlighted the need for stewardship. Stewardship is needed for ensuring the system as a whole functions, for setting goals and agendas legitimately, and for monitoring this complex system. As argued in the subsection on "The Sustainable Development Goals and Covid-19 Era," the need for stewardship has driven a return to WHO. Analysts examining the 1990s bemoaned the overall decline of WHO,[100] and in the MDG era highlighted how new global health initiatives competed with the organization for funding, influence, and relevance.[101] But what is less widely recognized is that most of these initiatives were channels for DAH; they focused on one function of the global health system – mobilizing solidarity – and did not play a major role with respect to the other three. DAH matters less in a context of emerging powers.

Three brief examples illustrate the implications. First, the drive to expand healthcare to achieve UHC is a central target of the health-related SDGs, and will largely depend on domestic financing in all but the poorest countries. WHO's role remains central in providing policy guidance, in convening countries and other actors to share experiences and evidence, and in monitoring and accountability for progress toward

[99] UNHCR 2020.   [100] Godlee 1997; Yamey 2002.   [101] Buse and Harmer 2004.

UHC. Similarly, outbreaks of infectious disease affect all countries, and most financing for outbreak preparedness is expected to come from domestic resources not DAH. As Covid-19 has demonstrated, WHO retains a central role in gathering and interpreting information daily on potentially risky disease events, assessing when an outbreak should be declared a PHEIC, and supporting governments on outbreak responses. Many actors besides WHO have the capacity to stamp out chains of transmission or run clinics, such as the US Centers for Disease Control or Médecins Sans Frontières. But no other actor has the authority to monitor countries to ensure an adequate level of preparedness or to issue travel warnings that can bring economies to a halt, for example. After President Trump declared in 2020 that the USA was withdrawing as a member state of WHO in the heat of the Covid-19 pandemic, the USA appeared isolated as other member states announced their political and financial support to the agency.[102] Third, DAH is expected to play a relatively small role in addressing NCDs (e.g., heart disease, mental illness, cancer, and diabetes) in developing countries. However, WHO plays a critical role in convening the global community and providing policy guidance to governments on issues such as taxes on sugar or tobacco, marshaling the evidence base on various foods, warning labels on alcohol, and the design of healthy buildings and cities.

These three examples illustrate the ways in which WHO acts as a focal point for self-organizing, autonomous actors in the global system. Contrary to its constitution, WHO's main function today is not as a directing and coordinating authority, but rather as a convener, advisor, legitimator, and political arena.

Questions regarding the role of WHO are often not only about the organization itself, but also about the appropriate role of states vis-à-vis NSAs, and about the relative strengths of intergovernmental institutions versus the many forms of hybrid public–private and pure private governance that have arisen. WHO's place at the center is likely to endure in an increasingly fragmented yet ambitious Westphalia-plus, Great Powers-plus system. A key question for the future is whether WHO will be appropriately mandated, financed, and led to adequately perform the stewardship function – and whether states will be willing to grant it the greater hierarchical authority to do so.

Society's response to cross-border health threats has evolved significantly since the 1850s. Today's dense and complex adaptive system of

---

[102] Schmitz 2020.

GHG reflects significant shifts in how the purpose of global governance is defined, from a system that originated primarily to protect the trade interests of the major powers to one that seeks to govern an expansive range of health issues across all countries. Complex adaptive systems are difficult to predict, however, and how Covid-19 will alter the trajectory of that evolution is an open question. What may be predicted with greater certainty is that the central role of states – and by extension the intergovernmental institutions they have built – as the actors with authority and responsibility for protecting public health will endure in an increasingly dense and crowded ecosystem.

References

Abbasi, Kamran. 1999. Changing Sides. *BMJ : British Medical Journal* 318 (7187): 865–869.

Andonova, Liliana B. 2017. *Governance Entrepreneurs: International Organizations and the Rise of Global Public–Private Partnerships*. New York: Cambridge University Press.

AP. 2020. China Delayed Releasing Coronavirus Info, Frustrating WHO. *Associated Press*. https://apnews.com/3c061794970661042b18d5aeaaed9fae.

Barrett, Scott. 2007. *Why Cooperate? The Incentive to Supply Global Public Goods*. Oxford: Oxford University Press.

BBC Reality Check Team. 2020. Coronavirus: What Are President Trump's Charges against the WHO? *BBC*. www.bbc.com/news/world-us-canada-52294623.

Bill and Melinda Gates Foundation. n.d. Foundation Fact Sheet. www.gatesfoundation.org/Who-We-Are/General-Information/Foundation-Factsheet.

Birn, Anne-Emanuelle. 2005. Gates's Grandest Challenge: Transcending Technology as Public Health Ideology. *The Lancet* 366 (9484): 514–519.

Brandt, Allan M. 2013. How AIDS Invented Global Health. *New England Journal of Medicine* 368 (23): 2149–2152.

Brown, Theodore M., Marcos Cueto, and Elizabeth Fee. 2006. The World Health Organization and the Transition from "International" to "Global" Public Health. *American Journal of Public Health* 96 (1): 62–72.

Burci, Gian Luca. 2019. The World Health Organization at 70: Challenges and Adaptation – Introductory Notes. *International Organizations Law Review* 16 (2): 229–241.

Buse, Kent and Andrew Harmer. 2004. Power to the Partners? The Politics of Public–Private Health Partnerships. *Development* 47 (2): 49–56.

Buse, Kent and Sarah Hawkes. 2016. Sitting on the FENSA: WHO Engagement with Industry. *The Lancet* 388 (10043): 446–447.

Chatham House Centre on Health Security, Working Group on Health Financing. 2014. *Shared Responsibilities for Health: A Coherent Global Framework for Health Financing*. London: Chatham House. www.chathamhouse.org/publication/shared-responsibilities-health-coherent-global-framework-health-financing.

Chorev, Nitsan. 2012. *The World Health Organization between North and South.* Ithaca, NY: Cornell University Press.

Clift, Charles. 2014. *What's the World Health Organization For?* London: Chatham House.

Cueto, Marcos, Theodore M. Brown, and Elizabeth Fee. 2019. *The World Health Organization: A History.* Cambridge: Cambridge University Press. www .cambridge.org/core/books/world-health-organization/ 9A0B11E8BA52C41A2AD5504A6BEA8300.

Dieleman, Joseph L., et al. 2016. Development Assistance for Health: Past Trends, Associations, and the Future of International Financial Flows for Health. *The Lancet* 387 (10037): 2536–2544.

Easterly, W. 2006. *The White Man's Burden: Why the West's Efforts to Aid the Rest Have Done So Much Ill and So Little Good.* London: Penguin.

Fan, Victoria Y., Karen A. Grépin, Gordon C. Shen, and Lucy Chen. 2014. Tracking the Flow of Health Aid from BRICS Countries. *Bulletin of the World Health Organization* 92 (6): 457–458.

Faul, Moira V. 2016. Networks and Power: Why Networks Are Hierarchical Not Flat and What Can Be Done about It. *Global Policy* 7 (2): 185–197.

Fidler, David. 2005. From International Sanitary Conventions to Global Health Security: The New International Health Regulations. *Chinese Journal of International Law* 4 (2): 325–392.

    2007. Architecture amidst Anarchy: Global Health's Quest for Governance. *Global Health Governance* 1 (1). www.ghgj.org/Fidler_Architecture.pdf.

Frenk, Julio, Octavio Gómez-Dantés, and Suerie Moon. 2014. From Sovereignty to Solidarity: A Renewed Concept of Global Health for an Era of Complex Interdependence. *The Lancet* 383 (9911): 94–97.

Frenk, Julio and Suerie Moon. 2013. Governance Challenges in Global Health. *New England Journal of Medicine* 368: 936–942.

GFATM. n.d. Staff – The Global Fund. The Global Fund to Fight AIDS, TB and Malaria. www.theglobalfund.org/en/staff/.

Gleckman, Harris. 2018. *Multistakeholder Governance and Democracy: A Global Challenge.* London: Routledge.

Godlee, Fiona. 1997. WHO Reform and Global Health. *BMJ: British Medical Journal* 314 (7091): 1359.

Gostin, Lawrence O., Oyewale Tomori, Suwit Wibulpolprasert, Ashish K. Jha, Julio Frenk, Suerie Moon, Joy Phumaphi, Peter Piot, Barbara Stocking, and Victor J. Dzau. 2016. Toward a Common Secure Future: Four Global Commissions in the Wake of Ebola. *PLoS Medicine* 13 (5): e1002042.

Hale, Thomas, David Held, and Kevin Young. 2013. *Gridlock: Why Global Cooperation Is Failing When We Need It Most.* Cambridge: Polity.

Hall, Rodney Bruce and Thomas J. Biersteker. 2003. *The Emergence of Private Authority in Global Governance.* Cambridge: Cambridge University Press.

Hanefeld, Johanna and Gill Walt. 2015. Knowledge and Networks – Key Sources of Power in Global Health: Comment on "Knowledge, Moral Claims and the Exercise of Power in Global Health." *International Journal of Health Policy and Management* 4 (2): 119–121.

Harman, Sophie. 2016. The Bill and Melinda Gates Foundation and Legitimacy in Global Health Governance. *Global Governance: A Review of Multilateralism and International Organizations* 22 (3): 349–368.

Hein, Wolfgang and Suerie Moon. 2013. *Informal Norms in Global Governance: Human Rights, Intellectual Property Rules and Access to Medicines.* Aldershot: Ashgate.

Held, David, Ilona Kickbusch, Kyle McNally, Dario Piselli, and Michaela Told. 2019. Gridlock, Innovation and Resilience in Global Health Governance. *Global Policy* 10 (2): 161–177.

Hill, Peter S. 2011. Understanding Global Health Governance as a Complex Adaptive System. *Global Public Health* 6 (6): 593–605.

Hirono, Miwa. 2018. *Exploring the Links between Chinese Foreign Policy and Humanitarian Action.* London: Humanitarian Policy Group, Overseas Development Institute. www.odi.org/sites/odi.org.uk/files/resource-documents/12015.pdf.

Hoffman, Steven J., Clark Cole, and Mark Pearcey. 2015. *Mapping Global Health Architecture to Inform the Future.* Research Paper. Chatham House. www.chathamhouse.org/sites/files/chathamhouse/field/field_document/20150120GlobalHealthArchitectureHoffmanColePearceyUpdate.pdf.

Institute for Health Metrics and Evaluation (IHME). 2016. *Financing Global Health 2015: Development Assistance Steady on the Path to New Global Goals.* Seattle: IHME. www.healthdata.org/policy-report/financing-global-health-2015-development-assistance-steady-path-new-global-goals.

Kahler, Miles. 2013. Rising Powers and Global Governance: Negotiating Change in a Resilient Status Quo. *International Affairs* 89 (3): 711–729.

Kickbusch, Ilona, Gian Luca Burci, and Austin Liu. 2017. A Good Start for WHO: But the New DG Election Process Needs an Independent Monitoring Body. The BMJ. http://blogs.bmj.com/bmj/2017/08/16/a-good-start-for-who-but-the-new-director-general-election-process-needs-an-independent-monitoring-body/.

Kickbusch, Ilona and K. Srinath Reddy. 2015. Global Health Governance: The Next Political Revolution. *Public Health* 129 (7): 838–842.

Kingdon, John W. 1995. *Agendas, Alternatives and Public Policies,* Vol. 2. New York: Harper Collins.

Knight, Lindsay. 2008. UNAIDS: The First Ten Years. Geneva: UNAIDS.

Labonte, Ronald and Ted Schrecker. 2007. Globalization and Social Determinants of Health: The Role of the Global Marketplace. *Globalization and Health* 3 (1): 6.

Lee, Kelley and Adam Kamradt-Scott. 2014. The Multiple Meanings of Global Health Governance: A Call for Conceptual Clarity. *Globalization and health* 10 (1): 28.

Maciocco, G. 2008. From Alma Ata to the Global Fund: The History of International Health Policy. *Social Medicine* 3(1). www.socialmedicine.info/index.php/socialmedicine/article/view/186/0.

Mackey, Timothy K. and Thomas A. Novotny. 2012. Improving United Nations Funding to Strengthen Global Health Governance: Amending the Helms–Biden Agreement. *Global Health Governance Journal* 6 (1). http://blogs.shu.edu/ghg/

2012/12/31/improving-united-nations-funding-to-strengthen-global-health-governance-amending-the-helms-biden-agreement/.

McGoey, Linsey. 2015. *No Such Thing as a Free Gift: The Gates Foundation and the Price of Philanthropy*. London and New York: Verso.

Moon, Suerie, et al. 2015. Will Ebola Change the Game? Ten Essential Reforms before the Next Pandemic. The Report of the Harvard-LSHTM Independent Panel on the Global Response to Ebola. *The Lancet* 386 (10009): 2204–2221.

—— 2018. Global Health Law and Governance: Concepts, Tools, Actors and Power. In *Research Handbook on Global Health Law*, edited by Gian Luca Burci and Brigit Toebes, 24–54. Cheltenham: Edward Elgar. https://doi.org/10.4337/9781785366543.00008.

—— 2019. Power in Global Governance: An Expanded Typology from Global Health. *Globalization and health* 15 (1): 74.

Moon, Suerie, Jennifer Leigh, Liana Woskie, Francesco Checchi, Victor Dzau, Mosoka Fallah, Gabrielle Fitzgerald, Laurie Garrett, Lawrence Gostin, and David L Heymann. 2017. Post-Ebola Reforms: Ample Analysis, Inadequate Action. *BMJ: British Medical Journal (Online)* 356. www.bmj.com/content/356/bmj.j280.

Moon, Suerie and Oluwatosin Omole. 2017. Development Assistance for Health: Critiques, Proposals and Prospects for Change. *Health Economics, Policy and Law* 12 (2): 207–221.

Musgrove, Philip. 1993. Investing in Health: The 1993 World Development Report of the World Bank. *Bulletin of the Pan-American Health Organization* 27 (3). https://iris.paho.org/handle/10665.2/26989.

Ooms, G. and R. Hammonds. 2009. Scaling Up Global Social Health Protection: Prerequisite Reforms to the International Monetary Fund. *International Journal of Health Services* 39 (4): 795–801.

Ottersen, Ole Petter, et al. 2014. The Political Origins of Health Inequity: Prospects for Change. *The Lancet* 383 (9917): 630–667.

Packard, Randall M. 2016. *A History of Global Health: Interventions into the Lives of Other Peoples*. Baltimore, MD: Johns Hopkins University Press.

Policy Cures Research. 2017. *G-Finder Neglected Disease Research and Development: Reflecting on a Decade of Global Investment*. http://policycuresresearch.org/downloads/Y10_G-FINDER_full_report.pdf.

Rio+20 UN Conference on Sustainable Development. 2012. *The Future We Want*. www.uncsd2012.org/content/documents/727The%20Future%20We%20Want%2019%20June%201230pm.pdf.

Rohde, Jon, Simon Cousens, Mickey Chopra, Viroj Tangcharoensathien, Robert Black, Zulfiqar A. Bhutta, and Joy E. Lawn. 2008. 30 Years after Alma-Ata: Has Primary Health Care Worked in Countries? *The Lancet* 372 (9642): 950–961.

Schmitz, Rob. 2020. Germany and France Promise New Financial Support to World Health Organization. *National Public Radio*. www.npr.org/sections/coronavirus-live-updates/2020/06/25/883302474/germany-and-france-promise-new-financial-support-to-world-health-organization.

Shajalal, Mohon, Junfang Xu, Jun Jing, Madeleine King, Jie Zhang, Peicheng Wang, Jennifer Bouey, and Feng Cheng. 2017. China's Engagement with Development Assistance for Health in Africa. *Global Health Research and Policy* 2 (1): 24.

Smith, Raymond A. and Patricia D. Siplon. 2006. *Drugs into Bodies : Global AIDS Treatment Activism*. Westport, CN: Praeger. http://discovery.lib.harvard .edu/?itemid=%7Clibrary/m/aleph%7C009980995.

Smith, Richard. 1995. The WHO: Change or Die. *BMJ: British Medical Journal* 310 (6979): 543.

Sridhar, Devi, Janelle Winters, and Eleanor Strong. 2017. World Bank's Financing, Priorities, and Lending Structures for Global Health. *BMJ : British Medical Journal* 358. www.bmj.com/content/358/bmj.j3339 .abstract.

Sridhar, Devi and Ngaire Woods. 2013. Trojan Multilateralism: Global Cooperation in Health. *Global Policy* 4 (4): 325–335.

Szlezák, Nicole A. 2008. *Global Health in the Making: China, HIV/AIDS, and the Global Fund to Fight AIDS, Tuberculosis and Malaria*. Cambridge, MA: Harvard University Press.

Szlezák, Nicole A., Barry R. Bloom, Dean T. Jamison, Gerald T. Keusch, Catherine M. Michaud, Suerie Moon, and William C. Clark. 2010. The Global Health System: Actors, Norms, and Expectations in Transition. *PLoS Medicine* 7 (1): e1000183.

't Hoen, Ellen, Jonathan Berger, Alexandra Calmy, and Suerie Moon. 2011. Driving a Decade of Change: HIV/AIDS, Patents, and Access to Medicines. *Journal of the International AIDS Society* 14 (15). www.jiasociety.org/content/ 14/1/15.

UNAIDS. 2018. Its about the People We Serve: UNAIDS Staff Connecting the World. UNAIDS. www.unaids.org/en/resources/presscentre/featurestories/ 2018/march/20180327_staff-share-global-experience.

2020. Global HIV and AIDS Statistics 2020. UNAIDS. www.unaids.org/en/ resources/fact-sheet.

UNHCR. 2020. *Global Trends: Forced Displacement in 2019*. UN High Commissioner for Refugees. www.unhcr.org/statistics/unhcrstats/ 5ee200e37/unhcr-global-trends-2019.html.

United Nations. 1946. Constitution of the World Health Organization. https:// treaties.un.org/doc/Treaties/1948/04/19480407%2010-51%20PM/Ch_IX_ 01p.pdf.

Walt, Gill. 1993. WHO under Stress: Implications for Health Policy. *Health Policy* 24 (2): 125–144.

WHO. 2019a. *Global Tuberculosis Report 2019*. World Health Organization. www .who.int/tb/publications/global_report/en/.

2019b. *World Malaria Report 2019*. World Health Organization. www.who.int/ publications/i/item/world-malaria-report-2019.

World Bank. 2014. Transcript – Toward Universal Health Coverage for 2030 – April 11, 2014. www.worldbank.org/en/topic/pandemics/brief/transcript- toward-universal-health-coverage-for-2030.

Yamey, Gavin. 2002. WHO in 2002: Have the Latest Reforms Reversed WHO's Decline? *BMJ : British Medical Journal* 325 (7372): 1107–1112.

Youde, Jeremy. 2013. The Rockefeller and Gates Foundations in Global Health Governance. *Global Society* 27 (2): 139–158.

Ziemba, Elizabeth. 2005. *Public–Private Partnerships for Product Development: Financial, Scientific, and Managerial Issues as Challenges to Future Success.* www.who.int/intellectualproperty/studies/Ziemba.pdf.

9 Governing Armed Conflicts
The ICRC between Hierarchy and Networks

Vincent Bernard and Anne Quintin

This chapter examines the governance of the regulation of armed conflict and the central role played by international humanitarian law (IHL) and the International Committee of the Red Cross (ICRC). Historically, states and non-state actors have tried to regulate armed conflict through various means, but with the adoption of the first Geneva Convention in 1864 law became a critical element. In brief, IHL is a "set of rules that seek to limit the effects of armed conflict[,] protect[ing] people who are not or are no longer participating in hostilities and restrict[ing] the means and methods of warfare."[1] The modern governance of the regulation of armed conflicts begins in 1863 with the creation of what was to become the International Committee of the Red Cross (ICRC), a private Swiss initiative led by Henry Dunant who mobilized states to adopt the first Geneva Convention the following year. States endorsed Henry Dunant's vision of an international binding legal framework accompanied with a network of neutral, impartial, and independent actors (originally the National Societies of the Red Cross) to assist the wounded on the battlefields. This led to a model with states as the law-makers and duty-bearers of IHL, the ICRC as a guardian and promoter of IHL, and a network of National Societies tasked to support their states in the implementation and promotion of IHL. As such the original mode of governance was a combination of hierarchy and network with several actors including the ICRC and National Societies supporting states and each other in the application and promotion of the existing rules. And this arrangement has largely stayed in place ever since.

This makes the ICRC quite unusual when situated against the other chapters. It indeed has a somewhat unusual status and is a different kind of creature in comparison to other actors in this volume. Although it

The views expressed in this chapter are those of the authors and do not necessarily reflect the views of the ICRC. The authors would like to thank Michael Barnett for his advice and Saman Rejali for her support in the drafting of this chapter.
[1] ICRC 2018b.

received a mandate from states under the 1949 Geneva Conventions, it is a private association under Swiss law. This combination makes it a unique, sui generis body in international relations. In addition, here is an organization and a mode of governance that seemingly withstood considerable shocks, wars, and trends in the global environment. In almost all the other cases there are various factors that cause a change in the mode of governance and the social relations between actors. But not here. The obvious question is: why? First, the resilience of the ICRC owes to several factors, including: the endorsement by states and Switzerland in particular; its cohesion, status in international affairs, expert authority; and its transformation into an operational actor in armed conflicts. Second, as states remain the main actors of governance the very nature of armed conflicts (power struggles, rivalries, emergence of non-state armed actors, etc.) hampers them from building a governance model where the main functions (i.e., rule-making, implementation, dissemination, application, enforcement) would be carried out by them or through international mechanisms in a predictable, systematic, and universal way. Hence the need for impartial, independent, and neutral actors has always remained.

This chapter is organized in the following way. The first section examines the modern origins of the global governance of the regulation of armed conflict. The second section looks more closely at the current landscape to consider whether and how new pressure points and opportunities may have forced a change in the mode of governance. First it examines how the expansion of contemporary IHL and the growth of other areas of international law have increased legal complexity. Second, it examines the growing diversity of the actors involved in the regulation of armed conflict. Although such trends suggest that the hierarchy is being worn down, we claim that it remains strong in place, even when it seems to be in the shadows. We conclude by considering the relationship between the resilience of this governance model and the effectiveness of protection during armed conflict.

Origins of the Governance of the Regulation of Armed Conflict

There is a long history of norms, rules, and customs regulating armed conflict, but it was not until the mid-nineteenth century that there developed a body of international law. There are various ways to narrate the background factors that contributed to its rise at this moment, but most impactful was the combination of the growing brutality of war, the rise of national armies, and new reporting and visual technologies that brought the war into the public's gaze. There were also several prominent personalities. In the United States for instance, Florence Nightingale and Francis Lieber had been advocating for the development of rules during warfare through national codes, the former to include medical services within the armed forces, the latter to regulate the detention of captured prisoners and place some restraints in the conduct of hostilities.[2] Such initiatives did not reach permanence because they were drafted for specific events and relied on unilateral commitments from belligerents.

The breakthrough from voluntary national codes such as the Lieber Code to international binding law occurred at the instigation of Henry Dunant. A Swiss businessman who was traveling to obtain letters of support for a commercial venture, he witnessed the horrific aftermath of the Battle of Solferino in 1859. His experiences led him to write a memoir: one of the first unsanitized portraits of war, it ended with a plea for an international agreement by states to guarantee relief for both sides of the conflict, which was to be made possible through the support of neutral and impartial relief societies, independent from but recognized by states. His memoir became widely read and four fellow Genevois, Gustave Moynier, General Guillaume-Henri Dufour, Dr. Louis Appia, and Dr. Théodore Maunoir, took up the cause. The "Committee of the Five," operating under the name of the "International Committee for Relief to the Wounded," invited all the European states, several other states from the western hemisphere, and four philanthropic institutions to an international meeting to discuss wartime protections for soldiers in Geneva in 1863. The conference adopted several resolutions, including the creation of national committees, which soon became the National Societies of the Red Cross and Red Crescent.

The following year, sixteen states held another conference that adopted the Geneva Convention for the Amelioration of the Condition of Wounded in Armies in the Field. The draft of the 1864 Geneva Convention had been prepared by the committee – renamed in 1875 the International Committee of the Red Cross (ICRC). The ICRC draft was then adopted by the conference without major alterations.[3] Neutrality, which was a core concept in international relations at

---

[2] In a letter to Dunant, Florence Nightingale even dismissed his idea of creating independent relief societies: "Miss Nightingale ... entertains no doubt with regard to Mr Dunant's proposal. She says it is objectionable because first, such a Society would take upon itself duties which ought to be performed by the Government of each country and so would relieve them of responsibilities which really belong to them and which they can only properly discharge and being relieved would make war more easy" (Moorehead 1999, 30).

[3] Bugnion 2009.

the time, was cleverly used by the drafters of the 1864 Geneva Convention: as attested by several of its articles, the protection of medical services, operating under the Red Cross flag – the reverse of the colors of Switzerland – is intrinsically linked to their neutrality.[4]

The governance of the regulation of armed conflict was a cross between a hierarchical and a networked mode. There were hierarchical elements, starting with states agreeing on an international treaty and being in the driving seat to regulate the conduct of armed conflict. Yet the Red Cross Movement, with its association of National Red Cross Societies, had the qualities of a network. The National Societies created a powerful group of like-minded actors, often well connected with military and political circles, capable of efficiently mobilizing resources and good will to advocate toward governments. These National Societies were created as "auxiliaries to government" but were to be recognized as part of the Movement, and granted a special independent status protected under the domestic law of each state.

Great Challenges without Change

The ICRC, IHL and this governance arrangement marched through its first half century without any major test, but that would change in its second half with two world wars, decolonization, and a growing concern with mass atrocities. The succession of these earth-shaking events posed severe questions for IHL and the ICRC, whose scope of concerns were simultaneously expanding and falling short of expectations. The surprise is not that the mode of governance changed, but rather that it remained largely the same. Below we identify three major challenges and how the ICRC responded to them and how IHL adapted in a way that preserved a mode of governance that had elements of both networks and hierarchies.

The first challenge occurred after the First World War and represented a direct assault on the ICRC's place in a growing humanitarian system. During its first fifty years, with the exception of the Franco-Prussian War (1870–1871), the ICRC's "main activity consisted of 'literary' work, exchanging correspondence with the Red Cross societies, and theoretical considerations on the relief in time of war."[5] In response to the First World War though, it grew from a "small philanthropic organisation" of a dozen of people to 1,200 staff in a few months and expanded its scope of activities into operations and monitoring compliance with IHL by the belligerents.[6] These and other activities not only promoted IHL but also

---

[4] Segesser 2013.   [5] Palmieri 2013, 1277.   [6] Palmieri 2013, 7.

elevated the authority of the ICRC.[7] Just as the ICRC was embracing its expanded, operational role, it had to confront a new rival in the form of the League of the Red Cross Societies (now the International Federation of the Red Cross and Red Crescent Societies). Henry P. Davison, then chairman of the American Red Cross's "War Committee" – who had considerable support from US president Woodrow Wilson – pushed the idea of replacing the loose network of Red Cross societies and the ICRC with a more hierarchical mode modeled on the newly created League of Nations (even if only composed of the National Societies on the winning side of the war).

With the support of the Entente (with Britain and the US at its head) and the League of Nations, which wanted to be its humanitarian counterpart, and riding the wave of universal pacifism following "the war to end all wars," the League intended to expedite and modernize the work of the Red Cross by addressing social activities and preventive health care in peacetime. Given these new aims, the ICRC no longer had an active role because the League intended to take over many of its skills and responsibilities. The ICRC was therefore destined to become a "museum piece."[8]

In this context, the focus of this emerging system of governance could not be IHL, which was promised to also become a "museum piece" as there would be no more war.

The ICRC managed to survive this first major existential crisis due to several factors. First, its raison d'être remained highly relevant. At a time when pacifist movements wanted to banish war, the ICRC could have been seen as being out of step by continuing to implement its mandate to protect victims of armed conflict. But these visions of world peace quickly vanished and the need for regulating war remained. In parallel, the very homogenous Swiss, Geneva-based composition of the ICRC's governing entity presented a unified front in favor of the status quo, while the American-driven proposal for a new model did not receive the expected support.

Also, the ICRC did not seek to establish a "monopoly," and offered various ideas for the creation of new treaties and the expansion of the network operating on the regulation of armed conflict. For instance, Gustave Moynier was the first one to suggest the creation of an international court to judge suspects of war crimes in 1872.[9] The ICRC gave its patronage to the Geneva-based International Save the Children Union in 1920. In 1921, Gustave Ador, then president of the ICRC, addressed members of the League of Nations and "urged the Council to appoint a

---

[7] Cameron 2015.   [8] Palmieri 2013, 1280.   [9] Hall 1998.

commissioner to deal with the thousands of Russian refugees then spread out across Europe. He called the League the 'only supranational political authority capable of solving a problem which is beyond the power of purely humanitarian organisations'.[10] This call was heard, and the Council of the League eventually created a high commissioner for refugees, appointing the Norwegian explorer Fridtjof Nansen to that position.

A second major development could have challenged the model of governance and the role of the ICRC: the creation of the United Nations after the Second World War. However, in the beginning the UN had a tricky relationship with IHL. As an organization created at the end of the Second World War with the view to ensuring international peace and security, the UN was confronted with a dilemma. States had agreed in the UN Charter to "refrain in their international relations from the threat or use of force against the territorial integrity or political independence of any state."[11] Getting involved in substantive discussions on IHL, and in particular on the regulation of international armed conflict, could be seen as conflicting with its raison d'être. For the UN, working toward or even encouraging the development of IHL would have meant getting involved in the regulation of a situation that it was precisely meant to prevent – this would have been considered as an implicit recognition of the failure of the new world order.

While several articles of the UN Charter, including its first article, enjoins the UN "to promote and encourage respect for human rights and for fundamental freedoms for all,"[12] there is no mention of IHL. In return the 1949 Geneva Conventions do not mention the United Nations. Also, the distinction between *jus ad bellum* and *jus in bello* discouraged the UN from being initially involved in the development of IHL. Having said this, the UN later reconsidered its position and became more active because of the United Nations operations in Korea and in the Congo. The first historical mark of this change was Resolution XXIII of the International Conference on Human Rights (Tehran, 1968), which became General Assembly Resolution 2444 (XXIII) of December 19, 1968. Entitled "Respect for human rights in armed conflicts," the resolution "codified basic humanitarian principles applicable in all forms of armed conflict, and at the same time gave decisive impetus to the process which eventually led to the adoption, in 1977, of the two

---

[10] Skran 2018.   [11] UN Charter 1945, Art. 2(4).
[12] See Art. 1(3) UN Charter. See similar mentions in Preamble, and Arts. 13(1)(b), 55(c), 62(2), 68, and 76(c) UN Charter.

Protocols additional to the Geneva Conventions."[13] In parallel the UN became involved in the regulation of weapons, which it viewed as within its mandate of international peace and security.

The third challenge to the ICRC and IHL was their overall efficacy, which was questioned as a result of the numerous atrocities committed during the world wars. However, the ICRC responded by promoting the development of IHL to answer new contemporary challenges. The ICRC usually followed the same process over time: assemble the most complete documentation with a view to highlighting what specific legal issues – and in particular those directly linked to humanitarian challenges – needed to be added, confirmed, or changed; draft projects of conventions with the help of experts from governments, National Societies, and other aid organizations; and submit these projects to the International Conferences of the Red Cross and Red Crescent and then to a diplomatic conference for adoption. Following the First World War a diplomatic conference adopted the two Geneva Conventions of 1929. After the Second World War (and while the Movement had issued resolutions to address the legal gap in the protection of the civilian population already in 1921, 1923, and 1925) another diplomatic process led to the adoption of the four Geneva Conventions of 1949. Following the numerous examples of decolonization wars or guerrilla wars in the 1950s–1970s, yet another diplomatic process led to the adoption of the two Additional Protocols of 1977. In these and other moments the ICRC played a critical role in preparing the Diplomatic Conferences, through the drafting of texts to be discussed, organization of conferences of government experts, and being an active member during the diplomatic processes themselves.

The best illustration of the perpetuation of the original hybrid model of governance by states, the Movement, and non-state entities today is perhaps the periodic International Conferences of the Red Cross and Red Crescent. First held in 1867, the latest one took place in December 2019 with its 33rd edition. These conferences bring together institutions born out of private initiative – that is the components of the Movement – and the states party to the 1949 Geneva Conventions. Such a hybrid composition is virtually unique among international bodies (with the exception of the International Labour Conference, which brings together the member states of the International Labour Organization and the trade union federations and employers' federations of those countries). Not only do governments take part in the International Conferences, but they do so "on an equal footing with other entities."[14]

---

[13] Gasser 1995.   [14] Casalin and Lamb 2009. 91, Number 876, December 2009, p. 733.

It is generally accepted that the International Conference is a key moment of IHL governance. The conference serves as the "supreme deliberative body for the Movement."[15] In particular, François Bugnion highlights the role of the International Conferences for the following two critical functions of IHL governance.

- The development of international humanitarian law: there is no doubt that the Conference has contributed to every stage of the development of international humanitarian law, by virtue of the fact that it is a key place of dialogue between the Movement and the states;
- Respect for international humanitarian law: each conference enables a dialogue to take place between the Red Cross and Red Crescent institutions and the states on the subject of respect for humanitarian law.[16]

Indeed, while the resolutions adopted during these conferences are non-binding, they have often led to concrete developments. The Geneva Conventions of 1949 were developed at the International Conference in Stockholm in 1948, prior to their adoption the next year. In 1965, the conference adopted the Movement's fundamental principles – which guide an immense array of humanitarian activities across the globe. In 1995, the 26th International Conference had a major impact in shaping the landscape of IHL for the following two decades. First, the ICRC was invited to prepare a report on customary rules of IHL. Thanks to this mandate the ICRC carried out an extensive study on customary law, which was published in 2005[17] and later turned into a regularly updated online database.[18] Second, the 1995 conference also requested the ICRC to strengthen its capacity to provide advisory services to states, in their efforts to implement and disseminate IHL. On that basis the ICRC's Advisory Service on IHL was created to assist in the national implementation of IHL, and remains active today.[19] Third, the 1995 International Conference contributed to create the momentum around the international campaign to ban landmines.

More recently, the ICRC has been seizing this periodic opportunity to share its report of activities, as well as recommendations or plans of action on the implementation of IHL, and its assessment of the evolving challenges to IHL.[20] In parallel, numerous pledges, including in relation to IHL, are traditionally adopted at each International Conference by all participating entities. Such endeavors provide concrete opportunities not only for the ICRC but also for each National Society to continue

---

[15] Movement Statutes, Art. 8.   [16] Bugnion 2009, 707.
[17] Henckaerts and Doswald-Beck 2005.   [18] ICRC, *Customary IHL*.
[19] See ICRC 2015b.   [20] See for instance: IRRC 2015.

engaging in a constant dialogue with states on the application, promotion, and implementation of IHL. Finally, the International Conferences can pave the way for expert meetings and other types of conferences to interpret or clarify IHL.

What is remarkable is that despite the extraordinary challenges posed by the world wars and the lack of compliance with IHL, and even criticism of the ICRC's actions during the wars, there was little change in the mode of governance. Yet over the next several decades there occurred various developments that have continued to challenge this mode of governance, including changes in the conduct of war and the desirable responses and the expansion of actors involved in the regulation of armed conflict.

The Contemporary Challenges to the Mode of Governance

The mode of governance survived the strains and challenges posed by successive wars. This section addresses the evolution of the main tool of the governance model: IHL itself. While the most basic rules of IHL are frequently violated in modern armed conflicts and much work remains to be done to promote and enforce them, it is striking to note that there is a growing sophistication of the debates on IHL. Below we identify the impact of three important developments on international humanitarian law.

An Increasingly Complex Legal Environment

The evolution of armed conflict and the expansion of the range of issues to be governed have led to an increasingly complex legal regime. These and other factors triggered various efforts to clarify or expand IHL, including on themes such as direct participation in hostilities,[21] the law applicable to detention during peace operations,[22] and the regulation of autonomous weapons systems.[23] Additionally, human rights law has expanded in scope and become much more involved in the regulation of armed conflict. In this section we identify several important trends.

The first is the growing refrain regarding the "humanization of IHL."[24] IHL initially developed through two parallel branches: the Law of Geneva and the Law of The Hague, in reference to the two cities where the main conventional instruments of IHL were adopted. Geneva

[21] ICRC 2009.   [22] Copenhagen Principles 2012.   [23] LAWS 2016.
[24] Meron 2000.

law is often presented as focusing on the principle of humanity, away from the battlefield and aimed at the protection of persons who do not or no longer participate in hostilities (the wounded and sick, shipwrecked, prisoners of war and internees, and civilians). The ICRC is often seen as the principal guardian of Geneva law. Hague law – from the two Hague Conferences of 1899 and 1907 – is usually presented as focusing on the principle of military necessity: the legitimate purpose of war is to weaken and defeat the opposing army, but with due considerations for humanity.[25]

These two areas of IHL began to converge after the Second World War. The first important step came with the Fourth Geneva Convention (GC IV) as it expanded to include the protection of civilians, using the term "rights" in some instances, and complementing the regulation of occupation already dealt with in the Hague Regulations. But the merger truly began with the two Additional Protocols to the Geneva Conventions in 1977, which also introduced tensions. As Charles Garraway writes, "This convergence in itself has caused tension due to the differing philosophies that governed the two independent strands":[26]

The bringing together of "Hague" and "Geneva" law in 1977 was the start of a major upheaval in the laws of armed conflict. The ICRC now saw themselves as the guardians not only of traditional "Geneva law" but also of "Hague law." Both were now incorporated in the new terminology "international humanitarian law" and this led to an increasing concentration on the humanity side of the balance. The United Nations, now perhaps somewhat more realistic than in the halcyon days immediately after the Second World War, moved into the "Hague law" field with a concentration on weaponry.[27]

In his view, instead of conciliating "the necessities of war with the laws of humanity," the concentration was now on fixing "the technical limits at which the necessities of war ought to yield to the requirements of humanity." As Garraway concludes, "the principles that had always governed 'Geneva law' were now spilling over into 'Hague law,' which had always been much more concerned with maintaining the balance."[28]

This perceived "humanization" trend was reinforced by the parallel development of international human rights law after the Second World War. Human rights mechanisms have played a crucial role in developing and implementing IHL – and this involvement is not without opposition. In parallel, several scholars push for a merger between international human rights law (IHRL) and IHL.[29] This trend was, and still is,

---

[25] Meron 2000.   [26] Garraway 2013, 261   [27] Garraway 2013, 268.
[28] Garraway 2013.   [29] Schabas, Doswald-Beck, Hampson and Lubell.

considered to be dangerous by most states and military lawyers, and many IHL scholars. Recent examples from military circles have shown increased concern regarding the role of the European Court of Human Rights for instance and the move toward a "human rights" understanding of IHL.[30]

The second big development was the growth of international criminal justice. The creation of the two international criminal tribunals in the 1990s, respectively for the former Yugoslavia and for Rwanda, led to a number of cases that developed if not redefined IHL. One question to ask is whether international criminal justice, and more specifically international criminal judges, have played a role in the making of IHL, and whether such law-making competes with the will of the traditional makers of international law, namely states.[31]

A few cases have been considered groundbreaking for IHL. The case of *Tadić* in front of the International Criminal Tribunal for the former Yugoslavia (ICTY) is emblematic in this respect. Among various key achievements, the case of *Tadić* (1) proposed a refined definition of international and non-international armed conflict, which is still used today by most states and scholars,[32] (2) defined both the geographical and the temporal scopes of both types of armed conflicts,[33] (3) proposed and applied an expansive interpretation of the notion of protected persons under GC IV,[34] (4) decided that war crimes could also be committed during non-international armed conflicts,[35] and (5) advocated in favor of a convergence between the law applicable in international armed conflict and the law applicable in non-international armed conflict, with the result that most protective rules applicable in the former were also applicable in the latter.[36]

Such developments created a euphoric belief that international criminal justice could "fill in the gaps" of IHL. International jurisprudence indeed "has the potential to become a highly persuasive source of authority regarding future understanding and implementation of IHL."[37]

---

[30] The United Kingdom's threats of quitting the European Convention on Human Rights exemplify this push-back for a merging between IHRL and IHL.

[31] In this regard it is interesting to note that international criminal justice was influenced in its development by both common law and civil law traditions. In common law systems jurisprudence/case law and the judicial sector in general play important roles in interpreting and developing the law.

[32] See in particular the following ICTY 1995, para. 70.   [33] ICTY 1995, para. 68–69.

[34] ICTY 1995, para. 76; ICTY 1997, paras. 163–169.   [35] ICTY 1997, paras. 86–136.

[36] ICTY 1995, paras. 73–76 and 96–98. See also: Cassese 1996, para. 11.

[37] IHL Clinic at Emory University 2011, 2.

However, precisely for that reason some cases were also heavily criticized for proposing an erroneous interpretation of IHL.[38] That said, the fact that military experts – who are the primary implementers of IHL – disagree with the interpretation of an international tribunal does not necessarily imply a competition between the actors. What is particularly interesting is that, although some case law is contested, the ICTY's mandate is widely accepted. The same experts who criticized the ICTY jurisprudence have also recognized that "one of the mandates of the tribunal is the progressive development of IHL."[39] In other words, the mode of governance is a network. Disputes and differences of opinion are resolved through negotiation and persuasion, and the fact that international criminal justice can shape IHL shows that parallel means and mechanisms can be used to reach a common goal.

Growing Diversity

The purpose of IHL is to regulate the behavior of belligerents. While this seems quite obvious, the complexification of warfare has transformed the task of promoting respect for IHL. The diversification of the parties to armed conflict means that it is no longer sufficient to engage in a dialogue with state authorities: one now has to consider the high increase in the number of non-international armed conflicts (NIACs), and hence of non-state armed groups being party to them. Furthermore, there are new networks and coalitions formed at the national, regional, and international level by government and civil society experts.[40] Also, the main organizations active in the regulation of armed conflict, the ICRC and the UN, have evolved within this context of diversification of actors.

One area of growing diversity reflects the changing nature of war. Until roughly the end of the Second World War, regulating the behavior of belligerents mainly meant regulating the conduct of state armies during interstate conflicts. Yet, today most armed conflicts are not of an international character. In parallel, most of the rules of IHL apply to interstate conflicts. While IHL does contain many rules regulating NIACs, be they conventional (common Article 3, Additional Protocol II, or weapons conventions applicable in NIAC) or customary, it often remains difficult to further regulate noninternational armed conflicts, as this raises

---

[38] See e.g. ICTC, Gotovina case. See also IHL Clinic at Emory University 2011.
[39] IHL Clinic at Emory University 2011, 13.
[40] For instance, Slaughter (2005) contends that the new forms of global governance are fairer because they are less hierarchical and less state-centric.

questions of sovereignty and the perception of a risk of legitimizing "rebels," "bandits," or, nowadays, "terrorists."

The governance of IHL has always included dissemination of the law to weapons bearers. One way of doing so is to integrate IHL into military training and military manuals – an area that is actually a core obligation of states under IHL. The increasing involvement of non-state armed groups as parties to armed conflicts, however, also created the need to disseminate IHL to this category of belligerents. Activities aimed at integrating IHL into military practice only involve a small number of active actors (if we focus on non-military actors), which in the majority of cases cooperate well toward a common goal of ensuring awareness of the laws governing war among the primary actors involved in armed conflicts. This tends to demonstrate a network mode of governance. The ICRC is an obvious actor in this field, but not the only one. The International Institute of Humanitarian Law, based in San Remo, Italy, typically trains representatives of armed forces, and Geneva Call, a Geneva-based nongovernmental organization (NGO) created in 2000 is today generally dedicated to promoting respect for IHL and protections of civilians.

New networks and coalitions represent a second major change in the growing diversity in the regulation of armed conflict. Contemporary armed conflicts tend to present practical issues that the law does not always address with extreme clarity; hence a number of initiatives have been launched in the last decade or so with the purpose of identifying the law applicable to certain areas of armed conflicts. The goal was usually not to create new law (as mentioned, law-making is a state competence) but rather to try and clarify existing law, with the view to helping belligerents determine the applicable law and hence better respect it. The first of these attempts was the 1994 San Remo Manual on International Law Applicable to Armed Conflicts at Sea. The manual was developed by a group of legal and naval experts participating in their personal capacity, following a series of meetings convened by the San Remo Institute.[41] The number of initiatives meant to "clarify" or "identify" existing law increased afterward: ICRC Study on Customary IHL, HPCR Manual on International Law Applicable to Air and Missile Warfare, Copenhagen Principles of Detention by Multinational Forces, Tallinn Manual on the International Law Applicable to Cyber Warfare, and similar initiatives are underway regarding the use of force in outer space.

---

[41] San Remo Manual 1994.

Second, state structures created to ensure proper implementation of IHL may see a strong involvement of civil societies, and in particular of the National Societies. In this respect the national committees of IHL are the perfect example of how states and non-state actors can work together. IHL national committees are (optional) interministerial or interdepartmental entities that a state may decide to create within the executive branch to gather the various stakeholders on IHL-related matters. Such national committees are usually made up of representatives of the ministries or departments concerned with implementing IHL (e.g., depending on the state this may include defense, foreign affairs, internal affairs, justice, finance, education, and culture), representatives of legislative committees, as well as scholars, humanitarian organizations, the National Society of the Red Cross or Red Crescent, and the media. The national committees are traditionally tasked with a variety of activities, from advising and assisting the government in implementing and spreading knowledge of IHL, to making recommendations for new legislation, amendments, or administrative regulations. Although often unknown to the general public and ignored even by lawyers, the ICRC lists 115 national committees active as of December 31, 2020.[42]

There is also a growing influence of local and transnational civil society in the governance of weapons regulation. The birth of IHL corresponded with the start of the industrial revolution in warfare, and hence IHL governance has always been interested in technologies. The rapid changes in warfare technologies have fueled several initiatives from the legal community and NGOs. The role of civil society in this area has significantly grown since the late 1990s, and particularly since the Coalition Against Landmines. The latter created a new way to draft treaties. Instead of following the traditional way of opening diplomatic conferences to all states (at the risk of having different states pursuing different objectives), the coalition gathered several NGOs, supported by some strong sponsor states, and set a different methodology: only states that accepted the end goal – the total ban of anti-personnel landmines – were allowed to take part in the drafting discussions. The approach by thematic campaigns developed afterward (e.g., Article 36, cluster munitions, autonomous weapons systems), with the latest example being that of the Treaty on the Ban of Nuclear Weapons. In general, notwithstanding, the growing diversity of actors, the mode of governance has largely remained static.

---

[42] Advisory Service on IHL 2018.

The "Shadow of Hierarchy"

Based both on its legal expertise and on the legitimacy conferred by its field presence, the ICRC has developed its "humanitarian diplomacy" led from its headquarters and its network of missions in Addis, Brussels, New York, and the capitals of regional and global powers. Marion Harroff-Tavel defines this concept as follows: "The ICRC's humanitarian diplomacy is a strategy for influencing the parties to armed conflicts and others - States, non-State actors and members of civil society. Its purpose is purely humanitarian and it is carried out through a network of sustained relationships – bilateral and multilateral, official and informal."[43] Convincing states to apply or develop IHL is one of the main goals of these diplomatic efforts.

The UN has also evolved. Contrary to the early days of its existence the UN does not shy away from invoking IHL anymore. The UN Secretary-General and the president of the ICRC even issued a joint call for respect for IHL in 2015.[44] IHL is now referred to very often by UN specialized agencies and in United Nations meetings, reports, and resolutions. A good illustration is the annual Report of the Secretary-General on the protection of civilians in armed conflict,[45] which are emblematic of an "IHL diplomacy" by the UN.

The UN has expanded its diplomatic efforts in recent years, and some of its organs regularly invoke IHL, such as the Office of the High Commissioner for Human Rights. Similarly, some NGOs, local and international, refer to IHL on a more systematic basis.[46] But the humanitarian sector has not necessarily followed this trend, and the use of IHL in field or advocacy work remains occasional. While further research is needed, it appears that few NGOs use IHL systematically in their dialogue with parties to armed conflict in the field or in their public advocacy campaigns. For instance, Médecins Sans Frontières (MSF) – while a strong promoter of the humanitarian principles – hardly ever invokes IHL in its public communication or advocacy efforts,[47] with the notable example of its reaction after the attack against its hospital in Kunduz, Afghanistan.

The ICRC is still seen as the main champion of IHL, the reference organization for promoting respect for and implementing IHL. One

---

[43] Harroff-Tavel 2006, 1.   [44] ICRC 2015a.   [45] UNSG Resolution 2018, 462.

[46] For instance, the NGOs ALMA in Israel and Al Haq in Palestine, or reports from Amnesty International or Human Rights Watch.

[47] Rony Brauman explains that MSF should not refer to IHL (Brauman 2018).

could wonder whether the diffuse authority of the ICRC over the governance of IHL could reflect the concept of "shadow of hierarchy." For instance, this authority manifests itself when interpretations of the law by the ICRC are accepted by other actors, including courts, states, and their militaries, as the reference. *A contrario*, the "shadow of hierarchy" can also be demonstrated by the virulent objections raised by some states to certain ICRC initiatives to interpret or clarify existing law, for instance the ICRC study on customary IHL,[48] or the more recent initiative to update the Commentaries to the 1949 Geneva Conventions.[49] One could argue that states would not bother to raise objections if they did not consider the ICRC to be a key player in the governance of the regulation of conflicts. The ICRC's source of authority lies within the Geneva Conventions and the Additional Protocols, which give it a clear mandate on many tasks to be carried in relation to armed conflict. On a more informal level the ICRC has managed to maintain its legitimacy over time through its long history and the enduring quality of its legal expertise, taking into account the reality of the field that the ICRC understands extremely well because of its presence in contexts torn apart by armed conflict.

Conclusion: Change, Legitimacy, and Efficacy

The governance of the regulation of armed conflict was born out of a private initiative to address the growing devastating impact of modern warfare, through the early collaboration of governments and civil society actors. States recognized that armed conflicts were by essence conducive to *inhumanity, partiality,* and *iniquity* and adhered to Dunant's vision of an international network of independent entities acting as auxiliaries to states and basing their actions on *humanity, impartiality,* and *neutrality.* Combining hierarchical and network features, this model has proved particularly resilient.

Indeed, although one the oldest regimes of global governance, the governance of the regulation of armed conflict could have found its end following the wars and genocides of the twentieth century, fallen into obsolescence, been replaced by a new model, or been absorbed into the larger governance of peace and security under the aegis of the UN. The legitimacy of the very existence of IHL has been questioned regularly,

---

[48] Bellinger and Haynes 2007.
[49] ICRC 2020. Several scholars criticized the ICRC's initiative, see e.g. Watts 2020.

with critiques coming from all sides: idealists blaming it for making wars easier to wage and cynics for exactly the opposite reason, with both agreeing it has anyway become obsolete. However, up to now no alternative model of regulation has been advanced.

Atrocities still happen in war, humanitarian access remains hampered, and there were countless victims of violations of the law over the course of the last 150 years with, all too often, impunity for the perpetrators. Nonetheless the persistence of actors of governance produced great progress for humankind such as the adoption of the four Geneva Conventions, the Ottawa treaty banning anti-personnel landmines, and the creation of a permanent international criminal court. They created the legal framework allowing impartial humanitarian organizations to operate in conflict situations. These achievements have saved countless lives over the same period.

Talking about respect, it is important to reiterate that IHL is a tool to an end: protect persons who are not or are no longer participating in the hostilities and restrict the means and methods of warfare. There are other norms (such as social norms, armed actors' own ethics, and codes or religious prescriptions) that may contribute to the same objectives.[50] Parties to armed conflict can even decide to implement more protective rules than what international law prescribes.

Even if the pace of progress has been irregular the governance model stood the test of time. It evolved over time and new actors joined in: in the past three decades international courts, NGOs, and academia have played an increasing role in the governance of the conduct of armed conflicts. In our view this diversification of actors and forums, beyond states and the Movement, did not dramatically change a preexisting "hybrid" model of governance. The latter was flexible enough to co-opt new actors. We can illustrate this evolution by looking at the main functions of governance: the development of new norms, the implementation of the rules and monitoring of their respect, and the repression of violations.

When it comes to the development of the law, states remain the central actor. As the sole entities with the authority to develop international law, states have brought forward new initiatives throughout the whole history of IHL. This includes states that are not necessarily the most powerful ones on the international scene. Switzerland played a crucial role in the creation and development of the 1864 Geneva Convention and its successor instruments, the Russian Empire initiated

---

[50] See for instance the ICRC 2018a.

the Saint Petersburg Declaration of 1868 as well as the diplomatic conferences that led to the adoption of the Hague Regulations, at a time where it was not as strong as it later became, and several states, including the Nordic states, have sponsored recent weapons-related conventions. Furthermore, the legitimacy of the model was strengthened after decolonization with the two Additional Protocols to the Geneva Conventions of 1977, adopted also by newly decolonized states.

For some scholars the fact that non-state armed groups are bound by rules elaborated by states without having participated in their elaboration undermines the legitimacy of the governance, in an era when the vast majority of armed conflicts are of a non-international character. The same argument is used to explain why armed groups would be less incentivized to respect the law. However, it needs to be nuanced: armed groups are far from forming a homogeneous category and their motivations to respect the law largely depend on non-legal factors.[51]

Beyond states, other actors have played an important role in paving the way for the adoption of new conventions. First, the ICRC has regularly been involved in the preparatory work leading to development of the law. Its legitimacy to doing so increased over time as it progressively developed its own operations from the First World War on. In parallel, a growing number of other actors from civil society have emerged that run advocacy campaigns promoting the development of specific norms, such as the coalition to ban landmines or the Campaign to Stop Killer Robots.

Finally, in areas where the development of binding instruments is unlikely, the governance model has allowed for the adoption of soft law instruments and specific studies aimed at clarifying how existing rules apply to new challenges posed by warfare. Those instruments are often developed by the same actors traditionally involved in the governance of the regulation of armed conflict: state representatives, ICRC, NGOs, scholars, and independent experts.

The ICRC remains the central actor when it comes to supporting the implementation of IHL by states (mainly through the ICRC's Advisory Services) and monitoring the application of IHL in modern conflicts. The ICRC now interacts with a growing number of experts, who play a critical role when it comes to the function of implementation of existing norms of IHL: governments, the military, National Societies, specialists

---

[51] Bangerter 2011; ICRC 2018a.

in academia, and NGOs are working to ensure a better integration of the rules into national legislation, military instruction, military manuals, academic teaching, etc.[52] This community of experts benefits from an ever-growing amount of academic literature, manuals, and training courses. They contribute discreetly but actively to the aim of building a stronger culture of respect among weapons bearers (developing sanctions, certifications, etc.).

Innovative strategies have been adopted to ensure that the law is implemented and ultimately respected by non-state actors. For instance, Geneva Call works to make armed groups implement the law through the signing of "deeds of commitment," the adoption of codes of conduct or trainings on IHL. Another interesting innovation in the field of implementation of the law is the International Code of Conduct Association (ICoCA). Private military and security companies (PMSCs) can join the ICoCA.[53] By providing platforms of discussions, certifications of compliance, and codes of conduct, the ICoCA provides a "cluster of governance" specifically adapted to translate international norms to PMSCs, within the broader governance of the conduct of armed conflicts. However, this is not a self-contained regime of governance or a kind of self-regulation club as the ultimate responsibility to regulate the conduct of PMSCs lies with states. The ICoCA helps them to implement their obligations to make sure the law is respected by these non-state actors.

When it comes to the repression of violations of the law, the development of international criminal courts and tribunals has been a much-needed addition to the model. Their jurisprudence has also enriched the interpretation of IHL and clarified some gray areas. At the same time the legitimacy of the mechanisms, in particular the International Criminal Court (ICC), is periodically being questioned. The ICC has been criticized for its slow processes, for targeting only African states, or for infringing on the sovereignty of states not party to the Rome Statute. However, it should be recalled that the governance model places the primary responsibility to repress violations on states. On that front it should be noted that many states in the world have in the recent past updated their penal codes or adopted specific acts in order to allow for the repression of international crimes at the domestic level.[54]

We could add a remark on the evolution of other areas of governance and the potential impact on the governance of the conduct of armed

---

[52] Bernard and Nikolova 2016.
[53] For an analysis of the governance of PMSCs, see Chapter 1.
[54] ICRC, National Implementation of IHL Database.

conflict itself. Today the humanitarian field is witnessing the increasing involvement of actors not traditionally concerned with armed conflicts.[55] For instance, development actors are moving away from the optimistic paradigm of development ultimately putting an end to conflicts. They are instead realizing that the benefits brought by development work is threatened, if not destroyed, by armed conflicts.[56] However, at the moment, while these new actors are not active in the field of the regulation of armed conflicts. This could nonetheless be the case in the future: with the realization that the mitigation of violence could contribute to peace – itself a precondition for human development – the network could perhaps expand beyond the initial actors and the increasing layers added over time (which include to a certain extent human rights and humanitarian circles) but also include development, environment, or business actors in the years to come.

The undeniably frequent violations of IHL can lead one to despair on the efficacy of the law. Governance actors need to adopt a more nuanced narrative on IHL highlighting its successes and impact, both when violated and when respected.[57] Showing how respect for IHL can help the international community address other types of global challenges such as displacement, development, education, or public health could also contribute to opening up the field of IHL and creating bridges with other areas of global governance.

References

Advisory Service on IHL. 2018. National Committees and Similar Bodies on International Humanitarian Law, July 31. ICRC. www.icrc.org/en/docu ment/table-national-committees-and-other-national-bodies-international-humanitarian-law.

Bangerter, Olivier. 2011. Reasons Why Armed Groups Choose to Respect International Humanitarian Law or Not. *International Review of the Red Cross* 93 (882): 353–384.

Bellinger, John B. and William J. Haynes. 2007. A US Government Response to the International Committee of the Red Cross's Customary International Humanitarian Law Study. *The International Review of the Red Cross* 89 (866): 443–471.

Bernard, Vincent and Mariya Nikolova. 2016. Generating Respect for the Law: The Need for Persistence and Imagination. In *Tribute to Jean Pictet*, edited by

---

[55] For an analysis of trends in humanitarian governance, see Chapter 5.
[56] As an example of development actors getting increasingly interested in armed conflicts, we can mention the strategic partnership established recently by the ICRC and the World Bank (World Bank 2018).
[57] Sassòli and Issar 2015; Bernard and Nikolova 2016.

Julia Grignon, 545–578. Schulthess and Montreal: Éditions Yvon Blais. www.icrc.org/en/document/generating-respect-law-need-persistence-and-imagination.

Brauman, Rony. 2018. *Guerre Humanitaire? Mensonges et Intox: Conversation Avec Regis Meyran*. Paris: Textuel.

Bugnion, François. 2009. The International Conference of the Red Cross and Red Crescent: Challenges, Key Issues and Achievements. *International Review of the Red Cross* 91 (876): 675–712.

Cameron, Lindsey. 2015. The ICRC in the First World War: Unwavering Belief in the Power of Law? *International Review of the Red Cross* 97 (900): 1099–1120.

Casalin, Deborah and Christopher Lamb. 2009. Participation of States in the International Conference of the Red Cross and Red Crescent and Assemblies of Other International Organizations. *International Review of the Red Cross* 91 (876): 733–758.

Cassese, Antonio. 1996. Memorandum to the Members of the Preparatory Committee for the Establishment of the International Criminal Court, on "Definition of Crimes and General Principles of Criminal Law as Reflected in the International Tribunal's Jurisprudence," March 22.

Copenhagen Principles. 2012. Copenhagen Process Principles and Guidelines on the Handling of Detainees in International Military Operations. October 19.

Garraway, Charles. 2013. Armed Conflict and Law Enforcement: Is There a Legal Divide? In *Armed Conflict and International Law: In Search of the Human Face – Liber Amicorum in Memory of Avril McDonald*, edited by Marielle Mathee, Brigit Toebes, and Marcel Brus, 259–283. The Hague: T.M.C. Asser.

Gasser, Hans-Peter. 1995. The United Nations and International Humanitarian Law: The International Committee of the Red Cross and the United Nations' Involvement in the Implementation of International Humanitarian Law. International Symposium on the occasion of the fiftieth anniversary of the United Nations, Geneva, October 19–21, 1995.

Hall, Christopher Keith. 1998. The First Proposal for a Permanent International Criminal Court. *International Review of the Red Cross* 28 (322): 57–74.

Harroff-Tavel, Marion. 2006. The Humanitarian Diplomacy of the International Committee of the Red Cross. *African Yearbook on International Humanitarian Law*: 1–16.

Henckaerts, Jean-Marie and Louise Doswald-Beck. 2005. *Customary International Humanitarian Law*, Vol. 1. Geneva and Cambridge: ICRC and Cambridge University Press.

Héritier, Adrienne and Dirk Lehmkhul. 2008. Introduction: The Shadow of Hierarchy and New Modes of Governance. *Journal of Public Policy* 28 (1): 1–17.

ICRC. *Customary IHL*. IHL Database. https://ihl-databases.icrc.org/customary-ihl/eng/docs/home.

National Implementation of IHL Database. https://ihl-databases.icrc.org/ihl-nat.

2015a. World at a Turning Point: Heads of UN and Red Cross Issue Joint Warning. www.icrc.org/en/document/conflict-disaster-crisis-UN-red-cross-issue-warning.

2015b. Domestic Law and IHL. www.icrc.org/en/document/international-humanitarian-law-domestic-law.

2018a. The Roots of Restraint in War. www.icrc.org/en/publication/roots-restraint-war.

2018b. War and Law. www.icrc.org/en/war-and-law.

2009. *Its Mission and Work.* Geneva: ICRC. www.icrc.org/en/doc/assets/files/other/icrc_002_0963.pdf.

2020. Updated Commentary on the Third Geneva Convention of 1949 – New from the International Committee of the Red Cross. www.icrc.org/en/publi cation/4434-updated-commentary-third-geneva-convention-1949-new-international-committee-red.

ICTY. 1995. *The Prosecutor v. Dusko Tadić.* Appeals Chamber, Decision on the Defence Motion for Interlocutory Appeal on Jurisdiction, Case No. IT-94-91-AR72, October 2.

1997. *The Prosecutor v. Dusko Tadić.* Trial Chamber II, Judgement, IT-94-91, May 7.

IHL Clinic at Emory University. 2011. Operational Law Experts Roundtable on the *Gotovina* Judgment: Military Operations, Battlefield Reality and the Judgment's Impact on Effective Implementation and Enforcement of International Humanitarian Law.

IRRC (International Review of the Red Cross). 2015. International Humanitarian Law and the Challenges of Contemporary Armed Conflicts. *International Review of the Red Cross* 97 (900): 1427–1502.

LAWS (Group of Governmental Experts on Lethal Autonomous Weapons Systems). 2016. www.unog.ch/80256EE600585943/(httpPages)/7C335E71DFCB29D1C1258243003E8724.

Meron, Theodor. 2000. The Humanization of Humanitarian Law. *The American Journal of International Law* 94 (2): 239–278.

Moorehead, Caroline. 1999. *Dunant's Dream: War, Switzerland and the History of the Red Cross.* New York: Caroll and Graf Publishing.

Palmieri, Daniel. 2013. An Institution Standing the Test of Time? A Review of 150 Years of the History of the International Committee of the Red Cross. *International Review of the Red Cross* 95 (889): 1–26.

Sassòli, Marco and Yvette Issar. 2015. Challenges to International Humanitarian Law. In *100 Years of Peace through Law: Past and Future*, edited by Andreas von Arnaud, Nele Matz-Lück, and Kerstin Odendahl, 181–235. Berlin: Duncker & Humblot. http://archive-ouverte.unige.ch/unige:79005.

Segesser, Daniel Marc. 2013. Le Concept de Neutralité et la Convention de Genève de 1864. In *Le Temps des Hommes Doubles, les Arrangements Face à l'occupation, de la Révolution Française à la Guerre de 1870*, edited by Jean-François Chanet, Annie Crepin, and Christian Windler, 69–84. Rennes: Presses universitaires de Rennes.

Skran, Claudena M. 2018. Gustave Ador, the ICRC, and Leadership on Refugee and Migration Policy. *Humanitarian Law and Policy Blog.* http://blogs.icrc .org/law-and-policy/2018/01/30/gustave-ador-the-icrc-and-leadership-on-refugee-and-migration-policy/.

Slaughter, Anne-Marie. 2005. *A New World Order.* Princeton: Princeton University Press.

UN Charter (Charter of the United Nations). 1945. www.un.org/en/charter-united-nations/.

UNSG Resolution. 2018. 2018. Protection of Civilians in Armed Conflict: Report of the Secretary-General. http://undocs.org/en/S/2018/462.

Watts, Sean. 2020. Interpretation in the GCIII Commentary. Blog post, *Articles of War*. https://lieber.westpoint.edu/interpretation-updated-gciii-commentary/.

World Bank. 2018. ICRC, World Bank Partner to Enhance Support in Fragile and Conflict-affected Settings. www.worldbank.org/en/news/feature/2018/05/09/icrc-world-bank-partner-to-enhance-support-in-fragile-and-conflict-affected-settings.

10 Clean Energy and the Hybridization of Global Governance

Liliana B. Andonova

The transformation of global governance has taken multiple forms. When the international relations scholarship speaks of such transformations it refers implicitly or explicitly to an ideal type of twentieth-century intergovernmental regimes, characterized by an integrated structure and legal frameworks often managed by international organizations (IOs). Increasingly, the idea of integrated international regimes centered on organizational hierarchies has been challenged by a growing complexity of institutional modalities and actors making governance claims. At least three distinctive pathways of change in governance architectures can be discerned.

First, among the traditional intergovernmental institutions and organizational hierarchies there has been expansion of mandates to include new and interdependent issues, resulting in regime complexes with overlapping functions, norms, practices, and contractions.[1] A second pattern of change and complexity, which has become apparent over several decades, is one where a traditional intergovernmental institution remains central to a governance regime, but finds itself flanked by a growing orbit of other IOs, as well as a diverse set of transnational network-based initiatives and market instruments. Political processes of "horizontal rescaling," whereby issues become linked to and grafted on the mandates of preexisting or new institutions, often result in this type of complexification.[2] Prototypical examples of such transformation are the governance of health and climate change.[3] Finally, for a third set of global cooperation dilemmas an integrated intergovernmental regime never was. Instead, distinct spheres of decentralized governance seem to have developed organically out of a series of new institutional

---

[1] Raustiala and Victor 2004; Alter and Meunier 2009; Hofmann 2009; Orsini et al. 2013 among others.
[2] Andonova and Mitchell 2010.
[3] Keohane and Victor 2011; Moon 2013; Moon et al. 2010; Morse and Keohane 2014; Andonova 2017.

experiments, reforms, and practices, often carving political space in-between preexisting regimes. In such decentralized spheres, trans-national governance, conceptualized here as networks linking actors across jurisdictions and steering action toward a set of collective and public purposes, is a centrally important mode of organization and deliv-ery of governance functions.[4] Such networks may operate in the shadow of governmental hierarchies, in the sense that they may include public actors, draw resources from governmental agencies, or seek to ultimately influence the creation of new hierarchical instruments. Nonetheless, substantial articulation of governance purposes, norms, and functions takes place across more horizontally structured networks and associated markets. The governance of forestry, private military companies, busi-ness and human rights, clean energy, and the internet have in many ways followed such pattern of governance formation with a relatively decen-tralized structure.[5]

This chapter focuses on clean energy governance to analyze the pat-terns and causes of decentralized governance, when political gridlocks have continuously blocked the issue in the frameworks of traditional hierarchies. This is a policy sphere that has been constructed as such first through transnational network-based initiatives, and more recently with the creation of several new IO hierarchies and hybrid structures. The analysis links to the line of inquiry in this volume about how networks capture the growing interdependence across issue areas and actors claiming governance roles. It also brings evidence of tendencies of hybridization and considerable layering of modes of governance, as networks often engage markets, rely on state agencies for resources, and create pathways to new intergovernmental or hybrid structures.[6]

The chapter follows the overall framework of the volume by examining how the modes of governance for clean energy have changed over time, and what political dynamics can account for the relative decentralized governance of the issue. The first section defines clean energy as an issue area of global governance, and specifies the rationale for the intertem-poral research design of the empirical analysis. The second section ana-lyzes the evolution of clean energy governance across three distinct periods and institutional developments – from limited cooperation within hierarchical institutions to the proliferation of networks and ultimately the creation of new hierarchies and hybrid arrangements. The third section examines the political drivers of decentralized governance.

---

[4] See Andonova et al. 2009; Andonova et al. 2017; Bulkeley et al. 2014.
[5] Avant 2005, 2016; Cashore et al. 2004; Pattberg 2007; Raustiala 2016; Ruggie 2013.
[6] Abbott et al. 2016; Andonova 2017; Bartley 2018.

The Conclusion reflects on whether decentralized governance is good news for cooperation.

Clean Energy Governance: Definition and Methods

The governance of clean energy involves the articulation of shared norms and objectives on the transition toward energy systems that are more efficient and less damaging to health and the environment, as well as their implementation through a set of policies, networks, and practices. Different organizations and networks working on clean energy have adopted alternative, broader or narrower terminology and policy focus on the issue, such as "renewable energy," "low-carbon energy," or "sustainable energy."[7] For the purposes of this analysis, clean energy is defined as the technologies, services, and processes that reduce energy consumption and enable a transition to systems with low environmental and health impacts, in particular through achieving greater efficiency and increasing the share of renewable sources.[8] The empirical examination of the paths to decentralized governance for clean energy adopts an inter-temporal methodology of analysis to document institutional change, following the approach of Colgan, Keohane, and Van de Graaf.[9] Specifically, the chapter identifies three relevant, albeit overlapping, periods during which distinctive modalities of clean energy governance developed, or in some circumstances failed to do so. This research design corresponds to the interest of this volume as a whole to inquire how changes in world politics have reshaped the modes of governance over time, and the objective of the chapter to understand the pathways to decentralized governance of clean energy.

The first period of analysis, the 1980s–1990s, marked the rise in salience of issues related to alternative energy sources and energy efficiency in the aftermath of the Organization of the Petroleum Exporting Countries (OPEC) embargo and oil crisis (1970s) and heightened concern about global warming (1980s and early 1990s). Yet, the rise in issue salience also coincided with strong geopolitical interests to retain

---

[7] See for example the different terminologies adopted by the Renewable Energy Network (REN21, www.ren21.net/about-ren21/about-us/); the International Renewable Energy Agency (IRENA, https://irena.org/aboutirena); the International Energy Agency (IEA, www.iea.org/about/), the Sustainable Energy for All initiative (SEforAll, www.seforall.org/about-us).

[8] This conceptualization follows the definition adopted in Andonova and Chelminski 2016. It is derived from the objectives on clean energy outlined in major policy and academic initiatives such as SEforALL, the IEA, and the MIT Clean Energy Prize (see http://cep.mit.edu/tracks-1).

[9] Colgan et al. 2012.

sovereign control over the relative reliance on fossil fuels and the national energy mix, resulting in limited intergovernmental collaboration on cleaner energy.

The second period, from the late 1990s to 2010, marks the long stalemate in climate cooperation that followed the adoption of the Kyoto Protocol under the United Nations Framework Convention on Climate Change (UNFCCC) and the crowning debacle of its 2009 Conference of Parties in Copenhagen. This has been also a period of increased proliferation of networks for clean energy governance, starting to carve out a new space for cooperation with a noticeable degree of separation from the gridlocks of the traditional energy and climate institutions.

Finally, the third and most recent time period studied in the chapter, 2009–2017, has brought about a certain consolidation and formal, normative recognition of the decentralized sphere of clean energy governance. This period also marked the creation of a new intergovernmental hierarchy, the International Renewable Energy Agency (IRENA), as well as the more hybrid structures of networks and hierarchies such as the UN Sustainable Energy for All initiative and organization (SEforALL) and the Sustainable Development Goal (SDG) 7 on Affordable and Clean Energy.

For each period of time the analytic narrative examines the political drivers of deadlock or variable creation of governance mechanisms for clean energy. More specifically, it places the spotlight on the evolution and sequencing of governance modalities, which have become the building blocks of decentralized governance architecture. The empirical analysis relies on a cross-examination of studies that so far have tended to situate clean energy initiatives as a subset of the regime complexes of climate change or energy, rather than as a distinct governance sphere.[10] In addition, it draws on text analysis of treaty instruments, international reports, and other primary documents, as well as on interviews and a new database on Transnational Clean Energy Governance to document the evolutions of organizational modalities.[11]

---

[10] See for example, Bulkeley et al. 2014; Florini and Sovacool 2009; Dubash and Florini 2011; Lesage et al. 2010; Keohane and Victor 2011, 2013; Van de Graaf 2013a.

[11] The dataset draws on the following data sources: Barnsley and Ahn 2014; Andonova and Chelminski 2016; and Climate South 2018 (see www.geg.ox.ac.uk/research/climate-south). Through additional coding the new dataset on Transnational Clean Energy Governance, 1980–2018 includes transnational initiatives with explicit and central focus on the governance of clean energy as defined in this chapter. On the basis of the type of actors that constitute the transnational governance network, the initiatives in the Transnational Clean Energy Governance, 1980–2018 are also coded and classified as

The Making of Clean Energy Governance: Networks, Hierarchies, and Hybrids

Hierarchical Institutions and Stasis in Clean Energy Governance, 1980–1997

Global energy governance has been traditionally structured around inter-governmental hierarchies, like the majority of issues that emerged in twentieth-century Cold War politics. In the wake of the 1973 oil crisis triggered by the embargo of OPEC, Western industrialized nations established the International Energy Agency (IEA, 1974) as the principal institution to facilitate cooperation for the security and predictability of oil supply among members of the Organisation for Economic Co-operation and Development.[12] Within intergovernmental hierarchies, however, there was very limited scope for cooperation on cleaner or alternative energy sources to fossil fuels for much of the twentieth century. This was despite the fact that the 1970s oil shocks put on the policy agenda the issue of greater energy efficiency and diversification of resources with a certain urgency, and prompted the adoption of domestic policies including in the USA, but also in some countries with autocratic regimes such as Brazil and the Philippines. The salience of the issue led to the first United Nations Conference on New and Renewable Sources of Energy in Nairobi (1981). However, the proposal to create a specialized energy department within the World Bank with policy and financing power was opposed by the USA. More generally, the geopolitical context and state interests during that period were such that the management of the energy mix rested firmly within the sovereign prerogatives of states.

Within the IEA, a Working Party on Renewable Energy Technologies was created as an advisory body in 1982. However, the tight control over the agency by member states, concerned primarily about the stability of oil prices, made any substantial policy work or agreement on renewable sources outside the reach of the agency. As Colgan et al. characterize it, the IEA "remained structurally frozen in time."[13] Similarly, the Energy Sector Management Assistance Program (ESMAP) was created in 1983 as a program within the World Bank, but at that time it focused largely on access to energy and energy security. Text analysis of ESMAP Annual Reports between 1983 and 1995 shows that these documents only marginally mention "environmental externalities" and "energy

---

private, public, or partnered, following the methodology specified by Andonova et al. 2018.
[12] Keohane 1984; Van de Graaf 2012.   [13] Colgan et al. 2012, 126.

efficiency," a far cry from any serious policy or strategy for project investments away from fossil fuels.[14]

The issue of energy externalities and cleaner sources gained salience
again in the late 1980s and early 1990s with the rise in scientific and
public concern about climate change and reliance on fossil fuels.
Countries adopted the UNFCCC in 1992 as the main instrument of
climate cooperation. However, the convention entirely avoided the issue
of the transition to more sustainable energy sources and technology.
While its text calls for reduced emissions of greenhouse gases, which
implies progressive reduction in the use of fossil fuels, its language does
not contain any provision that directly mentions energy resources. The
term "energy" appears only in the Preamble, referring to developing
countries and stating that: "their energy consumption will need to grow
taking into account the possibilities for achieving greater energy efficiency and for controlling greenhouse gas emissions in general."[15]
States were simply not ready to delegate authority on energy matters
through the hierarchical mechanisms of an intergovernmental treaty,
despite their centrality for addressing climate change. As the then US
President George H.W. Bush remarked at the UNFCCC negotiations,
"the American way of life is not up for negotiation."[16] The Global
Environmental Facility (GEF) was established as the main funding
mechanism to serve the UNFCCC along with several other environmental conventions, providing some resources for clean energy projects,
which however were limited and bound by additionality conditions.

The adoption of the Kyoto Protocol under the UNFCCC was the
most notable event in the intergovernmental politics of climate change
during the second part of the 1990s, with important, although not fully
anticipated effects on the politics of clean energy governance. The Kyoto
Protocol established emission reduction targets for industrialized states
(Annex I countries), interpreting the UNFCCC provision for "common
but differentiated responsibilities" in a way that reified the divisions
between industrialized and developing countries on climate cooperation
(see Chapter 3). Article 2 of the Kyoto Protocol also specified that Annex
I industrialized countries will advance policies and measures to implement their emission reduction obligations according to their national
circumstances, including through "enhancement of energy efficiency"
and "promotion, development and increased use of, new and renewable

---

[14] "Annual reports," ESMAP. www.esmap.org/annual-reports.
[15] United Nations Framework Convention on Climate Change, adopted on May 9, 1995,
    1771 U.N.T.S. 107, 3
[16] "A Greener Bush," *The Economist*, February 13, 2003.

forms of energy."[17] The Kyoto Protocol was thus the only legal instrument under the UNFCCC that included soft but explicit expectations about energy sector reforms. However, by placing the provision under Annex I the Kyoto Protocol also deepened the geopolitical discord on climate change between the USA, the European Union states, and developing countries. Its provision on clean energy is likely an additional factor that contributed to its rapid demise in the US political context, and conversely supported the European Union's embrace of stronger commitments on renewable sources since the late 1990s.[18] The protocol furthermore did not include dedicated financing or a strong technology transfer mechanism for clean energy, implicitly pushing to the sideline questions of developing countries' engagement in a low-carbon transition.[19] Divergence of geopolitical interest ossified into inflexible negotiating blocks, and gridlock settled in for the next decade, particularly after the US withdrawal from the Kyoto Protocol.[20]

The analysis of institutional hierarchies and treaty provisions thus reveals a highly limited scope to address the transition to a more sustainable energy mix within institutions such as the IEA, the UNFCCC, or the World Bank at times of geopolitical discord and heightened concern among states to maintain sovereign control and limited international delegation over energy policy decisions.

Expanding Clean Energy Governance through Networks, Late 1990s–Present

The longstanding geopolitical gridlock in climate politics between 2000 and 2015 is widely interpreted as one of the main triggers for alternative, network-based action by non-state and substate actors on climate-related issues. Indeed, this was a period of rapid proliferation of transnational clean energy governance initiatives (see Figure 10.1). However, the stasis in intergovernmental regimes on energy and climate change is only a partial account of the politics that produced a decentralized and layered architecture of clean energy governance. The diversification of political agency in international affairs and the ability of non-state and substate actors to directly claim governance roles have shaped in significant ways networked modes of governance.[21]

---

[17] Kyoto Protocol to the United Nations Framework Convention on Climate Change, adopted December 11, 1997, 37 I.L.M. 22 (1998), Article 2
[18] Schreurs et al. 2009.   [19] Benedick 2001.   [20] Depledge 2006; Hale et al. 2013.
[21] Andonova et al. 2009, 2017; Bulkeley et al. 2014; Green 2014; Hoffmann 2011; Prakash and Potoski 2006; Ruggie 2004; Slaughter 2004.

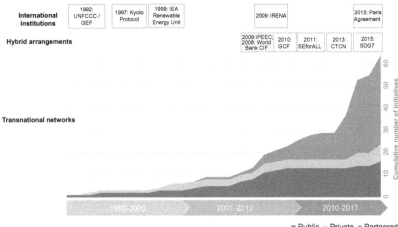

Figure 10.1 Evolving modalities of clean energy governance.
Source: Author, data from Transnational Clean Energy Database, 1990–2018

The 1992 Rio Summit on the Environment and Sustainable Development, where the UNFCCC was negotiated, provided one of the first formal platforms for participation by private, advocacy, and substate actors. As a result, several transnational initiatives with explicit priorities on energy sustainability were launched, independently from the intergovernmental processes that steered clear from the issue. The E-7 consortium of electricity companies (later renamed E-8 and now the Global Sustainable Electricity Partnership) pledged to promote "expertise, competence, know-how" and investment for more efficient and environmentally sound electricity use and production, including through greater share of renewables.[22] The Local Governments for Sustainability (ICLEI) network engaged municipalities in horizontal collaboration to leverage commitments, resources, and support for local sustainability, such as the advancement of cleaner energy systems, energy efficiency, and urban planning.[23] ICLEI became the network with the widest global participation of cities with commitments for climate and energy action.[24] In many ways the E-7 partnership and ICLEI were precursors of a larger tendency in subsequent decades to advance the clean energy discourse and objectives through the expansion of transnational governance networks. Figure 10.1 captures the intertemporal tendency in the rise of transnational networks as modes of governance for clean energy

---

[22] E-7 1992.   [23] Betsill and Bulkeley 2004.   [24] Andonova et al. 2017.

since the late 1990s, alongside intergovernmental institutions and hybrid initiatives.

Figure 10.1 also reveals a rapidly developing tendency toward shared authority between public and private actors through transnational governance networks and public–private partnerships, operating in parallel with intergovernmental institutions. The political incentives behind the proliferation of networks have several dimensions.

First, the divergence of preferences among groups of industrialized countries, which contributed to the gridlock in climate cooperation for much of the 2000s, motivated the mobilization of coalitions of the "green and greedy" or of the "brown and greedy"[25] between public and private or advocacy interests, to promote energy technology diffusion and policies via transnational networks. Entrepreneurs of donor-driven networks typically included government departments within states, often alongside with industry associations and IOs.[26] The Asia-Pacific Partnership, for example, was sponsored by the US government and involved counterparts in Australia, India, and China, among others. Through a series of ministerial meetings it promoted a technology-oriented approach to the reduction of greenhouse gases from the fossil fuel industry, including clean coal. The partnership was also interpreted as an effort to undermine the Kyoto Protocol.[27] European countries with proactive renewable policies in turn supported initiatives such as the Renewable Energy and Energy Efficiency Partnership (REEEP), the Johannesburg Renewable Energy Coalitions, and REN21.[28] All of these initiatives used a transnational, network-based structure that facilitated involvement of private actors, policy officials, and actors from developing countries in a process of governance experimentation and project-based investment.[29]

Second, IOs, or more precisely departments and individual leaders within IOs, sometimes reacted with surprising speed and entrepreneurship to establish new programs on clean energy governance. More often than not such programs took the shape of hybrid partnership networks, rather than hierarchically implemented instruments or formal policies.[30] In 1997, for example, the United Nations Environment Programme (UNEP) established its Energy Branch. In an interview the founding director of the Energy Branch explained:

Before the Kyoto Protocol, it was impossible to discuss renewable energy and energy efficiency in the political context of the UN. The Protocol brought the issue into the open. There was a growing interest among industry and

---

[25] Hicks et al. 2008.   [26] Andonova 2014, 2017; Bulkeley et al. 2014.
[27] Taplin and McGee 2010.   [28] Andonova, Castro et al. 2018.
[29] Bulkeley et al. 2014; Szulecki et al. 2011.   [30] Andonova 2010, 2017; Newell 2011.

policy circles in renewable energy, but the quality of information and expertise were limited; particularly for developing countries, which were not members of the IEA.[31]

Organizational entrepreneurs within UNEP thus saw a political opportunity to advance a portfolio of clean energy programs and partnerships that would fall within UNEP's mandate and expertise related to technology, industry, and climate change.[32] This work proceeded in large part through networks, including the REN21 partnership network that expanded to become one of the most authoritative governance bodies providing information and facilitation of policy coordination on issues of renewable energy.[33] UNEP's clean energy portfolio benefited to a great degree from the parallel creation of another entrepreneurial structure – the United Nations Foundation and the UN Fund for International Partnerships (UNFIP) – set up by then Secretary-General Kofi Annan with the support of a $1 billion grant from US philanthropist Ted Turner.[34] The fund identified clean energy as a priority for supporting partnership collaboration between UN agencies and private and civil society actors. Over time UNEP's Energy Branch established a diverse portfolio of transnational programs and partnerships, with the support of UNFIP, a variety of public and private donors, relevant departments in developing countries, industry, and think tanks. The focus of energy initiatives, in which UNEP is engaged, ranges from energy efficiency (e.g., the Global Market Transformation for Efficient Lighting, the Sustainable Buildings and Construction Programme, the Global Fuel Efficiency Initiative) to improved access to clean energy (e.g., the African Rural Energy Enterprise Development Programme, the Clean Cookstove Alliance, REEEP, Sustainable Biofuels) and provision of expertise and technical support on energy-related strategies.

A third type of clean energy network involves a growing number of non-state and substate actors, which have created horizontal initiatives across borders for climate and clean energy. Most municipal and regional climate governance networks, such as ICLEI, C40, or Regions20, place strong emphasis on efficient energy management, transportation, efficiency of buildings, and displacement of polluting technologies. Clean energy issues have thus found a space on subnational policy agenda, through their interdependence with concerns about local air pollution, dependence on imported fossil fuel, and the effects of

---

[31] Interview, director of UNEP Energy, Paris, July 2015.   [32] Andonova 2017.
[33] Andonova 2017; interview with senior staff member of REN21, Paris, May 2015. See also Barnsley and Ahn 2014; REN21 2015; Stadelmann and Castro 2014.
[34] Andonova 2017.

climate change. Nongovernmental organizations (NGOs) and industry associations have similarly established partnerships or voluntary commitments to advance cleaner and more efficient energy systems. However, the most significant contribution from the private sector to the clean energy transition has taken place primarily through markets, including through trade and foreign direct investment and in response to incentives put in place by government policies and diffusion effects.[35]

Finally, and somewhat paradoxically, the influence of formal hierarchical institutions such as the Kyoto Protocol of the UNFCCC, or agencies such as the World Bank and the IEA on clean energy collaboration, has materialized primarily through associated networks and market-based mechanisms rather than hierarchical implementation of intergovernmental commitments. The Clean Development Mechanism (CDM) and the Joint Implementation (JI) mechanisms of the Kyoto Protocol became de facto the most important market-based instruments under the UNFCCC for clean energy technology transfer.[36] This is despite the fact the CDM and JI were not designed to exclusively target clean energy investment, and in some instances produced perverse incentives for low-cost offsets in methane capture from coal mines or the continued production and destruction of hydrochlorofluorocarbons.[37] Nonetheless, approximately 72 percent of all CDM projects up to February 2019 involved renewable energy, providing project-based investments for the diffusion of cleaner technologies,[38] and importantly, for the creation of domestic constituencies in favor of such transitions.[39]

Under the shadow of the formal UNFCCC market mechanisms emerged private carbon markets and transnational private rules to regulate them. Green qualifies private carbon markets as "entrepreneurial governance" capturing the bottom-up agency of private developers, epistemic communities, consultants, associations, and NGOs.[40] In 2013 the new Climate Technology Centre and Network (CTCN) involving multiple institutions and experts was established to facilitate "technology solutions, capacity building and advice on policy" under the UNFCCC Technology Mechanism, with limited direct funding allocated to it.[41]

Kyoto Protocol market mechanisms, furthermore, provided an impetus for the Environment Department of the World Bank to create, with donor countries and private actor participation, a series of carbon funds as financial instruments to support the implementation of market-

---

[35] Dechezleprêtre et al. 2011; Gallagher 2014.   [36] Stadelmann and Castro 2014.
[37] Wara and Victor 2008.   [38] UNEP DTU Partnership 2019.
[39] Andonova and Sun 2019; Schröder 2012.   [40] Green 2014.
[41] See www.ctc-n.org/.

based carbon offsets. In the course of less than ten years the expanding number of climate funds made the World Bank a focal point for the creation, in 2008, of the Climate Investment Facility (CIF), the largest mechanism at the time for targeted financing for clean technology transfer and climate change.[42] Amid the proliferation of organizational platforms, transnational networks, and markets for clean energy, there was a sense that the IEA was lagging behind.[43] However, the IEA had an important epistemic advantage as the principal depository of credible information on energy, technology roadmaps, and advisory functions.[44] Ultimately, with facilitation and financing by the G8, the International Partnership for Energy Efficiency Cooperation (IPEEC) and the Low-Carbon Energy Technology Platform were created as partnership platforms through which the IEA has expanded its expertise and advisory functions on cleaner energy, particularly with respect to developing countries.[45] As the present analysis reveals, during the period of stagnating climate negotiations in the late 1990s and the 2000s, networks with highly variable constellations of actors became the most vibrant modes of clean energy governance. Such networks were created at multiple sites of governance, reflecting the interdependency of issues and actors, and frequently in conjunction with market mechanisms linked to carbon offsets and technology investments. Moreover, the transnational governance networks captured by Figure 10.1 are, in many ways, just the tip of a more complex web of initiatives and practices, linking the global and the local transnationally.

Specific cases can illustrate further the functioning of this sphere of interdependent and overlapping networks. Consider the initiative of the mayor of Saint Cristóbal in the Galapagos Islands to launch the first wind power project ever built on an island for the displacement of 50 percent of the island's diesel-generated electricity. This initiative was prompted by concerns about dependency on imported diesel fuel and its significant externalities resulting from air pollution and oil spills. It became possible primarily through a global partnership network, which included the Global Sustainable Electricity Partnership, investments from private utilities such as American Electric Power and RWE Power AG, the United Nations Development Program, the national government of Ecuador,

---

[42] Andonova 2017; Newell 2011; Nakhooda 2011; interview with staff members of the World Resources Institute, Washington, DC, July 2014.
[43] Van de Graaf 2012; Colgan et al. 2012.
[44] Interview, director of UNEP Energy, Paris, July 2015. See also Keohane 1984.
[45] Interview with staff member of the International Energy Agency, May 2015, Paris. See also Barnsley and Ahn 2014; Lesage et al. 2010.

and facilitation and financial support from UNFIP.[46] As this very local episode illustrates, multiple institutions, partnerships, and platforms *interplay* to create spheres of decentralized network-based governance. By focusing on the global level the analysis of this chapter thus captures some of the gateways to a much thicker and broader network of actors.

Layering and Institutionalization of Clean Energy Governance, 2009–2017

After the first decade of rising networks for clean energy governance, the creation of IRENA in 2009 marked a turn to formal intergovernmentalism for the first time in this policy issue. The mandate of the new organizational hierarchy focuses on renewable energy, rather than on a broader scope of technologies and systems for a sustainable energy transition. Nonetheless, it also represents the first formal institutionalization of clean energy governance. Existing accounts explain IRENA as a major institutional breakthrough, driven by a new geopolitical constellation and a sufficient coalition of powerful state actors that were increasingly dissatisfied with the limitations of the IEA.[47] However, the present analysis raises a prior question: to what extent did the growing constellation of clean energy networks and markets prior to 2009 ultimately help to articulate a closer agreement among industrialized countries and with the Global South? Lead countries on clean energy, such as Germany and the UK, used high-level network-based platforms such as the G8 and G20 to advance greater consensus on energy transition and to pledge financing as a commitment mechanism. Transnational partnerships and market-based instruments, in turn, promote learning, policy diffusion, and project-based investment in emerging and developing countries, strengthening policy constituencies. Transnational networks thus constructed, over the first decade of the twenty-first century, a sphere of governance that is related to and yet distinct from the contentious climate politics, and which appeared more technical and focused on information, technology transfer through projects, and new investment mechanisms. Not coincidentally, the new intergovernmental agency IRENA was fashioned as a depository of expertise, capacity building, and project-based investment to promote renewable resources.

After 2009 the formal institutionalization of the emergent sphere of clean energy governance in some ways responded to concerns about

---

[46] Interview with senior staff of UNFIP, New York, September 2014. See also Global Sustainable Electricity Partnership 2016.
[47] Colgan et al. 2012; Van de Graaf 2013a, 2013b.

institutional fragmentation and the role of decentralized networks as conduits of influence by powerful actors.[48] It proceeded with the parallel construction of institutions under the auspices of more broadly representative UN frameworks (Figure 10.1), and with a formal articulation of norms and the rationalization of clean energy governance as a sphere of hybrid authority. Because of their voluntary and self-selecting participation, transnational governance arrangements have tended to privilege the agendas of actors with stronger capacity and interests, rather than those that are marginalized with fewer resources and greater need for governance support.[49] The resulting patterns of participation often reified familiar inequities across the industrialized North and the Global South.[50] Led by such concerns, developing countries challenged the increasing dominance of the World Bank in climate financing networks and markets, and motivated, in part, the negotiations of the Green Climate Fund (GCF) under the more representative structure of the UNFCCC. Ultimately the GCF was fashioned as a formal intergovernmental institution, which however did not replace the World Bank CIF, and included partnership-type horizontal structures through its Private Sector Facility.[51]

The UN initiative on *Sustainable Energy for All* (2011), launched by then UN Secretary-General Ban Ki-Moon subsequently became the main vehicle for the formal recognition and institutionalization of the decentralized sphere of clean energy governance. The process had all the elements of organizational orchestration.[52] The UN Secretary-General launched the initiative as a "movement" and "consultation" rather than a summit or negotiation, engaging UN agencies but also a multitude of partnerships and networks for clean energy governance.[53] In effect, *Sustainable Energy for All* deliberately brought the hybrid structure of the decentralized governance for clean energy to the floor of the UN General Assembly. It became the first multi-stakeholder process to result in the adoption of a UN General Assembly Resolution 65/151 on the *International Year of Sustainable Energy for All*, which articulated for the first time a set of broad normative objectives and a policy consensus for a "sustainable energy transition."[54] It implicitly recognized the two decades of prior work of the multitude of transnational networks, IOs, and partnerships and provided the normative glue of a new sphere of hybrid governance. Notably, the *Resolution on Sustainable Energy for All* does not mention the UNFCCC, having been adopted during the period

---

[48] Barnett and Duvall 2005; Hafner-Burton et al. 2009.   [49] Andonova and Levy 2003.
[50] Bulkeley et al. 2014.   [51] Andonova 2017.   [52] Abbott et al. 2016.
[53] The Secretary-General's High-Level Group on Sustainable Energy for All 2012.
[54] UN General Assembly 2011, 2012, 3.

of stagnation in climate negotiations, even though it calls for a climate-resilient future.[55] The resolution also paved the way for the inclusion, in the 2015 Sustainable Development Goals (SDGs), of Goal 7 on the advancement and implementation of "access to affordable, reliable, sustainable and modern energy for all."[56] In an interesting twist of institutional evolution, the Sustainable Energy for All Initiative was subsequently incorporated as a formal IO in Vienna, albeit with a multi-stakeholder constituency including "leaders in government, the private sector and civil society" and a mandate linked to SDG 7 and the UNFCCC Paris Agreement.[57] This identity card of the organization and Figure 10.1 summarize the hybrid and decentralized structure of clean energy governance that developed in the course of two decades, through the interplay of networks, markets, and hierarchies.

Decentralized Governance for Clean Energy: Why Is It Happening?

The decentralized sphere of networks, hierarchies, and hybrid arrangements for clean energy governance represents an increasingly common institutional constellation in international relations. It is characterized by the absence of a core integrated regime, instead involving the layering of organizational modalities and sources of authority. Such constellations have become part of a broader tendency of hybridization of governance that relies increasingly on the interplay between public and private governance, and between traditional bureaucratic hierarchies, transnational networks, and informal instruments of governance.[58] What accounts for the growing reliance on a relatively non-hierarchical layering of networks, markets, and formal IOs for the governance of many global issues?

In the case of clean energy, geopolitics has been a fundamental structural and political variable that in the first instance prevented the effective integration of clean energy issues in preexisting or new international regimes, as documented most notably for the cases of the IEA and the UNFCCC. Furthermore, as issues gain in complexity there is both a greater degree of uncertainty about the payoffs of collaboration and greater normative contestation, leading to consistent reluctance by states

---

[55] UN General Assembly 2011.   [56] UN General Assembly 2015, 14.
[57] "About Us," SEforAll. www.seforall.org/about-us.
[58] Abbott et al. 2016; Andonova 2017; Andonova et al. 2018; Bartley 2018; Büthe and Mattli 2011; Farrell and Newman 2014; Kahler 2016; Pauwelyn et al. 2012; Vabulas and Snidal 2013; Sending and Neumann 2006; Green 2014; Raustiala 2016; Tallberg et al. 2013.

to delegate substantial authority on energy under the UNFCCC framework.[59] Even the Paris Agreement, which is considered as a milestone in breaking the climate cooperation gridlock, "encourages" "technology development and transfer" but does not include a specific mention of "energy" or "energy transition."[60] Categories matter. They reflect how different institutions may facilitate or obstruct the articulation of contested political priorities, and influence international relations and policy choices.[61]

While geopolitics and other structural accounts capture important changes in world politics, such as the constellation of power and interests, resources, and connectivity, the present analysis shows that the pluralization of agency has to a large extent shaped the networks and market-based mechanisms that gave rise to the sphere of clean energy governance. It furthermore highlights the role of governance entrepreneurs, for example actors with strong normative, epistemic, or incentive-based motivations, to engage in the construction of new experimentalist governance through transnational networks. Such entrepreneurs can be private, non-state actors,[62] but also institutional actors such as IOs or government agencies that have driven or orchestrated the political coalitions behind the proliferation of governance modalities.[63]

The empirical analysis of the making of clean energy governance also reveals that networks and markets have deployed governance functions primarily through expertise, financing, and the project-based implementation of technology.[64] They focused at first on providing credible information and facilitating stronger epistemic consensus on renewable energy, energy efficiency, and other transition pathways, implicitly or explicitly assuming advocacy and policy diffusion functions. A large number of transnational partnerships and subnational initiatives in turn have adopted strong capacity-building, financing, and project-implementation approaches. The influence of these modalities of governance has materialized by revealing and updating preferences and by the facilitation of learning and negotiation among formerly distant political positions on clean energy. Policy-making and regulation on clean energy matters, in turn, have remained largely in the domain of domestic politics.

---

[59] Keohane and Victor 2013.
[60] See Paris Agreement, 2015. https://unfccc.int/process-and-meetings/the-paris-agreement/the-paris-agreement.
[61] Barnett and Finnemore 2004.
[62] Boasson and Huitema 2017; Green 2014; Cashore et al. 2004; Prakash and Potoski 2006.
[63] Andonova 2017; Abbott et al. 2015; Hale and Roger 2014.
[64] See also Andonova et al. 2009; Andonova, Castro et al. 2018.

Finally, the analysis in this chapter demonstrates that the entrepreneurship of decentralized and network-based modalities of governance has not taken place in an institutional vacuum. Political entrepreneurs take cues from the intergovernmental space or from domestic politics to foster alliances across borders and identify windows of opportunity for action. Ultimately, we also observe a turn to more formal institutionalization, albeit through a hybrid structure that has included the creation of a new intergovernmental hierarchy IRENA, the adoption through a multi-stakeholder process of a UN resolution, a set of goals on clean energy, and subsequently the incorporation of SEforALL into an organizational bureaucracy with a multi-stakeholder constituency to manage the UN SDG on sustainable energy. These mechanisms advance the functions of institutionalizing and legitimating the emergent sphere of clean energy governance by articulating more explicitly its underlying purpose, norms, and policy objectives. The analysis thus reveals processes of experimentation across multiple planes of politics as key dynamics that can help to explain the decentralized development of new hybrid spheres of governance from the ground up.

Conclusion: Is Decentralized Governance Good News for Cooperation?

Climate change, by now an existential threat to earth systems, has given the impetus for political interests to advance cleaner energy technologies and cooperation. Paradoxically, and somewhat counterintuitively, the UNFCCC has not proved to be the most conducive institutional setting for developing a substantive agreement on advancing a clean energy transition. Clean energy collaboration proceeded first through transnational networks and experimental initiatives, linking to or in parallel with the climate and energy regimes. Such network-based collaboration became visible at the highest political level (G8, the Major Economies Forum, the Clean Energy Ministerial), as well as through hundreds and possibly thousands of transnational public–private partnerships, networks of cities, regions, NGOs, and industry. Some of these networks expanded and became institutionalized as "multisector" IOs. Others have lost political influence and disbanded. These institutions have put in place a set of tools in terms of credible expertise, capacity building, policy advice, and funding to support transition pathways.

Such developments raise the question: is decentralized governance good news for cooperation? Is it signaling the coming end of international treaty-making as we know it? Is it second best to the traditional integrated and legalized regimes?

The complexification of global governance may not always be good news for researchers or policy-makers, who now may have to make sense of and work with myriad institutions, networks, and market-based activities. For many issue areas, however, gone are the days of the relatively integrated and organized regimes around specific rules and commitments, against which we could attempt to measure effectiveness. And yet the governance of clean energy is part of a broader set of issues, where decentralized governance has made the advancement and articulation of global objectives possible, while still depending to a large degree on national governments and substate actors for their codification and implementation. The development of decentralized governance for clean energy, I would argue, has followed in many ways the problem structure of the issue and the underlying interest by the majority of states to retain considerable sovereignty in setting priorities and policies to shape the use and mix of energy resources.

The variety of initiatives, norms, and funding instruments attempts to steer domestic practice, implementation, and learning to support more sustainable energy strategies. In this sense, one could stipulate that the pluralization of agency in world politics and of modes of organization has contributed to fostering collaboration, which may not have been possible through state-centric and formal diplomacy-driven modalities. Several streams of politics, fluctuating between gridlock and cooperation, seemed to have come together to facilitate a normative commitment to a more sustainable energy future and enabled streams of information, projects, and investment. From such a perspective, complex decentralized governance has made collaboration on clean energy possible, despite a clear tendency to keep the issue under the lid of sovereignty. At the same time, the multitude of institutions that make the structure of governance and their boundaries can appear fragmented, elusive, and contested. The distributional implication of myriad governance modes, their sufficiency for addressing global problems, and the lines of accountability are far from established. Understanding the contemporary transformation of governance is thus, in many ways, only the first step toward a larger and more difficult inquiry about effectiveness and accountability.

Transnational networks, flatter in structure compared to hierarchies, are nonetheless important conduits of power and influence.[65] Nonlegalized network governance thus tends to privilege certain agendas that are pursued by actors with stronger capacity and interests, compared to marginalized actors with fewer resources and greater need for

---

[65] Barnett and Duvall 2005; Hafner-Burton et al. 2009.

governance support.[66] The resulting patterns of participation in transnational governance networks often reify, at least in their initial stages, familiar inequities across the industrialized North and the Global South.[67] In practice, transnational market-based networks have privileged participation by large emerging countries such as China, India, Brazil, or Russia.[68] New financing mechanisms may consolidate the influence of traditionally powerful institutions such as the World Bank and donor agencies.[69] Such concerns, particularly among developing countries, have prompted demands for the greater institutionalization of new financing instruments, including through oversight and alignment with the UNFCCC as a broadly representative institution.

References

Abbott, Kenneth W., Jessica F. Green, and Robert O. Keohane. 2016. Organizational Ecology and Institutional Change in Global Governance Journal. *International Organization* 70 (2): 247–277.

Abbott, Kenneth W., Philipp Genschel, Duncan Snidal, and Bernhard Zangl. 2015. *International Organizations as Orchestrators*. Cambridge: Cambridge University Press.

Alter, Karen J., and Sophie Meunier. 2009. The Politics of International Regime Complexity. *Perspectives on Politics* 7 (1): 13–24.

Andonova, Liliana B. 2010. Public–Private Partnerships for the Earth: Politics and Patterns of Hybrid Authority in the Multilateral System. *Global Environmental Politics* 10: 25–53.

2014. Boomerangs to Partnerships? Explaining State Participation in Transnational Partnerships for Sustainability. *Comparative Political Studies* 47 (3): 481–515.

2017. Governance Entrepreneurs: *International Organizations and the Rise of Global Public–Private Partnerships*. Cambridge: Cambridge University Press.

Andonova, Liliana B. and Kathryn Chelminski. 2016. Emergence of a Regime Complex for Clean Energy: The Critical Role of Legitimacy. Paper presented at the 2nd Annual Conference on Environmental Politics and Governance, June 16–19, Gerzensee, Switzerland.

Andonova, Liliana B. and Marc A. Levy. 2003. Franchising Global Governance: Making Sense of the Johannesburg Type II partnerships. In *Yearbook of International Co-operation on Environment and Development 2003/2004*, edited by Olav S. Stokke and Oystein B. Thommessen, 19–31. London: Earthscan.

Andonova, Liliana B., Michele M. Betsill, and Harriet Bulkeley. 2009. Transnational Climate Governance. *Global Environmental Politics* 9 (2): 52–73.

---

[66] Andonova and Levy 2003.   [67] Bulkeley et al. 2014.
[68] Castro and Michaelowa 2011; Andonova and Sun 2019.
[69] Nakhooda 2011; Newell 2011.

Andonova, Liliana B., Paula Castro, and Kathryn Chelminski. 2018. Transferring Technologies. In *Governing Climate Change: Polycentricity in Action?* edited by Andrew Jordan, Dave Huitema, Harro van Asselt, and Johanna Forster, 266–284. Cambridge: Cambridge University Press.

Andonova, Liliana B. and Ronald Mitchell. 2010. The Rescaling of Global Environmental Politics. *Annual Review of Environment and Resources* 35: 255–282.

Andonova, Liliana B., Thomas N. Hale, and Charles B. Roger. 2017. National Policy and Transnational Governance of Climate Change: Complements or Substitutes? *International Studies Quarterly* 61 (2): 253–268.

Andonova, Liliana B., Thomas N. Hale, and Charles B. Roger, eds. 2018. *The Comparative Politics of Transnational Climate Governance.* London: Routledge.

Andonova, Liliana B. and Yixian Sun. 2019. Private Governance in Developing Countries: Drivers of Voluntary Carbon Offset Programs. *Global Environmental Politics* 19 (1): 99–122.

Avant, Deborah D. 2005. *The Market for Force: The Consequences of Privatizing Security.* Cambridge: Cambridge University Press.

2016. Pragmatic Networks and Transnational Governance of Private Military and Security Services. *International Studies Quarterly* 60 (2): 330–342.

Barnett, Michael N. and Martha Finnemore. 2004. Rules for the World: *International Organizations in Global Politics.* Ithaca, NY: Cornell University Press.

Barnett, Michael N. and Raymond Duvall, eds. 2005. *Power in Global Governance.* Cambridge: Cambridge University Press.

Barnsley, Ingrid and Sun-Joo Ahn. 2014. *Mapping Multilateral Collaboration on Low-Carbon Energy Technologies.* IEA Insights Series. Paris: IEA.

Bartley, Tim. 2018. *Rules without Rights: Land, Labor, and Private Authority in the Global Economy.* Oxford: Oxford University Press.

Benedick, Richard E. 2001. Striking a New Deal on Climate Change. *Issues in Science and Technology* 18 (1): 71–76.

Betsill, Michele M. and Harriet Bulkeley. 2004. Transnational Networks and Global Environmental Governance: The Cities for Climate Protection Program. *International Studies Quarterly* 48 (2): 471–493.

Boasson, Elin Lerum and Dave Huitema. 2017. Climate Governance Entrepreneurship: Emerging Findings and a New Research Agenda. *Environment and Planning C: Politics and Space* 35 (8): 1343–1361.

Bulkeley, Harriet, Liliana B. Andonova, Michele M. Betsill, Daniel Compagnon, Thomas N. Hale, Matthew J. Hoffmann, Peter J. Newell, Matthew Paterson, Charles B. Roger, and Stacy D. VanDeveer. 2014. *Transnational Climate Change Governance.* Cambridge: Cambridge University Press.

Büthe, Tim and Walter Mattli. 2011. *The New Global Rulers: The Privatization of Regulation in the World Economy.* Princeton: Princeton University Press.

Cashore, Benjamin, Graeme Auld, and Deanna Newsom. 2004. *Governing through Markets: Forest Certification and the Emergence of Non-State Authority.* New Haven: Yale University Press.

Castro, Paula and Axel Michaelowa. 2011. Would Preferential Access Measures Be Sufficient to Overcome Current Barriers to CDM Projects in Least Developed Countries? *Climate and Development* 3 (2): 123–142.

Climate South. 2018. Cooperative Climate Action 2013–2018: Global Performance and Geographic Scope. Research Report Published by the German Development Institute/Deutsches Institut für Entwicklungspolitik (DIE), the Blavatnik School of Government at the University of Oxford, the African Centre for Technology Studies (ACTS), and The Energy and Resources Institute. www.geg.ox.ac.uk/ sites/geg.bsg.ox.ac.uk/files/2018–2012/ClimateSouth%2020Global%20climate% 20action%202013–2018%20Nov2018.pdf.

Colgan, Jeff D., Robert O. Keohane, and Thijs Van de Graaf. 2012. Punctuated Equilibrium in the Energy Regime Complex. *Review of International Organizations* 7 (2): 117–143.

Dechezleprêtre, Antoine, Matthieu Glachant, Ivan Haščič, Nick Johnstone, and Yann Ménière. 2011. Invention and Transfer of Climate Change – Mitigation Technologies: A Global Analysis. *Review of Environmental Economics and Policy* 5 (1): 109–130.

Depledge, Joanna. 2006. The Opposite of Learning: Ossification in the Climate Change Regime. *Global Environmental Politics* 6 (1): 1–22.

Dubash, Navroz K. and Ann Florini. 2011. Mapping Global Energy Governance. *Global Policy* 2 (s1): 6–18.

E-7. 1992. The Environment, Global Warming, and the Development of the Electricity Industry. Chairpersons Joint Statement. E-7 James Bay Inaugural Summit, April 9, 1992. https://globalelectricity.org/content/uploads/E7_ JamesBay_Summit.pdf. Accessed 15 February 2019.

Farrell, Henry and Abraham L. Newman. 2014. Domestic Institutions beyond the Nation-State: Charting the New Interdependence Approach. *World Politics* 66 (2): 331–363.

Florini, Ann and Benjamin K. Sovacool. 2009. Who Governs Energy? The Challenges Facing Global Energy Governance. *Energy Policy* 37 (12): 5239–5248.

Gallagher, Kelly S. 2014. *The Globalization of Clean Energy Technology. Lessons from China*. Cambridge, MA: MIT Press.

Global Sustainable Electricity Partnership. 2016. *Galápagos San Cristobal Wind Energy Project 2003-2016: Performance Summary and Recommendations for Enhancing Ecuador's Longest-Operating Wind Project*. https://globalelectricity .org/content/uploads/Galapagos-Report-2016-English.pdf.

Green, Jessica F. 2014. *Rethinking Private Authority: Agents and Entrepreneurs in Global Environmental Governance*. Princeton: Princeton University Press.

Hafner-Burton, Emilie M., Miles Kahler, and Alexander H. Montgomery. 2009. Network Analysis for International Relations. *International Organization* 63 (3): 559–592.

Hale, Thomas N. and Charles B. Roger. 2014. Orchestration and Transnational Climate Governance. *Review of International Organizations* 9 (1): 59–82.

Hale, Thomas N., David Held, and Kevin Young. 2013. *Gridlock: Why Global Cooperation Is Failing When We Need It Most*. Cambridge: Polity Press.

Hicks, Robert L., Bradley C. Parks, J. Timmons Roberts, and Michael J. Tierney. 2008. *Greening Aid? Understanding the Environmental Impact of Development Assistance*. Oxford: Oxford University Press.

Hoffmann, Matthew J. 2011. *Climate Governance at the Crossroads: Experimenting with a Global Response After Kyoto*. Oxford: Oxford University Press.

Hofmann, Stephanie C. 2009. Overlapping Institutions in the Realm of International Security: The Case of NATO and ESDP. *Perspectives on Politics* 7, 1: 45–52.

Kahler, Miles. 2016. Complex Governance and the New Interdependence Approach. *Review of International Political Economy* 23 (5): 825–839.

Keohane, Robert O. 1984. After Hegemony: *Cooperation and Discord in the World Political Economy*. Princeton: Princeton University Press.

Keohane, Robert O. and David G. Victor. 2011. The Regime Complex for Climate Change. *Perspectives on Politics* 9 (1): 7–23.

——— 2013. The Transnational Politics of Energy. *Daedalus* 142 (1): 97–109.

Lesage, Dries, Thijs Van de Graaf, and Kirsten Westphal. 2010. *Global Energy Governance in a Multipolar World*. Farnham: Ashgate.

Moon, Suerie. 2013. WHO's Role in the Global Health System: What Can Be Learned from Global R&D Debates? *Public Health* 128 (2): 168–172.

Moon, Suerie, Nicole A. Szlezák, Catherine M. Michaud, Dean T. Jamison, Gerald T. Keusch, William C. Clark, and Barry R. Bloom. 2010. The Global Health System: Lessons for a Stronger Institutional Framework. *PLOS Medicine* 7: 1.

Morse, Julia C. and Robert O. Keohane. 2014. Contested Multilateralism. *Review of International Organizations* 9 (4): 385–412.

Nakhooda, Smita. 2011. The Multilateral Development Banks, Energy Governance, and Asia. *Global Policy* 2: 120–132.

Newell, Peter J. 2011. The Governance of Energy Finance: The Public, the Private and the Hybrid. *Global Policy* 2: 94–105.

Orsini, Amandine, Jean-Frédéric Morin, and Oran R. Young. 2013. Regime Complexes: A Buzz, a Boom, or a Boost for Global Governance? *Global Governance* 19 (1): 27–39.

Pattberg, Philipp H. 2007. *Private Institutions and Global Governance: The New Politics of Environmental Sustainability*. Cheltenham: Edward Elgar.

Pauwelyn, Joost, Ramses A. Wessel, and Jan Wouters, eds. 2012. *Informal International Lawmaking*. Oxford: Oxford University Press.

Prakash, Aseem and Matthew Potoski. 2006. *The Voluntary Environmentalists: Green Clubs, ISO 14001, and Voluntary Environmental Regulations*. Cambridge: Cambridge University Press.

Raustiala, Kal. 2016. Governing the Internet. *American Journal of International Law* 110 (3): 491–503.

Raustiala, Kal and David G. Victor. 2004. The Regime Complex for Plant Genetic Resources. *International Organization* 58 (2): 277–309.

REN21. 2015. *Renewables 2015 Global Status Report*. Paris: REN21.

Ruggie, John G. 2004. Reconstituting the Global Public Domain: Issues, Actors and Practices. *European Journal of International Relations* 10 (4): 499–531.

——— 2013. *Just Business: Multinational Corporations and Human Rights*. New York: W.W. Norton.

Schreurs, Miranda, Henrik Selin, and Stacy D. VanDeveer, eds. 2009. *Transatlantic Environment and Energy Politics: Comparative and International Perspectives*. Farnham: Ashgate.

Schröder, Miriam. 2012. Local Climate Governance in China: *Hybrid Actors and Market Mechanisms*. New York: Palgrave Macmillan.

Sending, Ole J. and Iver B. Neumann. 2006. Governance to Governmentality: Analyzing NGOs, States, and Power. *International Studies Quarterly* 50 (3): 651–672.

Slaughter, Anne-Marie. 2004. *A New World Order*. Princeton: Princeton University Press.

Stadelmann, Martin and Paula Castro. 2014. Climate Policy Innovation in the South: Domestic and International Determinants of Renewable Energy Policies in Developing and Emerging Countries. *Global Environmental Change* 29: 413–423.

Szulecki, Kacper, Philipp H. Pattberg, and Frank Biermann. 2011. Explaining Variation in the Effectiveness of Transnational Energy Partnerships. *Governance* 24 (4): 713–736.

Tallberg, Jonas, Thomas Sommerer, Theresa Swuatrito, and Christer Jönsson. 2013. The Opening Up of International Organizations: *Transnational Access in Global Governance*. Cambridge: Cambridge University Press.

Taplin, Ros and Jeffrey McGee. 2010. The Asia-Pacific Partnership: Implementation Challenges and Interplay with Kyoto. *Wiley Interdisciplinary Reviews: Climate Change* 1 (1): 16–21.

The Secretary-General's High-Level Group on Sustainable Energy for All. 2012. Sustainable Energy for All: a Global Action Agenda (April). www.seforall .org/sites/default/files/SEFA-Action-Agenda-Final.pdf.

UN General Assembly. 2011. General Assembly Resolution 65/151, *International Year of Sustainable Energy for All*, A/RES/65/151 (February 16, 2011).

   2012. General Assembly Resolution 67/314, *International Year of Sustainable Energy for All, 2012: Report of the Secretary-General*, A/RES/67/314 (August 16, 2012).

   2015. General Assembly Resolution 70/1, *Transforming Our World: The 2030 Agenda for Sustainable Development*, A/RES/70/1 (October 21, 2015).

UNEP DTU Partnership. 2019. CDM Projects by Type. http://cdmpipeline.org/ cdm-projects-type.htm#1.

Vabulas, Felicity and Duncan Snidal. 2013. Organization without Delegation: Informal Intergovernmental Organizations (IIGOs) and the Spectrum of Intergovernmental Arrangements. *The Review of International Organizations* 8 (2): 193–220.

Van de Graaf, Thijs. 2012. Obsolete or Resurgent? The International Energy Agency in a Changing Global Landscape. *Energy Policy* 48: 233–341.

   2013a. *The Politics and Institutions of Global Energy Governance*. New York: Palgrave Macmillan.

   2013b. Fragmentation in Global Energy Governance: Explaining the Creation of IRENA. *Global Environmental Governance* 13 (3): 14–33.

Wara, Michael and David G. Victor. 2008. A Realistic Policy on International Carbon Offsets. *PESD Working Paper 74*. Stanford, CA: Stanford University Press.

11   Legitimacy and Modes of Global Governance

Jonas Tallberg

The architecture of global governance has undergone profound changes in recent decades. On the one hand, states have continued to empower the hierarchical international organizations (IOs) that were established in the post-Second World War era and constitute the backbone of global governance.[1] While IOs no longer constitute the growth area in global governance, those that exist have been conferred ever more authority in an increasing range of policy domains. On the other hand, we have witnessed a proliferation of new modes of global governance, involving a shift toward network- and market-based organization.[2] Transgovernmental networks (TGNs), transnational hybrid institutions (THIs), and transnational private arrangements (TPAs) have emerged in a broad range of policy areas.[3] As a result, various forms of non-state actors have assumed a more prominent role in the governing of global concerns.[4] This chapter follows on from previous chapters in this volume that have documented this transformation in the architecture of global governance. Instead of offering further testimony of this trend, it explores one of its potential sources: the legitimacy of old and new forms of global governance. Specifically, it examines whether the gradual shift from hierarchical IOs and toward TGNs, THIs, and TPAs could be explained by a decline in the legitimacy for old-style governance and the promise of higher legitimacy for new-style governance. Legitimacy is understood here as the perception or belief within a given audience that an

Deborah Avant, Michael Barnett, Lisa Dellmuth, Kal Raustiala, Jon C.W. Pevehouse, Jan Aart Scholte, and Soetkin Verhaegen have all provided very helpful comments on earlier drafts of this chapter. In addition, I am indebted to Karin Sundström and Soetkin Verhaegen for invaluable assistance with public and elite survey data. Finally, I would like to thank Riksbankens Jubileumsfond (Grant M15–0048:1) for generous financial support.
[1]   Hooghe et al. 2017; Zürn 2018.
[2]   Slaughter 2005; Kahler 2009; Avant et al. 2010; Weiss and Wilkinson 2014; Kelley and Simmons 2015; Introduction.
[3]   As documented in Chapters 3, 6, and 10, for instance.
[4]   Tallberg et al. 2014; Andonova 2019.

institution's authority is appropriately exercised.[5] Legitimacy in this sociological sense is an attribute of an institution, based on audience beliefs, and may vary over time and across audiences. This chapter examines the perceived legitimacy of old and new modes of governance among both publics and elites, mapping their degrees of confidence in global institutions across time and space.

The chapter suggests that legitimacy concerns are of limited importance in explaining the shift toward newer modes of global governance. It arrives at this conclusion in three steps. First, it shows how legitimacy concerns feature as a causal mechanism in prominent accounts of the transformation of global governance. Explanations highlighting geopolitical shifts, changing governance norms, and domestic backlash to globalization all suggest that concerns with the legitimacy of liberal hierarchical IOs help to drive the development toward alternative forms of governance. Second, it draws on public and elite opinion data to assess empirically (1) whether the perceived legitimacy of traditional IOs is in decline and (2) whether new-style governance is considered more legitimate than old-style governance. It finds mixed support for the first expectation and no support for the second. Third, it discusses potential reasons why the legitimacy of traditional IOs appears to hold up well in comparison to TGNs, THIs, and TPAs. Specifically, it highlights institutional reforms to IOs that may have helped to defuse legitimacy concerns, the limitations of new-style institutions in meeting societal standards of appropriate governance, and the role of heuristics in the formation of legitimacy beliefs among citizens and elites.

Why Legitimacy Might Drive New Modes of Governance

In the Introduction to this volume, Barnett, Pevehouse, and Raustiala identify potential sources of the shift toward new modes of global governance. A decline in the legitimacy of traditional hierarchical IOs does not feature explicitly among these structural drivers. Yet legitimacy concerns are arguably an integral part of why some of these factors would propel a shift toward network- and market-based global governance. In this section, I suggest that arguments emphasizing geopolitical shifts, changing governance norms, and domestic backlash to globalization rely

---

[5] E.g., Weber 1978 [1922]; Suchman 1995; Hurd 2007; Tallberg et al. 2018; Tallberg and Zürn 2019. This sociological conception of legitimacy is different from a normative understanding, where an institution's legitimacy is derived from its conformance to philosophical values such as justice and democracy (Buchanan and Keohane 2006).

partly on legitimacy as a causal mechanism, linking structural change and governance transformation.

Geopolitical Shifts

Existing scholarship on geopolitical shifts and global governance frequently accords legitimacy considerations an important theoretical role.[6] According to the conventional story, the USA and its allies successfully constructed a liberal international order in the aftermath of the Second World War. The core of this liberal order comprised a number of hierarchically organized IOs, among them the International Monetary Fund (IMF), the World Bank, the General Agreement on Tariffs and Trade (GATT), and the United Nations (UN). These IOs were structured to favor the interests of the Western powers both in terms of procedural rules and substantive policies. Procedurally they institutionalized inequalities by giving the Western powers particular advantages in decision-making. The IMF and the World Bank distributed voting power based on capital contributions, the UN granted exclusive veto power to five great powers, and the GATT informally relied on agreements between the USA and Europe. Substantively these IOs tended to pursue policy agendas aligned with Western liberal ideals of free trade, human rights, and liberalization. This liberal international order reached its climax in the 1990s, when the Western powers, inspired by the end of the Cold War, moved to expand the North Atlantic Treaty Organization (NATO) and the European Union (EU), create the International Criminal Court (ICC), and introduce norms such as responsibility to protect, human security, and sustainable development.

With the ascent of the rising powers the legitimacy of this international order has been called into question. What may have appeared as a legitimate system in times of Western dominance is increasingly seen as biased, unjust, and unreflective of economic and political realities. The distribution of capabilities has fundamentally shifted in favor of the rising powers, while the USA and its allies are in relative decline, economically, demographically, and militarily. This shift in geopolitical weight has gone hand in hand with demands for greater representation, influence, and recognition in global governance. At the forefront of these demands are the BRICS – Brazil, Russia, India, China, and South Africa – but other regional powers also call for greater voice.

---

[6] Morse and Keohane 2014; Ikenberry 2018; Zürn 2018; Stephen and Zürn 2019.

According to this account the challenges to the prevailing order are intimately bound up with the question of legitimacy. "[T]he crisis of the liberal order is a crisis of legitimacy and social purpose," argues Ikenberry.[7] Similarly, Stephen submits that: "The legitimacy of the rules and leadership roles of global governance is in dispute."[8] Contributions typically highlight how the existing order is criticized as illegitimate, leading to demands for fairer representation on governing bodies. For instance, regional powers without permanent seats call for institutional reforms that would make the UN Security Council (UNSC) more legitimate. China demands a recalibration of the system of voting weights in the IMF and the World Bank. Brazil and India request to become part of the core negotiating group of the World Trade Organization (WTO), previously restricted to the USA, the EU, Japan, and Canada. According to one interpretation these demands in themselves reflect the declining perceived legitimacy for the hierarchical IOs at the core of the liberal international order.[9] When criticizing these IOs the emerging powers demonstrate their lack of faith in the current system of governance. According to another interpretation these challenges rather amount to deliberate efforts at delegitimation, designed to put moral pressure on the current power holders of these IOs for purposes of achieving a rebalancing of privileges.[10]

On this view the geopolitical shift, through its effects on legitimacy, has produced a number of consequences for the architecture of global governance. When the incumbent powers heed demands for more equitable representation the result is institutional reforms to existing hierarchical IOs.[11] Such reforms are often interpreted as attempts at relegitimation intended to shore up support for an organization.[12] Examples include the rebalancing of voting weights in the IMF and the marginal reforms to the UNSC. Other adaptations to the geopolitical shift entail a step away from the traditional IOs of the post-Second World War era and toward greater complexity in global governance. One of the most significant trends is the growing informalization of cooperation, both in terms of country groupings and negotiated agreements.[13] For instance, the G7 has been supplemented by the G20 to accommodate demands from regional powers for representation on this informal TGN. Moreover, rising powers are forming informal clubs of their own, including the BRICS Forum, the IBSA (India, Brazil, South Africa) Dialogue Forum, and the BASIC

---

[7] Ikenberry 2018, 19.   [8] Stephen 2017, 483.
[9] Ikenberry 2018; Stephen and Zürn 2019.
[10] Binder and Heupel 2015; Kruck and Zangl 2020.   [11] Zangl et al. 2016; Lipscy 2017.
[12] Zürn 2018; Tallberg and Zürn 2019.   [13] Vabulas and Snidal 2013; Stephen 2017.

(Brazil, South Africa, India, China) bloc. The effect is a layering of global governance, where new-style network institutions coexist and sometimes build upon old-style hierarchical IOs.[14]

Changing Governance Norms

A second structural argument granting legitimacy a causal role highlights historical shifts in governance norms. According to this argument the dominant ideologies of governance have undergone important change in recent decades, altering the standards of what is perceived as legitimate forms of global governance. This shift in governance norms has put pressure on traditional hierarchical IOs, which have sought to adapt to this new normative landscape through institutional reforms, and stimulated new modes of global governance, constitutively more in line with the new standards of appropriateness.

On this view the traditional hierarchical IOs were established in a period when the prevailing governance norm prescribed pursuit of collective welfare through state-based cooperation. Consistent with this norm, IOs were organized as forums for intergovernmental negotiation, assisted by Weberian international bureaucracies, and infused with ambitions of technocratic problem-solving.[15] The legitimacy of IOs in this period was best described as output-based, resting on these organizations' capacity to produce collective benefits for states and societies.[16] With the end of the Cold War the dominant governance norm began to change. The combination of two factors helped to drive this development: the third wave of democratization and the growing authority of IOs. The effect was a shift in the societal norms used to evaluate the legitimacy of global governance, away from technocratic performance and toward democratic procedure.

On the one hand, the third wave of democratization helped to elevate democratic standards as governance norms. The end of the Cold War brought widespread democratization of former authoritarian states in Central and Eastern Europe as well as other areas of the world.[17] Illustrating the general burst of optimism about liberal democracy at the time, Fukuyama famously spoke of "the universalization of Western liberal democracy as the final form of human governance."[18] This upgrading of democratic norms at the domestic level had knock-on

---

[14] Stephen 2017; Zürn 2018, chapter 7.
[15] Barnett and Finnemore 2004; Rittberger et al. 2012.
[16] Scharpf 1999; Buchanan and Keohane 2006.   [17] Gleditsch and Ward 2008.
[18] Fukuyama 1992, 3.

consequences for the standards used to evaluate the appropriateness of global governance. While democratic standards of participation, accountability, and transparency historically had taken a back seat in the justification of IO policy-making, such concerns now gained in importance as liberal states sought to extend abroad the ideals to which they adhered domestically.[19] Some even suggest that democracy became the new gold standard of global governance.[20]

On the other hand, the growth in IO authority challenged the conventional understanding of these organizations as intergovernmental negotiation machineries, consistent with state consent, national sovereignty, and domestic democratic control. In a dual move away from the intergovernmental ideal type, supranational bodies within IOs had been delegated ever more authority, while interstate decision-making increasingly took place through procedures that pooled authority at the expense of national autonomy.[21] The quintessential example was the EU, but the trend extended well into the broader population of hierarchical IOs. Yet, as IOs gained greater authority at the expense of national governments, producing collective benefits gradually came to be seen as an insufficient basis for the legitimacy of these organizations. Instead, being perceived to satisfy democratic criteria of decision-making was regarded as increasingly central for IOs.[22] While the term "democratic deficit" hardly existed in the 1980s, it became a prominent way of characterizing and criticizing traditional IOs from the 1990s onwards.[23]

In this perspective, the shift from technocratic performance to democratic procedure as a governance norm helps to explain recent changes in the nature of global governance. Recognizing the shift in societal norms, actors have sought to move toward institutional designs that allow them to claim legitimacy. On the one hand, hierarchical IOs have engaged in institutional reforms that introduce stronger elements of democratic procedure. A growing number of IOs have established international parliamentary institutions, opened up policy-making to civil society actors, strengthened accountability mechanisms, and introduced transparency policies.[24] While strongest in IOs dominated by democracies, these trends extend to organizations whose memberships are authoritarian, pointing to the strong impact of externally legitimated models.

---

[19] Risse-Kappen 1996; Moravcsik 1997; Tallberg et al. 2016.
[20] Held 1995; Bodansky 1999.   [21] Hooghe et al. 2017; Zürn 2018.
[22] Scharpf 1999.
[23] Dahl 1999; O'Brien et al. 2000; Zürn 2000; Norris 2011; Binder and Heupel 2015; Dingwerth et al. 2019.
[24] Grigorescu 2007, 2010; Tallberg et al. 2013, 2014; Rittberger and Schroeder 2016; Rocabert et al. 2019.

On the other hand, state and non-state actors have negotiated new forms of global governance that aim to be more participatory by construction. Notably, multi-stakeholder partnerships have emerged as an alternative model, often seen to hold the promise of greater legitimacy (and effectiveness) due to its network construction, involving both state and non-state actors.[25] These new modes aim to meet democratic governance norms, not through old-style state representation but through stakeholder engagement and non-electoral forms of accountability.

Domestic Backlash to Globalization

A third structural argument in which legitimacy features prominently as a causal mechanism is that of a domestic backlash to globalization. According to this argument globalization has brought about new economic and political cleavages at the domestic level, which anti-globalist political entrepreneurs have exploited to breed discontent with existing global governance arrangements.[26] The most prominent expression of this backlash is the recent populist surge in Europe, the USA, and elsewhere, involving a rejection of IOs as expressions of a global faceless elite. Another example is the backlash in many countries against international courts, increasingly seen to interfere with national sovereignty.[27] In this explanation legitimacy concerns are at the core of the shift toward alternative forms of governance, or away from global cooperation altogether.

The deeper roots of the domestic backlash are usually sought in globalization's consequences for economic distribution and cultural values.[28] On the one hand, economic globalization and specialization have fundamentally transformed societies, leaving some segments more economically insecure even when benefiting countries as a whole. On the other hand, societal transformations that brought about a cultural shift among the younger and more educated toward post-materialist values, such as environmental protection, gender equality, and multiculturalism, clashed with more traditional values in older and less educated groups. To these economic and cultural processes, commonly emphasized in work on populism, should be added the expanding authority of IOs themselves, whose policies increasingly reach behind borders and impact core areas of state sovereignty.[29]

---

[25] Benner et al. 2004; Bäckstrand 2008; Andonova 2019.   [26] Hooghe et al. 2019.
[27] Alter et al. 2016; Voeten 2020.   [28] Inglehart and Norris 2017.
[29] Hooghe et al. 2017; Zürn 2018.

According to this narrative IOs have long profited from a state of "permissive consensus," in which populations enjoyed the fruits of cooperation and supported its broad goals but took little interest in the process as such.[30] With the impact of globalization and the rising power of IOs this consensus has given way to a state of "constraining dissensus," in which international issues are divisive and the legitimacy of cooperation itself is increasingly called into question.[31] Global governance is no longer a distant process of generally positive outcomes but a subject of domestic partisan contestation. As Hooghe et al. put it, global governance is now embedded in partisan conflict: "Counter-movements of leftists and nationalists have been at the forefront in challenging the legitimacy of IOs. Opposition began on the left, though in most recent years it has been strongest among nationalists who frame their opposition to international governance as defense of the nation against transnational influences, above all immigrants."[32]

In this new setting IOs are targeted by populists as proxy representatives of an otherwise faceless process of economic and cultural globalization, but also as contributors to these processes through the impact of their policies. The examples of populist leaders on the right and the left who pursue agendas of anti-globalism are manifold. Then US President Donald Trump challenged the authority of the WTO, took the USA out of the Paris Agreement on climate change, questioned transatlantic security cooperation within NATO, and vowed to take the USA out of the World Health Organization (WHO). Marine Le Pen, leader of the French far-right party Rassemblement National, declared globalization her enemy number one in the presidential election of 2017.[33] Michael Gove, then justice secretary and leading advocate for Brexit, criticized the EU for being "distant, unaccountable, and elitist," before famously adding that "this country has had enough of experts from organizations with acronyms."[34] Rodrigo Duterte, president of the Philippines, has countered international criticism by claiming the UN to be worthless and by threatening to pull the country out of the organization.[35] Attacking IOs from the left, Yanis Varoufakis as Greek finance minister submitted: "What [the EU and IMF] are doing with Greece has a name: terrorism."[36]

On this perspective the populist challenge has already contributed to changing the nature of global governance. The consequences are particularly negative for the traditional hierarchical IOs, whose political

---

[30] Lindberg and Scheingold 1970.   [31] Hooghe and Marks 2009.
[32] Hooghe et al. 2019.   [33] *Politico*, February 5, 2017.   [34] *Sky News*, June 3, 2016.
[35] BBC, August 21, 2016.   [36] *The Guardian*, July 7, 2015.

authority and contributions to transnational exchange have made them especially unpopular. Several IOs face withdrawals or threats thereof, including the EU, the ICC, the UN Human Rights Council, the United Framework Convention on Climate Change (UNFCCC), and WHO. Other IOs become subject to renegotiation of foundational rules, such as the North American Free Trade Agreement, or efforts at undermining their authority, such as the WTO. The beneficiaries of this trend remain to be identified but could potentially include more market- or network-based forms of global governance. The strategies of the Trump administration and the British government following Brexit appeared to strengthen an already ongoing development toward a bilateralization of global governance.[37] Likewise, the growing prominence of market-based ratings and rankings, also as governance tools of conventional IOs, could reflect an effort to move toward governance forms perceived as less intrusive and more legitimate.[38]

Legitimacy in Global Governance: The Empirical Record

In the previous section I suggested that legitimacy concerns feature as a causal mechanism in some of the most prominent efforts at explaining the shift toward new modes of global governance. Geopolitical shifts, new governance norms, and domestic backlash to globalization are structural changes whose consequences for global governance are partly expected to work through their effects on legitimacy. In this section I discuss these expectations in light of the empirical record. In focus are two observable implications. First, we would expect to observe a steady decline in the legitimacy of traditional hierarchical IOs over time, as these structural changes challenge the perceived appropriateness of these organizations. Second, we would expect to see new forms of global governance being awarded greater legitimacy than old conventional IOs, since they partly grow out of efforts to meet these legitimacy challenges. The empirical answer is tentative, as data limitations restrict the scope of comparisons over time and across institutions. Yet the available evidence suggests a picture that is partly different than the one expected. While there are some indications that traditional hierarchical IOs have witnessed declining legitimacy over time, those are not conclusive. In addition, traditional hierarchical IOs appear to enjoy more legitimacy on average than new modes of global governance.

---

[37] Baccini and Dür 2014.   [38] Kelley and Simmons 2015.

In line with a growing body of research in comparative politics and international relations, I rely on survey data and people's confidence or trust in institutions as a way of capturing legitimacy beliefs.[39] This operationalization is anchored in systems theory, which conceives of legitimacy as the reservoir of confidence in a political system, independent of short-term satisfaction with its distributional outcomes.[40] Different from some alternative operationalizations of legitimacy, it has the advantage of not integrating into the measure (1) potential sources of legitimacy, such as fairness or effectiveness or (2) potential consequences of legitimacy, such as compliance or protest. For data I consult established large-scale surveys of public opinion, but also a new and unique survey of elite opinion on global governance. The combination of public and elite opinion data helps to capture legitimacy beliefs among the multiple audiences of global governance.

Declining Legitimacy for Traditional IOs?

To begin with I explore over-time patterns in the perceived legitimacy of traditional hierarchical IOs. Unfortunately survey data exist only for a limited number of IOs, and then often in a non-comparable format, which helps to explain the dearth of systematic comparative research on the legitimacy of global governance institutions.[41] The World Values Survey (WVS) measures public opinion toward a number of IOs, but the organizations covered vary across survey waves, as do the countries included. Regional surveys, such as the Eurobarometer, Latinobarometer, and Afrobarometer, typically only cover attitudes toward a specific regional IO. I therefore choose to focus on the two IOs for which we have the most extensive and complete time-series – the UN and the EU. While these two IOs cannot be taken to represent the full population of organizations, they are probably the most prominent IOs in global and regional governance, respectively. In addition, they are among the traditional IOs enjoying the highest level of authority and most often claimed to suffer from legitimacy deficits.[42] If the legitimacy of hierarchical IOs is in steady decline, this is where we would expect to see it.

Starting with the UN, Figure 11.1 shows the extent to which citizens have had a great deal or quite a lot of confidence in this IO over the time

---

[39] E.g., Newton and Norris 2001; Inglehart and Welzel 2005; Johnson 2011; Voeten 2013; Dellmuth and Tallberg 2015.
[40] Easton 1975, 447.   [41] Dellmuth 2018.
[42] Hurd 2007; Binder and Heupel 2015; Scharpf 1999; Lord and Beetham 2001.

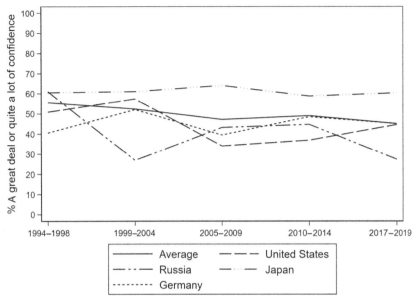

Figure 11.1 Confidence in the UN, 1994–2019.

Note: Author's presentation based on data from WVS waves 3–7. Countries included in the calculation of the average confidence in the UN are those in which the question was asked in all five waves: Argentina, Belarus, Chile, Estonia, Germany, Japan, Mexico, Peru, Poland, Romania, Russia, Slovenia, South Korea, Spain, Sweden, Turkey, and the United States. The figure uses sampling (probability) weights. Observations are weighted to correct for within-country imbalances. The graph for the average confidence uses data weighted to correct for differences in sample size but not for population size.

period 1994–2019, based on survey waves 3–7 of the WVS. The solid line captures the average confidence in the UN among respondents in the seventeen countries for which this question was asked in all five waves. It suggests that the perceived legitimacy of the UN among citizens in this diverse group of countries has declined slightly over time. While 56 percent of all respondents had a great deal or quite a lot of confidence in the UN at the beginning of the observation period, that figure was 45 percent at the end of the period. However, the over-time trend is quite sensitive to the countries included in the sample. Among the seventeen countries included (simply because they are available) are several that experienced very dramatic drops over this period, such as Belarus (from 71 to 50 percent), Estonia (from 70 to 52), Mexico (from 51 to 38), Peru (from 52 to 34), and Russia (from 61 to 27). It is also revealing to compare the figures for the UN to the average confidence in the national government in these seventeen countries, which was consistently lower throughout the observation period (not shown). Citizens thus appear to perceive the UN as more legitimate than their respective national governments.

Disaggregating confidence in the UN by country reveals interesting variation. Figure 11.1 shows the extent to which citizens in four specific countries have had a great deal or quite a lot of confidence in the UN over this period. These countries consist of two major powers with permanent seats on the UNSC (Russia and the USA) and two regional powers without permanent seats on the UNSC (Germany and Japan), both of whom have actively demanded reform of the UNSC. Comparing the start and end points of the observation period shows that confidence in the UN over these two decades has increased somewhat in Germany, remained stable in Japan, decreased slightly in the USA, and decreased significantly in Russia. This pattern offers limited support for the expectation that regional powers without a prominent voice in existing hierarchical IOs are generally dissatisfied with those organizations, while incumbent powers remain committed to their organizations of dominance.[43]

Shifting to the EU, Figure 11.2 shows the extent to which citizens tend to trust this regional IO over the time period 2003 to 2019, based on Eurobarometer data. The solid line captures the average level of trust in the EU in all member states. It indicates that trust in the EU has varied somewhat over time, but is almost the same at the start and the end of the observation period. The same pattern exists over an even longer time period (1973–2019) if we rely on support for membership as an alternative measure of legitimacy beliefs (not shown). Figure 11.2 shows that trust in the EU rose from an average of 52 percent in 2003 to 61 percent in 2007. It then declined during the financial crisis to a level of 34 percent before it turned upward again from 2013, reaching 49 percent in 2019. There is no evidence of a persistent downward trajectory indicative of a growing legitimacy deficit, as suggested by accounts emphasizing changing governance norms and domestic backlash to globalization. Yet, if observers diagnosed the legitimacy of the EU based on the trend during the recent financial crisis, the conclusion may understandably have been negative. The stability of public opinion toward the EU is one of the principal conclusions from the voluminous literature on this topic.[44] As in the case of the UN, citizens in EU member states on average tend to have less trust in their national governments than in the IO (not shown).

---

[43] See also Tallberg and Verhaegen 2020.
[44] Hooghe and Marks 2005; Hobolt and de Vries 2016.

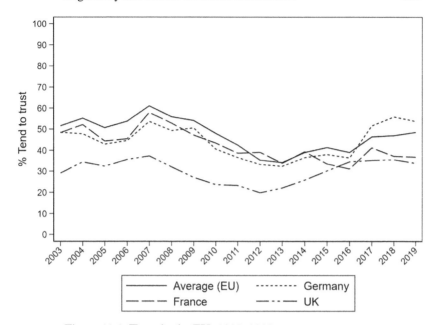

Figure 11.2 Trust in the EU, 2003–2019.
Note: Author's presentation based on data from the Eurobarometer no. 59–91
(2003–spring 2019). The average confidence in the EU is calculated based on
public opinion in all member states of the IO at any given point in time. The
figure uses sampling (probability) weights. The data for France, Germany, and
the UK are weighted using national weights, using the special weights for a
unified UK (up until the fall of 2018, after which there is no separate sample for
Northern Ireland) and Germany, and the standard national weight for France.
The data for the average confidence among EU citizens use the appropriate
population weights (EU factor).

Figure 11.2 also disaggregates the group of member states to explore
potential variation among the EU's major powers – France, Germany,
and the UK. It shows that trust in the EU in France and Germany has
largely followed the same trajectory over time and stayed close to the EU
average, with the exception of the last five years of the observation period
when French public opinion turned more negative and German public
opinion more positive than the EU average. As could be expected, trust
in the EU has been considerably lower in the UK during the entire time
period, highlighting the type of legitimacy challenge that brought about
the vote to leave the EU in 2016.

Summing up, public opinion data on the UN and the EU lend mixed
support to the expectation of a growing legitimacy deficit for traditional
hierarchical IOs over the past two decades. While there has been a

decline in legitimacy over time for the UN, this picture is sensitive to the countries included in the analysis. In the case of the EU, legitimacy has been relatively stable over time. In addition, both IOs appear to enjoy greater legitimacy than national governments in the member states.

Higher Legitimacy for New Modes of Governance?

As a second step I explore whether new modes of global governance enjoy higher levels of legitimacy than old-style hierarchical IOs. For this purpose I turn to novel findings from a recently concluded elite opinion survey. While public opinion surveys are useful for capturing broad trends in the popular legitimacy of select IOs they leave out newer modes of network- and market-based global governance. Part of the reason may be the suspicion than citizens at large are less informed about these newer types of governance. Surveying elite opinion allows us to move past this limitation since political and societal elites presumably are more aware of new modes of global governance. In addition, surveying elites has the advantage of tapping the legitimacy perceptions of the actors involved in the design of global institutions, as well as the actual global governing.

For data I rely on the LegGov Elite Survey conducted in the period 2017–2019.[45] This survey conceptualized elites as people holding leading positions in key organizations in society that strive to be politically influential. The survey covered 860 elite respondents in six elite sectors: partisan-political, bureaucratic, civil society, media, research, and business. The survey targeted elites in six countries – Brazil, Germany, the Philippines, Russia, South Africa, and the USA – comprising both incumbent and rising powers. In addition, it surveyed elites in the same elite sectors at the global level (e.g., staff of IOs, international nongovernmental organizations (NGOs), and multinational corporations). The survey covered elite opinions on twelve global governance institutions that vary in terms of organizational type – IOs, TGNs, THIs, and TPAs – and governance field: economic governance, sustainable development governance, and security and human rights governance.[46] This allows for a comparison between traditional IOs and new forms of governance in each of the three governance fields.

Specifically, the survey asked elites about their confidence in the following hierarchical IOs: the UN, the IMF, the ICC, the World

---

[45] For more information on survey and sample design, see Verhaegen et al. 2019.
[46] In addition the survey covered eight regional institutions.

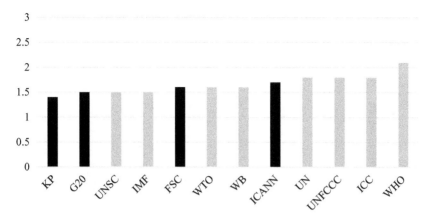

Figure 11.3 Elite confidence in IOs and new forms of governance.
Source: LegGov Elite Survey
Note: Gray bars indicate IOs and black bars non-IOs. Scale ranges from "a great deal of confidence" (3) to "quite a lot of confidence" (2), "not very much confidence" (1), and "no confidence at all" (0). $N_{Total} = 860$; $N_{Brazil} = 124$; $N_{Germany} = 123$; $N_{Philippines} = 122$; $N_{Russia} = 108$; $N_{South\ Africa} = 123$; $N_{USA} = 122$; $N_{Global} = 138$.

Bank, the WHO, the WTO, the UNFCCC, and the UNSC.[47] Additionally, it asked respondents about their confidence in four global institutions representative of new modes of governance: the G20, the Internet Corporation for Assigned Names and Numbers (ICANN), the Forest Stewardship Council (FSC), and the Kimberley Process (KP). The G20 is a transgovernmental network founded in 2008 that brings together the leaders of the twenty most powerful countries in the world. ICANN is a transnational private arrangement established in 1998 to regulate critical aspects of global Internet infrastructure. The FSC, too, is transnational private arrangement, founded in 1993 and well known for its sustainability certification of timber products. The KP, finally, is a transnational hybrid institution initiated in 2000, which brings together public and private actors in a cooperative process to stop trade in "conflict diamonds."

Figure 11.3 shows the average level of elite confidence in each of the twelve institutions, divided into old and new types of global governance. It reveals that elites tend to have slightly more confidence in traditional hierarchical IOs than in institutions representing new modes of global

---

[47] The UNSC was included next to the UN in order to assess if opinions toward this UN body differed from general opinions toward the UN as a whole, given the institutionalized power disparities and absent reforms of the UNSC.

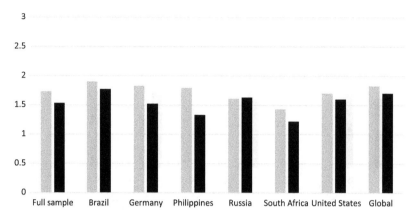

Figure 11.4 Elite confidence by country: IOs versus new forms
of governance.

Source: LegGov Elite Survey

Note: Gray bars indicate IOs and black bars non-IOs. Scale ranges from "a great
deal of confidence" (3) to "quite a lot of confidence" (2), "not very much
confidence" (1), and "no confidence at all" (0). N_{Total} = 860; N_{Brazil} = 124;
$N_{Germany}$ = 123; $N_{Philippines}$ = 122; N_{Russia} = 108; $N_{South\ Africa}$ = 123;
N_{USA} = 122; N_{Global} = 138.

governance. The WHO is accorded the highest confidence among elites
by some margin, followed by the ICC, the UNFCCC, and the UN at
about the same level. The middle of the field consists of the two traditional economic IOs – the World Bank and the WTO – as well as two
non-IOs with relatively high levels of confidence: ICANN and the FSC.
Elites have least confidence in the IMF, the UNSC, the G20, and the
KP. It cannot be excluded that another and richer selection of non-IO
institutions would have yielded higher levels of confidence for this
category. Yet, at a minimum, this pattern questions the idea that newer
modes of global governance enjoy greater legitimacy than traditional
hierarchical IOs, which would explain a shift toward TGNs, THIs, and
TPAs in global governance.

Figure 11.4 disaggregates elite confidence in IOs and non-IOs by
country. It shows that elites in different countries and at the global level to
a large extent agree in their assessments of the legitimacy of global governance institutions. With one exception, elites in all geographical samples have
more confidence in traditional hierarchical IOs than in new institutional
forms of global governance. The exception is Russia, where elites have as
much confidence in non-IOs as they have in IOs. Yet, across the full
sample, the difference between IOs and non-IOs is statistically significant.

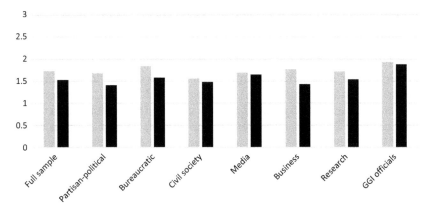

Figure 11.5 Elite confidence by sector: IOs versus new forms
of governance.
Source: LegGov Elite Survey
Note: Gray bars indicate IOs and black bars non-IOs. Scale ranges from "a great
deal of confidence" (3) to "quite a lot of confidence" (2), "not very much
confidence" (1), and "no confidence at all" (0). $N_{Total} = 860$; $N_{Brazil} = 124$;
$N_{Germany} = 123$; $N_{Philippines} = 122$; $N_{Russia} = 108$; $N_{South\ Africa} = 123$;
$N_{USA} = 122$; $N_{Global} = 138$.

Neither is the Russian case indicative of a more general pattern of relatively
higher confidence in new forms of governance among rising powers compared to the incumbent powers of the liberal international order. Excluding
Russia, the differential between IOs and non-IOs is lowest among US elites
and highest among Philippine elites.

Figure 11.5 disaggregates confidence in IOs and non-IOs by elite
sector. It shows that elites in all sectors on average have more confidence
in IOs than in institutions representing new modes of governance. The
differential is largest for bureaucratic and business elites and smallest for
media and civil society elites as well as elites working for global
governance institutions.

To sum up, elite opinion data do not support the expectation that new
modes of global governance enjoy higher levels of legitimacy than old-
style hierarchical IOs. In fact the reverse appears to hold true for the
twelve institutions examined here: elites tend to have more confidence in
IOs than in non-IOs.

What Explains the Resilient Legitimacy of Old Modes of Governance?

While geopolitical shifts, new governance norms, and domestic backlash
to globalization would lead us to expect declining legitimacy for

traditional hierarchical IOs, this does not appear to be the dominant empirical pattern. What can explain this disjuncture between established expectations and empirical realities? Why is the legitimacy of old-style IOs holding up fairly well, even among citizens and elites in rising powers, while new-style institutions confront problems in winning the hearts and minds of audiences? In this section I suggest three complementary explanations for this puzzle, focused on (1) institutional reforms to traditional IOs, (2) limitations of new modes of global governance, and (3) audiences' use of heuristics when forming legitimacy beliefs.

Institutional Reforms to Traditional IOs

The first explanation suggests that traditional IOs have adapted to structural changes in world politics and thereby managed to maintain legitimacy among audiences. Rather than remaining passive in the face of geopolitical shifts, new governance norms, and domestic backlash, IOs have undertaken reforms aimed at addressing these challenges. What we are observing in terms of sustained legitimacy is the fruit of those labors.

This explanation builds on the premise that audiences care about institutional form in global governance and reward IOs that meet standards which audiences value. Recent research offers some support for this assumption. For instance, survey experiments demonstrate that citizens award IOs with greater legitimacy when these organizations are inclusive, transparent, fair, and effective, while they punish IOs that are characterized by the opposite.[48] Similarly, a recent study shows that elites are more likely to consider an IO to be legitimate when they perceive its processes and outcomes as democratic, fair, and effective.[49] It is therefore plausible to imagine that audiences have responded positively to the string of institutional reforms that IOs have undertaken since the end of the Cold War. Since elites are likely more aware than citizens about such institutional reforms, we can expect this explanation to be more relevant for elite compared to citizen perceptions of IO legitimacy.

In terms of responding to geopolitical shifts, IOs have in several cases sought to accommodate demands from rising powers for greater influence, representation, and recognition.[50] The IMF has adjusted its voting shares to better reflect the relative economic weight of member countries, answering to demands from China especially, but also from other BRICS countries. In the WTO the core negotiating group (the Quad) has been

---

[48] Bernauer and Gampfer 2013; Anderson et al. 2019; Bernauer et al. 2020; Dellmuth et al. 2019.
[49] Verhaegen et al. 2021.   [50] Zangl et al. 2016; Lipscy 2017; Kruck and Zangl 2020.

extended from the USA, the EU, Japan, and Canada to also include Brazil and India, following intense pressure. All major Western powers except the USA and Japan have joined the Asian Infrastructure Investment Bank as a complement to the Asian Development Bank and the World Bank. The UNFCCC continues to take decisions through consensus and to structure obligations such that developing countries shoulder a smaller burden. The notorious exception to this pattern is the UNSC, although it should be recalled that this body already grants special status to two rising powers (China and Russia) and denies this privilege to prominent incumbent powers of the liberal international order (Germany and Japan).

The responses of traditional IOs to changing governance norms are even more far-reaching. Over the past two decades old-style IOs have been refitted for new procedural standards, including transparency, participation, and accountability. These reforms have in many cases been explicitly driven by a desire to legitimize IOs in light of new governance norms and growing societal contestation.[51] IOs have seriously expanded the institutional opportunities for civil society actors to participate in policy-making.[52] Many IOs have also adopted public information policies that expand transparency and instituted novel accountability procedures.[53] In addition, a growing number of IOs have sought to strengthen democratic representation through the creation of international parliamentary assemblies.[54]

At this point in time it is more difficult to identify corresponding reforms aimed at defusing the consequences for IOs of domestic backlash to globalization. In many respects the populist backlash targets the very raison d'être of authoritative IOs, making it more difficult to respond to this type of challenge. However, there is an important nuance to consider between left-wing and right-wing populist critique of IOs. While left-wing populists typically accept the need for IOs but criticize their distributive consequences, right-wing populists reject IO authority in principle.[55] In this perspective, efforts by the IMF in recent years to acknowledge its historical mistakes and reorient its policies toward a stronger emphasis on inequality reduction could potentially be interpreted as a strategy to maintain legitimacy.

Limitations of New Modes of Global Governance

The second explanation suggests that the limitations of new modes of global governance can help to account for the relatively higher legitimacy

---

[51] Steffek et al. 2008; Zürn 2018; Dingwerth et al. 2019; Tallberg and Zürn 2019.
[52] Tallberg et al. 2013.   [53] Grigorescu 2007, 2010.   [54] Rocabert et al. 2019.
[55] Hooghe et al. 2019.

of traditional IOs compared to TGNs, THIs, and TPAs. We may conceive of these limitations in terms of procedure and performance, both of which are qualities of global governance institutions that audiences care about.[56] On the procedural side, new modes of global governance may sometimes be worse positioned than traditional IOs in meeting standards embraced in society. While new-style institutions often trumpet their strengths relative to IOs in terms of integrating expertise, promoting efficiency, and expanding stakeholder participation, their organizational form simultaneously comes at a cost. The shift from hierarchy to network as the organizing principle makes it more difficult to ensure proper accountability and equal representation.[57] Internal accountability is a well-known challenge for institutions that operate without designated (member state) principals, leading to efforts at securing accountability externally vis-à-vis a more diffuse cast of stakeholders.[58] Similarly, the greater inclusion of private actors in governing automatically raises questions about the democratic status of these actors and the principles of representation.[59]

On the performance side, new modes of global governance may face particular challenges when taking on governance gaps left behind by traditional IOs. According to one proposition, new modes of global governance have grown out of difficulties for hierarchical IOs in tackling more wicked policy problems.[60] While the traditional IOs effectively picked off the low-hanging fruit in the second half of the twentieth century they have since encountered more difficult problems, which they have been unable to settle with the same success. Born out of efforts to address these problems new modes of global governance face a more difficult task. On the one hand, the problems they take on may be less amenable to simple solutions. On the other hand, their looser organizational form may partly reflect an unwillingness among states to invest in institutional solutions that are more politically costly.

The Role of Heuristics

A third reason why the legitimacy of conventional IOs may hold up well relative to that of new forms of governance is the role of heuristics in opinion formation. Public opinion scholars have long argued that most citizens have low-quality opinions and therefore rely on cognitive heuristics to help them form attitudes toward political institutions.[61]

---

[56] Bernauer et al. 2020; Dellmuth et al. 2019.   [57] Bernstein 2011; Scholte 2011.
[58] Grant and Keohane 2005.   [59] Bexell et al. 2010.   [60] Introduction.
[61] Mondak 1993; Chong and Druckman 2007.

A heuristic is a cognitive problem-solving strategy (or mental shortcut) that allows an individual to ignore some information with the goal of making a decision more efficiently.[62] Recent research indicates that such dynamics are also at play in the formation of legitimacy beliefs toward global institutions and would benefit well-known and hierarchical IOs over newer and more fluid forms of governance. Specifically, these studies point to the use of two types of heuristics: recognition and representativeness.

When individuals make use of the recognition heuristic they assume that objects they recognize are of greater value simply because they recall them. A recent study shows this type of heuristic to influence how NGOs rate the legitimacy of election-monitoring organizations.[63] When NGOs were asked to rate the legitimacy of hypothetical organizations there was some evidence that NGOs based such assessments on the institutional qualities of organizations in terms of procedure and performance. However, when NGOs instead were asked to rate the legitimacy of real-world organizations they decisively favored the EU and the UN over the Carter Center, a private election-monitoring organization less familiar to respondents but typically regarded as one of the best-performing. If this dynamic is at play among citizens and elites in general it can help to explain why traditional and well-known IOs continue to score high in terms of legitimacy, while newer and less well-known TGNs, THIs, and TPAs enjoy less legitimacy.

When individuals make use of the representativeness heuristic they form opinions about an object based on its resemblance to a model they know. Recently, research on legitimacy in global governance has discovered an empirical regularity that likely reflects widespread use of this heuristic. A large number of studies have established that citizen beliefs in the legitimacy of national political institutions and IOs are highly linked.[64] The more citizens perceive national governments, legislatures, and courts as legitimate, the more likely they are to regard international executives, parliamentary assemblies, and courts as legitimate. This finding is consistent across IOs, time, alternative measures of legitimacy, and surveys. Moreover, it is substantively important: the perceived legitimacy of domestic political institutions is usually the strongest predictor of an IO's legitimacy. The logic behind this finding suggests that citizens use their attitudes toward the national political institutions they know relatively better when forming opinions about the IOs they know relatively

---

[62] Simon 1957; Kahneman et al. 1982.   [63] Nielson et al. 2019.
[64] E.g., Harteveld et al. 2013; Voeten 2013; Armingeon and Ceka 2014; Schlipphak 2015; Dellmuth and Tallberg 2018.

less well. The implication is that hierarchical IOs, which resemble national governments more closely than new forms of global governance, also are more likely to be rated as legitimate by citizens approving of domestic political institutions.

Conclusion

Following on from earlier chapters describing the transformation of global governance, this chapter has examined one of its potential sources: the legitimacy of old and new forms of global governance. Could the gradual shift toward new-style institutions be driven by concerns with the legitimacy of old-style IOs? I have explored this question in three steps and end in a negative verdict.

While several accounts of the changing architecture of global governance assign a causal role to legitimacy concerns there is no strong pool of evidence in public and elite opinion for the expected patterns. Trends in the perceived legitimacy of traditional IOs show a mixed picture. In addition, there is no evidence to support the notion that new modes of global governance would enjoy greater legitimacy than hierarchical IOs, even among the elites that negotiate the institutions of global governance.

My explanation for this disjuncture between expectations and empirics is threefold. Traditional IOs have engaged in reforms that may have partly diffused legitimacy concerns. New modes of global governance face their own challenges in meeting societal expectations on procedure and performance. Citizens and elites make use of heuristics when forming legitimacy beliefs – to the advantage of well-known and hierarchical IOs over less familiar and more diffuse forms of new global governance.

In all, this chapter gives us reason to be skeptical of legitimacy as a factor driving changes in the dominant modes of global governance. While accounts emphasizing geopolitical shifts, changing governance norms, and domestic backlash to globalization all invoke legitimacy concerns as a factor in the transformation of global governance, this chapter offers limited support for this expectation. There is little to suggest that low legitimacy for old modes of governance has been a push factor, nor that high legitimacy for new modes of governance has been a pull factor, in this transformation. Instead, the greater legitimacy still accorded to old modes of governance compared to new modes of governance suggests that other drivers, distinct from legitimacy, are the principal source of the new global governance architecture.

References

Alter, Karen J., James Thuo Gathii, and Laurence Helfer. 2016. Backlash against International Courts in West, East, and Southern Africa: Causes and Consequences. *European Journal of International Law* 27: 293–328.

Anderson, Brilé, Thomas Bernauer, and Aya Kachi. 2019. Does International Pooling of Authority Affect the Perceived Legitimacy of Global Governance? *Review of International Organization* 14: 661–683.

Andonova, Liliana B. 2019. *Governance Entrepreneurs: International Organizations and the Rise of Global Public–Private Partnerships.* Cambridge: Cambridge University Press.

Armingeon, Klaus and Besir Ceka. 2014. The Loss of Trust in the European Union during the Great Recession since 2007: The Role of Heuristics from the National Political System. *European Union Politics* 15 (1): 82–107.

Avant, Deborah D., Martha Finnemore, and Susan K. Sell, eds. 2010. *Who Governs the Globe?* New York: Cambridge University Press.

Baccini, Leonardo and Andreas Dür. 2014. Investment Discrimination and the Proliferation of Preferential Trade Agreements. *Journal of Conflict Resolution* 59 (4): 617–644.

Bäckstrand, Karin. 2008. Accountability of Networked Climate Governance: The Rise of Transnational Climate Partnerships. *Global Environmental Politics* 8 (3): 74–86.

Barnett, Michael and Martha Finnemore. 2004. *Rules for the World: International Organizations in Global Politics.* Ithaca, NY: Cornell University Press.

Benner, Thorsten, Wolfgang H. Reinicke, and Jan Martin Witte. 2004. Multisectoral Networks in Global Governance: Towards a Pluralistic System of Accountability. *Government and Opposition* 39 (2): 191–210.

Bernauer, Thomas and Robert Gampfer. 2013. Effects of Civil Society Involvement on Popular Legitimacy of Global Environmental Governance. *Global Environmental Change* 23 (2): 439–449.

Bernauer, Thomas, Steffen Mohrenberg, and Vally Koubi. 2020. Do Citizens Evaluate International Cooperation Based on Information about Procedural and Outcome Quality? *Review of International Organizations* 15: 505–529.

Bernstein, Steven. 2011. Legitimacy in Intergovernmental and Non-State Global Governance. *Review of International Political Economy* 18 (1):17–51.

Bexell, Magdalena, Jonas Tallberg, and Anders Uhlin. 2010. Democracy in Global Governance: The Promises and Pitfalls of Transnational Actors. *Global Governance* 16: 81–101.

Binder, Martin and Monica Heupel. 2015. The Legitimacy of the UN Security Council: Evidence from Recent General Assembly Debates. *International Studies Quarterly* 59 (2): 238–250.

Bodansky, Daniel M. 1999. The Legitimacy of International Governance: A Coming Challenge for International Environmental Law? *American Journal of International Law* 93 (3): 596–624.

Buchanan, Allen and Robert O. Keohane. 2006. The Legitimacy of Global Governance Institutions. *Ethics & Global Politics* 20 (4): 405–437.

Chong, Dennis and James N. Druckman. 2007. Framing Theory. *Annual Review of Political Science* 10 (1): 103–126.

Dahl, Robert A. 1999. Can International Organizations Be Democratic? A Skeptic's View. In *Democracy's Edges*, edited by Ian Shapiro and Casiano Hacker-Cordon, 19–36. Cambridge: Cambridge University Press.

Dellmuth, Lisa M. 2018. Individual Sources of Legitimacy Beliefs: Theory and Data. In *Legitimacy in Global Governance: Sources, Processes, and Consequences*, edited by Jonas Tallberg, Karin Bäckstrand, and Jan Aart Scholte, 37–55. Oxford: Oxford University Press.

Dellmuth, Lisa M., Jan Aart Scholte, and Jonas Tallberg. 2019. Institutional Sources of Legitimacy in Global Governance: Unpacking Procedure and Performance. *Review of International Studies* 45 (4): 627–646.

Dellmuth, Lisa M. and Jonas Tallberg. 2015. The Social Legitimacy of International Organisations: Interest Representation, Institutional Performance, and Confidence Extrapolation in the United Nations. *Review of International Studies* 41 (3): 451–475.

2018. Why National and International Legitimacy Beliefs Are Linked: Social Trust as an Antecedent Factor. *Review of International Organizations* 15: 311–337.

Dingwerth, Klaus, Antonia Witt, Ina Lehmann, Ellen Reichel, and Tobias Weise (2019) *International Organizations under Pressure: Legitimating Global Governance in Challenging Times*. Oxford: Oxford University Press.

Easton, David. 1975. A Re-assessment of the Concept of Political Support. *British Journal of Political Science* 5 (4): 435–457.

Fukuyama, Francis. 1992. *The End of History and the Last Man*. New York: Free Press.

Gleditsch, Kristian Skrede and Michael D. Ward. 2008. Diffusion and the International Context of Democratization. *International Organization* 60 (4): 911–933.

Grant, Ruth W. and Robert O. Keohane. 2005. Accountability and Abuses of Power in World Politics. *American Political Science Review* 99 (1): 29–43.

Grigorescu, Alexandru. 2007. Transparency of Intergovernmental Organizations: The Roles of Member States, International Bureaucracies and Nongovernmental Organizations. *International Studies Quarterly* 51 (3): 625–648.

2010. The Spread of Bureaucratic Oversight Mechanisms across Intergovernmental Organization. *International Studies Quarterly* 54 (3): 871–886.

Harteveld, Eelco, Tom van der Meer, and Catherine E. de Vries. 2013. In Europe We Trust? Exploring Three Logics of Trust in the European Union. *European Union Politics* 14 (4): 542–565.

Held, David. 1995. *Democracy and the Global Order: From the Modern State to Cosmopolitical Governance*. Cambridge: Polity Press.

Hobolt, Sara B. and Catherine E. de Vries. 2016. Public Support for European Integration. *Annual Review of Political Science* 19: 413–432.

Hooghe, Liesbet and Gary Marks. 2005. Calculation, Community and Cues: Public Opinion on European Integration. *European Union Politics* 6 (4): 419–443.

2009. A Postfunctionalist Theory of European Integration: From Permissive Consensus to Constraining Dissensus. *British Journal of Political Science* 39 (1): 1–23.

Hooghe, Liesbet, Gary Marks, Tobias Lenz, Jeanine Bezuijen, Besir Ceka, and Svet Derderyan. 2017. *Measuring International Authority: A Postfunctionalist Theory of Governance*. Oxford: Oxford University Press.

Hooghe, Liesbet, Tobias Lenz, and Gary Marks. 2019. The Delegitimation of International Governance. *Review of International Organizations* 14: 731–743.

Hurd, Ian. 2007. *After Anarchy: Legitimacy and Power in the United Nations Security Council*. Princeton: Princeton University Press.

Ikenberry, G. John. 2018. The End of Liberal International Order? *International Affairs* 94 (1): 7–23.

Inglehart, Ronald and Christian Welzel. 2005. *Modernization, Cultural Change, and Democracy*. Cambridge: Cambridge University Press.

Inglehart, Ronald and Pippa Norris. 2017. Trump and Populist-Authoritarian Parties: The Silent Revolution in Reverse. *Perspectives on Politics* 15 (2), 443–454.

Johnson, Tana. 2011. Guilt by Association: The Link between States' Influence and the Legitimacy of Intergovernmental Organizations. *Review of International Organizations* 6: 57–84.

Kahler, Miles, ed. 2009. *Networked Politics: Agency, Power, and Governance*. Ithaca, NY: Cornell University Press.

Kahneman, Daniel, Paul Slovic, and Amos Tversky, eds. 1982. *Judgment under Uncertainty: Heuristics and Biases*. Cambridge: Cambridge University Press.

Kelley, Judith G. and Beth A. Simmons. 2015. Politics by Numbers: Indicators as Social Pressure in International Relations. *American Journal of Political Science* 59 (1): 55–70.

Kruck, Andreas and Bernhard Zangl. 2020. Bringing Negotiations Back In: Instiutional Adaptations to Global Power Shifts. *Global Policy* 11 (3): 5–16.

Lindberg, Leon N. and Stuart A. Scheingold. 1970. *Europe's Would-Be Polity: Patterns of Change in the European Community*. Englewood Cliffs, NJ: Prentice Hall.

Lipscy, Philip Y. 2017. *Renegotiating the World Order: Institutional Change in International Relations*. Cambridge: Cambridge University Press.

Lord, Christopher and David Beetham. 2001. Legitimizing the EU: Is There a "Post-Parliamentary" Basis for Its Legitimation? *Journal of Common Market Studies* 39 (3): 443–462.

Mondak, Jeffrey J. 1993. Public Opinion and Heuristic Processing of Source Cues. *Political Behavior* 15 (2): 167–192.

Moravcsik, Andrew. 1997. Taking Preferences Seriously: A Liberal Theory of International Politics. *International Organization* 51 (4): 513–553.

Morse, Julia and Robert O. Keohane. 2014. Contested Multilateralism. *Review of International Organizations* 9 (4): 385–412.

Newton, Ken and Pippa Norris. 2001. Confidence in Public Institutions: Faith, Culture or Performance? In *Disaffected Democracies: What's Troubling the Trilateral Countries?*, edited by Susan J. Pharr and Robert D. Putnam, 52–73. Princeton: Princeton University Press.

Nielson, Daniel L., Susan D. Hyde, and Judith Kelley. 2019. The Elusive Sources of Legitimacy Beliefs: Civil Society Views of International Election Observers. *Review of International Organizations* 14: 685–715.

Norris, Pippa. 2011. *Democratic Deficit: Critical Citizens Revisited.* Cambridge: Cambridge University Press.

O'Brien, Robert, Anne Marie Goetz, Jan A. Scholte, and Marc Williams. 2000. *Contesting Global Governance: Multilateral Institutions and Global Social Movements.* Cambridge: Cambridge University Press.

Risse-Kappen, Thomas. 1996. Collective Identity in a Democratic Community: The Case of NATO. In *The Culture of National Security: Norms and Identity in World Politics*, edited by Peter J. Katzenstein, 357–399. New York: Columbia University Press.

Rittberger, Bernhard and Philip Schroeder. 2016. The Legitimacy of Regional Institutions. In *The Oxford Handbook of Comparative Regionalism*, edited by Tanja Börzel and Thomas Risse, 579–599. Oxford: Oxford University Press.

Rittberger, Volker, Bernhard Zangl, and Andreas Kruck. 2012. *International Organization*, 2nd edition. Basingstoke: Palgrave Macmillan.

Rocabert, Jofre, Frank Schimmelfennig, Loriana Crasnic, and Thomas Winzen. 2019. The Rise of International Parliamentary Institutions: Purpose and Legitimation. *Review of International Organizations* 14: 607–631.

Scharpf, Fritz. 1999. *Governing in Europe: Effective and Democratic?* Oxford: Oxford University Press.

Schlipphak, Bernd. 2015. Measuring Attitudes toward Regional Organizations outside Europe. *Review of International Organizations* 10 (3):351–375.

Scholte, Jan Aart, ed. 2011. *Building Global Democracy? Civil Society and Accountable Global Governance.* Cambridge: Cambridge University Press.

Simon, Herbert. 1957. *Social and Rational: Mathematical Essays on Rational Human Behavior in a Social Setting.* New York: Wiley.

Slaughter, Anne-Marie. 2005. *A New World Order.* Princeton: Princeton University Press.

Steffek, Jens, Claudia Kissling, and Patrizia Nanz. Eds. 2008. *Civil Society Participation in European and Global Governance: A Cure for the Democratic Deficit?* Basingstoke: Palgrave Macmillan.

Stephen, Matthew D. 2017. Emerging Powers and Emerging Trends in Global Governance. *Global Governance* 23: 483–502.

Stephen, Matthew D. and Michael Zürn, eds. 2019. *Contested World Orders: Rising Powers, Non-State Actors, and the Politics of Authority beyond the Nation-State.* Oxford: Oxford University Press.

Suchman, Marc C. 1995. Managing Legitimacy: Strategic and Institutional Approaches. *The Academy of Management Review* 20 (3):571–610.

Tallberg, Jonas, Karin Bäckstrand, and Jan Aart Scholte, eds. 2018. *Legitimacy in Global Governance: Sources, Processes, and Consequences.* Oxford: Oxford University Press.

Tallberg, Jonas and Michael Zürn. 2019. Legitimacy and Legitimation in International Organizations: Introduction and Framework. *Review of International Organizations* 14: 581–606.

Tallberg, Jonas and Soetkin Verhaegen. 2020. The Legitimacy of International Institutions among Rising and Established Powers. *Global Policy* 11 (3): 115–126.

Tallberg, Jonas, Thomas Sommerer, and Theresa Squatrito. 2016. Democratic Memberships in International Organizations: Sources of Institutional Design. *Review of International Organizations* 11 (1): 59–87.

Tallberg, Jonas, Thomas Sommerer, Theresa Squatrito, and Christer Jönsson. 2013. *The Opening Up of International Organizations: Transnational Access in Global Governance.* Cambridge: Cambridge University Press.

2014. Explaining the Transnational Design of International Organizations. *International Organization* 68 (4): 741–774.

Vabulas, Felicity and Duncan Snidal. 2013. Organization without Delegation: Informal Intergovernmental Organizations (IIGOs) and the Spectrum of Intergovernmental Arrangements. *Review of International Organizations* 8 (2): 193–220.

Verhaegen, Soetkin, Jan Aart Scholte, and Jonas Tallberg. 2019. *Elite Attitudes Toward Global Governance.* A Report of Summary Findings from the LegGov Elite Survey. Gothenburg and Stockholm: University of Gothenburg and Stockholm University.

2021. Explaining Elite Perceptions of Legitimacy in Global Governance. *European Journal of International Relations.* https://doi.org/10.1177% 2F1354066121994320.

Voeten, Erik. 2013. Public Opinion and the Legitimacy of International Courts. *Theoretical Inquiries in Law* 14 (2): 411–436.

2020. Populism and the Backlashes against International Courts. *Perspectives on Politics* 18 (2): 407–422.

Weber, Max. 1978 [1922]. *Economy and Society.* Berkeley and Los Angeles: University of California Press.

Weiss, Thomas G. and Rorden Wilkinson. 2014. Rethinking Global Governance: Complexity, Authority, Power, Change. *International Studies Quarterly* 58 (1): 207–215.

Zangl, Bernhard, Frederick Haussner, Andreas Kruck, and Xenia Lanzendörfer. 2016. Imperfect Adaptation: How the WTO and IMF Adjust to Shifting Power Distributions among Their Members. *Review of International Organizations* 11: 171–196.

Zürn, Michael. 2000. Democratic Governance beyond the Nation-State: The EU and Other International Institutions. *European Journal of International Relations* 6 (2): 183–221.

2018. *A Theory of Global Governance: Authority, Legitimacy, and Contestation.* Oxford: Oxford University Press.

Conclusion
Global Governance and Institutional Diversity

Orfeo Fioretos

The 2020 coronavirus pandemic exposed once again the limits of global governance. The focal organization for managing such events, the World Health Organization (WHO), lacked the capacity to mitigate the spread of Covid-19 in its acute phases. Though enjoying a reputation as one of the most effective and legitimate intergovernmental organizations before the crisis,[1] the WHO quickly came in for heavy criticism. Much of it was not deserved, but the ferocity of the scrutiny reinforced perceptions that neither effectiveness nor legitimacy may be hallmarks of contemporary global governance. Even if global health governance offered a particularly vivid illustration of such perceptions in 2020, it is not alone among policy domains in having this reputation. In the last two decades a strong sense had already emerged among policy-makers and scholars that while global challenges were proliferating, global solutions kept falling short.[2] At a forum a year before the pandemic struck, United Nations Secretary-General Antonio Guterres presciently identified a conundrum in contemporary global governance:

> If I had to select one sentence to describe the state of the world, I would say we are in a world in which global challenges are more and more integrated, and the responses are more and more fragmented, and if this is not reversed, it's a recipe for disaster.[3]

Exchanges with many colleagues have contributed to this chapter. My deepest thanks to Michael Barnett, Jon C.W. Pevehouse, and Kal Raustiala for sharing their wonderment of global governance and deeply constructive feedback on earlier versions. Many thanks also to Liliana B. Andonova, the Graduate School of International Affairs in Geneva, volume contributors, workshop participants, as well as press reviewers for sharing thoughts and suggestions along the way.

[1] In a 2019 survey of foreign policy experts, global health received the highest grade among all areas (Council of Councils 2019). Tallberg (Chapter 11, Figure 11.3) reports that in 2019 surveys of politicians, civil servants, media, business, civil society, and global institutions themselves, WHO enjoyed the greatest confidence of all big international organizations.

[2] See e.g. Haass 2007; Hale et al. 2013; Copelovitch and Pevehouse 2019; Weiss and Wilkerson 2019.

[3] Guterres 2019, 1.

Guterres' carefully chosen sentence speaks to a common perception that contemporary global governance is qualitatively different from the past, especially in terms of a deficit of integrated arrangements that can effectively manage global challenges. One way to appreciate the extent to which contemporary global governance lacks integration is to compare the present with past arrangements. Most audience members at Guterres' 2019 address would have been in agreement that contemporary levels of fragmentation are unprecedented, while audience members at the opening of the League of Nations a century earlier would have seen things very differently. For the 1919 observers there would have been no point in previous history when responses to global challenges had been more integrated. The same would be the case for audience members at the 1945 opening of the United Nations. While many would have agreed that holes remained in global arrangements, few would have argued that the world was more fragmented than in their recent past. The level of fragmentation would also have appeared smaller after 1989 with the publication of the UN's "An Agenda for Peace" and "In Larger Freedom," the latter officially branded an "integrated and coordinated implementation of and follow-up to the outcomes of the major United Nations conferences and summits in the economic, social and related fields."[4] It represented a sense after the Cold War that, though "unfinished," a gradual "revolution" was taking place in global governance in the direction of less fragmentation.[5]

In 2020 the sentiment was very different. A sense prevailed at the 75th anniversary of the UN that global governance was fragmented and that great obstacles existed to providing integrated solutions to pressing challenges. Few events made the costs of lacking integration more apparent than the Covid-19 pandemic. It was already evident in its early stages that an integrated global response was not at hand, one in which all major stakeholders in global health effectively coordinated responses and collectively marshaled resources to minimize deaths and economic disruption. The world instead witnessed a patchwork of arrangements. It featured governments that withdrew from international cooperation and contested intergovernmental organizations, and loose partnerships among the former and non-governmental philanthropic organizations.[6] Nobody characterized this arrangement as integrated. But the global health domain is not the only area where crises have exposed disjointed arrangements. An "existential" global climate crisis has been brewing for

---

[4] United Nations General Assembly 2005, 1.   [5] Malloch-Brown 2011.
[6] Gates 2020; Blanco and Rosales 2020; Kreuder-Sonnen 2020.

decades without an integrated solution.[7] In the trade domain, where the opportunity costs of fragmentation are considered high, fragmentation has increased for more than two decades.[8] By any historical standard of rules-based governance that is a significant period of time that belies the notion that past milestones of integrated global governance will soon be matched.

At the center of the conundrum Guterres flags is the issue of institutional diversity. Solving the conundrum requires coming to terms with the immensely varied types of institutions that inform the totality of global governance. When the world fails to solve a global problem, the solution is rarely simply about plugging some gap in governance capacity. It is also about integrating extant institutions, joining these and new ones, and it is about more effectively coordinating the responses of major governmental and private stakeholders. This can be very challenging because those with vested interests in existing designs, often built in a different era, may be reluctant to adapt specific designs in the name of some overarching goal. If institutional arrangements are very different, misaligned, or incomplete, such that constellations in one area of governance prevent solutions to urgent problems or undermine the effectiveness or legitimacy of arrangements in other areas, then integration is lacking.[9] This form of institutional fragmentation may be inevitable to some extent, and perhaps even welcome by some. Nevertheless, many observers agree and worry with Secretary-General Guterres that contemporary global governance is particularly fragmented and that a pathway is needed toward establishing a more integrated arrangement.[10]

In their Introduction to this volume Michael Barnett, Jon C.W. Pevehouse, and Kal Raustiala offer a novel framework for capturing why global governance is so diverse and what implications it has for how a variety of policy challenges are managed. They do not directly engage Guterres' conundrum, but their analysis has significant implications for how the conundrum is understood and potentially resolved. Barnett, Pevehouse, and Raustiala base their inquiry of global governance on a comparative institutional approach that urges scholars to shift from comparing the formal properties of organizations to comparing "modes" of governance. They distinguish between three modes that are

---

[7] Victor 2011; Bernstein and van der Ven 2017; Keohane 2020.

[8] Narlikar 2010; Faude 2020; Collier 2006.

[9] If global governance institutions were uniform, aligned, and complete, then there would be no deficit of integration. Notions of cohesive and integrated models are particularly sharp in world government and world federalism models. See Wynner and Lloyd 1949; Baratta 2004; Rosenboim 2017.

[10] Kagan 2018; Haass 2020.

used to induce collective decision-making and rule-based behavior on a global level. The three modes – hierarchies, networks, and markets – constitute a typology that they use to map essential features and differences in global governance arrangements across more than a century and a dozen issue areas. The typology provides a tool to answer many questions, such as how far or near arrangements are to the aspirations of their architects, and the extent to which features change with time. Barnett, Pevehouse, and Raustiala's framework also provides the means to map and theorize the sources of institutional development, including patterns that entail more or less institutional integration or fragmentation. They use the typology to reveal the relative prominence of hierarchal, network, and market-based modes over a century of global governance across the security, economic, health, humanitarian, and many other domains, and paint a picture of ebbs and flows in the integration and fragmentation of global governance arrangements.

In this contribution I explore analytical payoffs from the modes of governance typology for comparative, historical, and institutional analysis of global governance. I discuss the advantages and limitations from bringing together structural explanations of global politics with theories of governance. And I probe alternative understandings of the totality of global governance, suggesting that this volume presents an image of global governance as a system of deep institutional diversity that is distinct from common conceptualizations. The implications of this representation for pathways to and from greater integration and fragmentation are discussed in a separate section. In the Conclusion I highlight some lessons that comparative institutional analysis holds for understanding contemporary junctures in global governance and the prospects for significant redirections in the future.

Payoffs from Shifting the Study of Global Governance

Global governance in the twenty-first century is often described in terms of a mixed system of unprecedented numbers of formal and informal intergovernmental organizations, global civil society organizations, and, *primus inter pares*, powerful sovereigns (states, governments). In their Introduction, Barnett, Pevehouse, and Raustiala provide a comprehensive sense of this system across a century and a dozen domains, distilling the essence of global governance into "the institutional arrangements used to identify problems, facilitate decision-making, and promote rule-based behavior on a global scale" (p. 4). The authors underscore that these arrangements have taken diverse forms across time and urge scholars to adopt a comparative institutional approach to disentangle this diversity. To capture the variety of institutional arrangements, they champion a typology that distinguishes between three generic modes of governance: hierarchy, markets, and networks. These represent alternative ways of facilitating "decision-making" and "rule-based behavior" with long histories in the social sciences.[11] Developing and applying this typology has several payoffs for the study of global governance.[12]

Comparative Institutional Analysis

First, the typology recasts the comparative institutional analysis of global governance. Many studies of global institutions focus on variations in the number and formal properties of organizations (e.g., membership, decision-making procedures). These have contributed greatly to explanations of why spatial and temporal variations exist (or are absent) in global institutions.[13] For Barnett, Pevehouse, and Raustiala, however, comparative institutional analysis should be less about differences in the formal properties of individual organizations and more about variations in the nature of institutions, or what they conceive of as distinct constellations or "modes" of governance. This is an important difference for it makes comparative institutional analysis less about the presence or absence of institutions or the value these take (e.g., large versus small membership, majoritarian versus non-majoritarian), but about diversity in the type of institutions.

Anchored within the social science tradition of discrete structural analysis, the hierarchies-networks-markets typology features within a substantial literature devoted to organizations and institutions where the analytical fulcrum is placed on diverse solutions to social coordination.[14] This tradition views alternatives as functional substitutes, meaning that they are incentive incompatible and thus not easily integrated. For Barnett, Pevehouse, and Raustiala the three modes represent fundamental "organizing principles" that underlie the institutional arrangements that govern. In the context of global governance each mode thus represents a departure from a world of anarchy, the canonical starting

---

[11] E.g. Coase 1937; Simon 1962; Williamson 1991; Powell 1990.

[12] The typology has featured also in the international relations field (IR), though generally with an emphasis on one or two modes of governance (e.g., Koenig-Archibugi and Zürn 2006; Lake 1996; Avant and Westerwinter 2016).

[13] E.g. Koremenos 2016; Hooghe et al. 2017; Grigorescu 2020.

[14] Common features along which modes of governance are compared include incentive structures, provision of information, administrative oversight, modes of conflict resolution, quality of autonomous and cooperative adaptation, and relational calculus (Williamson 1991, 1996; Powell 1990).

point for much international political theory.[15] Unlike in anarchy where there is an absence of a central legitimate authority, in a hierarchical model there is a clear relationship between who establishes and enforces rules and norms, even if the ways in which it is experienced varies.

Hierarchical models are found in many state-centric accounts of global governance that place an emphasis on formal and informal arrangements through which hegemonic powers exercise decisive influence over the nature and content of global rules.[16] Hierarchies can also be observed in more discrete contexts, such as in the practices that structure the interactions among diplomats in a multilateral setting, the deference that some ideas are afforded over others, or the ways in which states and global actors are stratified even before they gain agency.[17] While some disagreement exists among scholars regarding what exactly is the best way to understand hierarchy in global governance, there is now a great appreciation that hierarchal arrangements are common features of global governance, including in the security, economic, legal, and other domains.[18]

Barnett, Pevehouse, and Raustiala want to move beyond contrasting hierarchy with anarchy and push for comparisons with two other modes of governance. Markets are the second mode and are understood to be systems in which autonomous actors hold the authority.[19] In the contemporary setting, market-based models of governance are most familiar from a variety of economic contexts where actors compete in offering services and preferred blueprints without a designated central authority. They also inform areas of cooperation where global standards are set by private actors, as Deborah Avant notes in Chapter 1 in her study of private security services and as Miles Kahler shows with respect to commercial arbitration in Chapter 2. Like the other forms of governance, markets have certain institutional advantages, with flexibility and adaptability being the dimensions that receive the most attention. Their

---

[15] E.g. Waltz 1979; Milner 1991; Wendt 1992.
[16] E.g. Mearsheimer 2018; Keohane 1984; Lake 2011; Musgrave and Nexon 2018.
[17] Pouliot 2016; Zarakol 2017.   [18] Bially-Mattern and Zarakol 2016.
[19] Analogies have been made between anarchy and markets, though there are important distinctions to consider, especially in the slippage of terms and connotations when describing the worlds of politics and economics. While anarchy is understood to involve the absence of a central legitimate (global) authority, markets are understood to be systems in which autonomous actors hold the authority. This distinction can be reconciled, even if awkwardly (Waltz 1979). Others are more difficult to reconcile in the context of global politics and economics. For instance, unlike the notion of the market, where cooperation is generally presumed to be welfare enhancing, the notion of anarchy begins from the assumption that the world is one of scarcity and ever present threats of domination and violence.

liability is that they are prone to an eponymous governance failure. To many observers of global governance an overly strong reliance on these models risks "market failures" and thus an undersupply of public goods without which the ability to achieve greater global security, prosperity, health, or justice is put in jeopardy.[20]

Networks represent a third mode by which actors arrange themselves. Networks are semi-voluntary arrangements in which actors with considerable degrees of equality address common goals through negotiation, established rules, and persuasion.[21] Networks may lack some efficiencies associated with hierarchies, but are generally thought to make up for that in terms of legitimacy, greater learning opportunities, and more.[22] Because the modern sovereign state occupies such a central position in global affairs, encompassing networked arrangements among these are thought to be positively associated with effective solutions to collective action problems.[23] The notion of networked global governance, as opposed to a hierarchical model, became prominent in the aftermath of the Cold War and is linked to trends of actor pluralization.[24] From models capturing alliances among activist networks and novel arrangements between public and private entities, networked global governance may be welcomed on normative grounds.[25] But while networked governance arrangements are often a potent means for addressing global issues, they also entail some comparative institutional disadvantages. For example, while networks may be effective in solving specific categories of governance challenges they can also become the means through which select entities extend their power. Networked governance systems are sensitive to hold-up problems and give those members with great network centrality outsized influence over the ways in which global challenges are managed.[26] Network governance, in other words, can be far from the harmonious arrangement it is frequently made out to be. And it can be normatively suspect on grounds of limited representation.

One of Barnett, Pevehouse, and Raustiala's messages is that contemporary global governance is different from the past because it has become more diverse. To them there is not one or a few hierarchically integrated arrangements, or harmoniously arranged networks, or smoothly functioning markets that imperfectly resolve global governance challenges.

---

[20] Kaul et al. 1999.
[21] Network models of global cooperation are explored in a large and diverse literature, including Avant and Westerwinter 2016; Kahler 2011; Goddard 2009.
[22] Powell 1990; Podolny and Page 1998.   [23] E.g. Slaughter 2004; Slaughter 2017.
[24] Kahler 2011; Acharya 2014.
[25] Keck and Sikkink 1998; Tallberg et al. 2013; Andonova 2017.
[26] Farrell and Newman 2019.

Rather, global governance is full of hierarchies, networks, and market-based arrangements that exist side by side. Even if some modes may be more dominant in some periods or policy domains it is rarely the case that all arrangements in an area always employ the same mode. For example, hierarchical modes of governance remain central in the contemporary global economic system, but they exist alongside other modes. Notably, a variety of decentralized arrangements have emerged in the last several decades that use markets and networks to furnish solutions to complex governance challenges. As Michael Barnett and Suerie Moon show respectively in Chapter 5 and Chapter 8, responses to humanitarian and health crises are also highly multifaceted: complex interlinkages between more state-centric, top-down, hierarchical governance arrangements where significant power is vested in a small number of nation-states have developed into systems where such structures exist alongside networks of public, private, and other actors of different size who operate across global, national, and local levels. Seen from this vantage point, global governance is a patchwork of arrangements. One may say that the three modes are the three primary colors that give the patches their hue. The patchwork will not always have the same arrangement across domains; in some instances one color will appear more dominant, in other cases a different color shines brighter. Barnett, Pevehouse, and Raustiala leave somewhat open why particular configurations emerge, but underscore that at no point has global governance been monochromatic.

Historical Analysis

A second payoff from using the typology concerns its applications to historical analysis. The typology can be used to mark moments and narrate developments in global governance. If the analysis of global economic governance begins in 1945, for example, the narrative is one of change from a historic high watermark for hierarchical governance to its nadir in the 1990s when market-based models were ascendant. But if the narrative begins in 1920, as Miles Kahler notes in Chapter 2, then the period between 1945 and 1980 is one where hierarchical intergovernmental organization had a "transitory monopoly" that no longer applies. The typology, in other words, furnishes a means for identifying institutional baselines against which change and continuity in a mode can be referenced and for identifying ebbs and flows in diverse arrangements.

The irony with many big social science concepts – "transaction costs," "regulation," "power," "anarchy," "order," and indeed "market," "hierarchy," and "network" – is that there are no widely accepted or easy ways of measuring them. The governance typology comes with a notable benefit in this context by furnishing a threshold that can be used to distinguish between degrees and kinds of change.[27] In the tradition of discrete structural analysis, alternatives are functional substitutes.[28] Adjustments within a mode represents degrees of change and processes of incremental change, while shifts of the mode or kind of governance is associated with radical or transformative change. In such analyses the study of governance can be distilled to a distinction between the politics of incremental change or pathways of institutional continuity, and the politics of a wholesale transformation from one to another mode of governance.

Some big historical punctuations, notably the two world wars, are often understood to have generated transformative shifts in global governance.[29] The Bretton Woods organizations, for example, are said to have marked a radical break from the past through the addition of hierarchical models of governance that placed governments from large industrialized economies in leading roles within formalized international monetary and development systems. In the area of human rights the 1970s feature as a major punctuation.[30] But studies show that in both cases what went into agreements and what followed were the product of processes of incremental institutional adaptation that spanned decades.[31] Today both areas feature a mix of institutional designs, including network- and market-based modes of governance. Nonetheless, what passes for innovation may hide deep-seated continuities. Neither the monetary nor the development domains are devoid of hierarchies, for example. The International Monetary Fund and World Bank are still focal organizations in which a small number of industrialized economies retain disproportionate influence.[32] New arrangements that have been added, such as the Group of 20 (G20), may have altered some hierarchies but have certainly not overturned the presence of that mode of governance.[33] In other words, when temporal contexts are considered the governance typology provides the means to identify both types of change and how they are related over longer periods of time.

The global health system has also gone through distinct periods during which the mode of governance and the structure of international organizations have changed, including their relationships with each other and

---

[27] On governance typologies, see Williamson 1991. More broadly, see Collier et al. 2012.
[28] Simon 1962; Williamson 1991.   [29] Ikenberry 2001; Lundgren et al. 2018.
[30] Moyn 2010.   [31] Helleiner 2017; Sikkink 2017.   [32] Fioretos and Heldt 2019.
[33] Viola 2019.

national authorities. The WHO, the focal organization after 1945, has seen its authority wax and wane as a panoply of public, private, and public–private arrangements have come to populate the area. In Chapter 8, Suerie Moon argues that it is a "complex adaptive system" in which WHO remains central, but where its primary functions are less to direct and coordinate global scientific action than to serve as a convener and legitimator of a political space in which states, especially larger ones, retain outsized influence. Moon admits that the future path of such systems is difficult to predict, but ventures that this domain will continue to feature a mixture of governance types, including novel hybrids of national and international authorities as well as private organizations.

Revealing Gaps

A third payoff from the typology is that it helps capture instances where governance is in short supply. A gap is easier to identify when one is familiar with its opposite. From the perspective of the typology there is a gap of governance if no arrangement represents a hierarchical, network, or market-based mode of governance. That global governance is incomplete to some extent is to be expected. It is difficult to anticipate all future problems and find global agreement on integrated designs even in the best of times. When it is further recognized that global governance often is reactive, in the sense that many initiatives have come about after some major event has revealed the costs from inaction or gaps of governance, it is easier to recall that global governance never has been fully complete.

Ascertaining the presence and size of gaps is not a task that any study has yet mastered. Barnett, Pevehouse, and Raustiala take such an inquiry many steps forward, however. Their typology provides baselines when considering the sources, nature, and consequences of gaps in global governance patchworks. For example, looking back to the origins of global health governance in 1851, or theorizing about its future, the typology provides an effective tool to identify past, present, and potential future gaps in governance. In the process it also opens up room for new questions. If a hierarchical model of governance is absent, for example, it means there is an absence of a strong central authority, which in turn opens inquiry into why such authority is absent at a particular time. In this way the study of hierarchy, which primarily tends to be about its presence, also becomes one of its periodic absence. By expanding the number of periods and type of cases that are studied the typology thus facilitates a more encompassing set of cases from which to analyze ebbs and flows in global governance arrangements.

This volume is deeply aware that many gaps exist not because there are no feasible solutions, but because some political actors reason that they are better served by gaps than the alternative. Many voids exist because those with power prefer a gap to its opposite. Counterfactual analysis is a valuable complement here, for it encourages scholars to consider why some feasible alternatives fail to emerge and what drivers are most important in pushing or pulling the path of development in one or another direction.[34] The typology facilitates historically situated counterfactual analysis by providing the material for exploring what specific structures could have been present or absent at any particular moment, or what movement in a different direction would have looked like had conditions been different. In this way the typology provides both a palette from which to paint an image of extant global governance arrangements and to imagine what potential alternatives would look like.

Theorizing Past and Present

This volume aspires to extend beyond categorization to explain why global governance looks different in a variety of temporal and spatial contexts. To this end the volume explores a multitude of potential causes behind specific, varied, and changing modes of global governance. With a strong nod to conjunctural causality, authors are urged to move away from monocausal and monochromatic accounts of global governance and to recognize that it is often shaped by a confluence of factors that interact in diverse ways across temporal and spatial contexts.[35] At the center of their inquiry are fully nine causes or "structural drivers" of change. Several of these feature regularly in global governance studies and others receive overdue attention.

Some Usual Suspects

This project relies extensively on structural analysis, which is to say that it emphasizes developments that actors cannot meaningfully shape on their own. Geopolitics and domestic politics are structural factors that feature in many studies of global governance, and they also make an appearance here. That shifts in global distributions of power have altered the prospects of global governance is widely documented,[36] and this volume

---

[34] Capoccia and Kelemen 2007; Fioretos et al. 2016.

[35] Conjunctural analysis concerns the "interaction effects between distinct causal sequences that become joined at particular points in time" (Pierson 2004, 12).

[36] Kahler 2013; Stephen and Zürn 2019; Kruck and Zangl 2020.

provides additional examples where geopolitical developments have impacted how actors arrange themselves globally. The "rise" of large developing economies in the past two decades, for example, has made comprehensive and integrated agreements in the area of global climate cooperation more difficult and encouraged creativity in the type of governance arrangements that are used. In Chapter 3, Jessica F. Green shows, for example, that this has entailed greater reliance on informal and market-based designs. Meanwhile, as Liliana B. Andonova underscores in Chapter 10, the retreat of governments from some global organizations and limited budgets have pushed intergovernmental organizations to develop partnerships with nongovernmental organizations. The domestic politics of countries is also known to exert powerful influence on global governance. In 2020, for example, to consider the state of global governance without reference to the sovereigntist politics of governments in the United States, United Kingdom, Russia, China, or Brazil would be to underestimate the consequences of domestic politics for global governance and to overestimate the prospect that multilateral solutions will be supplied in ways that quickly reduce gaps in global governance. At the same time a reversed scenario is also important to consider, one in which global governance remakes domestic politics.[37] The latter scenario does not get as much attention in this volume, even though it may in some cases be an integral element behind why the fortunes of global governance change over time. The construction of a neoliberal economic globalization around the millennium, for example, was a significant source behind the electoral fortunes of several populist nationalist governments two decades later who made international institutions their preferred targets. But this ideological current is by no means the only factor that contributes to a sense of stagnation in global governance in 2020. In Chapter 4, Susanne Mueller and Jon C.W. Pevehouse reason, for example, that even "if Donald Trump woke up as David Ricardo reincarnate, multilateral trade negotiations would still be a long slog." In other words, even if a nationalist political leader ("Trump") were to have a sudden ideational conversion to more liberal trade ("Ricardo") it may be insufficient to alter the complex dynamics that shape the course of global trade governance.

The global economy features as another structural force behind changes in global governance. Industrialization and modernity, science and commerce, are all implicated in the origins of global governance.[38] In some cases the links are more direct, such as efforts by scientists to

---

[37] Hurrell 2007; Zürn 2018.   [38] Murphy 1994: Mazower 2012, 94–115.

create agreements on physio-sanitary standards in the middle of the nineteenth century or more recently in cooperation with other public agencies in constituting global climate governance.[39] In other cases the impact of changes to industrialization and economic globalization have been more indirect. New technologies and greater commerce facilitated the creation of more sovereign states, for example, which in turn made agreement more difficult in some areas and in the process created incentives to use decentralized modes of governance that acknowledged diversity among sovereigns. Increases in the number of actors have impacted what type of governance solutions are considered effective and legitimate. With four times the number of members than when it was founded, the UN is one prominent example of how an increase in actors can serve to stimulate demand and supply of global governance institutions in one period, only to later be considered a reason why global agreement has become more difficult with time.[40] But the increase of numbers and types of international actors goes much further. Actor pluralization, which Barnett, Pevehouse, and Raustiala treat as a separate driver from increases in the number of actors, has impacted many fields of governance. In the health field, for example, Suerie Moon shows in Chapter 8 that power has devolved to many non-state actors who now hold significant material and moral power and have become indispensable partners to national and international public agencies, including the WHO. In response to the Covid-19 pandemic, the prior pluralization of actors within the global health domain meant that efforts to find a remedy were fragmented. Select governments sought to coordinate a solution, while public–private partnerships such as Gavi played prominent roles.[41] This suggests that even if a more integrated response is desirable, prior levels of fragmentation make it likely that a response to a crisis will be disjoint and may enhance the prospects that the aftermath reinforces rather than overturns prior arrangements.

Newer Faces

Drivers that feature less commonly in the large global governance literature but are given their due in this volume include the ease with which problems are solved and the effects of rationalization. The world of global governance has come a long way since the front pages of the world's newspapers featured ribbon-cutting ceremonies for new universal intergovernmental organizations. That such stories should have been

[39] Allen 2017.   [40] Hale et al. 2013; Patrick 2014; Victor 2011.
[41] Gates 2020; Blanco and Rosales 2020.

particularly common in the aftermath of the Second World War is natural given the momentous punctuation of that global political event. It is nevertheless remarkable that in the contemporary period, one in which a large number of global challenges remain unsolved, there is scarcely ever a picture or major headline featuring the creation of a new large organization to manage global concerns. The forces militating against it are many and are on ample display in this volume, including opposition by powerful states, coalitions of smaller states, and global civil society.

Barnett, Pevehouse, and Raustiala suggest that an eighth reason for the current state of global governance is that the "low-hanging fruit" has already been picked. That is to say, the areas where agreement would have been particularly likely – international trade, global health, and to some extent human rights – are the ones that have seen the biggest advances. By contrast, in areas where problem structures are complex, or "super wicked" as in the case global climate change, effective and legitimate solutions are harder to come by and very rarely are they presented at ribbon-cutting ceremonies.[42] Past structures to manage cooperation also matter here, for many are defined by arrangements where small numbers of states, sometimes single ones, wield veto power over major changes. As a consequence, collaborative efforts to reach the high-hanging fruit are easily upended. Some global governance actors may attempt to keep the ladders to themselves, while others look to devise alternative ways of collecting the fruit. From this perspective the future of comprehensive solutions to global problems looks dire.

The final driver behind global governance is the process of rationalization. Barnett, Pevehouse, and Raustiala see global governance as a modernist project. After each of the big wars of the twentieth century delegates at conferences sought to construct international organizations that would be capable of solving major challenges, including preventing armed conflict and economic crises. International organizations that resembled legal-rational bureaucracies were those that were "increasingly valorized" and became the metrics for effective and legitimate governance.[43] Rationalization refers to a process in which the objective of governance is to enhance standardization and specialization with the goal of providing effective responses to new demands. In the contemporary period rationalization is a central feature in the introduction of new management techniques as well as greater investments in the development of performance indicators. Each of these represents a way of

---

[42] Levin et al. 2012.   [43] See also Barnett and Finnemore 2004.

incentivizing governments and others to behave in specified ways without the presence of coercive hierarchal models of enforcement.[44]

Networks have become deeply implicated in rationalization processes. In the area of humanitarian assistance Michael Barnett shows in Chapter 5 that networks of humanitarian elites have come to interact more intensely after 1989 and contributed to the emergence of a more rationalized field; yet he also argues that while the sector might appear to have flattened, hierarchy still very much remains. Networks of transnational experts have also propelled new areas of governance, such as the management of post-conflict reconstruction in fragile states. In Chapter 7, Leonard Seabrooke and Ole Jacob Sending detail a transformation in sites of collective decision-making toward greater incorporation of networks, which has contributed to a significantly more differentiated system for managing postwar reconstruction and strengthen national public authority. In Chapter 1, Deborah Avant underscores that even in the security area where hierarchies are thought to be particularly entrenched, processes of rationalization have pushed multi-stakeholder initiatives forward that regulate private security companies, including the use and conduct of mercenaries.

Agency and Contingency

The nine drivers all have structural qualities, which means that each exerts an influence on global governance arrangements beyond the power of individual actors, whether states, governments, international organizations, or individual leaders. In placing such a strong emphasis on structural variables, however, Barnett, Pevehouse, and Raustiala run the same risks as a long history of structural theorizing in international relations, namely overlooking the role of agency and contingency in shaping global arrangements. But, unlike systemically oriented IR theories where such blind spots are dismissed in the name of parsimony, this project's openness to causal conjunctures help contributors be attentive to the interplay between structure, agency, and contingency. They use this opening to explore how the structural drivers identified by the editors shape the agency of political actors, hide or amplify their political entrepreneurship, and how unexpected events impact paths of global governance.

In the security, health, and environmental domains, where national interest and resource scarcities may impose significant constraints on

---

[44] Cooley and Snyder 2015; Kelley and Simmons 2020.

ambitious global governance arrangements, the room for agency is often small. But it exists, and when exercised can have far-reaching legacies. In Chapter 1, Deborah Avant shows how the Swiss government and the International Committee of the Red Cross exercised decisive entrepreneurship in the creation of a mixed system of governance for military and security services that linked networks of actors to formulate rules and norms that are sustained through hierarchical governance channels at the national and local levels. In Chapter 8, Suerie Moon shows in the case of global health that the material and later normative power of the Bill and Melinda Gates Foundation redirected not only the priorities of national and global health governance but contributed to the consolidation of a multi-stakeholder model that is anchored by the WHO. In Chapter 10, Liliana B. Andonova shows how incentive-based, normative, and epistemic motivations led individuals and groups of actors to work with, against, and around structural constraints to shape the path of global environmental governance.

The role of contingency is a second blind spot of structural theories. Even when considered as a product of conjunctural circumstances where several factors interact to produce a given outcome, a whole lot in global governance appears contingent. From that which did not happen to that which did happen and prevented other developments, global governance could have taken different pathways. As contributors to this volume illustrate, committed diplomats and policy-makers attempt to use even the smallest windows of opportunity to overcome structural constraints. The success of such entrepreneurship finds little room in structural theories, yet may be important to consider when answering why rules of global governance are transformed or, indeed, remain intact under duress. For these reasons, studies of past, present, and future global governance should be mindful not to overinvest in structural theory without simultaneously renewing their commitment to identifying the conditions under which agency and contingency impact the institutional arrangements associated with global governance.

The Totality and Pathways Questions

Typologies are about differences and thus about specificities. They are not intended to stand in for general claims or be the foundation for large generalizations. They are fundamentally about making possible claims with respect to particulars and sometimes about the sum whole. In the context of governance typologies, Bob Jessop brings the sociologist's wisdom when he observes that "there is no governance in general nor general governance. Rather, there is only particular governance and the totality of governance."[45] Barnett, Pevehouse, and Raustiala are careful not to make statements about global governance in general or to offer a general view of global governance. They focus instead on the particulars of global governance, conceived of in terms of constellations of institutions representing diverse modes of governance. But in their careful assessment of the particulars of the three modes it is not clear what defines global governance in the aggregate, or in its "totality"? Does global governance come only in three colors – representing, respectively, hierarchies, networks, and markets? Do hybrid or mixed types exist and what effects do they have, if any, on how the totality of global governance is understood?

Without answers to these questions there can be only partial resolutions to the sort of conundrum raised by UN Secretary-General Guterres. How a deficit in institutional integration is addressed, for example, will look different if the totality of global governance is understood as primarily representing a system of one dominant mode, or a mixed system of three modes, or a system of hybrid types. The pathways to and from integration will take different form as well, and so will understandings of what constitutes fragmentation.

Four Images

Four images of the totality of global governance figure in this study. Though not explicitly discussed in such terms by Barnett, Pevehouse, and Raustiala, these totalities are a function of two considerations that feature in their study: (1) whether global governance in the aggregate has a dominant mode of governance and (2) whether mixed varieties enjoy equal status to the three ideal types. Table C.1 distinguishes these four images in the simplest of terms.

This volume departs from representations of global governance as a largely uniform arrangement. In particularly strong versions of the latter, an image emerges of global governance as deep uniformity. Theories of isomorphism and convergence lurk behind such images. They feature in theories of governance and IR alike, including in models focused on organizational competition under anarchy and sociological models of socialization and emulation where patchworks have dominant colors.[46] Though not painted in quite such stark terms, this is the image of global governance from which Barnett, Pevehouse, and Raustiala depart. It centers on the institutional arrangements of 1945 and highlights the

---

[45] Jessop 1997, 105, emphases added.
[46] E.g. Powell and DiMaggio 1991; Johnston 2008; Koppell 2010.

Table C.1 *Four images of the totality*

Is one mode dominant?

		Yes	No
Do hybrid modes exist?	No	I *Deep uniformity*	II *Mixed system*
	Yes	III *System of hybrids*	IV *Deep diversity*

hierarchical arrangements in which intergovernmental organizations reinforce a system of state sovereignty that gives special privileges to the most powerful. This system had far-reaching consequences for global developments, including the reproduction of inequalities among states despite legal equality among them.[47] However, as Barnett, Pevehouse, and Raustiala note together with their colleagues, hierarchy has rarely been the dominant mode across multiple domains and its relative imprint has varied over time.

At first sight Barnett, Pevehouse, and Raustiala's representation of global governance corresponds to a second image, one of a mixed system made up arrangements representing all three modes of governance. In this image no mode has an overly commanding presence. It represents the world as one where three different modes simultaneously coexist, though with some variations in their relative imprint across domains and time. But discrete structural analysis risks exaggerating differences between modes of governance at the expense of hybrid modes. Several contributions to this volume show that hybrid systems are relatively common.

Hybrids are arrangements that are not reducible to one single mode, but constitute the integration of elements from more than one type.

---

[47] Mazower 2012; Viola 2020.

Contemporary governance studies underscore that hybrid forms of governance have become more common with time.[48] For example, when the United Nations, an organization that reflects a relatively hierarchical model of political authority, developed an arrangement that encouraged corporate social responsibility by embracing a model that itself combined network and market-based modes of governance, it championed a hybrid arrangement that was not reducible to one or another mode of governance.[49] But hybrid forms have existed for longer. In Chapter 9, Vincent Bernhard and Anne Quintin document that the development of international humanitarian law over two centuries produced a hybrid arrangement that has been resistant to fundamental change. In Chapter 6, meanwhile, Michael W. Manulak and Duncan Snidal show that the emergence of new technologies has upended some and reinforced other governance arrangements in what they describe as a "Hierarchy plus Networks" model of global governance. If most domains are characterized by hybrids then the image of global governance is a third image, one of a system of hybrids rather than one of structurally diverse systems with or without dominant colors (first and second images).

Barnett, Pevehouse, and Raustiala's representation of global governance points to a fourth image. That image is one of global governance as deep institutional diversity that accommodates both the second and third images of global governance. In this image global governance entails areas that conform more closely to one of the ideal types, other arrangements to different ideal types, and includes a variety of hybrid models. From this perspective the totality of contemporary global governance is definitely not one of uniformity (first image), but nor is it reducible to simply a mixed system (second image) or a system of hybrids (third image). It represents a fourth alternative in which the primary colors of the three modes exist, in various combinations, alongside new colors generated by their mixing. It is an image of global governance that is more El Anatsui than Jackson Pollack or Mondrian.

Pathways to Integration

How the totality of global governance is conceived impacts how pathways to and from greater integration of institutions is understood. If the image is one of deep uniformity then integration entails institutional transformation in areas that are incompatible with the dominant mode. While such notions feature in utopian models of global governance, in some

---

[48] E.g. Clapp 1998; Andonova 2010.   [49] Ruggie 2013.

understandings of global governance under anarchy, as well as under highly socialized system, this volume finds little support for such an image. For example, by comparison to the structure of the modern sovereign (nation) state, which shares a great many governance attributes across space and time, global institutions have been institutionally very different. The two parts are of course linked. Since state interests take different forms and often compete, and since there are upper limits to how much authority governments are willing to vest in international forums, there are structural limitations on creating integrated solutions through uniformity.

Also the image of global governance as a system of hybrids suggests that none of the three modes is dominant and that pure versions of them are rare. The path to integration in this image is one in which reforms aim to move specific arrangements away from any one of the three ideal types with the goal of lessening incentive incompatibilities between arrangements. But encouraging a world of hybrids also entails challenges. Hybrid arrangements may fail to reconcile differences among diverse modes and become self-undermining. This may be one reason why Barnett, Pevehouse, and Raustiala are reluctant to place hybrids at the center of their analysis or to suggest that hybrid forms are the dominant mode.

If global governance in its totality is a system of deep institutional diversity then integration is not about convergence, specialization, or uniformity. But nor is it about denying the prospects for such developments in limited contexts. Deep diversity is about managing multiple arrangements, often traveling their own paths, and it is thus about managing institutional incompatibilities, large and small. Rather than having complementary effects the integration of diverse modes of governance can produce sums that are less than their parts. In the characteristic prose of economists this is a scenario of incentive incompatibility.[50] One way to reconcile different modes is to reduce the intensity of incentive incompatibilities by distancing arrangements from their respective ideal types and/or to make their imprint highly domain-specific. For example, in instances where hierarchy remains a dominant feature and market or network-based arrangements appear secondary, integration can theoretically be improved by moving arrangements some distance from their ideal type. "Shadow of hierarchy" models suggest that a mixed system generally has one dominant mode (hierarchy) and that alternative

---

[50] Hurwicz (1972) defines incentive incompatibility as scenarios in which participants find it advantageous to break rules or behave in ways that undermine arrangements.

arrangements (markets, networks) exist under the former's umbrella. In such models the pathway to integration entails an incremental process in which the dominant mode is prioritized, and other modes are adapted in such ways that they do not significantly undermine the returns from the former. In this pathway the goal is not to eliminate all incentive incompatibilities but to manage and contain them without significantly reducing the presence of multiple modes of governance. Over time such an arrangement of deep diversity will include single-colored pieces and a mixture of colors and novel mixes (hybrids) – in short, there is an expectation that the future will see more, not fewer, color combinations beyond those already known.

Deep Diversity and Path Dependence

A system in which deep institutional diversity persists suggests that there are strong internal or endogenous reasons to why arrangements with less diversity face long odds. These reasons may be found in logics of path dependence. While the underlying mechanisms that propel institutional developments along a particular path may be different across cases, it is a well-known phenomenon that the further down a particular path history moves the less likely it is that reversals take place.[51] This does not mean that radical change through some rupture does not take place, but simply that it is a less common mode of change. Much that is associated with global governance is characterized by incremental processes of change. Even the productive elements of critical junctures, those which give junctures their content, have been found to have developed incrementally.[52] In a global system where designs have emerged at different moments and in distinct contexts, institutional diversity has been the norm, even if periodically punctuated by moments in which integrated arrangements favor one mode of governance. Over time this has served to reinforce institutional diversity, if for no other reason than staying the course serves interests or inertia better than switching modes and the paths that go with them.

Path dependence has been identified as an obstacle to reform in global governance, as a source behind inefficient adaptation and for making it less likely that new, potentially more representative global institutions emerge in practice.[53] This is a plausible scenario. It is also possible that logics of path dependence have contributed to the long-term viability of

---

[51] Pierson 2004; Rixen and Viola 2015.   [52] E.g. Helleiner 2017; Sikkink 2017.
[53] Fioretos 2011; Hale et al. 2013; Rixen and Viola 2016.

many global governance arrangements. Had global leaders attempted to construct *de novo* a "league" or "united" anything in 2020 it would not have met with much success, even in the face of a calamitous pandemic. Contemporary gaps in governance would have been even larger. Instead, logics of path dependence have effectively locked in a diverse set of arrangements that have helped states and other actors manage global challenges better than in their absence. Seen from this perspective, path dependence may retard progress to an aspirational mode of global governance, but also has the power to protect institutions from a worse alternative if that is how a gap in governance is understood. The most creative agents from this perspective are not those who manage to create unified or integrated modes of governance, but those who successfully navigate and innovate amid institutional diversity.[54] In this view path dependence is not an obstacle, but can be a beneficial constraint that anchors experimentation and sustains a foundation of coordination under high levels of uncertainty.

Deep institutional diversity may be both a cause and effect of contemporary global governance. Against the bedrock of continuity that many established international organizations and global institutions have provided over decades, whether for reasons of path dependence or not, institutional diversity appears to be a more likely scenario in the long term than its opposite. Institutional integration through convergence has not been a trend in recent decades. The contemporary period is different from the past when solutions to global challenges often featured well-developed and integrated plans, frequently with hierarchical elements. There is no zeitgeist today analogous to San Francisco in 1945, even a pale version. As contributions to this volume suggest, the resources and agency required to reproduce arrangements are less than those needed to reach agreement on transforming designs given the multitude of structural factors that have already contributed to institutional diversity.

Theories of path dependence come in for regular criticism, generally for failing to account for one or another instance of change. But when political passions shift, and institutions remain more stable than widely anticipated, such theories offer a particularly valuable point of departure. They suggest, for example, that institutional diversity is a more likely outcome when existing arrangements are highly contested than is the emergence of a streamlined system. Under such conditions arrangements with strong support are reproduced while those that no longer

---

[54] Acharya 2016.

enjoy support are dismissed, often without much consideration of how either will affect arrangements in other domains. As the empirical studies in this volume confirm, a dominant approach to dealing with new challenges is to add new layers of governance rather than transforming select bits in ways that enhance institutional integration. While the creative agency of political leaders and unexpected historical events may alter this dynamic, Barnett, Pevehouse, and Raustiala underscore that there are at least nine structural forces pushing and pulling global governance along pathways that in the aggregate will reproduce a world of deep institutional diversity before its alternatives.

Conclusion

Barnett, Pevehouse, and Raustiala do not traffic in presentism. Their comparative institutional approach is deeply anchored in the rich history of global governance and has important implications for how the study of global governance is approached in the future. Since 2016 and what is broadly understood to be a populist nationalist surge, including in two countries that were intimately connected with the post-1945 order as well as in three other major powers, much meaningful attention has been paid to the potential fragility of global governance. Much of it is framed in terms of an end to the past, especially key features of the post-1945 world order with its emphasis on rules-based governance and liberal notions of progress. In 2020 the notion of effective global governance was further bruised and portended prospects of significant change, at least in the global health domain.

Barnett, Pevehouse, and Raustiala are attentive to the influence that populist politics and global health and economic crises may have on ebbs and flows in modes of global governance. But their telling of the history of global governance is not one that stresses populism over other factors or one of worries that it will plunge global governance to ever new low watermarks in global cooperation. They remind us that the beginnings of critical junctures, if that is what 2016 and/or 2020 represent, do not determine their closure. The impact of the policy choices of sovereigntist world leaders can be profound. Few observers of global politics, for example, dispute that had the response of US President Trump to a global pandemic been more in line with his predecessor the future of global governance would look more similar to its past. But it is also plausible, indeed likely from the perspective of Barnett, Pevehouse, and Raustiala, that many structural drivers make it unlikely that any particular national leader can fundamentally upend or undo the deep diversity of contemporary global governance.

While it is commonly said that there is nothing inevitable about what the future of global governance will look like, the long history of global governance strongly suggests that whatever patchwork arrangements emerge in the future they are more likely to feature colors of the past than to entail a radical shift to a new color spectrum. Even if many international organizations have died and lost vitality, a great many formal and informal organizations have remained durable.[55] More likely than not, suggests Barnett, Pevehouse, and Raustiala's analysis of the past and present, the future of global governance will come in multiple colors and include a growing number of hybrids that will make the future of global governance look like another version of deep diversity.

Secretary-General Guterres and others who hope for greater integration of global governance institutions are likely to remain disappointed. Such efforts may have profound impacts but are often not lasting. Uniformity, completeness, and seamless integration have not been the primary features of global governance. 1919, 1945, and 1989 may have briefly paused a trendline born from greater modernity, as one reading of Barnett, Pevehouse, and Raustiala may have it, or even reversed it momentarily. But overall the trend has been one of greater institutional diversity and with that elements of greater fragmentation. The challenge this represents, as Guterres noted, is particularly acute in moments of crises. The first phase of the Covid-19 pandemic did not foster movement in the direction of greater integration, whether by reconciling diverse modes of governance within the global health governance field or filling gaps in governance capacity. Rather, history underscored again that scholarly attention is wisely steered to answering why fragmentation is so conspicuous.

Seen through the lenses of Barnett, Pevehouse, and Raustiala's structural approach, the near future of global governance is more likely to look like its recent past than to look like the models idealized by populist nationalists or those hoped for by global civil servants. With colleagues, they document that global governance has gradually become characterized by many more types of governance arrangements, including a variety of hybrid arrangements that have widened the color palette with time. From their perspective, then, there are good reasons to expect the prominence of some colors to vary from context to context also in the future, and that the totality of global governance will be another version of deep diversity before it resembles a mixed system, much less one of deep uniformity.

---

[55] Eilstrup-Sangiovanni 2018; Gray 2018; Vabulas and Snidal 2013; Pevehouse et al. 2020.

References

Acharya, Amitav. 2014. *The End of American World Order*. Cambridge: Polity.

Acharya, Amitav. 2016. The Future of Global Governance: Fragmentation May Be Inevitable and Creative. *Global Governance* 22 (4): 453–460.

Allen, Bentley B. 2017. Producing the Climate: States, Scientists, and the Constitution of Global Governance Objects. *International Organization* 71 (Winter): 131–162.

Andonova, Liliana B. 2010. Public–Private Partnerships for the Earth: Politics and Patterns of Hybrid Authority in the Multilateral System. *Global Environmental Politics* 10 (2): 25–53.

Andonova, Liliana B. 2017. *Governance Entrepreneurs: International Organizations and the Rise of Global Public-Private Partnerships*. Cambridge: Cambridge University Press.

Avant, Deborah and Oliver Westerwinter, eds. 2016. *The New Power Politics: Networks and Transnational Security Governance*. Oxford University Press.

Baratta, Joseph P. 2004. *The Politics of World Federalism*, 2 vols. Westport, CT: Praeger.

Barnett, Michael and Martha Finnemore. 2004. *Rules for the World*. Ithaca, NY: Cornell University Press.

Bernstein, Steven and Hamish van der Ven 2017. Continuity and Change in Global Environmental Politics. In *International Politics and Institutions in Time*, edited by Orfeo Fioretos, 293–320. Oxford: Oxford University Press.

Bially-Mattern, Janice and Ayşe Zarakol. 2016. Hierarchies in World Politics. *International Organization* 70 (3): 623–654.

Blanco, Masaya Llavaneras and Antulio Rosales. 2020. *Global Governance and COVID-19: The Implications of Fragmentation and Inequality*. E-International relations. Available at: www.e-ir.info/2020/05/06/global-governance-and-covid-19-the-implications-of-fragmentation-and-inequality/.

Capoccia, Giovanni and R. Daniel Kelemen. 2007. The Study of Critical Junctures: Theory, Narrative, and Counterfactuals in Historical Institutionalism. *World Politics* 59 (3): 341–369.

Clapp, Jennifer. 1998. The Privatization of Global Environmental Governance: ISO 14000 and the Developing World. *Global Governance* 4 (3): 295–316.

Coase, Ronald. 1937. The Nature of the Firm. *Economica* 4 (16): 386–405.

Collier, David, Jody Laporte, and Jason Seawright. 2012. Putting Typologies to Work: Concept Formation, Measurement, and Analytical Rigor. *Political Research Quarterly* 65 (1): 217–232.

Collier, Paul. 2006. Why the WTO Is Deadlocked: And What Can Be Done about It. *The World Economy* 29 (10): 423–449.

Cooley, Alexander and Jack Snyder. 2015. *Ranking the World: Grading States as a Tool of Global Governance*. New York: Cambridge University Press.

Copelovitch, Mark and Jon C. W. Pevehouse. 2019. International Organizations in a New Era of Populist Nationalism. *Review of International Organizations* 14: 169–186

Council of Councils. 2019. Ranking the Top Global Challenges. www.cfr.org/interactive/councilofcouncils/reportcard2019/#!/ranking/2019.

Eilstrup-Sangiovanni, M., 2018. Death of International Organizations: The Organizational Ecology of Intergovernmental Organizations, 1815–2015. *The Review of International Organizations* 15: 339–370.

Farrell, Henry and Newman, Abraham. 2019. Weaponized Interdependence: How Global Economic Networks Shape State Coercion. *International Security* 44 (1): 42–79.

Faude, Benjamin 2020. Breaking Gridlock: How Path Dependent Layering Enhances Resilience in Global Trade Governance. *Global Policy* 11 (4): 448–457.

Fioretos, Orfeo. 2011. Historical Institutionalism in International Relations. *International Organization* 65 (2): 367–399.

Fioretos, Orfeo, Tulia G. Falleti, and Adam Sheingate. 2016. Historical Institutionalism in Political Science. In *The Oxford Handbook of Historical Institutionalism*, edited by Orfeo Fioretos, Tulia G. Falleti, and Adam Sheingate, 3–30. Oxford: Oxford University Press.

Fioretos, Orfeo and Eugenia Heldt. 2019. Legacies and Innovations in Global Economic Governance Since Bretton Woods. *Review of International Political Economy* 26 (6): 1089–1111.

Gates, Bill. 2020. Responding to Covid-19: A Once-in-a-Century Pandemic. *The New England Journal of Medicine*, February 28. www.nejm.org/doi/full/10.1056/NEJMp2003762.

Goddard, Stacey E. 2009. Brokering Change: Networks and Entrepreneurs in International Politics. *International Theory* 1 (2): 249–281.

Gray, Julia, 2018. Life, Death, or Zombie? The Vitality of International Organizations. *International Studies Quarterly* 62 (1): 1–13.

Grigorescu, Alexandru, 2020. *The Ebb and Flow of Global Governance: Intergovernmentalism versus Nongovernmentalism in World Politics.* Cambridge: Cambridge University Press.

Guterres, Antonio. 2019. Speech at Davos. January 24. www.weforum.org/agenda/2019/01/these-are-the-global-priorities-and-risks-for-the-future-according-to-antonio-guterres/.

Haass, Richard. 2007. *The World in Disarray: American Foreign Policy and the Crisis of the Old Order.* New York: Penguin.

2020. *The World: A Brief Introduction.* New York: Penguin.

Hale, Thomas, David Held, and Kevin Young. 2013. *Gridlock: Why Global Cooperation Is Failing When We Need It Most.* Cambridge: Polity.

Helleiner, Eric. 2017. Incremental Origins of Bretton Woods. In *International Politics and Institutions in Time*, edited by Orfeo Fioretos, 214–230. Oxford: Oxford University Press.

Hooghe, Liesbet, Gary Marks, Tobias Lenz, Jeanine Bezuijen, Besir Ceka, and Svet Derderyan, 2017. *Measuring International Authority*, Vol. 3. Oxford: Oxford University Press.

Hurrell, Andrew. 2007. *On Global Order: Power, Values, and the Constitution of International Society.* Oxford: Oxford University Press.

Hurwicz, Leonid. 1972. On Informationally Decentralized Systems. In *Decision and Organization*, edited by Charles B. McGuire and Roy Radner, 297–333. Amsterdam: North-Holland.

Ikenberry, G. John. 2001. *After Victory: Institutions, Restraint, and the Rebuilding of Order after Major Wars*. Princeton: Princeton University Press.

2011. *Liberal Leviathan: The Origins, Crisis and Transformation of the American World Order*. Princeton: Princeton University Press.

Jessop, Bob. 1997. The Governance of Complexity and the Complexity of Governance: Preliminary Remarks on some Problems and Limits of Economic Guidance. In *Beyond Markets and Hierarchy: Interactive Governance and Social Complexity*, edited by Ash Amin and Jerzy Hausner, 111–147. Cheltenham: Edward Elgar.

Johnston, Alastair Iain. 2008. *Social States: China in International Institutions, 1980–2000*. Princeton: Princeton University Press.

Kagan, Robert. 2018. *The Jungle Grows Back: America and Our Imperiled World*. New York: Knopf.

Kahler, Miles, ed. 2011. *Networked Politics: Agency, Power, and Governance*. Ithaca, NY: Cornell University Press.

2013. Rising Powers and Global Governance: Negotiating Change in a Resilient Status Quo. *International Affairs* 89 (3): 711–729.

Kaul, Inge., Isabelle Grunberg, and Marc A. Stern, eds. 1999. *Global Public Goods: International Cooperation in the 21st Century*. New York: UNDP and Oxford University Press.

Keck, Margaret E. and Kathryn Sikkink. 1998. *Activists beyond Borders: Advocacy Networks in International Politics*. Ithaca, NY: Cornell University Press.

Kelley, Judith and Beth A. Simmons. 2020. *The Power of Global Performance Indicators*. New York: Cambridge University Press.

Keohane, Robert O. 1984. *After Hegemony: Discord and Collaboration in the International Political Economy*. Princeton: Princeton University Press.

2020. Understanding Multilateral Institutions in Easy and Hard Times. *Annual Review of Political Science* 23 (1): 1–18.

Koenig-Archibugi, Mathias and Michael Zürn, eds. 2006. *New Modes of Governance in the Global System: Exploring Publicness, Delegation and Inclusiveness*. Houndmills: Palgrave.

Koppell, Jonathan G. S. 2010. *World Rule: Accountability, Legitimacy and the Design of Global Governance*. Chicago: University of Chicago Press.

Koremenos, Barbara. 2016. *The Continent of International Law: Explaining Agreement Design*. Cambridge: Cambridge University Press.

Kreuder-Sonnen, Christian. 2020. *The WHO after Corona: Discretionary Powers for the Next Pandemic*. Verfassungsblog. https://verfassungsblog.de/the-who-after-corona-discretionary-powers-for-the-next-pandemic/.

Kruck, Andreas and Bernhard Zangl. 2020. The Adjustment of International Institutions to Global Power Shifts. *Global Policy* 11 (S1): 5–16.

Lake, David A. 1996. Anarchy, Hierarchy, and the Variety of International Relations. *International Organization* 50 (1): 1–33.

2011. *Hierarchy in International Relations*. Ithaca, NY: Cornell University Press.

Levin, Kelly, Benjamin Cashore, Steven Bernstein, and Graeme Auld. 2012. Overcoming the Tragedy of Super Wicked Problems: Constraining Our Future Selves to Ameliorate Global Climate Change. *Policy Sciences* 45 (2): 123–152.

Lundgren, Magnus, Theresa Squatrito, and JonasTallberg. 2018. Stability and Change in International Policy-Making: A Punctuated Equilibrium Approach. *The Review of International Organizations* 13 (4): 547–572.

Malloch-Brown, Mark. 2011. *The Unfinished Global Revolution: The Pursuit of a New International Politics*. New York: Penguin.

Mazower, Mark. 2012. *Governing the World: The History of an Idea*. New York: Penguin.

Mearsheimer, John J. 2018. *The Great Delusion: Liberal Dreams and International Realities*. New Haven: Yale University Press.

Milner, Helen. 1991. The Assumption of Anarchy in International Relations Theory: A Critique. *Review of International Studies* 17: 67–85.

Moyn, Samuel. 2010. *The Last Utopia: Human Rights in History*. Cambridge, MA: Belknap Press of Harvard University Press.

Murphy, Craig. 1994. *International Organization and Industrial Change: Global Governance since 1850*. New York: Oxford University Press.

Musgrave, Paul and Daniel H. Nexon. 2018. Defending Hierarchy from the Moon to the Indian Ocean: Symbolic Capital and Political Dominance in Early Modern China and the Cold War. *International Organization* 72 (3): 591–626.

Narlikar, Amrita, ed. 2010. *Deadlocks in Multilateral Negotiations: Causes and Solutions*. Cambridge: Cambridge University Press.

Patrick, Stewart. 2014. The Unruled World: The Case for Good Enough Global Governance. *Foreign Affairs* 93 *(1):* 58–73.

Pevehouse, Jon C. W., Timothy Nordstrom, Roseanne W. McManus, and Anne Spencer Jamison. 2020. Tracking Organizations in the World: The Correlates of War IGO Version 3.0 Datasets. *Journal of Peace Research* 57 (3): 492–503.

Pierson, Paul. 2004. *Politics in Time: History, Institutions, and Social Analysis*. Princeton: Princeton University Press.

Podolny, Joel M. and Karen L. Page. 1998. Network Forms of Organization. *Annual Review of Sociology* 24: 57–76.

Pouliot, Vincent. 2016. *International Pecking Orders: The Politics and Practice of Multilateral Diplomacy*. New York: Cambridge University Press.

Powell, Walter W. 1990. Neither Market Nor Hierarchy: Network Forms of Organization. *Research in Organizational Behavior* 12: 295–336.

Powell, Walter W. and Paul J. DiMaggio, eds. 1991. *The New Institutionalism in Organizational Analysis*. Chicago: University of Chicago Press.

Rixen, Thomas and Lora Anne Viola. 2015. Putting Path Dependence in Its Place: Toward a Taxonomy of Institutional Change. *Journal of Theoretical Politics* 27 (2): 301–323.

2016. Historical Institutionalism and International Relations: Explaining Change and Stability in International Institutions. In *Historical Institutionalism and International Relations: Explaining Institutional Development in World Politics*, edited by Thomas Rixen, Lora Viola, and Michael Zürn, 3–36. Oxford: Oxford University Press.

Rosenboim, Or. 2017. *The Emergence of Globalism: Visions of World Order in Britain and the United States, 1939–1950*. Princeton: Princeton University Press.

Ruggie, John G. 2013. *Just Business: Multinational Corporations and Human Rights*. New York: Norton.

Sikkink, Kathryn, 2017. Timing and Sequence in International Politics: Latin America's Contributions to Human Rights. In *International Politics and Institutions in Time*, edited by Orfeo Fioretos, 231–250. Oxford: Oxford University Press.

Simon, Herbert. 1962. The Architecture of Complexity. *Proceedings of the American Philosophical Society Society* 106 (6): 467–482.

Slaughter, Anne-Marie. 2004. *A New World Order*. Princeton: Princeton University Press.

2017. *The Chessboard and the Web: Strategies of Connection in a Networked World*. New Haven: Yale University Press.

Stephen, Mathew D. and Michael Zürn. 2019. *Contested World Orders: Rising Powers, Non-governmental Organizations, and the Politics of Authority beyond the Nation-State*. Oxford: Oxford University Press.

Tallberg, Jonas, Thomas Sommerer, Theresa Squatrito, and Christer Jönsson. 2013. *Opening Up: The Access of Transnational Actors to International Organizations*. Cambridge: Cambridge University Press.

United Nations General Assembly. 2005. In Larger Freedom: Towards Development, Security and Human Rights for All: Report of the Secretary General. May26. www.ohchr.org/Documents/Publications/A.59.2005.Add.3.pdf.

Vabulas, Felicity and Duncan Snidal. 2013. Organization without Delegation: Informal Intergovernmental Organizations (IIGOs) and the Spectrum of Intergovernmental Arrangements. *The Review of International Organizations* 8 (2): 193–220.

Victor, David G. 2011. *Global Warming Gridlock: Creating More Effective Strategies for Protecting the Planet*. Cambridge: Cambridge University Press.

Viola, Lora. 2019. G20 through the Lens of Historical Institutionalism. In *The G20 and International Relations Theory*, edited by Steven Slaughter, 116–134. Cheltenham: Edward Elgar.

Viola, Lora. 2020.*The Closure of the International System: How Institutions Create Political Equalities and Hierarchies*. New York and Cambridge: Cambridge University Press.

Waltz, Kenneth A. 1979. *Theory of International Politics*. New York: McGraw-Hill.

Weiss, Thomas G. and Rorden Wilkinson. 2019. *Rethinking Global Governance*. Cambridge: Polity.

Wendt, Alexander. 1992. Anarchy Is What States Make of It: The Social Construction of Power Politics. *International Organization* 46 (2): 391–425.

Williamson, Oliver. 1991. Comparative Economic Organization: The Analysis of Discrete Structural Alternatives, *Administrative Science Quarterly* 36 (2): 269–296.

1996. *Mechanisms of Governance*. Oxford: Oxford University Press.

Wynner, Edith and Georgia Lloyd. 1949. *Searchlight on Peace Plans: Choose Your Road to World Government*. New York: E. P. Dutton and Company.

Zarakol, Ayşe, ed. 2017. *Hierarchies in World Politics*. Cambridge: Cambridge University Press.

Zürn, Michael. 2018. *A Theory of Global Governance: Authority, Legitimacy, and Contestation*. Oxford: Oxford University Press.

Index

CPSIA information can be obtained
at www.ICGtesting.com
Printed in the USA
BVHW041642301121
622887BV00002B/2